Music and Theology

Essays in Honor of Robin A. Leaver

Edited by
Daniel Zager

THE SCARECROW PRESS, INC.
Lanham, Maryland • Toronto • Plymouth, UK
2007

ML
3000
M88
2007

SCARECROW PRESS, INC.

Published in the United States of America
by Scarecrow Press, Inc.
A wholly owned subsidiary of
The Rowman & Littlefield Publishing Group, Inc.
4501 Forbes Boulevard, Suite 200, Lanham, Maryland 20706
www.scarecrowpress.com

Estover Road
Plymouth PL6 7PY
United Kingdom

British Library Cataloguing in Publication Information Available

Library of Congress Cataloging-in-Publication Data
Music and theology : essays in honor of Robin A. Leaver / edited by Daniel Zager.
   p. cm.
 Includes bibliographical references and index.
 ISBN-13: 978-0-8108-5414-7 (hardcover : alk. paper)
 ISBN-10: 0-8108-5414-7 (hardcover : alk. paper)
 1. Church music. 2. Bach, Johann Sebastian, 1685–1750. 3. Leaver, Robin A.
I. Zager, Daniel. II. Leaver, Robin A.
ML3000.M88 2007
781.71—dc22

2006021111

Contents

Preface

Music and theology: in his scholarly work and in his teaching Robin A. Leaver has spent much of his life bringing these two disciplines together. His work as a musicologist consistently places sacred music in its various liturgical contexts, thereby enriching our understanding of why these repertories were created, how they functioned, and what they signified to those who listened. As a theologian, Robin has written cogently about music *as* theology—about church music playing its part in theological proclamation. Thus, he brings to the study of sacred music repertories, and indeed to the practice of church music, a connection to theology that grounds this music in its larger contexts.

Robin was trained in theology at Trinity College, Bristol, graduating in 1964 and being ordained into the ministry of the Church of England in the same year. He served various parishes in England for the next twenty years. By 1971 he was publishing articles and reviews on a wide variety of music and church historical topics, and in that same year, supported by a Winston Churchill Fellowship, he was able to travel to the United States in order to investigate Johann Sebastian Bach's own copy of the Abraham Calov *Deutsche Bibel*, held by the library of Concordia Seminary, St. Louis. This work would lead eventually to Robin's 1983 monograph *Bachs theologische Bibliothek* (Neuhausen-Stuttgart: Hänssler-Verlag), a foundational work in theological Bach studies. But Robin's first monograph was a theological treatise published eight years earlier, *Luther on Justification* (St. Louis: Concordia Publishing House, 1975). Thus, relatively early in his career Robin had begun his work on Luther and on Bach, topics that continue to absorb his scholarly attention today (with a major monograph, *Luther's Liturgical Music: Principles*

and Implications, forthcoming in 2007). Luther, of course, was a brilliant theologian but also an informed musician, a person who loved music and considered it a gift of God. Similarly, Bach, the extraordinary composer and con-
summate Lutheran cantor, who went to considerable effort and expense to
build a personal library of Orthodox Lutheran theological writings, was well
informed as a theologian, his musical work being shaped in part by his understanding of Lutheran theology. It is, of course, no coincidence that
Robin—theologian and musician—has devoted much of his scholarly energy
to investigating the work of these two towering figures, who were themselves
each immersed in music and theology.

In 1977 Robin was appointed to a position at Latimer House, Oxford, in
which he was expected to "research, write, lecture, and publish in the cross-
disciplinary areas of theology, liturgy, hymnology, and church music." A
glance at the chronological list of his writings in this volume reveals that he
has been doing precisely that ever since. Ten years later—in 1987—he earned
the doctorate in theology at the Rijksuniversiteit Groningen, the Netherlands.
His dissertation, "'Goostly Psalmes and Spirituall Songes': English and
Dutch Metrical Psalms from Coverdale to Utenhove 1535–1566" was subsequently revised for publication as a monograph by Clarendon Press (1991),
a work that illustrates yet another strain of Robin's work—the history of
psalmody and hymnody, including that of his native country.

As a teacher of church music at Westminster Choir College (since 1984),
as a faculty member of the Liturgical Studies program of the Graduate School
of Drew University, and as a member of the graduate faculty at The Juilliard
School, Robin has trained numerous church musicians and liturgical scholars,
providing them a rich background in theology, liturgy, hymnology, and the
history and practice of church music. He has also served as president of two
organizations that, each in their own way, focus on music and theology—the
Internationale Arbeitsgemeinschaft für Hymnologie and the American Bach
Society. Robin has invested considerable time in founding and editing three
monographic series devoted to theology, liturgy, and music: Studies in Liturgical Musicology, Drew Studies in Liturgy, and Contextual Bach Studies (all
three series published by Scarecrow Press). While some of these monographs
relate to Robin's teaching in the Liturgical Studies program at Drew University, others come from his knowledge of research in progress and his encouragement of scholars who share his love for the study of music and theology.

Characteristic of Robin is his generosity in sharing his time and in providing encouragement and sound advice to other scholars. I think it safe to say
that everyone connected with this volume has benefited at one time or another
from Robin's scholarly assistance and encouragement, and that we all relish

those conversations with Robin that invariably clarify a line of inquiry, confirm a hypothesis, or provide fresh insights into a particular problem. Robin is a cherished colleague, and it is a privilege to present this volume to him—with thanks, and with every good wish for more productive years as a teacher, mentor, editor, and scholar of music and theology.

Daniel Zager

"The Soul Is Symphonic"[1]: Meditation on Luke 15:25 and Hildegard of Bingen's Letter 23

William T. Flynn

> "Now his elder son was in the field; and when he came and approached the house, he heard music and dancing."
>
> —Lk 15:25 NRSV

> "erat autem filius eius senior in agro et cum veniret adpropinquaret domui audivit symphoniam et chorum"
>
> —Lc 15:25 Vulgate

The title of this meditation, "The Soul Is Symphonic," is taken directly from a letter that Hildegard of Bingen (the famous South-German prophet and composer) wrote to the prelates of Mainz in 1178, the eightieth year of her life (1098–1179).[2] She wrote the letter because the prelates had imposed a regime of strict sanctions upon her community. They objected to Hildegard's having granted permission for the burial of a certain nobleman within the consecrated grounds of her abbey on Mount Saint Rupert, since they (wrongly) believed that this nobleman had died while excommunicated, and therefore could not be accorded the dignity of a Christian burial. Hildegard had disagreed with them: she provided them with the names of eyewitnesses to the fact that the man had repented; she even obtained testimony from the priest who had heard his confession and granted him absolution. The prelates, however, used the occasion of their Archbishop's extended absence to remain obstinate, demanding that Hildegard order the man's body to be dug up and cast outside her abbey's grounds. Since she refused to obey, the prelates put her community under interdict. By the time Hildegard wrote to them, her community had been barred from receiving the Eucharist, and its members were allowed merely to recite the seven monastic prayer hours rather than sing them. Hildegard's letter makes it very clear that she considered the restriction on singing to be particularly destructive, and she tried to explain to the prelates not only the centrality of music to the life of her community, but also its importance both to the wider church and to the world. She contended that the interdict would do only harm, as it interfered with her community's work, identity, and purpose: it hindered their ability to bear witness to the end-of-time, their effort to live in a way that displayed the harmony of body and soul through their continual singing of praises to God.

Although Hildegard's letter did not move the prelates to lift the interdict (which was only lifted when their Archbishop returned and overruled them), there is no evidence that they did not agree with Hildegard's views about the importance of music. Indeed, Hildegard would have had good reason to expect the prelates to agree with her about the central importance of music to the church's purpose and mission, since they held in common a long tradition of reflection and interpretation of the Scripture that supported her view. This tradition was based in part on their shared interpretation of the Gospel passage read today.[3]

Hildegard's phrase "the soul is symphonic" uses the Latin adjective *symphonalis*, a word derived from the Greek noun *symphonia*, an important word in Greco-Roman music theory,[4] and the same word that denotes the relatively modern genre and the orchestra devoted to playing it: the symphony. The word makes its unique New Testament appearance in verse 25 of today's Gospel reading, but because of its English translation, it is not easy to spot: "Now his elder son was in the field, and when he came and approached the house, he heard *music*."[5] Hildegard would have been more attuned to the precise nuance of the Gospel passage, since in Jerome's Latin Vulgate it does not say that the elder son heard *musicam*, but that the son heard *symphoniam*.[6] In Latin, as in Greek, the word *symphonia* can denote music, but it refers more precisely to the special ability of music to symbolize an agreement, similar to what we intend to express when we say (both metaphorically and when we make music together) that we're really "in-tune" with each other. Hildegard would also have been schooled in the traditional interpretations of Luke 15:25 that had their origin in the commentary on Luke written by Ambrose, the renowned fourth-century hymn-writer and Bishop of Milan. In commenting on this verse, Ambrose noted two things: first, that it was especially fitting that the father had provided *symphonia* to celebrate his son's homecoming, because it signalled the concord that had been restored between him and his wayward son, and second, that in the congregational singing of his own flock in Milan, one could hear the same *symphonia* when all ages and abilities were united in singing their common praise of God.[7]

Hildegard and the prelates would not only have agreed about the nature of musical *symphonia*, they also would have agreed about the nature of another Greek term used in music theory then and now: *harmonia*, from which we get the word harmony. Both terms signal agreement, but whereas *symphonia* was generally used as a definition of the pleasing *agreement* of sounds, *harmonia* was used as a definition of a pleasing *arrangement* of musical sounds. To say that something expressed *harmonia* was to say that all its parts were in a pleasing arrangement to its whole. Moreover, the concept of being "in harmony" was applied not only to musical structures, but to any structure in which diverse elements combined to create a larger whole, such as the limbs and the body, or the body and soul, or humanity and creation.[8] Hildegard referred to both terms in the title she gave to her own collected music and poetry: *The* symphonia *of the* harmonia *of heavenly revelations*.[9]

In this letter, however, Hildegard goes beyond these inherited interpretations of music. Her explanation takes the form of a long analysis of the last verse of Psalm 150, which we recited a few minutes ago. But, whereas we read "Let everything that breathes, praise the Lord,"[10] the translation used by Hildegard would have read "Let every spirit praise the Lord,"[11] and although this translation is less precise than ours, it does have the advantage of encouraging both inspirited bodies (like us) and pure spirits (like the angels) to join together in a universal song.[12]

Hildegard placed the concepts of *symphonia* and *harmonia* within a highly original narrative of salvation history, in which music is understood as a primal and redemptive gift of God, one that was closely connected with the vivifying gift of God's breath and the revivifying gift of the Holy Spirit. She begins this narrative by stating that Adam, before he disobeyed, had (as a consequence of being given life through God's breath) a voice that contained the sweetness of all musical *harmonia*. For when he was still innocent, Adam's voice was fully in accord with the angels in their praise of God. When he was deceived by a trick of the devil, he fell asleep to the knowledge that he had possessed.[13] (Note that Hildegard does not say that Adam lost his voice, but that he lost access to its proper use: he could no longer sing in harmony with the angels because his heart and voice were no longer "in tune.") However, Hildegard believed that Adam's original knowledge of angelic song was, in part, recoverable. She describes a profound connection between prophetic and musical inspiration: the holy prophets, inspired by God, were called to compose psalms and canticles that would inspire the hearts of listeners, and were called even to invent musical instruments as signs of their prophecies. She argues that by these means, the prophets move beyond the music of our [self-imposed] exile and recall to our minds the paradisial melody of praise that Adam once knew.[14]

In the next stage of her argument, which I take to be a discussion about the music of her own time, she states that music evoking humanity's celestial homecoming may be created through human skill in imitation of the prophets, and that through this music people had already begun to sing from God's inspiration, and thus were being transformed to bring back the sweetness of the songs of heaven, humankind's natural home.[15] In Romans 8:26–27, Paul described a similar transformation of our prayer: "the Spirit helps us in our weakness; for we do not know how to pray as we ought, but that very Spirit intercedes with sighs too deep for words. And God, who searches the heart, knows what is in the mind of the Spirit." Hildegard seems to refer to this passage when she states that sometimes when we sigh and groan at the sound of singing, we are responding to a memory of the nature of celestial harmony. This movement of our spirits, our souls, toward God is what Hildegard describes as our souls' inherently *symphonic* nature, and, as she points out, it is most likely to happen when we confess to the Lord both with the harp (which in medieval tradition signifies a practice that disciplines our bodies) and with the psaltery (which similarly signifies a practice that expresses the striving of our spirits).[16]

In the final stage of her argument, Hildegard explains that this transformation towards the harmony of body and soul through music is possible because it is founded in the incarnation: just as the body of Jesus Christ was born of the Virgin Mary through the operation of the Holy Spirit, so too the canticle of praise, reflecting celestial harmony, is rooted in the church through the Holy Spirit.[17] For Hildegard, the transformative process of the Holy Spirit in the church produces a musical repertory that mirrors the celestial harmony that can be rediscovered.

Although Hildegard does not claim that an earthly canticle of praise can be equated with the celestial harmony (which cannot be experienced face-to-face in this life) I do not think she means that we, so to speak, "hear through a glass darkly." Rather, she seems to indicate that our canticle of praise is a true reflection, a sign of the church's coming into *harmonia*, and an inspiration for its ongoing journey towards its true home, where *symphonia* awaits us—as it did for the prodigal son.

What is most striking to me about Hildegard's theology of music is that it stems from the perspective of a performer. She does not describe the establishment of *symphonia* or *harmonia* as an achievement (although they are goals), but as an ongoing process of practice, discipline, and transformation. Thus, she describes her community (and claims that this is true of the church universal) as the place where they practice *symphonia* and *harmonia*. They practice being "in-tune" with each other, and they rehearse living in a way that both their diversity and difference form a pleasing arrangement, an arrangement that not only reflects the celestial harmony of heaven, but also hints at the interplay and mutual indwelling (the counterpoint and harmony) that is the nature of our Triune God.

NOTES

1. A sermon delivered at Marsh Chapel, Boston University, 11 February 2004. I have retained the text as it was preached, but have added endnotes.

2. "symphonalis est anima" (Letter 23, lin. 141). The Latin text can be found in the critical edition, *Hildegardis Bingensis Epistolarium, Pars Prima I–XC*, ed. L. Van Acker, Corpus Christianorum Continuatio Mediaeualis, 91 (Turnhout: Brepols, 1991), 61–66 (hereafter cited as Ep. 23). Peter Dronke's fine partial translation in *Women Writers of the Middle Ages* (Cambridge: Cambridge University Press, 1984), 196–98, although not based on the critical edition, is nevertheless preferable (where they overlap) to that found in *The Letters of Hildegard of Bingen*, trans. Joseph L. Baird and Radd K. Ehrman, 3 vols. (New York: Oxford University Press, 1994), 1:76–80. I have consulted both translations in making my own translation for these notes.

3. Luke 15:11–32, the parable of the Prodigal Son.

4. A search [11 January 2005] of the database *Thesaurus Musicarum Latinarum* www.music.indiana.edu/tml/start.html found the term frequently used in 128 of the 252 music theory treatises in the database dating from the third through twelfth centuries. Most commonly, the term denotes the principal consonances of octave, fifth, and fourth and their octave transpositions, i.e., intervals important for tuning and, from the eleventh century on, for improvised polyphonic singing.

5. Luke 15:25 as translated in *The Holy Bible: New Revised Standard Version* (Nashville: Thomas Nelson, 1990).

6. Luke 15:25 as translated in *Biblia Sacra iuxta vulgatam versionem*, ed. Bonifatius Fischer and Robert Weber, 4th ed. (Stuttgart: Deutsche Bibelgesellschaft, 1994).

7. Ambrose of Milan, *Expositio euangelii secundum Lucam*, in Patrologia cursus completus series latina (PL), ed. J. P. Migne, 221 vols. (Paris, 1857–1864), vol. 15, cols. 1762–63: Ideo chorum et symphoniam audire non potest, hoc est, non illa theatralis incentiva luxuriae, nec aulicorum concentus, sed plebis concordiam concinentis, quae de peccatore servato dulcem resultet laetitiae suavitatem sonorum. . . . Quomodo aures ejus symphoniam populi spiritualem ferre non possunt? Haec est enim symphonia, quando concinit in Ecclesia diversarum aetatum atque virtutum, velut variarum chordarum indiscreta concordia, psalmus respondetur, amen dicitur. Haec est symphonia quam scivit et Paulus; et ideo ait: *Psallam spiritu, psallam et mente.* Therefore he [the elder son] cannot hear the dancing and music (*symphoniam*); that is, not that theatrical tune of extravagance, nor a concert of courtiers, but the concord of the people singing prophetically, which should resound sweet with joy, a pleasantness of sounds concerning the rescued sinner. . . . How can his ears not bear the spiritual

symphony of the people? For this is a symphony, when there resounds in the church a united concord of differing ages and abilities as if of diverse strings; the psalm is responded to, the amen is said. This is the symphony which Paul also knew; and therefore he said: I will sing with spirit, and I will sing with the mind (I Cor. 14:13). The third sentence of the English translation above was taken from James McKinnon, *Music in Early Christian Literature*, Cambridge Readings in the Literature of Music (Cambridge: Cambridge University Press, 1987), 284.

Ambrose's commentary was very influential for much subsequent commentary; moreover, access to traditional interpretations of the word *symphonia* was also available through music theory and liturgical poetry; for example, the word is frequently encountered in sequences and is indeed one of the names for an early sequence tune.

8. There is a certain amount of slippage between the terms *symphonia* and *harmonia*, but the literary trope of the "harmony of the spheres" attributed to Pythagoras and extensively developed in Plato's works, seems to have been responsible for its more systematic metaphorical use. See the discussion of Plato's use of the term *harmonia* in Herbert M. Schueller, *The Idea of Music: An Introduction to Musical Aesthetics in Antiquity and the Middle Ages* (Kalamazoo, Mich.: Medieval Institute Publications, 1988), 31–54.

9. For a critical edition of Hildegard's lyrics see *Symphonia armonie celestium revelationum*, ed. and trans. Barbara Newman (Ithaca, N.Y.: Cornell University Press, 1988). The title comes from a works list found in Hildegard's *Liber vite meritorum*. It is not clear whether Hildegard was referring to her entire lyrical output or some specific portion of it, and she also wrote lyrics later on.

10. The reading is from the NRSV translation of Psalm 150:6.

11. The Vulgate (Gallican) translation of Psalm 150:6 is "*omnis spiritus laudet Dominum.*" Jerome appears to have been aware of the translation problem, as his later (Hebraica) translation reads "*omne quod spirat laudet Dominum.*" Nevertheless, the Gallican translation was almost always used in the liturgy, and is the version quoted by Hildegard in this letter.

12. The tradition of the angels as pure spirits was transmitted, in part, from Gregory the Great, *XL homilarum in euangelium libri duo*, in PL 76 as cited in CETE-DOC, 1996 Cl.1711, lib. 2: 2, hom: 34, cap 8, lin. 2–10: "Graeca etenim lingua angeli nuntii, arcangeli uero summi nuntii uocantur. Sciendum quoque quod angelorum uocabulum nomen est officii, non naturae. Nam sancti illi caelestis patriae spiritus semper quidem sunt spiritus, sed semper uocari angeli nequaquam possunt, quia tunc solum angeli, cum per eos aliqua nuntiantur; unde et per psalmistam dicitur: qui facit angelos quos spiritus. Ac si patenter dicat: qui eos quos semper habet spiritus; etiam cum uoluerit, angelus facit." Indeed, in the Greek tongue, angels are called heralds, archangels, highest heralds. Also, it should be known that the word designating angels is a name of their office, not of their nature. For those holy spirits of the heavenly homeland are indeed spirits, but can in no way always be called angels, since they are angels only at the time when something is announced through them; whence also is said through the Psalmist: the one who makes angels who are spirits. As if openly he should say: the one who always regards them as spirits, whom also, when he wishes, he makes angels.

13. For clarity, I have condensed Hildegard's argument rather than reporting it verbatim. I have stayed close to her own choices of words, and I provide the relevant Latin passages that underpin my paraphrase: "ut et recolentes Adam digito Dei, qui Spiritus Sanctus est, formatum, in cuius uoce sonus omnis harmonie et totius musice artis, antequam delinqueret, suauitas erat" (lin. 99–101). As it were, recalling that Adam was formed by the finger of God, who is the Holy Spirit, in whose voice, before he sinned, was the sound of all harmony and the sweetness of all musical art.

"adhuc innocens, non minimam societatem cum angelicarum laudum uocibus habebat" (lin. 68–69). Still being innocent he used to have no little association with voices of the angels in praise.

"Simultudinem ergo uocis angelice, quam in paradiso habebat, Adam perdidit, et in scientia qua ante peccatum preditus erat, ita obdormiuit, sicut homo a somno euigilans de his, que in somnis uiderat, inscius et incertus redditur, quando suggestione diaboli deceptus" (lin. 71–75). Therefore, he used to have in paradise a likeness of angelic voice; Adam fell, and thus fell asleep to the knowledge which he had possessed before his sin. Like a man waking from a dream, from those things which he had seen in dreams, he was rendered unknowing and unsure, when he was deceived by the devil's prompting.

14. "Vt autem etiam diuine illius dulcedinis et laudationis, qua cum angelis in Deo, priusquam caderet, idem Adam iucundabatur, et non eius in hoc exsilio recordarentur, et ad hec quoque ipsi prouocarentur, idem sancti prophete, eodem spiritu quem acceperant edocti, non solum psalmos et cantica, que ad accendendam audientium deuotionem cantarentur, sed et instrumenta musice artis diuersa, quibus cum multiplicibus sonis proferrentur, hoc respectu composuerunt, ut tam ex formis uel qualitatibus eorundem instrumentorum quam ex sensu uerborum, que in eis recitantur, audientes, ut predictum est, per exteriora admoniti et exercitati, de interioribus erudirentur" (lin. 84–94). But indeed, Adam used to enjoy the same [music] of their divine sweetness and praise with the angels in God before he fell, and not in this exile might they be recalled. Those same holy prophets, taught by the same spirit they had received, were called forth toward them also, not only that they compose psalms and canticles, which might be sung to kindle the devotion of the hearers, but also [that they construct] diverse instruments of the musical art, so that as much from the forms or properties of these same instruments as from the meaning of the words, which are sung with them, the hearers, as said above, reminded and aroused by outward things, might be instructed about inward things. (Hildegard's focus is not on the sound of instruments but on their symbolic meanings.)

15. Quos, uidelicet sanctos prophetas, studiosi et sapientes imitati, humana et ipsi arte nonulla organorum genera inuenerunt, ut secundum delectionem anime cantare possent" (lin. 95–97). Eager and wise men imitated these holy prophets, and by their art invented not a few human kinds of polyphony, so that they might sing according to the delight of the soul.

"Cum autem deceptor eius, diabolus, audisset quod homo ex inspiratione Dei cantare cepisset, et per hoc ad recolendam suauitatem canticorum celestis patrie mutaretur, . . . ita exterritus est . . . ut non solum de corde hominis per malas suggestiones et immundas cogitationes seu diuersas occupationes, sed etiam de ore Ecclesie, ubicumque postest, per dissensiones et scandala uel iniustas depressiones, confessionem et pulchritudinem atque dulcedinem diuine laudis et spiritalium hymnorum perturbare uel auferre non desistit" (lin. 104–15). When however, his deceiver, the devil, heard that humankind had begun to sing from the inspiration of God, and through this might be transformed to recall the sweetness of the canticles of the heavenly homeland, he became so frightened, that not only from the heart of humankind through evil promptings and unclean thoughts, but also from the mouth of the church, wherever he could, through dissensions and scandals or unjust suppressions, he did not cease to disrupt or destroy the confession and beauty and sweetness of divine praise and spiritual hymns.

16. "Et quoniam interdum in auditu alicuius cantionis homo sepe suspirat et gemit, naturam celestis harmonie recolens, propheta, subtiliter profundam spiritus naturam considerans, et sciens quia symphonialis est anima, hortatur in psalmo ut confiteamur Domino in cithara, et in psalterio decem chordarum psallamus ei, citharam, que inferius sonat, ad disciplinam corporis, psalterium, quod de superius sonum reddit, ad intentionem spiritus, decem chordas ad completionem legis referri cupiens" (lin. 138–45). And since, at times, in the hearing of some song, a human being often sighs and groans, recalling the nature of heavenly harmony, the prophet subtly considering the profound nature of the spirit, and knowing that the soul is symphonic, exhorts in the psalm that we should confess to the Lord on the harp, and that we should sing psalms to him on the ten-stringed psaltery: desiring that the harp, which sounds lower, be connected to the discipline of the body, the psaltery, which gives a sound from above, to the intention of the spirit, and the ten strings, to the fulfilment of the Law.

17. "Pensate itaque quoniam sicut corpus Iesu Christi de Spiritu Sancto ex integritate Virginis Marie natum est, sic etiam canticum laudum secundum celestem harmoniam per Spiritum Sanctum in Ecclesia radicatum est. Corpus uero indumentum est anime, que uiuam uocem habet, ideoque decet ut corpus cum anima per uocem Deo laudes decantet" (lin. 126–30). Therefore know that just as the body of Jesus Christ was born from the Holy Spirit, from the purity of the Virgin Mary, so also the song of praise is rooted according to the celestial harmony through the Holy Spirit in the church. Now, the body is the clothing of the soul, which has a living voice, and thus, it is fitting that the body with the soul should sing praises to God through the voice.

2

Early Lutheran Hymnals and Other Musical Sources in the Kessler Reformation Collection at Emory University

Stephen A. Crist

Emory University was founded in 1836 by the Georgia Conference of the Methodist Episcopal Church.[1] It is therefore perhaps not the most likely location for a world-class collection of primary sources from the sixteenth-century German Reformation. During the past few decades, however, several factors have contributed to the development of the Richard C. Kessler Reformation Collection. In 1975, Pitts Theology Library purchased the holdings of the Hartford Theological Seminary—approximately 220,000 volumes, including the Beck Lutherana Collection—and instantly became the second-largest theology library in North America.[2] A dozen years later, in 1987, the Kessler Collection was established when Richard and Martha Kessler donated their private collection of Reformation imprints and manuscripts to Emory. Since then, the collection has continued to grow. Thirty years after the Hartford acquisition, it now contains more than 3,200 items.[3]

The centerpiece of the Kessler Collection is its extensive list of early printed works by Martin Luther, unmatched by any other library in North America. Among the more than 900 publications by Luther is a large number of sermons, as well as a copy of the *September Testament* (1522), Luther's translation of the Greek New Testament into German. The remainder of the collection includes books, pamphlets, and manuscripts by Luther's colleagues and opponents; Roman Catholic responses to Luther; and documents such as the first Latin and German editions of the Augsburg Confession. There are substantial numbers of works by Philipp Melanchthon, Desiderius Erasmus, Johannes Eck, and Andreas Bodenstein von Karlstadt. In all cases, the focus is on the pivotal years of the German Reformation, 1500–1570.

Among the holdings of the Kessler Collection are several early Lutheran hymnals and a number of other items containing or pertaining to music. Some of these publications appear not to be held by any other library in North America, and several may not even be held in major European collections. This chapter provides an overview of the musical materials in the Kessler Collection, with the hope of stimulating more intensive investigations in the future.

PAMPHLETS CONTAINING ONE OR MORE SONGS

Lutheran hymns were printed individually before they were gathered together in hymnals. As Joseph Herl points out, "The first Lutheran hymn publications were broadsheets (also called broadsides), single sheets of paper printed on one side, and pamphlets, single gatherings of leaves usually containing only one, two, or three hymns."[4] The Kessler Collection currently includes no broadsheets. It does, however, hold four pamphlets, each containing seven or eight printed pages.[5]

> (1) Drey geystliche lieder vom wort | gottes, durch Georg kern | Landtgraff Philips | zu Hessen Ge= | sangmay= | ster. | Der Juppiter verendert geystlich, | durch Hans Sachssen Schüster. | Anno.M.D.XXv.
> N.p., 1525.
> 4 unnumbered leaves.
> 1525 Kern[6]

The earliest of the pamphlets (1525) includes four hymns.[7] The first, "O Gott Vater, du hast Gewalt," is by a well-known Reformation figure, Hans Sachs (1494–1576), the famous cobbler and Meistersinger of Nuremberg.[8] The wording on the title page ("Der Juppiter verendert geystlich") indicates that this twelve-stanza dialogue between the sinner and Christ is a contrafactum of an earlier secular song.[9] It dates from early in Sachs's career, just two years after his famous didactic poem, *The Wittenberg Nightingale*. This probably is the hymn's first appearance in print.[10] It later was incorporated into many hymnals, however, including four in the Kessler Collection (nos. 6–8, 10).

The other three songs, in contrast, appear nowhere else and were penned by an individual about whom very little is known.[11] The title page indicates that Georg Kern served as "singing master" (*Gesangmayster*) at the court of Philipp, Landgrave of Hesse (1504–1567). A remark printed beneath each song mentions that Kern was from Geisenhausen, a town in Bavaria just a few miles southeast of Landshut. Since the first church order for Hesse was drafted just one year after this pamphlet was published, Eduard Emil Koch speculates that Kern's hymns may have helped to accelerate the introduction of the Reformation into this region.[12] Beyond this, however, even the venerable *Allgemeine deutsche Biographie* avers that "nothing else seems to be known about Kern's life."[13]

(2) Zwey Schön new Geist= | lich lied, aus Göttlicher schrifft, von dem | wüsten wesen der itzigen bösen Welt, zum | schrecken den Gottlosen, vnd zu trost den | Christen, Jm thon, Frisch auff ihr Lands | knecht alle &c. durch M. R. Müntzer. | Das ander, Gott zu bitte[n] | vm[b] vergebung der sünd, vnd vmb stercku[n]g | des glaubens, auch vmb ein seliges end, | Jm thon, wie der 13. Psalm, Herr Gott | wie lang vergissest mein &c. M. R.
Nuremberg: Christoph Gutknecht, n.d.
4 unnumbered leaves.
1550 Munt

Even less is known about the author of the second pamphlet. His last name was Müntzer, but he has not yet been identified more specifically. The colophon indicates that it was printed in Nuremberg by Christoph Gutknecht. No date is given, but Philipp Wackernagel places it around 1550.[14] The booklet contains two songs. The first, "Ach Gott, thu dich erbarmen," has twelve stanzas, and the second, "Wer meinen glaub, Gott schöpffer mein," only four. Each also includes a concluding couplet.[15] Like the earlier Sachs and Kern documents, this pamphlet has no printed music. Rather, the tunes are indicated by title: "Frisch auff ihr Lands knecht alle" for the first hymn, and "Herr Gott wie lang vergissest mein"—a setting of Psalm 13—for the second.[16]

(3) Ein vermanlied: | im Lager | zu Werd gemacht, zu singen | inn Pentzenawer odder | Toller weise.
N.p., 1546.
4 unnumbered leaves.
1546 Verm

The other two pamphlets each contain just a single song. The first, "WOlauff jhr Deudsche Christen," is a "soldier's song" (*Vermanlied*) that runs to nineteen stanzas and was published in 1546.[17] It is not a hymn but rather a pro-Lutheran call to arms: an exhortation to fight for God's honor and against the pope, king, emperor, and others who were considered to be worldly representatives of the devil.[18] The pamphlet's title indicates that it could be sung to either of two popular melodies: "zu singen inn Pentzenawer odder Toller weise."[19] In addition, music for a third melody is printed at the beginning.[20]

The title of the "soldier's song" states that it was "written in the encampment at Werd" ("im Lager zu Werd gemacht"). The historical and cultural context of this place opens a fascinating and rich field of inquiry outside the mainstream of sixteenth-century German popular song.

Werd is a small village whose population has ranged between 500 and 700 inhabitants over the past few centuries. It is located not in Germany but in the area of present-day Romania known as Transylvania, a mile or two southwest of Agnita, on the Altbach, a tributary of the Harbach River. Werd was a settlement of the Transylvanian Saxons, Germanic people who migrated east beginning in the twelfth century. The village is first documented in the early 1300s, and its church was built in the fifteenth century.[21]

Luther's writings began circulating in the 1520s among the German-speaking population of Transylvania. 1543 saw the publication of the *Formula reformationis ecclesiae Coronensis ac Barcensis provinciae* by Transylvania's leading reformer, Johannes Honter (1498–1549). This important document "abolished the Mass and other liturgical practices and replaced them with an evangelical service that included Communion in both kinds, Matins, and Vespers."[22] Over the next few years, Honter and Valentin Wagner (ca. 1510–1557) helped to prepare a new church order for the Transylvanian Saxons, *Reformatio Ecclesiarum Saxonicarum in Transylvania* (translated into German as *Kirchenordnung aller Deutschen in Sybembürgen*), which marked the official introduction of the Reformation among these people.[23] It was approved in 1547, just one year after the "soldier's song" was published. Because the "soldier's song" appeared around the time of the Schmalkald War (1546–1547) and includes a woodcut of a war scene, it has been viewed as a religious and artistic response to that particular conflict. Future interpretations will have to take into account, however, its origins among the newly-reformed Transylvanian Saxons.

(4) Klag lied: | Deren von Magdebürgk, zu Gott vnd | allen frommen Christen. Jm thon | des Zwelfften Psalms: Ach Gott | vom Hymel sihe darein, Vnd | las dich das erbarmen.
N.p., 1551.
4 unnumbered leaves.
1551 Klag

The last pamphlet contains a "song of lamentation" (*Klaglied*) and a plea for God's help, "Gantz elendt schreien Herr zu dir."[24] As the title of the print indicates, it is addressed sometimes "to God" (stanzas 1–3, 16–18) and sometimes to "all devout Christians" (stanzas 4–15, 19–24). The text is an acrostic: the first letters of the stanzas spell out the slogan "Gottes Wort bleibt ewiglich" ("God's Word endures forever"). The body of the song is followed by Christ's reply—an additional stanza whose prosody is different from the others, then a very specific date: "Am 8 Augusti, Anno 1551 &c." The place of publication is not given, but one assumes that it was Magdeburg. Not only does the name of this city appear in the title, but at the bottom of the title page there is a ten-line poem whose first letters spell out the word "Magdeburgk." Moreover, Magdeburg had become a focal point of Lutheran resistance in the religious wars at mid-century; it was, in fact, under siege in 1550–1551.[25] Stanza 19 laments that over 20,000 men had shed their blood ("mehr dan[n] Zweyntzig tausent Man, | Vergossen han jhr Blüdte"). Similarly, stanza 21 claims that more than 80,000 had suffered in one way or another ("Viel mehr dan[n] Achtzig tausent Seel, | Die leiden Hertzlich angst vnd queel"). Though the print has no music, its title indicates that the song should be sung to the melody of Luther's paraphrase of Psalm 12, "Ach Gott, vom Himmel sieh darein."[26]

HYMNALS

(5) Etlich Cristlich lider | Lobgesang, vn[d] Psalm, dem rai= | nen wort Gottes gemeß, auß der | heylige[n] schrifft, durch mancher= | ley hochgelerter gemacht, in der | Kirchen zü singen, wie es dann | zum tayl berayt zü Wittenberg | in übung ist. | wittenberg. | M.D.Xiiij.
[Nuremberg: Jobst Gutknecht, 1524.]
12 unnumbered leaves.
1524 Etli

The first of the five hymnals in the Kessler Collection is a copy of the so-called *Achtliederbuch*, generally regarded as the earliest hymnbook of the Reformation. Of the eight hymns, four are by Luther, three by his associate Paul Speratus (1484–1551), and one is anonymous. Music is provided for five of the songs. But two of the melodies are identical, and a heading indicates that this same tune was to be used for two other hymns as well ("Die drey nachfolgenden Psalm. | singt man in disem thon."). The three songs by Speratus include lists of the biblical passages upon which they are based.

The standard literature on the *Achtliederbuch* describes three versions of this print, which differ from one another in minute details.[27] It has long been known that they were printed in Nuremberg by Jobst Gutknecht, despite the fact that "wittenberg." is given as the place of publication. The date also is incorrect in many of the exemplars (including the one in the Kessler Collection): the Roman numeral should have another "X" (1524 instead of 1514). Emory's *Achtliederbuch* is the unique copy of a fourth version, a variant corrected printing of the first edition. The woodcut border at the top of the title page matches Ala[1] in the Weimar edition of Luther's works (Benzing, no. 3571) rather than Ala[2] (Benzing, no. 3572). On the other hand, a typographical error in a date ("1523") at the top of page A2b in Ala[1] is corrected in the Kessler copy. It appears, then, that the *Achtliederbuch* in the Kessler Collection fits between Ala[1] and Ala[2]. Moreover, it matches the description of Benzing's missing "Variante 2" of no. 3571.[28]

(6) Enchiridi= | on Geistliker | leder vnde Psalmen, | vppet nye gecorri= | geret.
| Sampt der Vesper | Complet, Metten | vnde Missen.
Magdeburg: Michael Lotther, 1536.
109 numbered leaves, 3 unnumbered leaves.
1536 Ench

By present-day standards, it may seem odd to refer to a print with a relatively small number of songs, such as the *Achtliederbuch*, as a "hymnal." The term most certainly is appropriate, however, for the Magdeburg *Enchiridion*, which contains seventy-five hymns, plus orders of worship for Vespers, Compline, Matins, and the Mass. One-third of the songs are by Luther, and another dozen by members of his circle. The rest are an eclectic collection, "written by pious men in places other than Wittenberg"—that is, in cities such as Nuremberg, Strasbourg, Breslau, Basel, and even distant Riga. Thirty-one of the hymns in the main part of the book, plus the *Te deum* in the Matins service, have printed music.

The *Enchiridion* is one of the earliest hymnals printed in Magdeburg, the first major free city in north Germany to adopt the ideas of the Reformers and among the first to accept the Augsburg Confession. This little book also is one of the few remaining Low German hymnals dating from Luther's lifetime. It was published ten years before his death, and no other copies are known to have survived. Low German was the spoken and written language of north Germany until the first half of the seventeenth century. Writings and songs of the Reformation were translated into Low German and began appearing as early as 1525. In addition to the printed material, the *Enchiridion* contains four handwritten hymns in its endpapers—in a dialect of Low German that can be traced to the northwest corner of Germany, near the Dutch border. These songs apparently were entered by an early owner of the book, probably within a decade after it was published, to supplement the printed repertory. They include Luther's "Christ, unser Herr, zum Jordan kam" of 1541; "Nun lob, mein Seele, den Herren," a metrical version of Psalm 103 by Johannes Gramann of Königsberg; "Ich danck dir, liebe Herre," a morning song by Johannes Kohlross, pastor in Basel; and "Herr Gott, der du erforschest mich," a metrical version of Psalm 139 by Heinrich Vogther.[29]

(7) Geistliche Lie | der Zu Wit= | temberg, | Anno 1543.
Wittenberg: Joseph Klug, 1544.
198 leaves, most numbered.
1544 Luth I

The next two items (7 and 8/9) both are editions of important hymnals that preserve the Wittenberg repertory of congregational song. Robin A. Leaver provides the following concise summary:

> The first collection that Luther prepared specifically for congregational use in Wittenberg was the *Geistliche Lieder*, printed by Joseph Klug in 1529. . . . [T]he 1529 Wittenberg hymnal was carefully planned and followed closely the structure of the church year. The Wittenberg hymnal was reissued in enlarged and revised forms during the remainder of Luther's life: later known editions appeared in 1533, 1535, 1543, 1544 (three times), and 1545. The beautiful edition published by Valentin Bapst, *Geystlicher Lieder* (Leipzig, 1545), was effectively a later edition of the "Wittenberg" hymnal, the last to be overseen by Luther.[30]

The title page of Emory's copy of the Klug hymnal has the year 1543, but the colophon indicates that it was printed the following year ("Gedruckt zu Wittemberg, Durch Joseph Klug, Anno M. D. XLiiij."). No copy of the original 1529 edition has been preserved, and we have only one surviving exemplar for each of the 1533 and 1535 editions. The volume in the Kessler Collection is, therefore, one of just a few remaining copies that were published during Luther's lifetime.[31]

Though the scope of this chapter does not permit detailed comparison of the 1543/1544 and 1533 editions, it is worth noting that the differences are quite considerable. On the one hand, many items appear in the later edition that were not present a decade earlier. On the other hand, quite a few items in the former edition subsequently were either altered or omitted altogether. Thoughtful analysis of the similarities and differences between the editions of Klug's hymnal would surely yield important clues about the development of hymnody, liturgy, and doctrine in the early decades of the German Reformation.

(8) Geystliche | Lieder. | Mit einer newen Vorrede, | D. M. Luth. | . . . Leipzig.
Leipzig: Valentin Babst, 1567.
200 unnumbered leaves.
1567 Geys:1

(9) Psalmen vnd | Geistliche lieder, welche | von frommen Christen | gemacht vnd zusamen | gelesen sind. | Auffs newe vbersehen, | gebessert vnd ge= | mehret. | Leipzig. | M. D. LXVII.
Leipzig: Valentin Babst, 1567.
144 unnumbered leaves.
1567 Geys:2

The hymnal published in Leipzig by Valentin Babst was, for all intents and purposes, a later version of Klug's hymnal. The content of Part One of the original 1545 printing of Babst is similar to the 1543 edition of Klug.[32] The first part of Emory's 1567 copy of Babst (no. 8), in turn, is virtually identical to the first edition. It runs to 199 unnumbered leaves containing eighty-nine songs, ordered with Roman numerals, and it includes elaborate metal-engraved borders on each page as well as numerous large engravings illustrating biblical themes. Part Two (no. 9) is bound together with Part One but has its own title page, and the numbering of the songs starts over with Roman numeral "I." Unlike Part One, it is quite different from the first edition. The quantity of hymns is greatly expanded—from forty to seventy—and the original songs are reordered. As with Klug's hymnal, careful examination of these differences would doubtless be quite fruitful.[33] The vast majority of songs in both parts have music.

Emory's copy of Babst's hymnal contains signatures and dates in the hand of several former owners: "Hinrich Burmester" (1731), "Johann Christoph Schmügel" (1758), and "Hermann Laut Heinrich Nobbe" (1853). Schmügel (1727–1798) was a student of Georg Philipp Telemann in Hamburg, who subsequently served as organist at St. John's in Lüneburg (1758–1766) and as organist (1766–1784) and Kantor (1784–1798) at St. Nicholas's in Mölln.[34] The book also has a stamp indicating that it once belonged to the manor library in the Thuringian village of Niedertopfstedt, about twenty-five miles northeast of Erfurt.

> (10) Kirche[n] | Gesäng, Aus dem | Wittenbergischen, vnd allen an= | dern den besten Gesangbüchern, so biß an | hero hin vnd wider außgangen, colligirt vnd ge= | samlet, Jn eine feine, richtige vnd gute Ordnung gebracht, vnd | auffs fleißigest, vnd nach den besten exemplaren, | corrigiret vnd gebessert | Fürnem-lich de[n] Pfarrherrn, Schulmeistern | vnd Cantoribus, so sich mit jren Kirchen zu der Christ= | lichen Augspurgischen Confession bekennen, vnd bey | denselben den Chor mit singen, regieren vnd | versorgen müssen, zu dienst vnd | zum besten. | M. D. LXIX.
> Frankfurt am Main: Johann Wolff, 1569.
> 4 unnumbered leaves, 353 numbered leaves, 7 unnumbered leaves, plus 24 additional leaves with manuscript material.
> 1569 Kirc

The most recent songbook in the Kessler Collection is a huge volume titled *Kirchen Gesäng*, which was published in Frankfurt in 1569. Containing about 400 hymns (roughly half with music)—including songs of the Bohemian Brethren, and psalm settings by Johann Magdeburg (ca. 1520–1565), Nicolaus Herman (ca. 1480–1561), and Burkard Waldis (1490–1556), as well as the standard repertory by Luther and his circle—this collection is effectively a summation of the first great epoch of Protestant church music. It was the subject of a detailed study by Oswald Bill, which appeared in 1969.[35]

Emory's copy includes two handwritten inscriptions, in Latin and German, that provide valuable clues about its provenance. Both are found inside the front cover, and they affirm the same things, though the German provides more details. It states that on May 24, 1587—eighteen years after the book was published—"Herr Karl vonn Lichtenstein" gave it to the choir of the church at "Felsburg."

The Princely House of Liechtenstein is one of the oldest noble families still in existence, dating back to the twelfth century, and now in its twenty-fifth recorded generation.[36] Karl (1569–1627) was the most important member of the House of Liechtenstein. Among his many honors, he held the highest office at the Imperial Court of Rudolph II, and in 1608 he was elevated to the rank of Hereditary Prince. Feldsberg was the family estate where Karl was born. It is located on the southern border of the Czech Republic, near the corner where Austria, Slovakia, and the Czech Republic meet, and it is known today as Valtice. Karl von Liechtenstein is a fascinating figure—not least because he was raised as a Protestant, and even attended a Bohemian Brethren school, but converted to Roman Catholicism in 1599 at age thirty.[37]

Knowledge of Karl von Liechtenstein's religious proclivities may help to explain why this large book—which transmits the cream of the Lutheran and Bohemian Brethren traditions—also includes forty-five pages of added manuscript material at the end, mostly in Latin. We may never know, however, how a music book that Karl gave to the church of his family estate when he was eighteen years old made its way into the hands of a rare-book dealer in Ossining, New York (William Salloch), from whom it was purchased for the Kessler Collection.

LITURGIES

(11) Ein weyse Christ= | lich Mess zu hal= | ten vnd zum tisch | Gottes zu gehen. | Martinus Luther. | Wyttemberg. | M. D. xxiiij.
Wittenberg: N.p., 1524.
18 unnumbered leaves.
1524 Luth BBB

(12) Ein weyse Christ | lich Mess zuhal= | ten vn[d] zum tisch | Gottis zu gehen. | Martinus Luther. | Wyttemberg. | M. D. xxiiii.
Wittenberg: N.p., 1524.
19 unnumbered leaves.
1524 Luth U

The next group of documents are orders of worship for church services. Nos. 11 and 12 are copies of Paul Speratus's German translation of Luther's *Formula*

Missae et Communionis pro Ecclesia Vuittembergensi (Form of Mass and Communion for the Church at Wittenberg). This important treatise was "Luther's first attempt to describe an evangelical mass in its entirety."[38] It was drafted at the behest of Luther's friend Nicolaus Hausmann, pastor at St. Mary's in Zwickau, and published first in Latin in December of 1523, then in German the next month.[39] At the end of the first printing of the first German edition (no. 11) are the words of the hymn "Fröhlich wollen wir Halleluja singen" by Johann Agricola (1492?–1566).[40] Similarly, an appendix to a subsequent printing (no. 12) includes both Agricola's hymn and one by Luther: the first appearance of "Es wollt uns Gott genädig sein."[41]

(13) Deutsche | Messe vnd Ordnu[n]g | Gotes diensts, zü Wit= | temberg, fürge= | nom[m]en. | M. D. XXVI.
N.p., 1526.
26 unnumbered leaves.
1526 Luth R

The Kessler Collection includes a copy of Luther's *German Mass and Order of Service*, a very important publication in which the reformer sets forth his ideas about public worship, especially the main service on Sundays. Most of the printed music in the volume is chant: formulas for intoning the opening psalm, the Epistle, and the Gospel; the Kyrie; and the Words of Institution. Also included is Luther's metrical version of the German Sanctus, "Jesaja, dem Propheten, das geschah."[42] After the *Deutsche Messe* appeared in Wittenberg early in 1526, it quickly was reprinted in several other cities. Emory's copy was published in Augsburg, just four years before the diet that led to the formulation of the Augsburg Confession.[43]

(14) Teütsche | Letaney, vmb | alles anligen der | Cristenlichen | gemayn.
N.p.: Jobst Gutknecht, n.d.
8 unnumbered leaves.
1529 Luth

The Kessler Collection also holds a rare copy of the *German Litany* of 1529, Luther's adaptation of the Roman *Litany of All Saints*.[44] Appended at the end of this lengthy liturgical chant is Luther's hymn "Verleih uns Frieden gnädiglich," his German translation of the antiphon "Da pacem Domine."[45]

(15) Ordnu[n]g des | Herren Nachtmal: so | man die messz nennet, sampt der | Tauff vn[d] Jnseg[n]u[n]g der Ee, Wie | yetzt die diener des wort gots zü | Straßburg, Erneüwert, vnd | nach götlicher gschrifft gebes= | sert habe[n] vß vrsach jn nach= | gender Epistel | gemeldet. | M D. xxv.
N.p., 1525.
24 unnumbered leaves.
1525 Ordn

This booklet contains orders of service for the Mass, and for the ceremonies of marriage and baptism, as they were practiced in the city of Strasbourg.[46] Its rich cache of liturgical data offers the opportunity for comparison of Strasbourg's distinctive traditions with the central practices of Wittenberg. The Strasbourg liturgy includes four hymns with music. In addition to Luther's versions of Psalm 130 ("Aus tiefer Not schrei ich zu dir") and Psalm 67 ("Es wollt uns Gott genädig sein"), there are settings of Psalm 13 ("Ach Gott, wie lang vergissest mein") by Matthäus Greiter, cantor of Strasbourg Cathedral, and of Psalm 3 ("Ach Herr, wie sind meinr sünd [*sic*] so vil") by Ludwig Oeler, another local figure.[47]

CHURCH ORDERS

The church orders in the Kessler Collection vary greatly in size and scope, from about forty pages to over 600. The earliest was printed in 1531, while others appeared as late as the 1560s. These publications document the introduction of the Reformation into many different regions of Germany, and into cities as well as larger territories. *The Oxford Encyclopedia of the Reformation* explains that

> as the Reformation was officially adopted by princes for their territories and by city councils, it had to be regulated by church orders (*Kirchenordnungen*). These documents addressed matters of church polity, administration, congregational life, charitable institutions, schools, the calendar, and worship, and therefore effected a "revolution" in social life.[48]

Although the church orders contain an enormous amount of information concerning matters of liturgical practice, the quantity of printed music in them is relatively small. Typically, it is limited to formulas for chanting portions of the Mass such as the Lord's Prayer, the Words of Institution, the Agnus Dei, and the Nicene Creed.[49]

In most cases, the Kessler Collection holds two or three different versions of a particular church order. It therefore can serve as a valuable resource for studying the development of liturgy, as well as other aspects of church life, in the early years of the German Reformation.

(16) Der Erbarn | Stadt Braunschwyg | Christenliche Ordenung, zu | dienst dem heiligen Euange= | lio, Christlicher lieb, zucht, fri | de vnd eynigkeit, Auch darun | ter vil Christlicher lere | für die Bürger, | Durch Joan[n]. Bugenhagen | Pomer beschriben. 1531.
Nuremberg: Friedrich Peypus, 1531.
130 unnumbered leaves.
1531 Buge

(17) Der Erbarn Stadt | Braunschweig Christliche Orde= | nung, zu dienst dem heiligen Euangelio, Christ= | licher lieb, zucht, friede vnd einigkeit, | Auch darunter viel Christli– | cher lehre für die | Burger. | Durch Johan. Bugenhagen | Pomer beschrieben. | M. D. XXXI.
N.p., 1563.
184 unnumbered leaves.
1563 Buge

No. 16 is the first High-German printing of the church order for the city of Braunschweig. It originally was drafted in Low German in 1528 by Johannes Bugenhagen (1485–1558), who also produced similar documents for Hamburg (1529) and Lübeck (1531).[50] No. 17 is a revised reprint.[51]

(18) Kirchen Ordnung, Jn | meiner gnedigen herrn der Marggra= | uen zu Brandenburg, vnd eins Er= | bern Rats der Stat Nürmberg | Oberkeyt vnd gepieten, Wie | man sich bayde mit der | Leer vnd Ceremo= | nien halten solle. | M. D. XXXIII.
Nuremberg: Christoph Gutknecht, 1533.
2 unnumbered leaves, 57 numbered leaves, 1 unnumbered leaf.
1533 Kirc:1

(19) Kirchen Ordnung In | meiner gnedigen Herrn der Marg= | grauen zu Brandenburg, Vnd eins Erbarn Raths | der Stadt Nürmberg Oberkeyt vnd Gebie= | ten, wie man sich bayde mit der Lehr | vnd Ceremonien hal= | ten solle. | Auffs new yetzo, dem alten Exemplar nach, mit | sondern fleiß widerumb gedruckt. | Zu Nürnberg, bey Chri= | stoff Heussler. | 1564.
Nuremberg: Christoph Heussler, 1564.
2 unnumbered leaves, 57 numbered leaves, 1 unnumbered leaf.
1564 Evan:1

This document was drafted in 1529 by a group of theologians under the supervision of Andreas Osiander (1496?–1552) for use in the territories of Brandenburg-Nuremberg. It was put into effect in the city of Nuremberg on January 1, 1533, and in rural areas on February 9. It subsequently became a model for other church orders, including no. 22.[52] No. 19 is a later edition.[53]

(20) Kirchen= | ordnunge zum an= | fang, fur die Pfarher in | Hertzog Hein | richs zu Sach | sen v. g. h. Fürsten= | thumb. | M. D. XXXIX.
Wittenberg: Hans Lufft, 1539.
22 unnumbered leaves.
1539 Kirc

(21) AGENDA, | Das ist, | Kyrchenordnung, wie | sich die Pfarrherrn vnd Seelsorger in | jren Ampten vn[d] diensten halten sollen, | Fur die Diener der

Kyrchen in | Hertzog Heinrichen | zu Sachssen V. G. H. | Fürstenthumb | gestel=
| let. | Gedruckt zu Leipzig, | durch | Nicolaum Wolrab. | M. D. XL.
Leipzig: Nikolaus Wolrab, 1540.
6 unnumbered leaves, 64 numbered leaves, 2 unnumbered leaves.
1540 Agen:1

Nos. 20 and 21 are the first and third editions, respectively, of the church
order for Albertine Saxony.[54] It was drafted by Justus Jonas (1493–1555) and
other reformers, in connection with the introduction of the Reformation into
this region (which included northern Thuringia, Leipzig, Meissen, and Dresden) by Duke Henry (1473–1541).

(22) Kirchenord= | nung, wie es inn des durch= | leuchtigen hochgebornen
Fursten vnnd Herrn, | Herrn Albrechts des Jungern Marggrauen zu | Branden-
burgs, zu Preussen, zu Stettin, Pomern, der Cassuben | vnd Wenden, auch in
Schlesien zu Oppeln vnd Ratibarn etc. | Hertzogs, Burggrauens zu Nurmberg,
vnnd Für= | stens zu Rugen, Fürstenthumb, Landt, Obrig | keit vnd gebiet, mit
der lehr vnd Ceremoni= | en bis auff vernere Christliche ver= | gleichung gehal-
ten werden sol. | Gedruckt zu Leipzig | durch Wolff Günter. | M. D. LII.
Leipzig: Wolff Günter, 1552.
2 unnumbered leaves, 57 numbered leaves, 1 unnumbered leaf.
1552 Evan

This is the third church order for Prussia (after those of 1525 and 1544). It
was introduced under Albert, Margrave of Brandenburg-Ansbach and Duke
of Prussia (1490–1568), and is a reprint of the 1533 Brandenburg-Nuremberg
church order (no. 18), which has been characterized as "perhaps the single
most influential and widely copied work of its kind during the Reformation."[55]

(23) Kirchenordnung: | Wie es mit Christlich= | er Lere, reichung der Sacra= |
ment, Ordination der Diener des Euan= | gelij, ordenlichen Ceremonien, in den
| Kirchen, Visitation, Consistorio | vnd Schulen, | Jm Hertzogthumb | zu Meck-
elnburg etc. ge= | halten wird. | Witteberg. | Gedruckt durch Hans Lufft. | 1552.
Wittenberg: Hans Lufft, 1552.
136 numbered leaves.
1552 Kirc

(24) Kirchenordnung: | Wie es mit Christlich= | er Lere, reichung der Sacra= |
ment, Ordination der Diener des Euan= | gelij, ordenlichen Ceremonien, in den
| Kirchen, Visitation, Consisto= | rio vnd Schulen, | Jm | Hertzogthumb zu |
Meckelnburg etc. gehal= | ten wird. | Witteberg. | Gedruckt durch Hans Lufft. |
1554.

Wittenberg: Hans Lufft, 1554.
144 numbered leaves.
1554 Evan

These are two early editions of a church order for the duchy of Mecklen-
burg, which was commissioned by Johann Albrecht, Duke of Mecklenburg-
Schwerin (1525–1576).[56] Johannes Aurifaber (1519?–1575), who had served
as Luther's personal attendant during his last year (1545–1546), helped to
draft it, and editorial assistance was provided by Philipp Melanchthon.

(25) Kirchen Ordnung | Wie es mit der Reynen Lehr des Euan= | gelij, Admin-
istration der heyligen Sacrament, Anneh= | mung, verhörung, vnd bestetigung
der Priester, Ordent= | lichen Ceremonien in den Kirchen, Visitation vnd | Syn-
odis, in der Herrschafft Waldeck gehal= | ten werden soll. Anno Domini 1556. |
Mense Martio auffgericht.
Marburg: Andres Colben, 1557.
68 unnumbered leaves.
1557 Evan

This church order was written by a team of theologians in 1556 and issued
the next year by the Counts of Waldeck, a principality about twenty miles
southwest of Kassel, for use in their territories.[57]

(26) Kirchenordnung: | Wie es mit Christlicher Lere, reichung | der Sacrament,
Ordination der Diener des | Euangelij, Ordentlichen Ceremo= | nien, Visitation,
Consisto= | rio vnd Schulen, | Jm Hertzogthumb Lünenburg gehal= | ten wird. |
Wittemberg. 1564.
Wittenberg: Georgen Rhawen Erben, 1564.
95 unnumbered leaves.
1564 Brau

This is the first church order for the principality of Braunschweig-
Lüneburg. It was commissioned by Dukes Henry and William.[58]

(27) Kirchenordnung | Vnnser, von | Gottes Genaden, | Julij, Hertzogen zu |
Braunschweig vnd Lüneburg, &c. Wie | es mit Lehr vnd Ceremonien vnsers
Fürsten= | thumbs Braunschweig, Wolffenbütlischen Theils, | Auch derselben
Kirchen anhangenden sachen vnd ver= | richtungen, hinfurt (vermittelst Gött-
licher | Gnaden) gehalten werden sol. | Gedruckt zu Wolffenbüttel, | durch Cun-
rad Horn. | M. D. LXIX.
Wolfenbüttel: Cunrad Horn, 1569.
64 unnumbered leaves, 448 pages (numbered 1–442, with many errors), 4 unnumbered leaves.
1569 Brau

(28) Kirchenordnung | Vnnser, von | Gottes Genaden, | Julij Hertzogen zu | Braunschweig vnd Lüneburg, etc. | Wie es mit Lehr vnd Ceremonien vnsers Für= | stenthumbs Braunschweig, Wulffenbütlischen | Theils, Auch derselben Kirchen anhangenden | sachen vnd verrichtungen, hinfurt | (vermittelst Gött- licher Gna= | den) gehalten wer= | den sol. | Gedruckt zu Wulffenbüttel, | durch Cunradt Horn. | M. D. LXIX.
Wolfenbüttel: Cunrad Horn, 1569.
68 unnumbered leaves, 456 pages (numbered 1–451, with many errors), 4 un- numbered leaves.
1569 Brau A

Nos. 27 and 28 are two printings of the massive church order commis- sioned by Duke Julius of Braunschweig-Wolfenbüttel to introduce the Refor- mation in his lands.[59] It was written by Martin Chemnitz (1522–1586), su- perintendent of the churches in the city of Braunschweig, and Jakob Andreae (1528–1590), professor of theology at the University of Tübingen.[60]

(29) Agend | Büchlein | für die Pfar= | Herren auff | dcm Land.
Nuremberg: Johann vom Berg and Ulrich Neuber, 1543.
88 printed, unnumbered leaves, plus 13 additional leaves with manuscript ma- terial sewn in.
1543 Diet

(30) Agend | Büchlein für die | Pfarrherrn auff | dem Land. Durch | Vitum Diet- rich. | M. D. XLV.
Nuremberg: Johann vom Berg and Ulrich Neuber, 1545.
124 unnumbered leaves.
1545 Diet B

(31) Agend | Büchlein, für die | Pfarrherren auff dem Land. | Durch: | M. Vitum Dietrich. | Gedruckt zu Nürnberg, durch Vlrich | Newber. | M. D. LXIX.
Nuremberg: Ulrich Neuber, 1569.
121 unnumbered leaves.
1569 Diet

The Kessler Collection holds the first (1543), fourth (1545), and fifth (1569) editions of the handbook for rural clergy by Veit Dietrich (1506–1549), pastor of St. Sebaldus in Nuremberg.[61] The 1545 and 1569 versions include not only the usual liturgical chants but also the song "Als Je- sus Christus vnser Herr"[62] by Sebald Heyden (1499–1561), rector of the St. Sebaldus school and author of the important theoretical treatise *De arte ca- nendi* (1540),[63] as well as the German Litany.

OTHER

(32) Die letzste[n] drey | Psalmen von Orgelen, | Paucke[n], Glocken vnd | der gleychen eüsserlichen Gotß | dienst, ob vnd wie Got dar | ynnen gelobt wyrdt, Ver | deütscht durch Wen= | tzeßlaum Linck Ec= | clesiasten zü Alden | burgk. | M D.XXIII. | Zwickaw.
Zwickau: Jörg Gastel, 1523.
12 unnumbered leaves.
1523 Linc B

This pamphlet contains a German translation and exegesis of Psalms 148–150 by Wenceslaus Linck (1483–1547), a friend of Luther and leader in the Lutheran church during the first half of the sixteenth century. He served as preacher in the Thuringian city of Altenburg (1522–1524) and in Nuremberg (1525–1547). The treatise on *Die letzsten drey Psalmen* dates from Linck's tenure in Altenburg.[64] It was published in Zwickau, about twenty miles south of Altenburg.[65]

(33) Ain kurtzer be | griff vnd innhalt der gantzen | Bibel, in drew Lieder zü sing- en | gestellt, durch Joachim | Aberlin. | M. D. XXXIIII.
N.p., 1534.
48 unnumbered leaves.
1534 Aber

This pedagogical work by Joachim Aberlin condenses the entire content of the Bible into three very long songs. The Old Testament is summarized in 132 stanzas, the psalter in fifty, and the New Testament in forty-five.[66] Each song is preceded by several musical options—a melody in musical notation, fol- lowed by a list of song titles—with the indication that it may be sung to any of these tunes.[67] The songs also are acrostics. The first letter of each stanza of the Old Testament song spells out a biographical sketch: "Joachim Aberlin auß dem dorf Garmenschwiler, zwischen dem vrsprung der Dünaw vnnd dem Bodense (in ainer gegne die haißt das Madach) gelegen, sang es also am Jstro" ("Joachim Aberlin, from the village of Garmenschwiler, located be- tween the source of the Danube and Lake Constance [in a region called the Madach]; it therefore was sung on the Istro"). For the psalter, the hidden mes- sage reads: "Wol allen denen die auff Gott den Herren jr vertrauwen haben" ("Happy are all those who put their trust in God the Lord"). The acrostic for the New Testament quotes 1 Timothy 2:5, in Latin—"Vnus Deus vnus etiam conciliator Dei et hominum homo Christus Iesus" ("There is one God and one mediator between God and men, the man Christ Jesus")—but it is incomplete, ending with the "C" in "Christus." The project is pervaded with the work of an educator, and Aberlin did indeed spend the bulk of his career as schoolmaster and pastor in the towns of Lauingen, Göppingen, Heiningen, and Fortschweier.[68]

NOTES

1. See Gary S. Hauk, *A Legacy of Heart and Mind: Emory Since 1836* (Atlanta: Bookhouse Group, 1999), 1–9.

2. Ibid., 148.

3. About 1,500 of these pieces are listed in *The Richard C. Kessler Reformation Collection: An Annotated Bibliography*, comp. Fred A. Grater, ed. Wm. Bradford Smith, 4 vols. (Atlanta: Scholars Press, 1999), including nos. 1–2, 5–6, 10, 12–14, 22, 24–25, 27–31, and 33 below.

4. Joseph Herl, *Worship Wars in Early Lutheranism: Choir, Congregation, and Three Centuries of Conflict* (New York: Oxford University Press, 2004), 88.

5. According to Hans Joachim Köhler and Hans J. Hillerbrand, "More than half the known pamphlets are only eight pages, while the average is roughly twice that length." Hans Joachim Köhler and Hans J. Hillerbrand, "Pamphlets," in *The Oxford Encyclopedia of the Reformation*, 4 vols., ed. Hans J. Hillerbrand (New York: Oxford University Press, 1996), 3:201.

6. Call numbers refer to Special Collections of Pitts Theology Library, Emory University. I am grateful to M. Patrick Graham and the other librarians for their cordial and efficient assistance. The library's website, www.pitts.emory.edu, includes an extensive Digital Image Archive of woodcuts and metal engravings from items in the Kessler Collection.

7. Philipp Wackernagel, *Bibliographie zur Geschichte des deutschen Kirchenliedes im XVI. Jahrhundert* (1855; repr., Hildesheim: Georg Olms, 1987), 67–68 (no. 177).

8. Philipp Wackernagel, *Das deutsche Kirchenlied*, 5 vols. (1864–1877; repr., Hildesheim: Georg Olms, 1990), 3:60–61 (no. 87).

9. For details of its origins, see Adelbert von Keller and Edmund Goetze, eds., *Hans Sachs*, 26 vols. (1870–1908; repr., Hildesheim: Georg Olms, 1964), 22:104–8, 24:88–89 (Enr. 13), 25:12 (no. 97); Bernd Balzer, *Bürgerliche Reformationspropaganda: Die Flugschriften des Hans Sachs in den Jahren 1523–1525* (Stuttgart: J. B. Metzlersche Verlagsbuchhandlung, 1973), 94–95; Rebecca Wagner Oettinger, *Music as Propaganda in the German Reformation* (Aldershot, England: Ashgate, 2001), 104–12.

10. Karl Wilhelm Ludwig Heyse, *Bücherschatz der deutschen Nationalliteratur des XVI. und XVII. Jahrhunderts* (1854; repr., Hildesheim: Georg Olms, 1967), 62 (no. 1017).

11. The songs are "ELlendigklich, rüff ich O gott, mein herr" (Wackernagel, *Kirchenlied*, 3:423 [no. 486]; Oettinger, 263–64 [no. 64]), "ACh feyndes neydt, wie hast so weyt" (Wackernagel, *Kirchenlied*, 3:423 24 [no. 187]; Oettinger, 222 [no. 7]), and "VOn edler art, auch reyn vnd zart" (Wackernagel, *Kirchenlied*, 3:424 [no. 488]; Oettinger, 352 [no. 202]). Each contains three stanzas. Though they have no printed music, there are references to the tunes of secular songs. The first hymn is to be sung "Jn dem Thon. Klag für ich groß, gantz ploß."; the second "Jn dem Thon. Mich wundert zwar, was frawen har."; and the third "Jn dem Thon. Von Edler art. eyn frewlein zart. &c." The latter melody is from a *Minnelied* whose history is traced in Franz M. Böhme, *Altdeutsches Liederbuch: Volkslieder der Deutschen nach Wort und Weise aus dem 12. bis zum 17. Jahrhundert* (1877; repr., Hildesheim: Georg Olms, 1966), 227–28 (no. 130).

12. Eduard Emil Koch, *Geschichte des Kirchenlieds und Kirchengesangs der christlichen, insbesondere der deutschen evangelischen Kirche*, 3rd ed., 9 vols. (Stuttgart: Belser, 1866–1877), 1:289.

13. *Allgemeine deutsche Biographie*, 56 vols., ed. Rochus von Liliencron (Leipzig: Duncker und Humblot, 1875–1912), 15:632.

14. Wackernagel, *Bibliographie*, 241 (no. 608). He lists two more editions as well, both published in Nuremberg, by Valentin Neuber (pp. 241–42 [no. 609]) and by Friderich Gutknecht (p. 242 [no. 610]).

15. Wackernagel, *Kirchenlied*, 3:772–74 (nos. 899 and 900).

16. On the origins of "Frisch auf, ihr Landsknecht alle!" see Böhme, 521–24 (no. 417).

17. Wackernagel, *Bibliographie*, 213 (no. 519). The words are reprinted in Wackernagel, *Kirchenlied*, 3:982–83 (no. 1167).

18. See Oettinger, 177, 399 (no. 226).

19. The "Benzenauer" melody is discussed in Böhme, 469–72 (no. 381), and the "Dollerlied" on 456–59 (no. 374). The latter also is given in Johannes Zahn, *Die Melodien der deutschen evangelischen Kirchenlieder aus den Quellen geschöpft und mitgeteilt*, 6 vols. (1889–1893; repr., Hildesheim: Georg Olms, 1997), 4:330 (no. 7213). I am grateful to Robin A. Leaver for his assistance in ascertaining the origins of these tunes.

20. Zahn, 3:385–86 (no. 5356). A facsimile is available in the Digital Image Archive mentioned in note 6.

21. Eduard Albert Bielz, *Handbuch der Landeskunde Siebenbürgens: Eine physikalisch-statistisch-topographische Beschreibung dieses Landes* (1857; repr., Cologne: Böhlau, 1996), 419; Otto Mittelstrass, ed., *Topographie der Ortschaften: Karte des Grossfürstentums Siebenbürgen*, Historisch-Landeskundlicher Atlas von Siebenbürgen, vol. 2 (Heidelberg: Arbeitskreis für Siebenbürgische Landeskunde, 1993), 44; Walter Myß, ed., *Die Siebenbürger Sachsen Lexicon: Geschichte, Kultur, Zivilisation, Wissenschaften, Wirtschaft, Lebensraum Siebenbürgen (Transsilvanien)* (Thaur bei Innsbruck: Wort und Welt, 1993), 571, 609; Tibor Szentpétery and Terézia Kerny, *Gottes feste Burgen: Sächsische Wehrkirchen des Mittelalters in Siebenbürgen* (N.p., 1990), 141 (includes photos of the church in Werd). See also the online article about Werd by Johann Arz, www.siebenbuerger.de/ortschaften/werd/index.html, and

the entry in the "German Genealogy: Transylvania Village List," www.genealogie netz.de/reg/ESE/7burg_tz.html.

22. David P. Daniel, "Honter, Johannes," in *Oxford Encyclopedia*, 2:250.

23. Georg Daniel Teutsch, *Geschichte der Siebenbürger Sachsen für das sächsische Volk*, vol. 1 (Von den ältesten Zeiten bis 1699), 4th ed. (1925; repr., Cologne: Böhlau, 1984), 243–67; Erich Roth, *Die Geschichte des Gottesdienstes der Siebenbürger Sachsen* (Göttingen: Vandenhoeck und Ruprecht, 1954), 69–108; Karl Reinerth, *Die Reformation der siebenbürgisch-sächsischen Kirche* (Gütersloh: Carl Bertelsmann, 1956), 23–54; Annemie Schenk, *Deutsche in Siebenbürgen: Ihre Geschichte und Kultur* (Munich: C. H. Beck, 1992), 46–47; Myß, 202–3, 236–37; Peter Schimert, "Transylvania," in *Oxford Encyclopedia*, 4:170–71. See also Christian Agnethler, "Die Reformation in Siebenbürgen," www.agnethler.de/sites/kirche5.html, and Konrad Gündisch, "The History of Transylvania and the Transylvanian Saxons," www.sibiweb.de/geschi/7b-history.htm.

24. Wackernagel, *Bibliographie*, 248–49 (no. 632). The song appears in Wackernagel, *Kirchenlied*, 3:1056–58 (no. 1228).

25. Oliver K. Olson, "Magdeburg," in *Oxford Encyclopedia*, 2:481–82.

26. The words of Luther's hymn were, in fact, associated with five different melodies. See Markus Jenny, *Luthers Geistliche Lieder und Kirchengesänge: Vollständige Neuedition in Ergänzung zu Band 35 der Weimarer Ausgabe* (Cologne: Böhlau, 1985), 62–65, 175–79 (no. 8).

27. Wackernagel, *Bibliographie*, 49–50 (nos. 129–31), 462–64; Wilhelm Lucke, ed., *D. Martin Luthers Werke: Kritische Gesamtausgabe*, vol. 35 (Weimar: Hermann Böhlaus Nachfolger, 1923), 336–37; Konrad Ameln, "Das Achtliederbuch vom Jahre 1523/24," *Jahrbuch für Liturgik und Hymnologie* 2 (1956): 89–91; Konrad Ameln, ed., *Das Achtliederbuch Nürnberg 1523/24 in originalgetreuem Nachdruck* (Kassel: Bärenreiter, 1957); Jenny, 19–20; Josef Benzing and Helmut Claus, *Lutherbibliographie: Verzeichnis der gedruckten Schriften Martin Luthers bis zu dessen Tod*, 2 vols. (Baden-Baden: Valentin Koerner, 1989–1994), 1:426 (nos. 3571–73), 2:282.

28. Benzing, 2:282: "TE [Titeleinfassung] wie 3571, '1523' wie 3572.... Verbleib dieses Exemplars unbekannt."

29. For more detailed information about this hymnal, see Stephen A. Crist, *Enchiridion Geistliker Leder vnde Psalmen, Magdeburg 1536: Introductory Study and Facsimile Edition* (Atlanta: Scholars Press, 1994).

30. Robin A. Leaver, "Hymnals," in *Oxford Encyclopedia*, 2:286–87.

31. See Jenny, 51; also Wackernagel, *Bibliographie*, 187–88 (no. 463), and Lucke, vol. 35, 331–32 (P²). On the other editions of Klug's hymnal, see Konrad Ameln, "Das Klugsche Gesangbuch, Wittenberg 1529: Versuche einer Rekonstruktion," *Jahrbuch für Liturgik und Hymnologie* 16 (1971):159–62; Konrad Ameln, ed., *Das Klug'sche Gesangbuch 1533 nach dem einzigen erhaltenen Exemplar der Lutherhalle zu Wittenberg* (Kassel: Bärenreiter, 1983); and Robin A. Leaver, *"Goostly Psalmes and Spirituall Songes": English and Dutch Metrical Psalms from Coverdale to Utenhove 1535–1566* (Oxford: Clarendon Press, 1991), 10–13, 281–85.

32. A detailed comparison can be found in the introduction to Konrad Ameln, ed., *Das Babstsche Gesangbuch von 1545: Faksimiledruck mit einem Geleitwort* (Kassel: Bärenreiter, 1988), 8–9.

33. Wackernagel, *Bibliographie*, 342 (no. 889), notes that the thirty additional songs in Part Two of the 1567 edition are the same ones as in the 1553 printing.

34. Georg Karstädt, "Schmügel, Johann Christoph," in *The New Grove Dictionary of Music and Musicians*, 2nd ed. (London: Macmillan, 2001), 22:547–48.

35. Oswald Bill, *Das Frankfurter Gesangbuch von 1569 und seine späteren Ausgaben* (Marburg: Görich und Weiershäuser, 1969). See also Wackernagel, *Bibliographie*, 356–57 (nos. 903–5; Emory's copy is the second of the three editions); Ernst-Ludwig Berz, *Die Notendrucker und ihre Verleger in Frankfurt am Main von den Anfängen bis etwa 1630* (Kassel: Bärenreiter, 1970), 54–57 (regarding Johann Wolff), 157–58 (no. 26); Walther Lipphardt, *Gesangbuchdrucke in Frankfurt am Main vor 1569* (Frankfurt am Main: Waldemar Kramer, 1974), 186–88.

36. For a brief history of the Princely House, a simplified genealogical table, and other information, see www.fuerstenhaus.li.

37. See David Beattie, *Liechtenstein: A Modern History* (London: I. B. Tauris, 2004), 10–14. The most extensive account of Karl's life and cultural influence is Herbert Haupt, *Fürst Karl I. von Liechtenstein: Hofstaat und Sammeltätigkeit* (Vienna: Hermann Böhlaus Nachfolger, 1983). According to Haupt, a "Kirchenbuch" is listed in a 1608 inventory of the Prince's music (p. 60). One wonders whether this might be the volume now held by the Kessler Collection.

38. Herl, 6.

39. Paul Pietsch, ed., *D. Martin Luthers Werke: Kritische Gesamtausgabe*, vol. 12 (Weimar: Hermann Böhlau, 1891), 197–205.

40. Wackernagel, *Kirchenlied*, 3:51 (no. 74).

41. Jenny, 66–68, 184–87 (no. 10). See also Martin Luther, *Liturgy and Hymns*, ed. Ulrich S. Leupold, Luther's Works, vol. 53 (Philadelphia: Fortress Press, 1965), 232–34; an English translation of the entire treatise is provided on pp. 15–40. (This source is subsequently cited as *LW* 53.)

42. See Paul Pietsch, ed., *D. Martin Luthers Werke: Kritische Gesamtausgabe*, vol. 19 (Weimar: Hermann Böhlaus Nachfolger, 1897), 44–69, for a detailed discussion of the *Deutsche Messe*. An English translation of the service is available in *LW* 53, 51–90. Substantial treatment of aspects of this document also is found in Herl, 8–16. On Luther's version of the Sanctus, see Jenny, 97–99, 243–45 (no. 26).

43. According to Benzing, 261 [no. 224], the printer was Heinrich Steiner. Emory's Digital Image Archive (see note 6) includes a facsimile of the entire print.

44. Jenny, 101–5, 250–73 (no. 29). For an English translation, see *LW* 53, 153–70.

45. Jenny, 105–7, 274–75 (no. 30); *LW* 53, 286–87.

46. It includes a preface by "Johannes Schwan Burger zü Straßburg." See Wackernagel, *Bibliographie*, 72 (no. 185); Friedrich Hubert, *Die Straßburger liturgischen Ordnungen im Zeitalter der Reformation nebst einer Bibliographie der Straßburger Gesangbücher* (Göttingen: Vandenhoeck und Ruprecht, 1900), XV (no. 12); Lucke, vol. 35, 370 (k); Miriam Usher Chrisman, *Bibliography of Strasbourg Imprints*,

1480–1599 (New Haven, Conn.: Yale University Press, 1982), 354–55 (P7.2.11); Benzing, 432 (no. 3634).

47. See Jenny, 68–70 and 188–93 (no. 11: "Aus tiefer Not schrei ich zu dir"), 66–68 and 184–87 (no. 10: "Es wollt uns Gott genädig sein"); Wackernagel, *Kirchenlied*, 3:89–90 (no. 119: "Ach Gott, wie lang vergissest mein"), 3:95 (no. 128: "Ach Herr, wie sind meinr feind so vil").

48. Frank C. Senn, "Liturgy: Protestant Liturgy," in *Oxford Encyclopedia*, 2:440. See also Jeffrey P. Jaynes, "Church Ordinances," in *Oxford Encyclopedia*, 1:345–51.

49. The following list includes only church orders containing printed music.

50. Wolf-Dieter Hauschild, "Bugenhagen, Johannes," in *Oxford Encyclopedia*, 1:226–27.

51. See Georg Geisenhof, *Bibliotheca Bugenhagiana: Bibliographie der Druckschriften des D. Joh. Bugenhagen* (1908; repr., Nieuwkoop: B. De Graaf, 1963), 274–76 (nos. 239–40). The Low-German edition is reprinted in Aemilius Ludwig Richter, ed., *Die evangelischen Kirchenordnungen des sechszehnten Jahrhunderts*, 2 vols. (1846; repr., Nieuwkoop: B. De Graaf, 1967), 1:106–20 (no. 24), and in Emil Sehling, *Die evangelischen Kirchenordnungen des XVI. Jahrhunderts*, 15 vols. to date (Leipzig: O. R. Reisland, 1902–1913; Tübingen: J. C. B. Mohr (Paul Siebeck), 1955–), 6/1:348–455. Both Richter and Sehling omit all musical notation. It is vital, therefore, to consult original editions of church orders when investigating questions relating to music.

52. Günter Vogler, "Nuremberg," in *Oxford Encyclopedia*, 3:160–62.

53. The 1533 version is reprinted in Richter, 1:176–211 (no. 42), and in Sehling, 11:140–205.

54. Sehling, 1/1:89. The 1539 edition is reprinted in Richter, 1:307–15 (no. 64), and in Sehling, 1/1:264–81 (no. 24).

55. Grater, 4: no. 1274. See also Richter, 2:128 (no. 93).

56. On the various editions, see Sehling, 5:132–36. The 1552 version is reprinted in Richter, 2:115–28 (no. 92), and in Sehling, 5:161–219 (no. 28).

57. See Herbert Baum, "Kirchengesang, Gesang- und Choralbücher in Waldeck," in *Beiträge zur Geschichte der evangelischen Kirchenmusik und Hymnologie in Kurhessen und Waldeck*, ed. Landesverband der evangelischen Kirchenchöre (Kassel: Bärenreiter, 1969), 32–43, esp. 32–33. The document is reprinted in Richter, 2:169–77 (no. 104).

58. Sehling, 6/1:486. The entire document is reprinted in Sehling, 6/1:533–75 (no. 4); a summary is provided in Richter, 2:285–87 (no. 121).

59. A full-page portrait of Julius is printed at the front of both editions.

60. Sehling, 6/1:5. A modern reprint is provided in Sehling, 6/1:83–280 (no. 3); a summary is given in Richter, 2:318–24 (no. 131).

61. See Bernhard Klaus, *Veit Dietrich: Leben und Werk* (Nuremberg: Selbstverlag des Vereins für bayerische Kirchengeschichte, 1958), 3–5 (no. 5), 206–9. The 1545 edition is reprinted in Sehling, 11:487–553.

62. Wackernagel, *Kirchenlied*, 3:557–58 (no. 606).

63. For an English translation of Sebald Hcyden's 1540 treatise, see *De arte canendi*, trans. Clement A. Miller, Musicological Studies and Documents, 26 (n.p.: American Institute of Musicology, 1972).

64. Jürgen Lorz, *Bibliographia Linckiana: Bibliographie der gedruckten Schriften Dr. Wenzeslaus Lincks (1483–1547)* (Nieuwkoop: B. De Graaf, 1977), 36 (no. 7).

65. See Helmut Claus, *Die Zwickauer Drucke des 16. Jahrhunderts* (Gotha: Forschungsbibliothek, 1985), 83 (no. 22).

66. Wackernagel, *Bibliographie*, 126–27 (no. 324).

67. Zahn points out that the three notated melodies were not incorporated into subsequent publications (6:12 [no. 40]). From their titles, one surmises that most of the other songs are secular in origin. But only three are found in Böhme: "Jch gieng ains mals spacieren" (p. 751 [no. 641]), "Die Sonn ist vns entplichen" (pp. 215–17 [no. 116]), and the "Toller" melody (pp. 456–59 [no. 374]).

68. Hans Ulrich Bächtold, "Aberlin, Joachim," in *Biographisch-Bibliographisches Kirchenlexicon*, 24 vols. to date, ed. Friedrich Wilhelm Bautz (Herzberg: Traugott Bautz, 1999), 15:1–3.

3

Tradition with Variations: Chorale Settings *per omnes versus* by Buxtehude and Bach

Kerala J. Snyder

Since the time of the Reformation, German Lutheran congregations had been singing all the verses of their hymns. With the advent of concerted style in the seventeenth century, composers from Michael Praetorius and Samuel Scheidt to Johann Schelle and Dieterich Buxtehude exploited the various scoring possibilities that it offered to create large concerted vocal works based on all the verses of a chorale. This option became less attractive to eighteenth-century composers once operatic recitative and aria had become incorporated into the church cantata, and yet J. S. Bach composed ten chorale cantatas *per omnes versus*. Buxtehude and Bach were separated by geography and generation, but they were joined by a famous walk from Arnstadt to Lübeck so that Bach could "comprehend one thing and another about his art."[1] In this chapter I examine the *per-omnes-versus* compositions of both composers and suggest a point of convergence between the two. In order to do this, we must first be able to determine what each composer understood to be all the verses of a given chorale. While the texts and hymnal sources for Bach's chorales have been thoroughly researched,[2] those for Buxtehude's have not.[3] And since two previously lost sources of hymnody in Lübeck have recently come to light, I shall begin with a discussion of the sources for chorale texts and melodies available to Buxtehude in Lübeck.

HYMNODY IN LÜBECK DURING BUXTEHUDE'S TIME

Although various hymnals had been printed in Lübeck since shortly after the Reformation,[4] the first official Lübeck hymnal authorized by the city council, the *Lübeckisches Gesang-Buch*, was published only in 1703, very late in Bux-tehude's tenure as organist of St. Mary's Church. It appeared in numerous un-altered printings until 1748, when an appendix was added,[5] and thus the earliest extant copy, from 1729[6] (figure 3.1), can be accepted as representing the 1703 edition. The 1703 decree of the senate and an extensive foreword,

Figure 3.1. *Lübeckisches Gesang-Buch* (1729)

signed by the superintendent and all pastors and preachers, dated March 17, 1703, are reprinted in this 1729 edition. Its 303 numbered hymns, printed without music, are ordered in the manner typical of the time, grouping them under headings beginning with the seasons and festivals of the church year and then progressing to various topics relating to Christian faith and life.

In 1705 the St. Mary's cantor, Jacob Pagendarm, supervised the preparation of four manuscript partbooks—soprano, alto, tenor, and bass—containing harmonizations of the melodies for most of these 303 hymns, for which he had written the music and two "Aritmetici," probably teachers at the Catharineum, had copied the texts. In the account book that Buxtehude kept as part of his duty as Werkmeister, he recorded that Pagendarm had received 60 Lübeck marks for his work copying the music, and the text writers together 150 marks.[7] When Hermann Jimmerthal, organist and Werkmeister of St. Mary's from 1845 to 1886, wrote of this in his manuscript chronicle of St. Mary's Church, he noted that these books were still in the archives, and that the melodies were "almost all in their original form."[8] In his catalog of the St. Mary's archives, they are listed under III, Musik, nos. 14–17 and described as "four thick books, bound in parchment and containing a great number of four-voice chorales for soprano, alto, tenor, and bass (complete)."[9]

Following the bombing of Lübeck in 1942, almost all its valuable archives, including the Pagendarm partbooks, were removed from the city and placed in a salt mine in Bernburg, Saxony for safekeeping. They did not return to Lübeck after the war but were dispersed in various directions in Eastern Europe. Some of these materials were taken by the Soviet occupation forces to Potsdam in 1950, and between 1954 and 1971 the director of the Lübeck archives was able to inspect them there and note their presence in the Lübeck finding aids. When I was given access to these partbooks in 1982, the tenor and bass parts were missing, but I was able to obtain a microfilm of the soprano partbook (no. 14; here abbreviated Pag) and use those melodies for the chorale examples in my book *Dieterich Buxtehude: Organist in Lübeck*.[10] By the time they returned to Lübeck in 1988, the tenor partbook (no. 16) had reappeared, but the bass partbook (no. 17) is still missing.[11]

For every chorale that I have examined, Pagendarm's chorale number, text, and number of verses correspond exactly to those of the 1729 printing of the *Lübeckisches Gesang-Buch*. But where both Buxtehude and Jimmerthal stated that the chorale book included all 303 hymns, it in fact does not, and some of its 22 omissions are quite surprising: "Die deutsche Litanei," "Kyrie Gott Vater in Ewigkeit," "Allein Gott in der Höh sei Ehr," "Wir glauben all an einen Gott," "Herr Jesu Christ dich zu uns wend," "Liebster Jesu wir sind hier," "Jesus Christus unser Heiland der von uns," "Gott sei gelobet und gebenedeiet." But the very omission of these hymns that were so important to the liturgy might give us a clue as to the purpose of this chorale book. Clearly the omitted hymns, which the congregation must have sung, were NOT sung by the Cantorei in four-part harmony. Perhaps these hymns were too important for the congregation not to sing all the verses, and when the Cantorei did sing hymns in harmony from these partbooks they sang alone, without the congregation, in an introductory or alternatim capacity. When they sang with the congregation, they probably sang in unison. In a church as large as St. Mary's, this would make acoustical sense.

The ministers who compiled the official 1703 *Lübeckisches Gesang-Buch* (here abbreviated L 1703) had selected its hymns from a much larger hymnal that had been printed privately in Lübeck five years earlier, the *Lübeckisch-Vollständiges Gesangbuch* (here abbreviated L 1698).[12] Lübeck's copy of this hymnal has been missing since 1942, but a copy at the British Library has recently come to light.[13] As its full title notes, its 974 hymns include many additions to the core repertory of hymns by Luther and his contemporaries, including seventy-six by Paul Gerhardt. The pastors were concerned with the theological orthodoxy of some of these newer hymns and feared that their parishioners would forget the old ones; in fact, in the introduction to their official hymnal of 1703 they suggested that before and after the sermon, and during the distribution of communion, the congregation sing two old hymns for each new one.[14] But Ada Kadelbach has surveyed the 258 hymns that are common to the *Lübeckisch-Vollständiges Gesangbuch* and the Freyling-hausen hymnal of 1704 and established that none is later than 1675 and that the prominent writers of the pietistic circle—Gottfried Arnold, Johann Wilhelm Petersen, Laurentius Laurenti, Michael Müller, and others—are entirely missing from the 1698 Lübeck hymnal. She concludes that the fears of the pastors of an onslaught of pietistic hymns were unfounded.[15]

Meanwhile, another manuscript chorale book from St. Mary's Church had returned in 1998 to the Lübeck archives after a long exile in Armenia: one of the two partbooks preceding Pagendarm's set in Jimmerthal's catalog, described as "12.13. 2 manuscript chorale books bound in leather and dark blue paper, soprano and alto voices."[16] He did not note that this set was incomplete, but it was probably already missing a tenor and bass part in the mid-nineteenth century, and now just the soprano part is there, numbered 13 (here abbreviated MK13). This collection, with only 110 hymns, is much smaller than Pagendarm's chorale book, and it does not appear to be based on any known hymnal. Table 3.1 lists its repertory in order. The hymns themselves are not numbered, but the pages are, and the entries in the first column, marked MK13, represent the page number on which the hymn begins, almost invariably carrying over to the next page on the right side of the opening. If the hymns are short, two will fit in an opening, indicated by "a" and "b." Most of the hymns in MK13 also appear in the 1703 *Lübeckisches Gesang-Buch*.

The repertory of MK13 is quite an old one; approximately half its hymns already appeared in Lübeck's first "unofficial" hymnal, the Low-German *Enchiridion Geistlike Lede und Psalmen*, published in Lübeck in 1545 and edited by its first superintendent after the Reformation, Hermann Bonnus.[17] And 94 of its 110 texts were first published before 1600. Only sixteen of MK13's texts stem from the seventeenth century, including three from Johann Heermann's *Devoti Musica Cordis* of 1630, three by Johann Rist, and the latest of them, Ernst Christian Homburg's "Jesu meines Lebens Leben," first published in 1659 and the last hymn to be entered into MK13, on page 174. As in the Pagendarm chorale book, all the verses of each hymn are entered beneath the melody.

The physical evidence provided by MK13 suggests that it was copied in several stages. In the alphabetical index at the back of the manuscript, all of the chorales through "O Traurigkeit, o Herzeleid" on page 146 are entered neatly in alphabetical order, but those from pages 148 through 164 are added out of order at the end of each letter, and the last five do not appear at all. This evidence is congruent with the fact that there are at least four, perhaps five, distinct musical hands visible in this manuscript, which I have listed in the column "Clef," indicating five distinctive manners of writing the C-clef. Clef 2 accounts for the bulk of the manuscript, from pages 36 through 147, with the exception of pages 98–99, containing the only two chorales with Clef 3. The chorales with Clefs 4 and 5 correspond exactly to those that did not appear in the original index, and new paper begins with page 153. This group contains the latest dated texts and melodies that I have found, as well as the only two examples of signatures with two flats: "Wer nur den lieben Gott läßt walten," in B-flat, and "Jesu meine Freude," in C with two flats, an unusual key in the transmission of this chorale. All the other chorales in MK13 are written either in *cantus durus* with no signature or *cantus mollis* with one flat.

Only one of the hands in MK13 can be identified: the writer of the chorales with Clef 4 is almost certainly Jacob Pagendarm, cantor from 1679 until his death in 1706, Buxtehude's close contemporary. This would suggest that the bulk of MK13 was copied prior to Pagendarm's arrival in Lübeck, perhaps by his predecessor, Samuel Franck, cantor from 1663 until 1679 and Buxtehude's brother-in-law; I have not yet found a sample of his handwriting. The latest text date for Clef 2 is Rist's "O Traurigkeit, o Herzeleid" of 1641, and the latest melody date 1668 for "Der Tag hat sich geneiget" on page 130 (Zahn no. 5420b).[18] I thus tentatively date the copying of pages 1–147 of MK 13 to the 1670s, the early part of Buxtehude's tenure as organist of St. Mary's in Lübeck.

One other Lübeck chorale book bears mentioning: the manuscript A 216 at the Bibliothek der Hansestadt Lübeck comes from St. Peter's Church and is virtually identical with MK13 through page 140, as can be seen in table 3.1.

Table 3.1. MK13

MK13	Clef	Title	Key	Sig	Petri	L1690	L1703
6a	1	Nun komm der Heiden Heiland	g	-b	7a/end=	77x	1=
6b	1	Herr Christ der einig Gotts Sohn	F	-b	7b/end=	437	124=
8	1	Wie schön leuchtet der Morgenstern	F	-b	8=	53	275=
10	1	Ihr lieben Christen freut euch nun	F	-b	10=	927	
12a	1	Es ist gewisslich an der Zeit	F	-b	12a=	913	267=
12b	1	Es woll uns Gott genädig sein	e	0	120b=	796	68=
14	1	Wacht auf ihr Christen alle	G	0	14=	914	268=
16	1	Wachet auf ruft uns die Stimme	C	0	16=	929	269=
18a	1	Christum wir sollen loben schon	e	0	18a=	90	5=
18b	1	Helft mir Gotts Güte preisen	G	0	18b=	127	17=
20	1	Christ unser Herr zum Jordan kam	a	0	20=	311	86=
22	1	Ein Kindelein so löbelich	F	-b	22=	112	8=
24	1	Der Tag der ist so freudenreich	F	-b	24=	94	7=
26a	1	In dulci jubilo	F	-b	26a=	93	9=
26b	1	Vom Himmel kam der Engel Schaar	b	0	26b=	100	13x
28a	1	Gelobet seist du Jesu Christ	G	0	28a=	95	4=
28b	1	Ein Kind geborn zu Bethlehem	C	0	28bx		
30	1	Puer natus in Bethlehem/Ein Kind geborn	g	-b	30x	112	15=
32	1	Vom Himmel hoch da komm ich her	b	0	32=	99	6x
34a	1	Wohl dem der in Gottes Fürchten steht	G	0	34a=	577	156=
34b	1	Was kann uns kommen an für Not	G	0	34b=	447	202=
36	2	Ich ruf zu dir Herr Jesu Christ	d	-b	36=	585	145=
38	2	Allein zu dir Herr Jesu Christ	a	0	38=	358	102=
40	2	Kommt her zu mir spricht Gottes Sohn	g	-b	40=	656	146=
42	2	Aus tiefer Not schrei ich zu dir	G	0	42=	355	101=
44	2	Erbarm dich mein, o Herre Gott	e	0	44=	348	99=
46	2	Wo Gott der Herr nicht bei uns hàlt	g	-b	46x	798	230=
48a	2	Wenn wir in höchsten Nöten seyn	G	0	48a=	722	176=
48b	2	Mit Fried und Freud ich fahr dahin	d	0	48b=	832	260=
50	2	Ach Gott vom Himmel sieh darein	a	-b	50x	792	224=
52	2	O Herre Gott, dein göttlich Wort	Bb	-b	52=	805	238=
54	2	Es ist das Heil uns kommen her	F	-b	54=	435	122=
56a	2	Es spricht der unweisen Mund wohl	G	0	56a=	795	225=
56b	2	Christ der du bist der helle Tag	a	0	56b=	996	289=
58	2	Durch Adams Fall ist ganz verderbt	a	0	58=	434	121=
60a	2	Ein feste Burg ist unser Gott	C	0	60a=	802	226=
60b	2	Zwei Ding, o Herr, bitt ich von dir	G	0	60b=	517	
62	2	Vater unser im Himmelreich	d	0	62=	301	83=
64a	2	Christe der du bist Tag und Licht	a	0	64=	995	288=
64b	2	Gott der Vater wohn uns bei	C	0	64=	591	67=
66a	2	Ach Gott mein Herr, wie groß und schwer	C	0	66a=	361	104=
66b	2	O Lamm Gottes unschuldig	G	0	66b=	167	27=
68	2	Lobet den Herren denn er ist sehr freundlich	e	0	68=	40	130=
70	2	Christus der uns selig macht	e	0	70=	163	25=
72	2	Ach wir armen Sünder	d	0	72=	178x	26=
74	2	Hilf Gott, laß mirs gelingen	G	0	74=	182	
76a	2	Herr Jesu Christ, wahr Mensch und Gott	d	0	76a=	832	250=
76b	2	Christ ist erstanden	d	0	76b=	229	46=
78a	2	Da Jesus an dem Kreuze stund	e	0	78a=	189	30=
78b	2	Jesus Christus unser Heiland der den Tod	g	-b	78b=	231	47=
80	2	Christ lag in Todesbanden	d	0	80=	230	44=
82a	2	Surrexit Christus hodie/Erstanden ist	F	-b	82a=	240	
82b	2	Jesus Christus wahr Gottes Sohn	g	-b	82b=	245	48=
84a	2	Mag ich Unglück nicht wiederstehn	a	0	84a=	659	181=
84b	2	Nun laßt uns Gott dem Herren	F	-b	84b=	41x	132=

86	2	Nun freut euch lieben Christen gmein	G	0	86=	438	55=
88a	2	Ascendit Christus hodie/Gefahren ist der Herre Christ	F	-b	88a=	256	
88b	2	Christ fuhr gen Himmel	d	0	88b=	249	53=
90	2	Am Tag der Pfingsten das geschah	a-p	-b	90=		
92	2	O Herre Gott begnade mich	e-p	0	92=	351	100=
94a	2	Dies sind die heilige zehn Gebot	G	0	94a=	288	76=
94b	2	Mensch willst du leben seliglich	e-p	0	94b=	289	77=
96	2	Warum betrübstu dich mein Herz	G	0	96=	654	179=
98a	3	Nun bitten wir den heiligen Geist	G	0	98a=	264	59=
98b	3	Komm Heiliger Geist Herre Gott	G	0	98b=	263	60=
100	2	Nun lob mein Seel den Herren	G	0	100=	18x	127=
102a	2	Erhalt uns Herr bei deinem Wort	g	-b	102a=	803	227=
102b	2	Verleih uns Frieden gnädiglich	g	-b	102b=	803	227 Pag
104	2	An Wasserflüssen Babylons	F	-b	104=	799	
106a	2	In dich hab ich gehoffet Herr	d	0	106a=	625	178=
106b	2	Nimm von uns Herr du treuer Gott	d	0	106b=	724	177=
108a	2	O Gott wir danken deiner Güt	g	-b	108a=	1033	287=
108b	2	Was Lobes solln wir dir O Vater singen, dein That	g	-b	108b=	43xx	128=
110	2	Ich hab mein Sach Gott heimgestellt	g	-b	110=	818	247=
112a	2	Jesus Christus unser Heiland der von uns	d	-b	112a=	320	89 oPag
112b	2	Ach wie elend ist unser Zeit	F	-b	112b=	896	205=
114	2	Mitten wir im Leben sind	e-p	0	114=	359	256=
116	2	Herr Jesu Christ ich weiß gar wohl	a	0	116=	844	245=
118	2	Herzlich lieb hab ich dich O Herr	C	0	118=	542	251=
120a	2	Wend ab deinen Zorn	a	0	120a=	723	123=
120b	2	Wenn mein Stündlein vorhanden ist	Bb	-b	12b=	835	249=
122	2	Von Gott will ich nicht lassen	g	-b	122=	473	188=
124	2	Singen wir aus Herzen Grund	g	-b	124=	1034	285=
126	2	Wo soll ich fliehen hin	g	-b	126=	418	113=
128	2	Meine Seele erhebt den Herren	d	-b	128=,142x	1	2=
130	2	Der Tag hat sich geneiget	a	0	130x	1014	290=
132a	2	Du Friedefürst Herr Jesu Christ	F	-b	132a=	736	198=
132b	2	Auf meinen lieben Gott	g	-b	132=	542	193=
134	2	Allein Gott in der Höh sei Ehr	F	-b	134=	9	66 oPag
136	2	Ach lieben Christen seid getrost	g	-b	136=	476	183=
138	2	Was mein Gott will das gescheh allzeit	a	0	138=	477	200=
140	2	Herzlich tut mich verlangen	a-p	-b	140=	848	254=
142	2	Lobt Gott ihr Christen alle gleich	G	0	148x	117x	14=
144	2	Erschienen ist der herrliche Tag	d	0	0	239	45=
146	2	O Traurigkeit, o Herzeleid	a	0	150x	192	36=
148	4	Herr Jesu Christ meins Lebens Licht	Bb	-b	0	858	253=
150	4	Wir danken dir Herr Jesu Christ ..gen Himmel	d	0	0	252	57=
152	4	Von Adam her so lange Zeit	g	-b	0		
153	4	Die Propheten han prophezeit	g	-b	0		43=
154	5	Herr Gott dich loben wir	e-p	0	0	7	65=
156	4	O großer Gott von Macht	g	-b	0	725	197=
158	5	Herr Jesu Christ du höchstes Gut	a	0	0	400	103=
160	4	Ach Gott wie manches Herzeleid	d	0	0	594	173=
162	4	O Jesu du mein Bräutigam	F	-b	0	324	92=
164	4	O Jesu meine Wonne	F	-b	0	337	94=
166	4	Jesu meine Freude	c	-be	0	144	154=
168	4	Wer nur den lieben Gott lässt walten	Bb	-be	0	687	186=
170	4	Jesu der du meine Seele	g	-b	0	423	42=
172	4	Herzliebster Jesu was hast du verbrochen	a	0	0	184	29=
174	4	Jesu meines Lebens Leben	e	0	0	192	35=

It seems quite likely, then, that a repository of Lübeck hymnody was kept at the Catharineum, where the St. Mary's cantor was the music teacher and other teachers were responsible for leading the schoolboys in singing in each of the other parishes, and that the bulk of both MK13 and A 216 were copied from this source.

BUXTEHUDE'S *PER-OMNES-VERSUS* CHORALE SETTINGS

With four established sources for hymnody in Lübeck during Buxtehude's tenure—MK13 (1670s), *Lübeckisch-Vollständiges Gesangbuch* (1698), *Lübeckisches Gesang-Buch* (1703), and Pagendarm's chorale book (1705)— we are now in a position to establish which of his vocal chorale settings Buxtehude composed *per omnes versus*. There are only six,[19] listed in table 3.2. In looking at this group of six works, one is immediately struck by two facts: all six are settings of very familiar chorales, and these six works display a wide variety of compositional styles and overall designs. With the exception of "Jesu meine Freude," all the chorales date from the sixteenth century or earlier. The one Luther hymn among them, "Wär Gott nicht mit uns diese Zeit," is inexplicably missing from MK 13, although it was included in the 1545 *Enchiridion* and reappeared in L 1698, L 1703, and Pag.

Buxtehude employed his simplest and most characteristic mode of vocal chorale setting, the concertato harmonization, in three of these *per-omnes-versus* works, BuxWV 52, 81, and 102. *Wär Gott nicht mit uns diese Zeit* (BuxWV 102) presents this technique at its most basic: the four voices (SATB) declaim the hymn homophonically, interrupted after each phrase by two violins playing a two-measure interlude, which lengthens to a seven-measure ritornello after each stanza. There is no break or change of scoring between stanzas, and the first two are virtually identical; in the third stanza the regularity is broken and the sound intensified by the violins playing with the voices as well as during interludes. Buxtehude varies this pattern slightly

Table 3.2. Buxtehude's Chorale Settings *per omnes versus*

BuxWV	Title	Vss	Source
41	Herzlich lieb hab ich dich, o Herr	3	Lübeck
52	In dulci jubilo	4	Düben, Gottorf
60	Jesu meine Freude	6	Düben, Lübeck
81	Nun laßt uns Gott dem Herren	8	Düben
100	Wachet auf, ruft uns die Stimme	3	Gottorf
102	Wär Gott nicht mit uns diese Zeit	3	Düben

in *In dulci jubilo* (BuxWV 52) by reducing the number of voices to three (SSB) and in engaging the violins more extensively in true concertato interchange, sharing musical motives with the voices. These three *per-omnes-versus* settings differ in only one respect from the five other works that Buxtehude set as concertato harmonizations but which do not contain all the verses of the chorale (BuxWV 10, 20, 27, 40, and 103): these others all end with an extensive Amen section in concertato texture. The three *per-omnes-versus* settings thus come the closest of any of Buxtehude's works to congregational singing. But in fact they are two steps removed: the congregation sang in unison without accompaniment, the choirboys sang in simple four-part harmony, and Buxtehude's singers, most likely soloists, performed the chorales with strings and continuo.

In his other three *per-omnes-versus* settings, Buxtehude created much more complex works by setting each stanza as a separate movement and changing the scoring to heighten the contrast among them. Following an opening sinfonia, each of the three movements of *Wachet auf, ruft uns die Stimme* (BuxWV 100) is set as a separate chorale concerto, the first for soprano, the second for bass, and the third for three voices (SSB), all with instruments in constant concertato interchange. The cantus firmus is ever present, but Buxtehude breaks it up and varies it throughout. *Jesu meine Freude* (BuxWV 60) also begins with a sinfonia, and here he varies not only the scoring but also the compositional style between movements. The six stanzas of the chorale are arranged in near-symmetrical fashion, anchored in the outer movements by the tutti (SSB and instruments) in artful concertato harmonizations, lightening to aria-like chorale paraphrases for Soprano I (verse 2) and Soprano II (verse 5), accompanied only by continuo, and strengthening again in the middle with a chorale concerto movement for bass and instruments (verse 3) and a tutti concertato harmonization (verse 4). Since the chorale has an even number of stanzas, an axis of symmetry is lacking, however. Finally, in the three verses of *Herzlich lieb hab ich dich, o Herr* (BuxWV 41), Buxtehude presents his longest vocal work, and surely one of his most magnificent, as a chorale sinfonia for soprano and strings followed by two extended chorale concertos for five vocal soloists (SSATB), capella,[20] and instruments.

The manuscript sources that transmit these works can give just a sketch of their possible chronology. The three concertato harmonizations and *Jesu meine Freude* are found in the Düben Collection, now in Uppsala, Sweden, in manuscripts dating from the 1680s; in fact, three of these four works (BuxWV 60, 81, 102) are contained in a single tablature volume, S:Uu vok. mus. i hskr 85:1-18, which dates from 1687. The manuscripts for *In dulci jubilo* and *Wachet auf* were copied at the Gottorf court by its Kapellmeister Georg Österreich during the 1690s. *Jesu meine Freude* and *Herzlich lieb* both

appear in the Lübeck manuscript A 373, which was assembled under Buxtehude's supervision, probably late in his life. *Herzlich lieb* could thus have
been the latest of these works, and A 373 is the only one of these extant
sources that Bach might have seen on his visit to Lübeck in 1705–6.[21]

Every single stanza of Buxtehude's *per-omnes-versus* settings draws on the
chorale melody, but he did not adhere slavishly to the tunes as transmitted,
with slight variations, in the Lübeck sources MK 13 and Pag. He transformed
"Wachet auf" from duple meter to triple, and "Nun laßt uns Gott den Herren"
from triple to duple, and he added ornaments freely. Particularly in those
movements that he set as chorale concertos, he responded to both the affect
and the individual words of the texts, nowhere more so than in his striking
setting of the word "ruhen" in the third movement of *Herzlich lieb*. And in
half of these works he transposed the key of a chorale upwards from that
in which the hymnals transmitted it: from C to D in *Wachet auf*, from C to F
in *Nun laßt uns Gott den Herren*, and from D Dorian to E minor in *Jesu meine
Freude*.[22] As he was composing for trained singers, Buxtehude did not have
to consider the needs of congregational singing in his choice of keys.

BACH'S *PER-OMNES-VERSUS* CHORALE SETTINGS

Bach composed cantatas to all the verses of ten chorales, as listed in chronological order in table 3.3. At first glance, these chorales seem much less familiar than those that Buxtehude chose for his *per-omnes-versus* settings, and
most of their texts come from the seventeenth century. For the newer texts,
however, the hymnals often specified older, well-known melodies, which
Bach in turn followed; these chorales are more familiar to the ear than they
are to the eye. We do not hear these melodies very much, however, for while
Buxtehude set all the verses of a chorale with a variation on its melody, this
is true for only two of Bach's *per-omnes-versus* cantatas, *Christ lag in Todesbanden* (BWV 4) and *Lobe den Herren* (BWV 137). In all the others, Bach
used the chorale melody only in the first and last movements, and occasion-
ally in the middle: a chorale harmonization in BWV 117 and portions of the
melody in the fifth movement of BWV 107. In the other movements he composed arias and, less frequently, recitatives or ariosos to the chorale text, without any reference to its melody.

When one considers the dates of these cantatas, however, the question becomes rather why Bach chose to use the chorale melody in all the movements
of *Lobe den Herren* than why he did not do so in the rest. *Christ lag in Todesbanden* stands in isolation of at least sixteen years from the next on the list,
Was willst du dich betrüben (BWV 107), which Bach composed for the

Table 3.3. Bach's Chorale Cantatas *per omnes versus*

BWV	Title	Vss	Date*	Melody
4	Christ lag in Todesbanden	7	1708 or earlier	
107	Was willst du dich betrüben	7	1724	Von Gott will ich nicht lassen
137	Lobe den Herren, den mächtigen König	5	1725	
129	Gelobet sei der Herr, mein Gott, mein Licht	5	1726–27	O Gott, du frommer Gott
192	Nun danket alle Gott	3	1728–31	
117	Sei Lob und Ehr dem höchsten Gut	9	1728–31	Es ist das Heil uns kommen her
112	Der Herr ist mein getreuer Hirt	5	1731	Allein Gott in der Höh sei Ehr
177	Ich ruf zu dir Herr Jesu Christ	5	1732	
100	Was Gott tut das ist wohlgetan	6	1732–35	
97	In allen meinen Taten	9	1734	O Welt ich muss dich lassen

*Dates are drawn from the *Bach Compendium*, *Vokalwerke* I–II.

Seventh Sunday after Trinity, 23 July 1724, as the only *per-omnes-versus* cantata within the series of chorale cantatas that constitutes the second *Jahrgang*. As is well known, Bach's librettist for the other cantatas in this series paraphrased the inner stanzas of the chorale to provide texts suitable for the composition of recitatives and arias in the style of the modern church cantata introduced by Erdmann Neumeister. Lacking such a text for *Was willst du dich betrüben*, Bach still strove to emulate the musical style that he had established during the preceding weeks and composed the second stanza as a recitative and the next four as free arias. Despite the regularity of the line lengths, Bach invoked the style of recitative by using widely disjunct intervals for the first six lines and breaking the regular phrase structure by the introduction of melismas in the last two. And in quoting the opening of the chorale melody and all of its last line in the soprano aria for verse 5, he recalled the similar technique that he had used just two weeks previously in the arias of movements 3 and 6 of *Wer nur den lieben Gott läßt walten* (BWV 93).

Bach composed *Lobe den Herren* (BWV 137) for the Twelfth Sunday after Trinity a year later, 19 August 1725. Since a cantata for this Sunday is lacking from the second *Jahrgang*, he may have been trying to fill this hole by choosing a pure chorale text, but here he did not follow his model for the overall design from the previous year and instead introduced the chorale melody into all five movements. In its musical style, however, this cantata is much closer to its chronological neighbors than to *Christ lag in Todesbanden*. The aria of verse 2, for example, well known from its arrangement as one of the Schübler organ chorales (BWV 650),[23] superficially resembles versus 3 of *Christ lag in Todesbanden*, "Jesus Christus Gottes Sohn," in that both are scored as trios with the cantus firmus in the voice accompanied by an obbligato violin part. But Bach's encounter with Vivaldi is clearly reflected in the expansive and well-structured ritornello of "Lobe den Herren, der Alles so herrlich regieret," placing it worlds apart from the short, ostinato-style ritornello of the earlier work.[24] And in the first movement of BWV 137, Bach built the motet-like chorale setting in the voices into an orchestral ritornello structure in the artful manner so characteristic of the chorale cantatas of the previous year. Bach's *per-omnes-versus* settings, then, are not as unified a group of works as one might at first suppose. *Christ lag in Todesbanden* stands apart from the others, and one must look to the seventeenth century for related works.

Johann Pachelbel's cantata *Christ lag in Todesbanden*[25] has been suggested as a possible model for Bach's *Christ lag*.[26] Pachelbel sets the text of all seven verses but bases only verses 1, 3, and 5 on the melody of the chorale. Most strikingly similar is the use of chorale motet style by both composers in their settings of the first verse with the cantus firmus in the soprano in extended note values and in an interior verse with the cantus firmus in an inner voice (Pachelbel for verse 5 with the tenor; Bach for verse 4 with the alto). One does not find chorale settings such as these in the vocal works of Buxtehude. Both composers also score verses 2 and 6 as duets, although Pachelbel uses the same music for both verses, and they both set one verse as an expansive bass solo with full string accompaniment. But Bach's cantata is symmetrical in its design, and Pachelbel's is not; Bach set all the verses to the chorale melody, and Pachelbel did not; Bach scored with two violas to Pachelbel's three; and Bach chose the key of E minor while Pachelbel used the D Dorian in which the hymnals transmit this chorale. Example 3.1 gives Pachelbel's version of the melody, which departs only slightly from that of the Babst hymnal of 1545,[27] and which may be compared with Bach's version in example 3.2. Each example is extrapolated from the cantus firmus in the soprano of the first versus.[28] Johann Kuhnau, another central German predecessor of Bach, also composed a cantata in D minor on "Christ lag in Todesbanden," dated 1693 or earlier, but his is not *per omnes versus*. His version of the chorale is nearly identical to that of Pachelbel.[29]

Buxtehude left no settings of "Christ lag in Todesbanden," either for voices or for organ, but in *Jesu meine Freude* (BuxWV 60) he also took a chorale that was transmitted in D Dorian in the hymnals and set it *per omnes versus* in E minor, which could have provided a model for Bach's *Christ lag*. Johann Crüger had composed the melody of Johann Franck's hymn "Jesu meine Freude" and published it first in the 1653 edition of his *Praxis pietatis melica.*

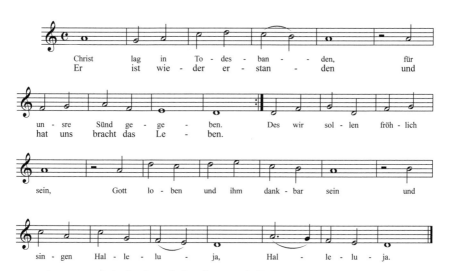

Example 3.1. "Christ lag in Todesbanden," Pachelbel

Example 3.2.   "Christ lag in Todesbanden," Bach

Example 3.3 gives his melody from the 1664 edition.[30] By 1682, with the version in Gottfried Vopelius's *Neu Leipziger Gesangbuch*,[31] someone had noticed that the opening line of text, "Jesu meine Freude," was identical to the last line of the final verse and changed the closing musical phrase to reflect this symmetry. Pagendarm's first copy of "Jesu meine Freude" in MK 13, made some time after his arrival in Lübeck in 1679, presents this version of the final phrase but transposes it into C, keeping a Dorian signature of two flats. In his own chorale book of 1705 he maintained the same intervallic structure but transposed it back to D, this time with a signature of one flat.[32] The symmetry of the first and last phrases is seen more easily in the Lübeck chorale books, with the entire chorale written on one line and with all six verses underlaid, than it is in the hymnals. This symmetry in the chorale itself may have suggested to Buxtehude the design for his *per-omnes-versus* setting of it. Buxtehude's melody, given in example 3.4, follows MK 13 in all but one small detail.

By the time Bach visited Lübeck, Buxtehude's *Jesu meine Freude* was at least eighteen years old, but Bach must have seen it or heard it; its similarities with his motet on this chorale (BWV 227), first noted by Philipp Spitta, are too striking to be coincidental. Spitta notes the similarities in their settings of "Trotz! trotz! trotz dem alten Drachen," "Tobe Welt und springe," and "Erd und Abgrund" in versus 3,[33] to which I would add "Gute Nacht, o Wesen" in versus 5. Bach may have copied the Buxtehude work in Lübeck, but he did not compose his own setting of all the verses of "Jesu meine Freude" until

Example 3.3. **"Jesu meine Freude," from Johann Crüger, *Praxis pietatis melica*, 1664.**

many years later.[34] Because of the five interpolated movements set to verses from Romans 8, Bach's motet is not strictly speaking a *per-omnes-versus* composition, but I would submit that it belongs to this family of works. Bach's motet, too, is a symmetrical work in E minor based on a chorale transmitted in D Dorian, and with the addition of these five movements he produced the axis of symmetry that Buxtehude's setting of the six chorale verses lacks. In both *Christ lag* and *Jesu meine Freude* the text of the central movement in a chiastic structure juxtaposes fundamental opposites: *Tod* and *Leben* in BWV 4, *fleischlich* and *geistlich* in BWV 227, and Bach sets both movements with fugal procedure. Table 3.4 outlines the symmetrical structures of these three works.

Example 3.4. **"Jesu meine Freude," from BuxWV60, Versus 6**

Table 3.4. Symmetrical Correspondences

BuxWV 60				BWV 4				BWV 227			
Sinfonia				Sinfonia			C				C
v1 "Jesu"	tutti	con-harm	C	v1 "Christ lag"	tutti	concertato	C	v1 "Jesu" [Rom. 8:1]	a4	harm	C
									a5		3/2
v2 "Schirmen"	S1	aria	C	v2 "Den Tod"	SA	aria	C	v2 "Schirmen" [Rom. 8:2]	a5	cptl-harm	C
									a3		3/4
v3 "Trotz"	B + insts	concertato	3/4	v3 "Jesu Christus"	T+vln	aria	3/4	v3 "Trotz" [Rom. 8:9]	a5	motet	3/4
				v4 Tod vs. Leben	SATB	fugue	C	fleischlich vs. geistlich	fugue		C
v4 "Weg"	tutti	con-harm +	3/4	v5 "Osterlamm"	B+insts	concertato	3/4	v4 "Weg" [Rom. 8:10]	a4	cptl-harm	C
									a3		
12/8											
v5 "Gute Nacht"	S2	aria	6/8	v6 "So feiern wir"	ST	aria	6/8	v5 "Gute Nacht" [Rom. 8:11]	a4	motet	2/4
									a5		3/2
v6 "Weicht"	tutti	con-harm	C	v7 "Wir essen"	tutti	harm.	C	v6 "Weicht"	a4	harm.	C

In arguing that Buxtehude's *Jesu meine Freude* exerted an influence on these two works of Bach, I do not wish to imply that the use of symmetrical design was a particularly Buxtehudian trait; Bach could have found symmetrically constructed chorale cantatas much closer to home in the works of Johann Schelle.[35] It is the combination of the symmetry with the transposition from a D-Dorian prototype to E minor that I find striking. Since Bach's *Christ lag in Todesbanden* survives only in the parts prepared for the Leipzig performances of 1724 and 1725, one might suggest the possibility that Bach had originally composed it in D minor for a Chorton performace, but Alfred Dürr found no evidence of such a transposition in the parts.[36]

On the basis of a thorough study of the text of BWV 4 and Bach's situation in Arnstadt, Robin Leaver has suggested that Bach composed *Christ lag in Todesbanden* for Easter 1706, fresh from his trip to Lübeck, as a response to the complaint of the consistory upon his return that he had not performed any concerted music, and that he chose to set Luther's Easter hymn to please the hymnologist Johann Christoph Olearius, a deacon in the Neue Kirche and son of the superintendent who had reprimanded him.[37] If this was the motivation for Bach's composition of *Christ lag*, then it would stand to reason that he would have used the compositional styles, particularly the chorale motet, that were familiar to his listeners. But his choice of key and overall design would also demonstrate that he had indeed learned "one thing and another about his art" during his recent trip to Lübeck.

NOTES

1. Bach's justification for the trip in the proceedings of the Arnstadt consistory, February 21, 1706, as translated in *The New Bach Reader*, ed. Hans T. David and Arthur Mendel, rev. Christoph Wolff (New York: W. W. Norton, 1998), no. 20, p. 46.

2. See Werner Neumann, *Sämtliche von Johann Sebastian Bach vertonte Texte* (Leipzig: VEB Deutscher Verlag für Musik, 1974); Hans-Joachim Schulze and Christoph Wolff, *Bach Compendium, Vokalwerke*, I–IV (Leipzig: Peters, 1985–1989); and the critical reports to the various cantata volumes of the *Neue Bach Ausgabe*.

3. Michael Belotti's forthcoming edition of Buxtehude's chorale settings for organ in *Dieterich Buxtehude: The Collected Works* (New York: The Broude Trust) will provide a discussion of the sources for these chorales.

4. See Carl Wilhelm Pauli, *Geschichte der Lübeckischen Gesangbücher und Beurtheilung des gegenwärtigen* (Lübeck: In Commission der Buchhandlung Rudolf Seeling, 1875), 2–29. See also *Speculum aevi: Kirchengesang in Lübeck als Spiegel der Zeiten*, ed. Ada Kadelbach and Arndt Schnoor (Lübeck: Schmidt-Romhild, 1995).

5. Pauli, *Geschichte*, 30–31.

6. *Lübeckisches Gesang-Buch, nebst Anfügung Eines Gebeth-Buchs, Auff Verord-nung Eines Hoch-Edlen Hochweisen. Raths von Finem Ehrwürdigen Ministerio Aus-gegeben. Cum Privilegio* (Lübeck: Christian Ernest Wiedemeyer, 1729).

7. "Sonnabend, wie die Herren Vorsteher am negst verwichenen Montagem aufm Werckhause bey abgelegter Kirchen Rechnung zusammen wahren, haben dieselbe ggl. consentiret, dem Cantori Pagendarm, für die Melodeyen derer 303 zusammen synd, in denn 4. neugemachten Gesangbüchern con canto, Alto, Tenor et Basso, ohne die Texte ein Zuschreiben pro Labore zu geben 60/-/-

Noch Christian Partike et Wolter Möllraht, beiden Aritmetici, für den Text unter denn 303: Gesängen in quadruplo zu legen, laut Quittung zahlet 150/-/-" (Archiv der Hansestadt Lübeck, Marienkirche, Wochenbuch 1705–1711, fol. 18).

8. Hermann Jimmerthal, "Zur Geschichte der St. Marien Kirche in Lübeck und deren innern und äussern Verhältnisse gesammelte Materialien aus den sämmtlichen Schriften des Kirchen Archivs, älteren Lübeckischen Chroniken, etc." (MS, 1857, Archiv der Hansestadt Lübeck, no signature), 315.

9. "Verzeichnis der Bücher, Schriften Zeichnungen, Musikalien, etc. des Archivs der St. Marien-Kirche. Eingerichtet von H. Jimmerthal, Organist und Werkmeister der St. Marien-Kirche, 1860" (MS, Archiv der Hansestadt Lübeck, no signature), 17.

10. Kerala J. Snyder, *Dieterich Buxtehude: Organist in Lübeck* (New York: Schirmer, 1987), exx. 7-12, 7-13, 7-18, 7-19.

11. On the removal and return of the Lübeck archives, see Anatjekathrin Graß-mann, "Die Hansestadt Lübeck erhält ihr Gedächtnis zurück," in *Alte Bestände—Neue Perspektiven: Das Archiv der Hansestadt Lübeck—5 Jahre nach der Archiv-alienrückführung*, ed. Antjekathrin Graßmann (Lübeck: Schmidt-Römhild, 1992), 5–17.

12. *Lübeckisch=Vollständiges Gesangbuch, Anjetzo biß auf 974. Gesänge ver-mehret, Darinn Des S. Hn. D. Lutheri und andere in unser Kirchen übliche alte Gesänge ebenwohl behalten, und Mit einen Kern Geistreicher Lieder aus andern Au-thorisirten Gesangbüchern, vermehret worden, Sammt Einem darzu nöthigen Gebet und Communion-Büchlein* (Lübeck and Leipzig: Johann Wiedemeyer, 1698). The date 1699 found in earlier literature appears to be incorrect.

13. Signature 765.aa.20. I would like to thank Robin Leaver for drawing my at-tention to this copy.

14. *Lübeckisches Gesang-Buch*, "Vorrede," unpaginated.

15. Ada Kadelbach, "Verloren und wieder entdeckt: *Lübeckisch=Vollständiges Gesangbuch*, Lübeck und Leipzig 1698/99. Ein 'geistreiches' Gesangbuch?" in *Pietismus und Liedkultur*, ed. Gudrun Busch and Wolfgang Miersemann, Hallesche Forschungen, no. 9 (Tübingen: Verlag der Franckeschen Stiftungen Halle im Max Niemeyer Verlag, 2002), 143–58.

16. Jimmerthal, "Verzeichnis," 17.

17. A list of the chorales in this collection is found in Pauli, *Geschichte*, 4–17.

18. Johannes Zahn, *Die Melodien der deutschen evangelischen Kirchenlieder*, 6 vols. (1889–1893; repr., Hildesheim: Georg Olms, 1963).

19. Martin Geck's statements that Buxtehude set all the stanzas of *Erhalt uns Herr bei deinem Wort* (BuxWV 27) and *Walts Gott, mein Werk ich lasse* (BuxWV 103) are

incorrect. (Martin Geck, *Die Vokalmusik Dietrich Buxtehudes und der frühe Pietismus* [Kassel: Bärenreiter, 1965], 205.) In BuxWV 27 Buxtehude set the first three stanzas of "Erhalt uns Herr" followed by the two verses of "Verleih uns Frieden gnädiglich," and MK 13, L 1703 and Pag all have five stanzas for "Erhalt uns Herr." Martin Luther wrote the first three stanzas, and Justus Jonas added the other two in 1545; for a published version of all five stanzas, see Philipp Wackernagel, *Das deutsche Kirchenlied von der ältesten Zeit bis zu Anfang des XVII. Jahrhunderts* (Leipzig: B. G. Teubner, 1864–1877), 3: p. 27, no. 46. "Walts Gott mein Werk ich lasse" is found neither in MK13 nor in L 1703, but all twelve stanzas, of which Buxtehude set six in BuxWV 103, are present in the *Lübeckisch=Vollständiges Gesangbuch*, 1017 (my thanks to Arndt Schnoor for confirming this.) See Albert Fischer and Wilhelm Tümpel, *Das deutsche evangelische Kirchenlied des 17. Jahrhunderts*, 6 vols. (1904–1916; repr., Hildesheim: G. Olms, 1964), 2:4–5, no. 3 for the complete text. I have argued elsewhere that the C-major setting of "Wachet auf" attributed to Buxtehude (BuxWV 101) is not an authentic work; see Snyder, *Dieterich Buxtehude*, 206–7.

20. I interpret the indication "a 10 vel 15" in the head title of the tablature (Bibliothek der Hansestadt Lübeck, Mus. Ms. A 373, fol. 29b) to indicate the optional participation of a reinforcing capella.

21. There were probably also sets of performing parts for these works in Lübeck at the time. Most of Buxtehude's manuscripts disappeared from Lübeck long before World War II; see Snyder, *Dieterich Buxtehude*, 311–12.

22. I use the expression "E minor" to invoke the practice used in the seventeenth and eighteenth centuries of marking the key tone with a sharp, flat, or natural to indicate whether it regularly had a major or minor third above it. The E tonality of Buxtehude's *Jesu meine Freude* can be understood as transposed Aeolian or E minor, but not as Phrygian or transposed Dorian.

23. The title *Kommst du nun, Jesu, vom Himmel herunter* that Bach gave to the organ arrangement reflects the earlier text with which this melody was originally associated.

24. For an extensive discussion of the early style characteristics of BWV 4, see Gerhard Herz, "More on Bach's Cantata no. 4: Date and Style. A Reply to Crawford R. Thoburn," *American Choral Review* 21, no. 2 (1979): 9–13. Herz does not offer a comparison with *Lobe den Herren*, inexplicably stating that "as a cantata using one chorale for all its movements, Christ lag is unique in Bach's vocal *oeuvre*" (p. 8). On Bach's ritornello construction, see Laurence Dreyfus, *Bach and the Patterns of Invention* (Cambridge: Harvard University Press, 1996), 59–102.

25. Johann Pachelbel, *Christ lag in Todesbanden: Osterkantate für vierstimmigen gemischten Chor: Sopran-, Alt-, Tenor-, Baß-Solo, 2 Violinen, 3 Violen, Fagott und Basso continuo*, ed. Hans Heinrich Eggebrecht (Basel: Bärenreiter, 1954).

26. See Friedhelm Krummacher, "Die Tradition in Bach's Choralbearbeitungen," in *Bach-Interpretationen*, ed. Martin Geck (Göttingen: Vandenhoeck und Ruprecht, 1969), 29–56, and Crawford R. Thoburn, "Pachelbel's *Christ lag in Todesbanden*: A Possible Influence on Bach's Work," *American Choral Review* 19, no. 1 (1977): 3–16.

27. *Das Babstsche Gesangbuch von* 1545, facsimile ed. Konrad Ameln (Kassel: Bärenreiter, 1966), no. VIII.

28. Example 3.1 is drawn from Eggebrecht's edition, example 3.2 from Johann Sebastian Bach, *Kantaten zum 1. Ostertag*, ed. Alfred Dürr, Neue Ausgabe sämtlicher Werke, series 1, vol. 9 (Kassel: Barenreiter, 1985).

29. For an edition see Evangeline Lois Rimbach, "The Church Cantatas of Johann Kuhnau" (PhD diss., University of Rochester, 1966), II/1, 50–80.

30. Johann Crüger, *Praxis pietatis melica*, Editio XI (Berlin: C. Runge, 1664), no. 490, p. 939. According to Zahn no. 8032 (vol. 4, p. 651), the first c-sharp in the second phrase was a c-natural in the 1653 edition.

31. *Neu Leipziger Gesangbuch*, ed. Gottfried Vopelius (Leipzig: Christoph Klinger, 1682), 780–83.

32. Later hymnals, such as Christoph Graupner's *Neu vermehrtes Darmstädtisches Choral-Buch* (Darmstadt, 1728), p. 74, and Georg Philip Telemann's *Fast allgemeines Evangelisch-Musicalisches Lieder-Buch* (Hamburg, 1730), no. 89, p. 50, maintained the Dorian signature in D.

33. Philipp Spitta, *Johann Sebastian Bach*, trans. Clara Bell and J. A. Fuller-Maitland (New York: Dover, 1951), 1:308.

34. *Bach Compendium, Vokalwerke* III, 961: "spätestens 1735." Daniel Melamed has argued that BWV 227 was composed in several stages, noting among other things an earlier form of the second phrase of the chorale melody in versus 5, "Gute Nacht." See Daniel Richard Melamed, "J. S. Bach and the German Motet" (PhD diss., Harvard University, 1989), 224–27; and Daniel Melamed, *J. S. Bach and the German Motet* (Cambridge: Cambridge University Press, 1995), 101–2.

35. See in particular his *per-omnes-versus* cantata *In dich hab ich gehoffet Herr* (in Johann Schelle, *Six Chorale Cantatas*, ed. Mary S. Morris, Recent Researches in the Music of the Baroque Era, vols. 60–61 [Madison: A-R Editions, 1988], 77–108). See also Friedhelm Krummacher, *Die Choralbearbeitung in der protestantischen Figuralmusik zwischen Praetorius und Bach* (Kassel: Bärenreiter, 1978), 290–97.

36. Alfred Dürr, *Kantaten zum 1. Ostertag: Kritischer Bericht*, Johann Sebastian Bach, Neue Ausgabe sämtlicher Werke, series 1, vol. 9 (Kassel: Bärenreiter, 1986), 24.

37. Robin Leaver, "Christ lag in Todesbanden (BWV 4): Hymnology and Chronology" (unpublished paper).

4

Bach's Preluding for a Leipzig Academic Ceremony

Gregory Butler

At Leipzig, in his capacity as cantor of St. Thomas's Church, Bach had no reason to write for and play the organ on a regular weekly basis during Sunday church services, as he had before 1714 as church and then court organist. His opportunities for performing on the instrument were largely limited to the following specific occasions: 1) the organ examination, the actual testing of a new or rebuilt organ in the presence of a small and select private audience, a performance that was rather technical in nature; 2) public concerts before large public audiences; 3) informal recitals, often given between church services; 4) academic ceremonies—memorial services, honorary academic functions, civic celebrations, and the like.[1] It is Bach's activity as organist in connection with the last of these categories upon which I will focus in this study.

In an article published in 1992[2] I brought to light documentary evidence of an academic ceremony that took place at St. Paul's Church, Leipzig (University Church) at 12:00 noon on 25 December 1745 to celebrate the signing earlier the same day in Dresden of the peace treaty that brought to an end the hostilities between the Prussian and Saxon forces and marked the close of the second Silesian War. In his capacity as director of music for the city's principal churches, Bach would surely have been called upon to provide concerted music for this special service, and in my study I make the compelling argument that the composer's *Gloria in excelsis Deo* (BWV 191) was performed on this occasion. With this enigmatic work removed from the category of "Kirchenkantate" and shifted into the category of academic "Festmusik" the problems[3] arising when it is viewed in the context of Bach's church cantata œuvre disappear. Its Latin text is perfectly consistent both with the academic function of such works and the tradition of the performance of concerted works based on biblical texts on such occasions. The relative brevity of the work is entirely in keeping with other occasional pieces of a similar nature. Since the ceremony at which his *Gloria in excelsis Deo* was performed fell between the regularly scheduled morning and afternoon services at St. Thomas's and St. Nicholas's, the two principal Leipzig churches, Bach would have had at his disposal the combined St. Thomas school choirs and the augmented instrumental forces required for the performance of this work, with its five-part choral writing and its particularly lavish instrumentation.

By far the most fully documented occasional academic ceremony at which Bach is known to have officiated was the memorial service for the recently deceased electress of Saxony, Christiane Eberhardine, held in St. Paul's Church on 17 October 1727. The following is a step-by-step summary of this service culled from the extant documentary sources:[4]

1. A formal academic procession made up of university officials and town councillors proceeds from St. Nicholas's Church to St. Paul's Church as the church bells peal.
2. As the procession approaches, the organ begins preluding (Sicul: "praeambuliret," Riemer: "intoniret") and continues until the procession has entered the church and the members of the procession and invited guests have taken their seats.
3. The printed text of Johann Christoph Gottsched's *Trauerode* is distributed to those present by the beadles.
4. The first part of the figural music, Johann Sebastian Bach's *Lass Fürstin! Lass noch einen Strahl* (BWV 198) is performed by the *Collegium Paulinum* under the direction of the composer.
5. The "oratio Germanica" is delivered by a university student, Hans Carl von Kirchbach.
6. The second part of the figural music is performed.
7. The members of the formal procession followed by the invited guests leave the church to preluding on the organ (Riemer: "praeludiret," Sicul: "Nachspiel").

It is reasonable to assume that the peace ceremony of 25 December 1745 followed a format much the same as that of the memorial service for Christiane Eberhardine.

Documentary evidence for the existence of number 5, in this case an "oratio Latina" rather than the "oratio Germanica" of the earlier memorial service, is furnished by the brief description of the *Festakt*, which appears in the entry for 25 December 1745 found in *Nachrichten von Leipzig auf das Jahr 1745*:

Den 25. Decembr.
als an dem H. Christ=Tage hielt Herr M. **Salomon Ranisch**, aus Chemnitz eine feyerliche Rede, *de Iesu Christi Servatoris, humiliter nati, maiestate*, in der

Pauliner=Kirche um 12. Uhr. Der Decanus der theol. Fac. Herr D. **Deyling**, hatte
vorher im Nahmen des Rectoris der Academie hierzu eingeladen, und in dem
Weynacht=Programmate von 2 Bogen die herrliche Erscheinung in dem bren-
nenden Busche Exod. III. als eine Abbildung der Erscheinung des Sohnes Gottes
im Fleische betrachtet.[5]

Dec. 25th

when on the holy Christmas Day Herr M. **Salomon Ranisch** from Chemnitz delivered a festive oration, *de Iesu Christi Servatoris, humiliter nati, maiestate*, in
the Pauliner church at 12 o'clock. The deacon of the theological faculty, Herr D.
Deyling, in the name of the rector of the academy, had extended an invitation
hereto beforehand and in the Christmas bulletin of two leaves elucidated the
marvellous apparition in the burning bush (Exod. III) as an image for the manifestation of the son of God in the flesh.

The oration referred to in Bach's heading to the second and third movements
of his *Gloria in excelsis Deo*, "Post orationem," would then be a reference to
the "feierliche Rede" delivered by Herr Magister Salomon Ranisch of Chemnitz. According to the order of the memorial service given above, the first part
of the concerted ceremonial music, "Gloria in excelsis Deo – Et in terra pax"
(BWV 191/1) would have been performed before the sermon and the second
part, "Gloria Patri" (BWV 191/2) and "Sicut erat in principio" (BWV 191/3)
after.

Text and music are closely bound together liturgically. The text to the opening movement, the climactic culmination of the Gospel reading for the First
Day of Christmas (Lk 2:14), has an iconic association with Christmas Day. At
the same time, it has close theological links both with the Old Testament subject[6] of Deyling's commentary in the bulletin, the appearance of the angel of
God in the blazing light of the burning bush and what it said to Moses, and
the New Testament subject of Ranisch's sermon, the regal majesty of Christ.

Although the documents state specifically that Bach directed the performance of the *Trauerode*, nowhere is he ever named as the organist responsible
for the preluding (numbers 2 and 8) mentioned in the order of service given
above. Although it might appear somewhat dangerous to assume that Bach
played the organ on this and other such occasions when he was the director
of the concerted music, there is good reason to believe that he did so. First, it
seems unthinkable that he would have entrusted this important function to the
organist of St. Paul's Church, Johann Gottlieb Görner, with whom he had so
recently fought for control over this service.[7] Nor would he have been likely
to have delegated this task even to a trusted pupil or family member, for, as
titular director of music at St. Paul's Church in charge of the music for this
service, Bach would certainly have left nothing to chance on such an important public occasion and with such an august audience in attendance. He

would surely have wanted to leave his personal stamp on every musical aspect of this ceremony, and indeed he may well have relished the opportunity to present himself as organist before such an assemblage of notables.[8]

In his discussion of the function of Bach's organ preludes, George Stauffer relates the general repertoire played for these occasional academic ceremonies to that played for the Sunday services in the two principal Leipzig churches, stating that "in these events free pieces fulfilled the same role they served in [the] *Hauptgottesdienst*: they functioned as preludes and postludes to the service proper and as preludes to concerted music when it was performed."[9] Nevertheless, while the repertoire was no doubt similar, the preluding for these academic ceremonies differed in its specifics in certain respects. From the foregoing account, we know that the preluding before this type of service was of a processional nature, but, just as in the regular Sunday church services, it must also have served an intonational function since it immediately preceded the first part of the concerted music. In this respect, then, the preluding before such ceremonies had a dual function, that of processional introduction to the service as a whole while simultaneously covering the tuning of, and providing the pitch for, the instrumentalists and singers involved in the performance of the concerted music (the "preluding on the principal composition"[10] enumerated by Bach as the ninth and fourteenth items in his outline of the Sunday morning service in Leipzig). As Stauffer notes, however, the preluding before the academic ceremony, unlike its chorale-bound counterpart in the Sunday service, was not restricted by the chorale tune whose choral performance followed it, unless, of course, on occasion a chorale was sung. As for preluding after the service, it is not certain that it was an established practice in the main Sunday services at the two principal Leipzig churches. However, it is clear that preluding after these occasional academic ceremonies had been established by tradition and was an integral part of the service, performing the necessary formal function of recessional for the academic procession as it left the church.

It is reasonable to assume that the peace ceremony of 25 December 1745, like the memorial service for Christiane Eberhardine, included preluding on the organ by Bach before the first half and immediately following the second half of the ceremonial concerted music. Although it is not referred to anywhere in the report of the memorial service outlined above, intonational preluding by the organ immediately preceding the performance of the second half of the figural music, at least during the morning service, was customary,[11] and there is every reason to believe that the same procedure was followed in the case of these academic ceremonies. Based on the source evidence and the internal evidence, we are in a rather favourable position for drawing informed and, I believe, well-grounded hypotheses concerning which of his compositions for organ Bach is most likely to have played on this occasion.

The intonational function of the preluding before the concerted music (the use of the term, "intoniret" by Riemer in referring to the preluding before the memorial service for Christiane Eberhardine is particularly significant here) is accorded prime importance by theorists. Friedrich Erhardt Niedt defines the term prelude in terms of its intonational function:

> an introduction which the organist plays alone before a real concerted piece of music begins in order to allow the singers to get the key and the instrumentalists to tune completely without arousing displeasure in the listeners by so doing. An organist can make such a prelude as long as he wishes or continue until the instrumentalists have tuned completely and have given him a sign to stop.[12]

For Johann Samuel Petri, there is an important adjunct to the practical function of such preludes as intonational pieces. Ideally, the organist should "look through the score in order to know what the tempo and affect of the concerted music really should be, and with what type of notes the first violin begins."[13] In so doing, the organist in his preludes, at the same time as he gives the pitch for the singers and instrumentalists, prepares the audience for the concerted music to follow by prefiguring its tempo, affect, and even its actual musical substance. Stauffer is undoubtedly correct when he states that if preluding before the service was required only "for tuning purposes, a short *intonatione* [sic] would have sufficed."[14] It should be stressed here again, however, that in addition to its intonational function, preluding before the occasional academic ceremony performed a processional function. In this case, then, the beginning of the processional prelude served to announce the approach of the procession, continuing until the members of the procession and the invited guests had taken their seats. Thus, it would have had to be somewhat more extended than the simple intonation referred to by Stauffer.

In commentaries by German theorists of the late baroque, fugue emerges over and over again as an effective means for bringing preluding on the organ to a conclusion. Fugue playing, Johann Mattheson's second type, "has to do with the prelude and postlude, as a part or conclusion of the same." According to Johann Adolph Scheibe, a pupil of Bach, one "should crown such a prelude or postlude with a fine and magnificent fugue." Among the means available to the organist for displaying all of his ingenuity in preluding, Petri includes "fugal preludes," and Daniel Gottlob Türk, in his relatively short fourth category of preluding, the postlude ("Nachspiel"), sees this as the "appropriate place" for a fugue. As for Bach's practice in postluding, we know from Johann Nikolaus Forkel that he "would conclude with full organ by means of a fugue."[15]

Lowell Mason, in a report written over a century after Bach's death, describes the intonational preluding before the performance of the concerted music at the morning service in St. Nicholas's Church as follows:

> When the slow solemn chant was ended, the organ burst out in a loud minor voluntary, which continued three or four minutes, during which time the violins, violoncellos, double basses, and wind instruments tuned. Yet so carefully was this done, that it was hardly perceptible, for the organ was giving out its full progressive chords, so as to nullify the tuning process, at least upon the ears of the people. Tune being secured, the choir, with organ and orchestra accompaniment, sung a motette, or hymn. . . .[16]

This account is important for it describes a practice that had changed little since the time of Bach's tenure as cantor of St. Thomas's Church; further, it is rather specific in laying out the duration of such intonational preluding. In fact, timing is a vitally important consideration in any discussion of the preluding for this academic ceremony. Since the Vespers service began at 1:30 P.M. there was less than an hour and a half for the service. The total duration for the three movements of BWV 191 is approximately fifteen minutes. If one assumes that the sermon was more or less the same length as that delivered at the morning and afternoon services, that is, one hour, this would allow for something in the order of ten to fifteen minutes in total for the three organ preluding segments of the service. The severe time restrictions this tight schedule imposed would indicate that three fairly short pieces—perhaps a longer prelude as processional, a shorter intonation of the type referred to by Stauffer as the preluding before the second half of the figural music, and a fugue as recessional.

In the Leipzig churches, the concerted music was performed at chamber pitch while the organs were tuned a whole step lower in chorus pitch.[17] The organ music performed at this service, then, would have been notated a major second lower than the concerted music. Thus, organ music for the preluding before and after the concerted music would have been notated in C chorus pitch, to accord with that of the opening and closing movements of the *Gloria in excelsis Deo* notated in D chamber pitch. Only four of Bach's surviving large-scale free organ works are in the key of C major and thus would come in for consideration—the three Prelude and Fugues BWV 531, 545, and 547; and the Toccata, Adagio, and Fugue (BWV 564). Of these, BWV 545 and BWV 564 are Weimar works and BWV 531 may be a pre-Weimar work.[18] This leaves the Prelude and Fugue in C major (BWV 547) for consideration.

From the beginning, Bach scholars have pointed to the close relationship between the fugue BWV 547/2 and Bach's treatment of fugue in the second volume of *Das wohltemperierte Clavier*, both as regards the melodic shape of the subject[19] and the contrapuntal treatment.[20] More recently, first Peter Williams[21] and then Russell Stinson[22] have marshalled compelling evidence pointing to a late dating of the fugue, particularly in light of the close parallels between this fugue and the *Fughetta super Allein Gott in der Höh sei Ehr'* (BWV 677) from Bach's *Dritter Theil der Clavier-Übung* (1739). Drawing on his extensive comparative analysis of the two fugues, Williams concludes that "it would be difficult to find two other keyboard works of J. S. Bach with quite such a correspondence," and based on his study of the extant sources and, more importantly, the style of the fugue, Stinson finds that "the relationship in this instance goes to the very core of the contrapuntal fabric."[23] Given the unique nature of the relationship between these two compositions, Stinson concurs with the view that dates the work to the last decade of Bach's life, stating in his conclusion that "the bulk of the evidence—indeed, virtually all of the evidence—overwhelmingly supports the notion that the C-major fugue dates from the late 1730's or the 1740's" and, slightly later, that "the evidence would seem to indicate that the Prelude and Fugue in C-major [BWV 547] was originally conceived as a prelude-fugue pair during the late 1730's or the 1740's."

Williams and Stinson both draw attention to the striking detached diminished seventh chords that immediately precede the extended closing tonic pedal passages in both the prelude and fugue, and both note the appearance of the same dramatic rhetorico-musical figure in *Wir glauben all an einen Gott* (BWV 681) from the *Dritter Theil der Clavier-Übung* and *Contrapunctus 1* from *Die Kunst der Fuge* (ca. 1742), further linking BWV 547 to other works from Bach's last decade. For Williams, "the final pedal point of BWV 547/2 anticipate[s] the piled-up climax of the *Canonic Variations*," but nowhere does he elaborate on this statement. In particular, the intense working out of the subject in stretto, alluded to by Williams, and the overall scalar descent in both is notable, but the almost identical sixteenth-note figuration, especially that in the voice above the pedal part in the final two measures of both passages, is even more striking. I believe this relationship is a particularly important point of comparison for a more precise placing of BWV 547/2 chronologically, and for that reason I have given the concluding measures of the two pedal passages here as examples 4.1 and 4.2. This close correspondence cannot be attributed to mere coincidence. It would suggest that Bach was involved in the composition of these two works at about the same time, and perhaps that he was even intent on unifying them in some way. I have argued elsewhere for a date of composition of *Variatio 5* of the *Canonic Varia-*

Example 4.1.   BWV 769/5 (mm. 55/3–end)

tions not too long before my proposed date of printing for the original edition, late 1746.[24] More recently, as a result of my study of the autograph P271, I have established that the composition of *Variatio 5* preceded that of the augmentation canon, *Variatio 4*, as the second layer and thus would fall in the period before 1746.[25] Is it possible, given this late dating, that both the prelude and fugue were composed and performed in connection with the Leipzig peace ceremony of Christmas, 1745?

Beyond the internal evidence linking together *Variatio 5* of the *Canonic Variations on "Vom Himmel hoch"* (BWV 769) and the fugue BWV 547/2, there are strong musico-liturgical allusions and associations that tie both the prelude and the fugue to the Christmas season. First, there are the close thematic and rhythmic links pointed out by Williams between the prelude BWV 547/1 and the opening of Bach's cantata *Sie werden aus Saba alle kommen* (BWV 65) and the chorale prelude *In dir ist Freude* (BWV 615) from the *Orgelbüchlein*. Interestingly, both the cantata and the chorale prelude have strong ties with the celebration of Epiphany and the coming of the magi.[26] In playing this work, with its commonplace musico-liturgical allusions to Epiphany, on Christmas Day as *Vorspiel*, Bach, in this music so strongly linked to the pastorale topus, would have projected a graphic depiction in music of the shepherds tending their flocks on Christmas Eve at the same time as it pointed ahead[27] across time into the New Year to the coming of the three wise men and the close of the Christmas season, always with the Christ child rocking in his cradle as a common central focus.

Example 4.2. BWV 547/2 (mm. 70/4–end)

The connection of the fugue BWV 547/2 with the occasion is, if anything, even more striking. Just as he parodied excerpts from the Gloria of his Latin *Missa* (BWV 232ᴵ) in fashioning the concerted music for this occasion, it is possible that Bach used the opening section of his setting of the *Allein Gott* (BWV 677) from his German "Orgelmesse" as a model on which to expand for the recessional that concluded the peace ceremony. The close liturgical connection between BWV 547/2 and the concerted Latin Gloria, the *Gloria in excelsis Deo* (BWV 191/1), and the common liturgical occasion for their performance are too obvious to warrant further elaboration. On the basis of the accumulated evidence, I would like to put forward the hypothesis that Bach undertook the expansion of the *Fughetta super Allein Gott in der Höh sei Ehr* (BWV 677) to produce the fugue BWV 547/2, performing it in conjunction with the prelude BWV 547/1 expressly for the peace ceremony on Christmas Day, 1745, and that he would have played the work as the recessional preluding after the second part of the figural music to conclude the service. The transposition up a minor third from the original tonality of A major to C major from the earlier model to the later expanded version would certainly lend added support to such a hypothesis.

The music opening the second part of *Gloria in excelsis Deo*, the "Gloria Patri" parody of the aria "Domine Deus," is in G major chamber pitch, and so the question arises as to whether among Bach's œuvre for solo organ there is a suitable work in F major, which unlike the opening processional/intonational prelude, might have served here as a relatively short tuning piece. A particularly good candidate would be the first section of the *Pastorella* (BWV 590). Williams points to similarities between this movement and the *Sinfonia* (BWV 248/10) that opens the second part of the *Christmas Oratorio*, the pastorale being traditionally closely associated with Christmas.[28] Bach may have

associated the topus of the pastorale with G major, the key of both BWV
248/10 and BWV 191/2, and thus his choice of the *Domine Deus* to parody
as the opening of the second part of his *Gloria in excelsis Deo* may have been
dictated by its subdominant G-major tonality as well as by its soft affective
cast and use of obbligato transverse flute, all elements closely associated with
the pastorale.

Of all German theorists of the late baroque, Türk is the only one who discusses the composition of intonational preludes in any analytical detail. He
singles out the third of his four categories of preluding, "the prelude before
the church [figural] music" (das Vorspiel vor der Kirchenmusik) as the only
one whose construction is largely determined by its intonational function:

> Since the tuning of the instruments is the principal aim here, I would advise the
> organist always to begin in a tonality in which the violins among others [i.e.,
> other string instruments] can be tuned easily, namely, if the organ stands in nor-
> mal (ordinary) Chorton, C major (also if need be G and F major or C and G mi-
> nor); . . . The organist should remain in these keys a while so that the musicians
> can tune their string instruments properly. Not until this has been accomplished
> does he go through a well chosen modulation out of the principal tonality of the
> piece; only because of the horns, trumpets, tympani among others [i.e., other
> wind instruments] must he remain a while still in the tonality in which these in-
> struments are pitched; . . .[29]

Even a cursory tonal analysis of the pastorale (BWV 590/1), such as that
given in table 4.1, demonstrates that it follows almost precisely the tonal construction advocated by Türk. The opening passage with the two upper voices
in imitation over a tonic pedal (mm. 1–10), repeated verbatim with contrapuntal imitation of the upper two voices (mm. 10–20), accounts for over a
half of this short intonation. It establishes the tonic and dominant whose tri-
ads give the pitches for the tuning of the G-, D-, and A-strings of the ripieno
string instruments and the fundamental pitch of the solo transverse flute, D.
A short modulation (mm. 20–23) leads to the subdominant C, where an abbreviated version of the opening passage is stated (mm. 23–26), allowing for
tuning of the C-strings of the viola, violoncello, and violone. An even shorter
modulation (m. 27) leads to the dominant of the sub-mediant, B, which is extended with a pedal (mm. 27–30) before resolving to E, which is elaborated
for six measures (mm. 31–36) allowing for the tuning of the E-string of the
violin as well as sounding the other important tonality in the following aria,
the relative minor. The foregoing tonal analysis in no way establishes BWV
590/1 as the piece performed by Bach as the intonation before the second part
of BWV 191. It does, however, point clearly to its original function as a short
intonation of the kind Stauffer suggests would have sufficed for the tuning of
the instruments necessary at this point in the ceremony.

Figure 4.1. A Comparison of the Tonal Structures of Türk's Intonational Prelude and J. S. Bach's Pastorale (BWV 590/1) and Prelude (BWV 547/1)

D. G. Türk, ideal intonational prelude (tonic C major)

tonality	C	G	F	->X	X

J. S. Bach, *Pastorale* BWV 590/1 (tonic G major chamber pitch)

measure	-10	-20	-23	-26	27	-30	-36	-37
tonality	G	D	->C	C	->B	B	e	b

J. S. Bach, Prelude BWV 547/1 (tonic D major chamber pitch)

measure	-13	-25	-31	-39	-45	-47	-54	-60	-67	-73	-79	-88
tonality	D,->A	A,->G	->b	->a	->e	->G	G,->D	D,->A	->g	->A	A	D

The tonal structure of the prelude BWV 547/1 presents an expanded version of Türk's basic scheme. Here in the first two-thirds of the movement, as in BWV 590/1, after an extended treatment of the tonic and dominant tonalities (mm. 1–13, 13–25), the music centers on minor tonalities (mm. 25–45). After a rapid modulation through a circle of fifths leading to the subdominant (mm. 44–47) there is a condensed recapitulation of elements from the first section, including a series of brief pedal passages on G and D (mm. 48–54, 54–60) followed by an extensive literal recapitulation of the passage at mm. 30–44 a step lower (mm. 59–73). A dominant pedal (mm. 73–76), interrupted by a musico-rhetorical *exclamatio* (mm. 77–79), leads to the concluding tonic pedal (mm. 80–88). Thus, BWV 547 can be seen as a binary structure (mm. 1–47, 48–88), the first dominated by the opening stable tonic and dominant prolongations, and the second by the approach to the dominant, and the dominant and tonic pedals that close the movement.

Although we know that Bach would have had only two or three days to prepare the music for this service, the hypothetical reconstruction given in table 4.2 shows signs of careful planning. The total duration of approximately eleven minutes for the performance of the three pieces I have suggested as the most plausible candidates for the preluding on this occasion—the prelude BWV 547/1, the pastorale BWV 590/1, and the fugue BWV 547/2—falls within the time constraint of ten to fifteen minutes imposed on Bach on this occasion. The peace ceremony presents an axially symmetrical structure with the sermon at its center. Framing it are pastoral movements in the softer subdominant key of G major—the "Et in terra pax" (BWV 191/1b) before and the "Gloria Patri" (BWV 191/2) preceded by its intonation, the pastorale (BWV 590/1), after. This frame is a musical reference to the humble birth of Christ in a stable implicit in the words "humiliter nati" of the title of the ser-

Table 4.2.   Hypothetical Reconstruction of the Peace Ceremony of 25 December 1745 Celebrated in St. Paul's Church, Leipzig

Function	Title	Key	Approximate Duration
Vorspiel	?Prelude BWV 547/1	D	4:15
ante orationem	"Gloria in excelsis Deo" BWV 191a	D	1:45
	"Et in terra pax" BWV 191/1b	G, D	4:30
invitatio			3:45
oratio	*De Jesu Christi servatoris, humiliter nati, maiestate . . .*		60:00
post orationem	?Pastorale BWV 590/1 (?)	G	2:30
	"Gloria Patri" BWV 191/2	G	4:30
	"Sicut erat" BWV 191/3	D	4:15
Nachspiel	?Fugue BWV 547/2	D	4:30

mon. This pastoral inner ensemble is framed by movements in the brilliant key of D major, stressing the heavenly glory and majesty of Christ the king implicit in the word "maiestate" of the sermon's title. The outer frame for the whole consists of the Prelude BWV 547/1 and the Fugue BWV 547/2. The former combines both the elements of pastoral humility and heavenly glory and thus serves as an ideal introduction affectively, while the fugue with its implicit reference to the German Gloria reflects back on its Latin counterpart preceding the sermon.

The two verses of the doxology that furnish the text for the two movements comprising the second part of the figural music serve as an echo of the invocation that would have closed the Latin sermon and thus act textually as a fitting close to the service as a whole. They also point ahead in time to the last two movements of the Magnificat about to be performed in a concerted version before the sermon during the Christmas afternoon service to be held immediately following the peace ceremony. In the same way, the Fugue BWV 547/2 constitutes a clear musical reference to (and, as chorale prelude, prepares the congregation for) the German Gloria sung choraliter during the afternoon service. At the same time, textually and liturgically it has its parallel in the Latin Gloria of the first half of the service.

The above hypotheses, like Spitta's suggestion that Bach played the Fantasia and Fugue in G minor (BWV 542) at St. Catharine's Church, Hamburg in 1720,[30] no matter how soundly they are argued, must remain within the realm of conjecture. We will probably never be in a position to know precisely what Bach played on the organ for his preluding at the beginning and conclusion of occasional services such as the peace ceremony of Christmas, 1745.[31] Nevertheless, what I hope to have accomplished here is to place the hypothetical preluding on this occasion in an informed historical, functional, and theological context. The fragmentary source evidence available to us and the somewhat more substantial internal evidence provided by the musical text allow us to arrive at rational, well-informed hypotheses, and, in so doing, go a long way toward clarifying and filling out the heretofore, at best, sketchy picture of this important facet of Bach's activity as organist during the Leipzig years.

NOTES

1. In the context of preluding for the Lutheran worship service, George Stauffer briefly mentions "special *Festtag* services" but he does not address specifically Bach's involvement on such occasions, referring instead impersonally to "an organist." See George Stauffer, *The Organ Preludes of Johann Sebastian Bach* (Ann Arbor: UMI Research Press, 1980), 138.

2. See Gregory Butler, "Johann Sebastian Bachs Gloria in excelsis Deo BWV 191: Musik für ein Leipziger Dankfest," *Bach-Jahrbuch* 78 (1992): 65–71

3. These problems may be summarized as follows:

a. The performance of a cantata with a Latin text in a Leipzig church service would have been most unusual.

b. Given the normal division of the St. Thomas school chorus into four choirs for simultaneous performances at the four Leipzig churches, a vocal work for five-voice choir would not have been performable at the morning and evening services in St. Nicholas's Church and St. Thomas's Church on Christmas Day, and all the more so in light of the augmented instrumental forces often required to support the choir particularly on such festive occasions. It is for this reason that Bach's church cantatas are written almost without exception for four-voice choir.

c. Bach's obituary expressly states that he left behind five yearly cycles of church cantatas, thus five for Christmas Day. Since all five can be accounted for among Bach's surviving church cantatas, *Gloria in excelsis Deo* would then be one too many.

More specifically, there is no occasion liturgically in the Leipzig Christmas service for a Gloria alone, particularly such an abbreviated one with its parodies of Doxology texts, after the sermon. Further, the indication of a specific feast day in the title (J. J. Festo Nativit: Xsti. Gloria in excelsis Deo. à 5 Voci. 3 Trombe e Tymp. 2 Trav. 2 Hautb. / 2 Violini e Cont. di J. S. B.) removes the work from the pieces of the Mass Ordinary and places it among those for the Proper of the Mass for Christmas, though as a Gloria the music could just as well be performed at Easter or Pentecost.

4. See *Bach-Dokumente*, vol. II, ed. Werner Neumann and Hans-Joachim Schulze (Kassel: Bärenreiter, 1969), nos. 230–35, pp. 174–77 (subsequently cited as *BDok* II).

5. *Nützliche Nachrichten von denen Bemühungen derer Gelehrten . . .* , V (Leipzig,1745), 96. I would like to thank the personnel of the Sächsische Landesbibliothek, Dresden for their searches on my behalf and for supplying me with a copy of the above entries from their exemplar of this source.

6. Pursuing the matter further, the biblical passage on which the commentary is based is enlightening. In chapter 3 of Exodus the angel of God appears to Moses in the flame of the bush, which burns but is not consumed. The angel announces that God has descended from heaven to deliver the children of Israel from their suffering at the hands of the Egyptian pharaoh. The burning bush, which burns but is not consumed, could have served as a vivid symbol for Saxony, which, although ravaged by war, nevertheless had survived. God may be seen as symbolizing the Dresden peace, which delivered Saxons from their suffering at the hands of the Prussian forces of Frederick the Great.

7. For the documents pertaining to this struggle for control of the service, see *BDok* II, nos. 225–28, pp. 169–73.

8. Not long after the memorial service, in a letter dated 12 November 1727 to his father-in-law, Johann Daniel Bähre, organist at the St. Peter's church in Brunswick,

Georg Heinrich Ludwig Schwanenberger wrote of having recently heard Bach perform on the organ: "Ich möchte wünschen dass er Herrn Bachen auff der Orgel mahl hörete, er wahrhafftig sich vor ihme, wie auch Keiner in Braunschweig, nicht auffdecken darff, ich habe so was noch niemahls gehöret, und ich mus meine Spielart ganz anders ändern, denn es nichts zu rechnen ist, . . ." (*BDok* II, no. 239, pp. 178–79); for an English translation see *The New Bach Reader*, ed. Hans T. David and Arthur Mendel, rev. Christoph Wolff (New York: W. W. Norton, 1998), no. 320, p. 325 (subsequently cited as *NBR*).

Given the date of this letter so soon after the memorial service, it seems likely that Schwanenberger was present at the ceremony and is here referring to the playing he heard on that occasion. Although this is a relatively well-documented reference to a performance given by Bach, as in all other instances, the documentary sources are annoyingly vague about what was actually played by the organ on such occasions.

9. Stauffer, 138.

10. "*Praeludiert* auf die Haupt*Music*." See *Bach-Dokumente*, vol. I, ed. Werner Neumann and Hans-Joachim Schulze (Kassel: Bärenreiter, 1963), no. 181, p. 251 (subsequently cited as *BDok* I). For an English translation, see *NBR*, no. 113, p. 113.

11. Bach gives as the fourteenth item in the "Order of the Divine Service in Leipzig on the First Sunday in Advent: Morning" (Anordnung des GottesDienstes in Leipzig am 1 *Advent*-Sonntag frühe), "(14) Preluding on the [concerted] music [second part of the cantata]" (*Praelud*[ie*r*et]: auf die *Music*). See *BDok* 1, no. 178, pp. 248–49; English translation in *NBR*, no. 113, p. 113. The preluding before the second part of the *Trauerode* may not have been mentioned in accounts of the memorial service because it was relatively brief.

12. ". . . ein Anfang ehe ein recht = gesetztes musicalisches Stück angefangen wird, da der Organiste alleine spielet damit die Sänger den Ton fassen und die Instrumentisten reine Stimmen mögen ohne den Zuhörern dadurch einen Verdruß zu erwecken. Solches Praeludium kann ein Organiste so lange machen als er will oder bis die Instrumentisten rein gestimmet haben und ihm ein Zeichen zum Aufhalten gegeben wird." Friedrich Erhardt Niedt, *Musicalische Handleitung Anderer Theil* (Hamburg, 1717), 102.

13. ". . . sieht . . . die Partitur einmal an, um zu wissen welches Tempo und der Affekt der Musik eigentlich seyn solle, und mit was für Noten die erste Violine anfange." Johann Samuel Petri, *Anleitung zur praktischen Musik* (Lauban, 1782), 298–99.

14. Stauffer, 143.

15. I have excerpted these references to fugal preluding by late baroque German theorists from Stauffer's useful survey. See Stauffer, 138–40.

16. *NBR*, p. 523.

17. For details concerning chorus and chamber pitch practices in Leipzig, see Alfred Dürr, *Studien über die frühen Kantaten Johann Sebastian Bachs* (Leipzig: Breitkopf und Härtel, 1951), 74–79. With regard to the organ of St. Paul's Church there is no unequivocal evidence supporting Christoph Wolff's statement that "unlike the old small choir organ, the new Scheibe organ was tuned to chamber pitch." See *Johann Sebastian Bach: The Learned Musician* (New York: W. W. Norton, 2000), 317

and 497, n. 38). While single stops for continuo playing and small positiv organs were sometimes tuned to chamber pitch, it was unusual in a large church organ as early as 1711–1716 when the Scheibe organ was under construction. In Ulrich Dähnert, *Historische Orgeln in Sachsen: Ein Orgelinventar* (Frankfurt am Mein: Verlag das Musikinstrument, 1980), 183–84 there is no indication that this organ was tuned to chamber pitch and no other organ built by Scheibe is known to have been tuned to the lower pitch. The tuning to chamber pitch of the Silbermann organ in St. Sophia's church, Dresden, completed two years after the Scheibe organ, must be considered as exceptional for the time. Johann Philipp Kirnberger, who was Bach's pupil in Leipzig and would certainly have played the Scheibe organ in St. Paul's Church, stated in 1769: "In Leipzig, the organs that were available in Mr. J. S. Bach's time are certainly all in chorus pitch" (Zu Leipzig stehen die Orgeln, die zu Herrn J. S. Bachs [Zeit] vorhanden waren, ganz gewiß alle in Chortone). See *Bach-Dokumente*, vol. III, ed. Hans-Joachim Schulze (Kassel: Bärenreiter, 1972), no. 755, p. 204.

18. For the dating of these works, see Stauffer, 101, 109, 112, and 122–24.

19. See Hermann Keller, *Die Orgelwerke Bachs* (Leipzig: C. F. Peters, 1948), 118.

20. See Philipp Spitta, *Johann Sebastian Bach* (Leipzig: Breitkopf und Härtel, 1916), 2:689.

21. See Peter Williams, *The Organ Music of J. S. Bach* (Cambridge: Cambridge University Press, 1978), 1:159–60. Volumes I and II have recently been published in a revised version as *The Organ Music of J. S. Bach*, 2d ed. (Cambridge: Cambridge University Press, 2003), and all subsequent references will be to this edition.

22. See Russell Stinson, "Toward a Chronology of Bach's Instrumental Music: Observations on Three Keyboard Works," *Journal of Musicology* 7 (Fall 1989): 466–69 and *The Bach Manuscripts of Johann Peter Kellner and His Circle: A Case Study in Reception History* (Durham, N.C.: Duke University Press, 1989), 114–19.

23. Stinson, "Toward a Chronology," 465.

24. See Gregory Butler, *Bach's Clavier-Übung III: The Making of a Print: With a Companion Study of the Canonic Variations on "Vom Himmel hoch" BWV 769* (Durham, N.C.: Duke University Press, 1990), 111–13.

25. See Gregory Butler, "J. S. Bachs Kanonische Veränderungen über 'Vom Himmel hoch' (BWV 769): Ein Schlußstrich unter die Debatte um die Frage der 'Fassung letzter Hand,'" *Bach-Jahrbuch* 86 (2000): 25ff.

26. See Williams, *The Organ Music*, 112–14, particularly example 53.

27. For another instance of Bach's pointing ahead across time, in this case in a work from the Lenten period, see Eric Chafe, "J. S. Bach's *St. Matthew Passion*: Aspects of Planning, Structure, and Chronology," *Journal of the American Musicological Society* 35 (Spring 1982): 111.

28. For a survey linking the *Pastorella* with the Christmas pastorale tradition, see George Stauffer, "Bach's Pastorale in F: A Closer Look at a Maligned Work," *The Organ Yearbook* 14 (1983): 49–52.

29. "Da hierbey das Einstimmen der Instrumente die Hauptabsicht ist, so würde ich dem Organisten rathen, allemal in einem Tone anzufangen worin sich die Violinen u.a. leicht stimmen lassen; das ware, wenn die Orgel im gewöhnlichen (ordinairen) Chortone steht, C dur (allenfalls auch G und F dur, oder C und G moll); . . .

In diesen Tonarten sich der Organist eine Zeitlang aufhalten, damit die Musicirenden ihre Saiteninstrumente richtig einstimmen können. Alsdenn erst geht er, durch eine gutgewählte Modulation, in den Hauptton des Stücks über; allein der Hörner, Trompeten, Pauken, u.a. wegen, muß er noch eine Weile in dem Tone, worin diese Instrumente stehen, moduliren; . . ."

Daniel Gottlob Türk, *Von den wichtigsten Pflichten eines Organisten* (Halle, 1787), 136–37.

30. See Spitta, 1:634–35.

31. The manuscript notation establishing that Bach performed the Toccata and Fugue in D minor BWV 538 at the inauguration of the organ of St. Martin's Church on 28 September 1732 must be considered as a chance exception.

5

Bach's Setting of the Hymn Tune "Nun komm, der Heiden Heiland" in His Cantatas and Organ Works

Anne Leahy

Martin Luther's hymn "Nun komm, der Heiden Heiland" is one that preoccupied Bach for most of his working life. He set various verses of it in three Advent cantatas: *Nun komm, der Heiden Heiland* (BWV 61 and 62) and *Schwingt freudig euch empor* (BWV 36) and in five organ chorale preludes: *Nun komm, der Heiden Heiland* (BWV 699, 599, 659, 660, and 661). This chapter examines Bach's settings of the hymn and shows how similar themes run through all of them, even when he is setting a different verse. First, the historical, theological, and liturgical context of Luther's hymn is considered. The Epistle and Gospel readings for the First Sunday of Advent are also examined in relation to the context of Bach's settings. Then these themes are highlighted in relation to Bach's settings.

THE HYMN TEXT

The text of "Nun komm, der Heiden Heiland" is Luther's translation of the fourth-century Latin Advent hymn "Veni redemptor gentium," attributed to Bishop Ambrose of Milan (334–397).[1] The hymn existed in several German paraphrases before the Reformation, the earliest dating from the twelfth century.[2] Verse 8 first appeared in the Middle Ages, and the hymn tune itself was not composed by Ambrosius.[3] The earliest source of the melody as we know it is a Swiss-Benedictine manuscript from 1120. It is possible that it stems from the nearby Benedictine Abbey at St. Gallen, which could perhaps date it as far back as 900.[4] It was published with the German text in 1524 in the Erfurt *Enchiridion* and in Johann Walter's *Geystliche Gesangk Buchleyn* at Wittenberg.[5] It is possible, therefore, that this hymn was written by Luther for

Advent 1523.[6] The two publications mentioned above contain versions of the text of "Nun komm, der Heiden Heiland" that are so similar that they may be considered copies. These two sources must be taken as a basis for this hymn.[7] Luther employs a 7.7.7.7 meter. He has transformed the eight-syllable lines of the original Latin to suit a seven-syllable per line setting. The text of the hymn as it appears in the Weimar hymnbook of 1713, where it is listed under the heading "Von der Menschwerdung JEsu Christi" (regarding the incarnation of Christ) is:

1. NUn komm der Heyden Heyland/
der Jungfrauen Kind erkannt/
des sich wunder' alle Welt/
GOTT solch Geburt ihm bestellt.

1. Come now, Savior of the nations,
Known to be the child of the Virgin,
All the world marvels that God
would prepare such a birth for him.

2. Nicht von Manns=Blut noch vom
    Fleisch/
allein von dem heilgen Geist/
ist GOttes Wort wordn ein Mensch/
und blüht ein Frucht Weibes=Fleisch.

2. Not by the flesh and blood of a man,

but alone by the Holy Ghost,
God's word is become human,
and becomes as the fruit of a woman's
    flesh.

3. Der Jungfrauen Leib schwanger ward/
doch bleibt Keuschheit rein bewahrt/
leucht herfür manch Tugend schon/
GOtt da war in seinem Thron.

3. The Virgin's body became with child,
but her chastity was purely preserved.
Many beautiful signs indicated that
God was in his throne.

4. Er gieng aus der Kammer sein/
dem Königlichen Saal so rein/
Gott von Art und Mensch ein Held/
seinn Weg er zu lauffen eilt.

4. He left his chamber,
the royal hall so pure.
God by origin, and man, a champion,
he hurries to run his course.

5. Sein Lauf kam vom Vater her/
und kehrt wieder zum Vater/
fuhr hinunter zu der Höll/
und wieder zu Gottes Stuhl.

5. His course originated with the Father
and returned again to the Father;
went below to hell
and back again to God's seat.

6. Der du bist dem Vater gleich/
führ hinaus den Sieg im Fleisch/
daß dein ewig Gottes Gewalt/
in uns das kranck Fleisch enthalt.

6. You, who are equal to the Father,
take the victory in the flesh
so that your eternal divine power
supports the sick flesh in us.

7. Dein Krippen gläntzt hell und klar/
die Nacht gibt ein neu Licht dar/
tunckel muß nicht kommen drein/
der Glaub bleibt immer im Schein.

7. Your manger shines bright and clear;
the night shines forth a new light.
Darkness must not enter therein.
Faith always remains in the light.

8. Lob sey GOtt dem Vater thon/	8. Praise be to God the Father,
lob sey Gott seinm eingen Sohn/	Praise be to God, his only Son,
lob sey GOtt dem heilgen Geist/	Praise be to God, the Holy Spirit,
immer und in Ewigkeit.[8]	Always and eternally.[9]

"Nun komm, der Heiden Heiland" was the *Hauptlied* or principal hymn for the First Sunday of Advent.[10] The hymn text, comprising seven four-line verses plus a doxology, concerns itself with Christ's incarnation and the purpose of his life on earth. The opening text, "nun komm" ("veni") expresses the wish of mankind for Christ's birth on earth. Therefore, this plea is also a wish for salvation, which comes with the birth of Christ.[11]

When Ambrosius wrote this hymn, the Christian church did not yet celebrate Advent. The observance of Advent as a special time in the church year began only in the fifth and sixth centuries. The First Sunday of Advent was a special Sunday at Leipzig. It was the first Sunday of the church year, and, as such, there were some special liturgical procedures.[12] This Sunday was also linked to Lent as the start of a period of repentance and preparation, in this case for Christmas.[13] Thus, a certain paradox existed—with the consequent polarity of a festive occasion and yet the beginning of a season of repentance and preparation.

According to Johannes Kulp, this hymn contains the entire story of salvation.[14] Martin Petzoldt demonstrates how Ambrosius has incorporated the important Christological ideas of the Old and New Testaments into this important Advent hymn.[15] Verse 1 speaks directly to Christ, verses 2–3 describe the mystery of his birth, while verses 4–5 describe the physical process of Christ's departure from heaven to carry out his work on earth. Verse 4 leaves behind the mystical world of the first three verses and refers to more earthly matters. Christ leaves the royal hall so pure (verse 4) to carry out his work on earth. In the last two lines of this verse there is a reference to Psalm 19:5–6, which speaks of the bridegroom leaving his chamber and rejoices as a strong man running a race:

> Er hat die Sonne eine Hütte an ihnen gemacht; und dieselbe geht heraus wie ein Bräutigam aus seiner Kammer und freut sich, wie ein Held zu laufen den Weg.[16]
> [In them hath he set a tabernacle for the sun, which is as a bridegroom coming out of his chamber, and rejoiceth as a strong man to run a race.][17]

In Psalm 19, which praises the wonders of God's creation with a special emphasis on light, the reference is to the sun shining to the edge of the heavens. Light is also an important image in the hymn "Nun komm, der Heiden Heiland." In the context of the psalm, verse 4 of the hymn could be seen as Christ spreading his light or goodness throughout the world by his incarnation, death, and resurrection. The image of Christ as a bridegroom was a common biblical theme. Luther commented on this passage from Psalm 19 in his sermon for the First Sunday of Advent:

> Das ist alles von dißem lieblichen anbrechenn des tags, das ist: vom Euangelio gesagt, wilchs die schrifft hoch uund lieblich preysset, denn es macht auch lebendig, frolich, lustig, tettig, unnd bringt alles gutt mit sich. Darumb es auch heyst Euangelium, das ist: eyn lustige bottschafft.[18]
>
> [It all refers to the beautiful daybreak of the Gospel. Scripture sublimely exalts the Gospel Day, for it is the source of life, joy, pleasure and energy, and brings all good. Hence the name "Gospel"—joyful news.[19]]

In referring to the beautiful daybreak, Luther stresses the important Advent theme of light. Verse 5 refers back to Christ's origin with the Father and his subsequent reunion with him after his life on earth. Verse 6 is important, as Christ is addressed once more directly as the equal of the Father, claiming his victory. In verse 7, describing the shining bright manger, the light of Christ contrasts with the darkness of evil, representing the triumph of good over evil. The beliefs of Christianity, which depend on the night when Christ was born, are depicted here in radiant light. Imagery pertaining to light is also contained in the Epistle for the First Sunday of Advent (Rom 13:11–14).[20]

> Die Nacht ist vorgerückt, der Tag aber nahe herbeigekommen: so lasset uns ablegen die Werke der Finsternis und anlegen die Waffen des Lichtes. Lasset uns ehrbar wandeln als am Tage, nicht im Fressen und Saufen, nicht im Kammern und Unzucht, nicht in Hader und Neid; sondern ziehet an den Herrn Jesus Christus und wartet des Leibes, doch also daß er nicht geil werde.
>
> [The night is far spent, the day is at hand: let us therefore cast off the works of darkness, and let us put on the armour of light. Let us walk honestly as in the day; not in rioting and drunkenness, not in chambering and wantonness, not in strife and envying. But put ye on the Lord Jesus Christ, and make not provision for the flesh, to fulfil the lusts thereof.]

In his sermon for the First Sunday of Advent, Luther equates light with faith and darkness with unbelief:

> drumb sind die wapen des liechts nichts anders denn die werck des glawbens. Widderumb, finsternis ist der unglawbe, durch abweßen des Euangeli und Christi, auß menschenleren unnd eygener vornunfft vom teuffell regirtt; darumb sind die werck der finsterniß, werck des unglawbens.[21]
>
> [The armour of light, then, is simply the works of faith. On the other hand, "darkness" is unbelief; it reigns in the absence of the Gospel and of Christ, through the instrumentality of the doctrines of men—of human reason—instigated by the devil.[22]]

These statements of Luther are important particularly in the context of verse 7 of "Nun komm, der Heiden Heiland."[23] Verse 8 is a concluding doxological stanza.

The Melody

The traditional, modal form of this melody was commonly used up to the early eighteenth century (example 5.1). Bach often used it in this form: in BWV 36 (movements 6 and 8), in BWV 62 (movements 1 and 6), in the *Orgelbüchlein* setting BWV 599, and in the short setting for organ BWV 699. The melody was transmitted most frequently in G or in A dorian. In the second half of the seventeenth century, the Berlin edition of Johannes Crüger's *Praxis pietatis melica* (1647) began to present a previously unusual version of the melody in which the third note of both the first and final phrase was raised chromatically.[24] Nicolaus Bruhns used the chromatic variant at these two points in his organ setting of the same hymn, as did Bach in BWV 36.2 and 61.1 as well as in BWV 660 and 661.

"Nun komm, der Heiden Heiland" was sung in Leipzig on all four Sundays in Advent and existed in most hymn books from around 1600.[25] Very much considered a traditional hymn, "Nun komm, der Heiden Heiland" was consistently listed as the *Hauptlied* or main chorale for the First Sunday of Advent and was used by Bach for all three extant cantatas for this Sunday.[26] In BWV 36 Bach sets verses 1, 6, and 8; in BWV 61 verse 1 only; with BWV 62 offering a setting of verses 1 and 8.

Lutheran hymnbooks of the sixteenth and seventeenth centuries consistently begin with "Nun komm, der Heiden Heiland," as does Bach's *Orgelbüchlein.* However, hymnbooks dating from the end of the seventeenth century began to precede the Advent hymns with hymns suitable for the commencement of worship. The 1681 edition of the Weimar hymnbook followed the older tradition, whereas the later editions followed the latter pattern.[27]

Example 5.1.   Traditional Modal Form of "Nun komm, der Heiden Heiland"

BACH'S SETTING OF "NUN KOMM, DER HEIDEN HEILAND" IN HIS CANTATAS

In trying to establish text-music relationships among Bach's settings of "Nun komm, der Heiden Heiland," it is logical to begin by examining those settings where we know precisely which verse Bach was setting, i.e., the cantatas. This approach then provides clues as to which verse Bach might be setting in the organ pieces. Let us begin with the different settings of verse 1 of "Nun komm, der Heiden Heiland." Bach sets this verse three times in his Advent cantatas: in the opening movements of cantatas BWV 61 and 62, and in movement 2 of BWV 36.

Nun komm, der Heiden Heiland (BWV 61)

In the opening movement of BWV 61, Bach sets verse 1 of "Nun komm, der Heiden Heiland" for SATB with five-part strings and continuo. This setting is rare in Bach's output in that he combines a chorale setting with the form of the French overture.[28] BWV 61 was first performed on the First Sunday of Advent, 2 December 1714.[29] The French overture was traditionally associated with the arrival of a secular king (Louis XIV) at the start of the opera at the French court. Bach links it in BWV 61 to the imminent arrival of the King of kings at Christmas, while also alluding to the arrival of Christ into Jerusalem on Palm Sunday, as told in the Gospel of the day (Mt 21:1–9). The metaphor of the arrival of a new church year is also invoked in the use of this form, the First Sunday of Advent also being the first Sunday of the new church year. There is a similar musical treatment in the opening two movements of the Palm Sunday cantata *Himmelskönig sei willkommen* (BWV 182), the first cantata to be composed by Bach following his appointment as *Konzertmeister* in Weimar in 1714.[30] The text of the chorale verbalizes what the music is implying in BWV 61: in turn, soprano, alto, tenor, and bass intone the first line of Luther's hymn. Each voice announces "Nun komm, der Heiden Heiland" in response to the use of the French overture, which also implies coming. As if Bach is not content with this very prominent proclamation of the hymn, he also presents it twice in the continuo: once at m. 1 and again at m. 13. Therefore, in all, the opening line of the hymn melody is heard six times by m. 24—there being only two measures without reference to the chorale. Thus, Bach makes a very powerful statement regarding the coming of Christ.

Bach chooses to use the chromaticized version of the chorale melody and the resulting diminished fourth, producing the *saltus duriusculus*, adds a further touch of poignancy to the music. The "Nun komm" melody contains a cross symbol within its first five notes (as seen in example 5.2), which was,

Example 5.2. The Cross Symbol

of course, very convenient for Bach, given the Lutheran association between incarnation and atonement.

In Lutheran terms, Christ was born to die, to provide salvation for humanity. Therefore, Christ's death begins with his birth.[31] Thus, in the opening bars there are many theological messages: the dotted rhythms of the French overture indicate arrival of some sort—the new church year, Christ in his incarnation, or Christ as King on Palm Sunday—and the six-fold repetition of line 1 of the hymn melody reiterates the coming of the Savior. It is interesting that the number 6 has long been associated with the coming of the Savior as seen in Isaiah 6:1–3:

> In the year that King Uzziah died, I saw also the LORD sitting upon a throne, high and lifted up, and his train filled the temple. Above it stood the seraphim: each one had six wings; with twain he covered his face, and with twain he covered his feet, and with twain he did fly. And one cried unto another, and said, Holy, holy, holy, is the LORD of hosts; the whole earth is full of his glory.

A further reference to the number 6 and the coming of Christ on Palm Sunday may be found in Revelation 4:8:

> And the four beasts had each of them six wings about him; and they were full of eyes within: and they rest not day and night, saying, Holy, holy, holy, LORD God Almighty, which was, and is, and is to come.

Therefore, it is not surprising that Bach repeats the hymn text regarding the coming of the Savior six times.[32] The voices enter in descending order, perhaps a reference by Bach to Christ's descent to earth to become man.[33]

Bach presents line 2 of the chorale in a straightforward homophonic fashion. By contrast with the preceding line, this section of text occupies only four bars. This may reflect the text stating that the Savior is known to be the child of the Virgin. The fact that it is known means there is no need for further elaboration; thus, Bach offers only a simple harmonization. For the following section, Bach changes to triple meter as all the world marvels at this birth. The dancing triple meter implies the celebration of all the world at the birth of the Savior. The circular motion of the vocal parts easily portrays the idea of all the world, as do the long held notes and melismas on the word "alle," as seen in example 5.3.[34]

Example 5.3. BWV 61.1 (mm. 33–37)

At m. 85 the slow dotted rhythm of the French overture returns for the final section. The final line of text is presented as the second, in a homophonic straightforward manner. Thus, it is clear that Bach incorporates many elements relating to Advent in the opening movement of BWV 61. He alludes to the special significance of the First Sunday of Advent by the use of the French overture, and he clearly portrays each line of text in succession. Many of the musical elements employed here will also be found in his other settings, both vocal and for organ, demonstrating a consistency of approach in a wide range of musical compositions for the season of Advent.

Nun komm, der Heiden Heiland (BWV 62)

Bach returned to this text ten years later in the first movement of BWV 62. Now established in Leipzig and in the middle of his second *Jahrgang*, he presents another strikingly original movement. This time he chooses the key of B minor, which was to be regarded very much as the key of humbling and incarnation in the *B-Minor Mass* (the opening "Kyrie," the "Qui tollis," and "Et incarnatus est"). Working with the more modern ensemble of four-part strings, he also adds a pair of oboes and one horn to the instrumental group. The meter is the more unusual compound duple of 6/4, perhaps pointing to the special significance of the arrival of the Savior. The opening instrumental ritornello is at once striking. The oboes play an offbeat *figura corta* motive that dominates the movement, while also incorporating much circular sixteenth-note figuration. Meanwhile in the opening two measures, the two violins and viola play a strong unison motive involving a descending arpeggio and repeated eighth notes. In m. 3 the continuo enters with the chorale melody in dotted half notes, while the strings continue in the strong triadic patterns established in the opening measures. This time Bach chooses the more traditional modal version of the melody. The ritornello material (shown in example 5.4) offers many possibilities with regard to theological symbolism.

It is possible to perceive trinitarian references in the musical material. Sixteenth notes in circular motion are consistently used by Bach to depict the Holy Spirit (e.g., the violin parts of the opening movement of the *St. John Passion*; the opening movement of the Pentecost cantata *O ewiges Feuer, o Ursprung der Liebe* (BWV 34); and the first of the "Leipzig" chorales, *Komm Heiliger Geist, Herre Gott* (BWV 651). In the case of BWV 62.1, the sixteenth-note figuration with its circular motion may also be indicative of the Holy Spirit; the strong triadic writing of the strings can portray the Father, while the "Heiden Heiland" is clearly portrayed in the bass part with the cantus firmus.[35] The Savior comes to provide salvation, but that salvation is the work of the Triune God: God the Father sends the Son who sends the Holy Spirit.[36] An additional motive is the slurred eighth note, first heard at m. 8. This kind of writing can be associated with the cross, as seen in the opening movement of the cantata *Ich will den Kreuzstab gerne tragen* (BWV 56), where this motive aptly portrays Christ carrying the cross.[37] In BWV 62.1, two measures before the entry of the first voice (alto), line 1 of the chorale melody is heard in unison in the two oboe parts. The alto, tenor, and bass enter in imitation with a motive based on the opening line of the chorale. Once more, as in BWV 61, the natural cross symbol embedded in the opening four notes of the chorale melody and its associated motives allow Bach to reiterate the coming of Christ as Savior. Following the entry of the three lower voices with this motivic writing, the soprano enters in m. 22 with the chorale melody in dotted half notes doubled by the horn.

For line 2 of the text, Bach allows the soprano to enter first. He has preceded this entrance with line 1 of the chorale melody on oboes (m. 31) and

Example 5.4. BWV 62.1 (mm. 1–7)

not line 2 as one might have expected. This is in keeping with his other settings of "Nun komm, der Heiden Heiland" (notably the organ chorale preludes BWV 659–61) where Bach continually emphasizes the opening line of the chorale throughout the setting. The reiteration of the line of the chorale that refers explicitly to the Savior, while also incorporating the cross symbol, serves to underline the purpose of his coming—that he is born to die.[38]

Bach sets line 3 of the text in a most vivid way. The soprano enters with the chorale melody in dotted half notes, while underneath, the alto, tenor, and bass engage in dancing imitative lines largely in sixteenth notes. Here Bach uses circular motives and impressive melismas on the word "alle," as he did in BWV 61, to portray the wonder of all the world. Measure 46 corresponds to m. 1 and the music remains the same for six measures. However, Bach opts for a new approach to the final line of the chorale, even though it is the same as the opening. He moves toward F-sharp minor, and the chorale melody is heard on the oboes a fifth higher than at the opening (m. 54). Equally, the imitative entries of the three lower parts are different melodically and in order of entry. The opening ritornello is then repeated, ensuring that the last three measures of music to be heard contain the oboes' citation of line 1 of the chorale melody. Thus, Bach is still reiterating the very important message of this opening movement, the plea by humanity to the Savior to come to earth and provide salvation.

Thus, it is clear in this opening movement of BWV 62 that Bach is further developing musical ideas, already explored in BWV 61.1, in relation to the theological issues relating to Advent and Luther's hymn. The powerful message of the coming Savior is clear in the instrumental citation of the opening line of the chorale, first in the continuo and then on oboes throughout the movement. The three distinct musical ideas of the opening ritornello indicate the Trinity, each member playing a unique role in the salvation of humanity. The third line of text is set in an even more dramatic manner than that of BWV 61.1 as the whole world dances in amazement at Christ's birth. Finally, the tonality is also significant. In the context of incarnation, Bach frequently employs the key of B minor (for example "Et incarnatus est" of the *B-Minor Mass*).

Schwingt freudig euch empor (BWV 36)

Bach sets verse 1 of "Nun komm, der Heiden Heiland" in a vocal setting one more time—in the second movement of the cantata *Schwingt freudig euch empor* (BWV 36). This cantata has a complex history, existing in as many as five different versions, and originating as a secular cantata.[39] It was only in the second version of the sacred transformation of the cantata that Bach inserted the three movements involving Luther's "Nun komm, der Heiden Heiland." This setting of verse 1 of Luther's hymn is markedly different from his settings of the same text in BWV 61 and 62. It is an intimate duet for soprano and alto with oboes d'amore I and II doubling the vocal lines with continuo (example 5.5). In many ways it has more in common with the organ settings BWV 659 and 660—the intimacy points to the mystical atmosphere of BWV 659, while the strict contrapuntal texture is reminiscent of BWV 660. As with the three organ settings of this chorale in the "Leipzig" chorales, Bach exploits the symbolic potential of the hymn melody repeatedly throughout the movement. The built-in cross symbol is made all the more poignant due to the use of the sharpened leading note. The continuo line is noteworthy for its constant reiteration of this figure (as in BWV 660) and for its prominent use of the *figura corta*. Bach changes the musical setting of each line of text in order to reflect its meaning in detail. The ways in which he approaches the text in BWV 36 find resonance in the organ settings and help to confirm conclusions drawn with regard to text-music relationships in BWV 659–61.

In terms of the text, the movement falls naturally into four sections. Bach begins his portrayal of line 1 with the voices entering in strict imitation. There are many interesting features to this opening section. First, the cross symbol is evident throughout, not just in the opening motive based on the chorale, but also later in the phrase (e.g., the alto part for "Heiland" in m. 5). Second, the falling motive for "nun komm," first heard in m. 6 and repeated three times, easily depicts descent, in this case of the Savior from heaven to earth. The use of oboes d'amore to double the voices counteracts the otherwise somewhat austere atmosphere created by the strict counterpoint. The constant reiteration of the *figura corta* in the continuo also helps to create an atmosphere of warmth and trust.

For line 2 of the text Bach turns to a more legato and less broken line with the hymn tune heard in notes twice as long as that of the first section. The hymn melody is heard first by soprano in m. 11, followed a measure later by alto. Although in both his portrayal of the first and second lines of text, Bach is initially quoting the chorale relatively unadorned, he nonetheless creates a different affect in both. The Virgin is emphasized in the long legato lines while the Savior in line 1 is shown in shorter more breathy phrases. As a reminder of the purpose of this Virgin birth, Bach chooses to repeat the text of line 1 from m. 16 before a final statement of line 2. This is in keeping with the prominence shown to the concept of "Heiden Heiland," as seen especially in BWV 659. At m. 20, the tonality turns decisively to A major for the close of section 2. This acts as a springboard for the next section "des sich wundert alle Welt," which in all of Bach's settings is more active and melismatic than any other line of the text. The vocal parts enter on an offbeat eighth note,

Example 5.5. BWV 36.2 (mm. 1–7)

more to give a dance-like feel to the music than any possibly more negative affect sometimes associated with syncopation. Once more, as in BWV 61 and 62, Bach employs the *circulatio* figure to portray "alle Welt."

The final section begins at m. 32 and is the most extended. Although this is the same music as the opening line, Bach sets it in a new way in keeping with the different text. Now the alto gets to sing the entire phrase before being imitated by the soprano one and a half measures later. At m. 37 the hymn tune is heard in quarter notes, somehow making the text stand out even more. Bach follows this with the falling motive he had used for "Nun komm" in m. 6 but this time to the text "Gott solch" followed by "Geburt." Thus, the same meaning may be extracted from this motive in section 4: the descending line is concerned with the descent of Christ to earth for his birth. The rising chromatic line of m. 44 is very marked, especially since Bach does not employ this kind of writing elsewhere in the movement. The use of chromaticism points out the text "Gott solch Geburt," but it would seem that it is the *purpose* of this birth that is preoccupying Bach at this time—Christ is born to die, and Bach once more points to the link between incarnation and atonement.[40]

This movement is 49 bars long. This is a number that can be associated with the Holy Spirit (7×7). Bach was to make this link with incarnation and

Example 5.6. "Et incarnatus est" (*B-Minor Mass*: **mm. 10–13**)

the Holy Spirit much later in 1749 when he composed the "Et incarnatus est" of the *B-Minor Mass*, a movement that is also 49 measures long.[41] The text of the "Et incarnatus est" is "et incarnatus est de spiritu sancto" [and was incarnate by the Holy Spirit]. In this movement Bach places especial emphasis on the Holy Spirit's role in the incarnation by providing the first augmented sixth chord in the entire *B-Minor Mass* for the text "spiritu sancto" at m. 12 of the "Et incarnatus est" (example 5.6). Similarly the use of 49 measures for this movement is indicative of the Holy Spirit. With BWV 36.2 Bach seems also to be linking the Holy Spirit with incarnation in the number of measures.

Settings of Other Verses of the Hymn

The only other verses of "Nun komm, der Heiden Heiland" that Bach sets are verse 8 in BWV 62 and verses 6 and 8 in BWV 36. The settings of verse 8 in BWV 62 are 36 are simple four-part harmonizations to close the respective

Example 5.7. BWV 36.6 (mm. 1–11)

cantatas. The setting of verse 6 in BWV 36 is most interesting. It is movement 6 of the cantata and is scored for tenor with two oboes d'amore and continuo (example 5.7). Bach chose to set this movement in B minor—the key of humbling and incarnation, in 3/4 time, and marked "Molt' allegro." The two oboes engage in strict contrapuntal and often canonic conversation while each phrase of the chorale is heard in dotted half notes.

The text, dealing with Christ's equality with the Father as he claims his victory on earth, can be related to Bach's use of canon in this movement. Bach often used this technique to symbolize law and order.[42] Although not always a strict canon, BWV 36.6 contains canonic writing. Since it is so marked throughout the movement, it is very likely that Bach intended the strict counterpoint to have symbolic meaning. Albert Clement sees the use of canon in the variations on *Vom Himmel hoch da komm ich her* (BWV 769/769a) as referring to Christ fulfilling the will of the Father.[43] Verses 4–6 of "Nun komm, der Heiden Heiland" deal with the Savior's coming to earth to save mankind by his sacrifice and his subsequent return to the Father, thereby fulfilling the will of the Father.

Further investigation of Bach's use of canon helps to establish his rationale. Helene Werthemann's comments on the "Et in unum Dominum" of the *B-Minor Mass* are insightful. The Father and Christ are shown as being the same, yet different in the canonic writing of this movement. Canon at the unison is an obvious means of portraying something that is the same yet different.[44] Philipp Spitta also pointed out the significance of canon at the unison in this movement of the *B-Minor Mass*:

> Bach treats the parts in canon on the unison at the beginning of the principal subject each time, not using the canon on the fourth below till the second bar; thus both the unity and the separate existence of the two Persons are brought out. The intention is unmistakable, since the musical scheme allows of the canonic imitation on the fourth below from the very beginning.[45]

Spitta assumed that Bach deliberately used canon at the unison to create unity and to depict independence, and his point seems very valid. Luther's commentary on Psalm 110:1 provides a useful insight into the idea of Christ as equal to the Father:

> Setze dich (spricht er) neben mich auff den hohen stuel, da ich sitze, und sey mir gleich. Denn das heisst er neben jm sitzen, nicht zum füssen, sondern zur rechten, das ist, jnn die selbige Maiestet und gewalt, die da heisst eine Gottliche Gewalt.[46]
>
> [Sit next to me on the exalted throne upon which I sit, and be my equal. To sit next to Him—at His right hand, not at His feet—means to possess the very majesty and power that is called divine.[47]]

Thus, it is clear that the idea of Christ's equality with the Father is also to be found in the Bible.[48] That Bach would want to stress it by portraying verse 6 of "Nun komm, der Heiden Heiland" in BWV 36 is, therefore, not surprising.

Another important consideration is the use of triple meter. Szymon Paczkowski has suggested to me that this movement is polanaise-like in its rhythm, while not perhaps being a strict polonaise. The polonaise was a strong and fiercely nationalistic Polish dance characterized by phrases beginning on the downbeat with dactyl rhythms.[49] He has drawn an analogy between this movement and the central section of the alto aria from the *St. John Passion*, "Es ist vollbracht," which he holds might also be a polonaise.[50] There are similarities in the text: "Der Held aus Juda siegt mit Macht" (*St. John Passion*) and "führ hinaus dem Sieg im Fleisch." Christ's victory over death may be reflected in Bach's choice of the triple rhythm.[51]

An important aspect of the text of verse 6 is Christ's victory in the flesh: i.e., his triumph over the cross here on earth. To achieve this he had to come to earth in the incarnation. B minor, the key of incarnation and humbling in the music of Bach, is not a surprising choice. This movement will prove very important in the interpretation of the organ chorale prelude BWV 660.

THE ORGAN SETTINGS OF "NUN KOMM, DER HEIDEN HEILAND"

When one turns to the organ compositions where Bach used "Nun komm, der Heiden Heiland," the detailed study of his settings of this hymn in the cantatas proves very useful. Similar musical ideas and treatments may have the same meaning in the organ works. All five settings of this chorale for organ were completed before Bach left his position at Weimar in 1717.[52] Bach revised the so-called "Leipzig" chorales while he was in Leipzig and began his autograph score in 1739.[53] Thus, the majority of the "Leipzig" chorales were composed before any of the cantatas discussed above. This does not mean, however, that the cantatas cannot be used as a means of interpreting the organ works. They can be regarded in many ways as a clarification of Bach's compositional methods in the earlier organ works.

Nun komm, der Heiden Heiland (BWV 659)

It is perhaps most useful to examine the more extended organ settings first, i.e., the three compositions from the "Leipzig" chorales, BWV 659–61. The first, BWV 659, is one of Bach's most mystical and ornate settings for organ. The chorale is presented in such an ornate fashion in the right hand that the melody all but disappears after the first four notes of each phrase. The influence of Dietrich Buxtehude is clear. When Bach returned from his visit to

Lübeck in 1706, where he heard Buxtehude play, he was severely criticized by the consistory at Arnstadt for his "curious *variationes* in the chorale, and . . . many strange tones in it."[51] Nowhere in Bach's music could Buxtehude's influence be more clear than in BWV 659. Striking musical aspects of the composition include the continuo style bass, many examples of the *figura corta*, persistent use of the "sighing" motive from m. 21, the ornamental Neapolitan chord at mm. 22–23, the many chromatic inflections throughout the piece, and the extended coloratura coda for the final three measures.

Bach's use of the "sighing" motive is particularly striking. As noted above, this kind of writing was frequently employed by Bach in relation to Christ's passion and death. In BWV 56 the carrying of the cross is consistently depicted in the use of this motive in the opening movement, and Bach also employs it in BWV 62.1. The connection between incarnation and atonement is clear here. The elaborate Neapolitan sixth chord at m. 23 of BWV 659 is also significant. The combination of Neapolitan harmonies with the "sighing" motive can also be found in the "Agnus Dei" of the *B-Minor Mass*. In the case of the "Agnus Dei," the reference to the cross of Christ is clear: the Lamb of God takes away the sins of the world by his death on the cross (Jn 1:36).[55] In BWV 659 the very ornate setting of the *cantus firmus* adds to the mystical atmosphere of this chorale prelude. Russell Stinson has suggested that this hiding of the chorale melody depicts the hidden mystery of the incarnation.[56]

What do these musical details tell us about which verse Bach is setting? There seems to be a clear connection to Christ the Savior and the incarnation. It is most likely, therefore, that Bach is setting verse 1 of "Nun komm, der Heiden Heiland." It would, of course, be the most logical place for Bach to start, especially given that he sets the hymn three times in the "Leipzig" chorales. Bach's treatment of the third line of text from verse 1,"des sich wundert alle Welt," is related to all other settings of this verse, in which Bach employs the *circulatio* figure to depict the whole world. Bach's extended coloratura coda, recalling Buxtehude's setting, confirms the mystical atmosphere as the world marvels at the mystery of the birth of Christ.

After consideration of four movements portraying verse 1 of "Nun komm, der Heiden Heiland," it is appropriate at this point to note similarities and differences between the settings. There are some elements common to all compositions: the naturally occurring cross symbol inherent in the chorale melody gives Bach ample scope for references to the cross in all movements. The reiteration of this motive throughout each movement implies a marked emphasis on the Savior. The circular motion for line 3 of the text appears in all four movements. The four settings can clearly be divided into two pairs: the two extrovert opening movements of cantatas BWV 61 and 62 and the more intimate settings of BWV 36.2 and 659. In the latter two settings Bach captures the mystical aspect of Christ's incarnation, while BWV 61 and 62 concentrate more on the processional and triumphant side of Advent prompted by the Gospel account of Christ's entry into Jerusalem on Palm Sunday.

Nun komm, der Heiden Heiland (BWV 660)

The second setting for organ in the "Leipzig" chorales (BWV 660) has puzzled many writers. This chorale prelude is a rather unusual trio with an ornamental cantus firmus played by the right hand and two obbligato bass parts played by the left hand and pedal. The two bass parts form a strict and often canonic counterpoint below the ornate cantus firmus. The coloratura writing is not as elaborate as that of BWV 659, and the chorale melody is discernible throughout. Roswitha Bruggaier has argued that the earlier Weimar version (BWV 660a) may have been originally composed as a piece with viola da gamba obbligato,[57] though it is clear from P271 that Bach clearly thought of it finally as an organ piece. An autograph copy of BWV 660a is to be found at the back of the P271 manuscript. It is possible that Bruggaier is correct, as Bach was constantly arranging and rearranging his own works. However, our interest in BWV 660 is as an organ composition in P271. And even if it were originally a piece for two gambas and cello as Bruggaier argues, the music remains the same and therefore the theological significance also.[58]

The most striking aspect of this piece is the strict contrapuntal writing. It is necessary, therefore, to examine Bach's use of this kind of writing elsewhere. In the case of the hymn "Nun komm, der Heiden Heiland," this leads naturally back to movement 6 of BWV 36, discussed above. In that movement Bach was portraying the equality between Father and Son through the use of canonic writing. This use of strict counterpoint can also be related to Christ fulfilling the will of the Father in coming to earth and providing salvation for humanity through his passion. Thus, Bach may have been setting verse 6 of the chorale in BWV 660. Other musical elements help to confirm this hypothesis. Throughout the course of BWV 660, the opening motive, which is based on the first four notes of the chorale, appears nineteen times. This motive may be linked both melodically and texturally to the "Laß ihn kreuzigen" chorus of the *St. Matthew Passion*. The openings of both pieces are noteworthy for their emphatic use of the cross symbol.[59] It does not seem accidental that the first five notes of the "Laß ihn kreuzigen" chorus (example 5.8) correspond to the opening five notes of "Nun komm, der Heiden Heiland."

Laß　ihn　　kreu_____

Example 5.8. BWV 244/45b (mm. 1–3)

The first version of this setting, *Nun komm, der Heiden Heiland* (BWV 660a) dates from the Weimar period. It might be possible that Bach got the idea for the theme of the "Laß ihn kreuzigen" fugue remembering the opening motive of BWV 660a. Similar crossings can be seen in the bass aria "Komm süßes Kreuz" (No. 57) from the *St. Matthew Passion*. There, two bass parts continually cross, the obbligato viola da gamba and the solo bass presenting a texture not unlike that of BWV 660.

As with the "Laß ihn kreuzigen" chorus, the use of the opening motive in BWV 660 results in many cross symbols and suspensions. The use of the interval of the diminished fourth, which results from sharpening the third note of the chorale, helps to support the Christological connection. That this opening motive appears as many as nineteen times in BWV 660 suggests its importance and significance for Bach.[60] The tortured suspensions, which result from imitation at the unison, as well as the continual crossing of voices, also confirm the Christological connection.[61] As shown above, there were many connections in Bach's Advent music with Christ's passion. Therefore, an Advent piece conceivably could provide a musical indication of this connection, even if the text did not specifically mention it. However, in a case such as BWV 660, where the text seems to be referring directly to Christ's fulfillment of the law, the employment of such techniques is all the more significant.

Another noteworthy musical feature of BWV 660 is the introduction of a chord in the left-hand part at m. 15 and m. 42 (example 5.9). The text may provide a clue for this departure from the trio texture. Examination of movement 4 of the cantata *Christ lag in Todesbanden* (BWV 4) offers some further clues (example 5.10). In this movement, Bach suddenly introduces chords in the violin part, which up to that point had been a single melodic line. It may be significant that the text at this point is "Gewalt." Normally, when Bach does something unusual, there is a textual reason for doing so. In this movement, Christ is depicted as conquering death and taking away the sin of the world, thereby providing salvation for mankind. His "Gewalt" is very important in this context. This word is equally important in the context of verse 6 of "Nun komm, der Heiden Heiland," which is addressed to Christ, who is equal to the Father and in possession of "ewig Gottes Gewalt." Bach may be stressing this issue by the sudden insertion of a chord as in BWV 4.4.[62] It is certainly unprecedented and very unusual in the context of an organ trio like this one.

A final musical element to be considered is the A-flat in the pedal part on beat 4 of m. 27. Bach writes an A-flat where he had previously written an A-natural in accordance with the cantus firmus. It is very likely that this striking alteration is related to the text. It is presented at the start of the interlude that leads to the final line of the verse. Inspection of the final lines of all verses may help to provide an answer. The only possibility appears to be the

Example 5.9. BWV 660 (mm. 14–15) and BWV 660 (m. 42)

final line of verse 6: "in uns das kranck Fleisch enthalt." Bach employs a similar "hard leap" or *saltus duriusculus* for the word "kranken" in the second movement of the cantata *Jesu, der du meine Seele* (BWV 78). It seems reasonable, therefore, to suggest that in the sudden introduction of A-flat, and in the context of the other possible relationships between text and music, Bach is depicting the word "kranck."

Thus, when one considers the significance of the canonic writing, the two chords of m. 15 and m. 42, the repetition of the opening motive, and the sudden introduction of A-flat in m. 27, one can only conclude that Bach was depicting verse 6 of the hymn text in BWV 660. The strongest clues are, of course, given by studying movement 6 of BWV 36. BWV 660a predates BWV 36 by several years, but it is still possible to glean information regarding Bach's compositional process and apply this knowledge to the earlier piece. In addition, the other musical elements cited above offer equally compelling reasons as to why Bach may have been thinking of verse 6 when he wrote BWV 660.

Example 5.10. BWV 4.4 (mm. 23–25)

Nun komm, der Heiden Heiland (BWV 661)

The final setting of this hymn in the "Leipzig" chorales (BWV 661) is a great chorale fantasia in *organo pleno* with the cantus firmus in the pedal. Since Bach presents three settings of "Nun komm, der Heiden Heiland" in succession in this collection, it is possible that he considered them as a mini-cycle within the larger context of the "Leipzig" chorales. I have suggested that the texts of verses 1 and 6 are relevant to BWV 659 and 660 respectively. It would seem logical that Bach was progressing through the text of the hymn and that in BWV 661 he might consider the text of verses 7 or 8. Important aspects of BWV 661 are the *organo pleno* indication, the penetrating cantus firmus, the fugal treatment, the prominence of inversion, and the change from 4/4 in BWV 661a to 2/2 in BWV 661.

I have suggested elsewhere that the image of light was an important aspect in the portrayal of text in the opening chorale prelude of the "Leipzig" chorales, *Komm heiliger Geist, Herre Gott* (BWV 651).[63] Light is mentioned in verses 1 and 2 of Luther's "Komm heiliger Geist, Herre Gott." As such, the *plenum* setting seemed appropriate within the context of BWV 651. In his sermon for the First Sunday of Advent, Luther states that faith is light.[64] Bach's use of the *plenum* setting may have similar meaning here. There is only one verse of "Nun komm, der Heiden Heiland" where faith and light are mentioned: verse 7. The link between faith, light, and the *plenum* registration suggests a link with the text of verse 7.

In BWV 661 Bach replaces the more modern time signature of 4/4 with the slower-moving 2/2 of the *prima prattica*. Bach frequently changed between 4/4 and 2/2 in differing versions of his autograph scores. There are three instances in the "Leipzig" chorales where he changed the time signature from the earlier Weimar to the Leipzig setting. In BWV 660 the time signature is common time, changed from the earlier indication of cut common time.[65] The change in BWV 661 may be related merely to performance practice and tempo, 2/2 considered as a more fitting meter for the final setting of this minicycle. By changing the time signature from 4/4 to 2/2, there is a change in the number of accents. In 4/4 time there are two strong accents per bar, on beats 1 and 3, whereas in 2/2 time there is only one accent on the first beat. If it is indeed the text of verse 7, then do the words fit in the right place? If one applies the text of the chorale to the bass line of BWV 661a, it would seem that the accents are not quite right. The text runs as follows (with accented syllables in italic):

Dein *Krip*pen glänzt hell *und* klar
Die Nacht gibt ein *neu* Licht dar
*Tunc*kel muß nicht *komm*en drein
Der Glaub bleibt *im*mer im *Schein*.

If one applies the text of verse 7 to the bass line of BWV 661, the accents appear more logical.

*Dein Krip*pen *glänzt* hell *und klar*
Die Nacht *gibt* ein *neu* Licht dar
*Tunc*kel *muß* nicht *komm*en *drein*
Der Glaub bleibt *im*mer *im Schein*.

One can apply this test to verse 8 of "Nun komm, der Heiden Heiland" as well, since Bach could have been depicting either verse 7 or verse 8 in BWV 661. But the text of line 1 of verse 8 applied with the appropriate accents result in:

Lob sey GOtt dem Vat*er thon*

This is not logical—neither "Gott" nor "Vater" receive a strong accent. Equally, if one looks to the other verses of the hymn, there are reasons why they are not depicted here by Bach. The text of the opening verse fits very well to the pedal notes. However, in the case of BWV 661, it is not logical that Bach would return to Verse 1, having set verses 1 and 6 in the two previous settings.

As with the motivic writing of BWV 660, Bach also uses the cross symbol in BWV 661. The emphatic reference in all three settings to these first four notes of the chorale, and their association with the idea of the cross, directly links the crib, passion, and consequently salvation. The Epistle of the day (Rom 13:11–14) opens with a reference to salvation:

> Und weil wir solches wissen, nämlich die Zeit, daß die Stunde da ist, aufzustehen vom Schlaf sintemal unser Heil jetzt näher ist, denn da wir gläubig wurden.
> [And this, knowing the season, that already it is time for you to awake out of sleep: for now is salvation nearer to us than when we first believed.]

The link between light and salvation can be seen in John 8:12.

> Ich bin das Licht der Welt; wer mir nachfolgt, der wird nicht wandeln in der Finsternis, sondern wird das Licht des Lebens haben.
> [I am the Light of the World; anyone who follows me will not be walking in the dark; he will have the light of life.]

Once more, the connection between incarnation and atonement is expressed through Bach's use of the cross symbol in the opening motive of BWV 661, although it is not used in the tortured manner of BWV 660.

The first appearance of the fugal theme in its inversion occurs almost exactly half-way through BWV 661 following the second line of the chorale at m. 45. The text here is: "Die Nacht gibt ein neu Licht dar." The contrast between light and dark, and good and evil is a common biblical theme. It may be possible that Bach was using the contrast of inversion to illustrate this theme. The inversion continues for the statement of the following line of text: "dunkel muß nicht kommen drein." Over the final line of the chorale, the fugal theme is heard in its *rectus* and *inversus* forms. They are very forcefully combined in mm. 86–88. Here the words are "Der Glaub bleibt immer im Schein." The implication is that faith and light are synonymous as opposed to the contrast of dark and evil. The element of contrast or opposites in BWV 661 may relate to Bach's interpretation of the text.[66] The contrast of light and dark was also present in the Epistle for the First Sunday of Advent. Faith is the cornerstone of the Lutheran church, and it is unlikely that Bach would have ignored a reference to it. Faith and light are portrayed in the splendor of the *organo pleno* setting. The dominant feature of BWV 661 is the power of the *plenum* where clarity and brightness are of paramount importance. Therefore, the text of verse 7 appears to be relevant here, as it confirms the musical characteristics of the piece.

If verse 7 is indeed the verse that Bach is portraying here, then he is setting a verse containing truths that were very dear to Luther. It may have seemed more logical to Bach to give this setting the 2/2 time signature, thus adding to the *gravitas* of the musical setting. I have suggested that the technique of inversion represents opposites in BWV 661. Christ came as a human child, but also as Savior of the world. The divine and human, good and bad, light and dark are represented in BWV 661 through the consistent use of inversion techniques.

"Nun komm, der Heiden Heiland" is one of two hymns set three times by Bach in the "Leipzig" chorales, the other being Nicolaus Decius's "Allein Gott in der Höh sei Ehr." The use of "Nun komm, der Heiden Heiland" in three Advent cantatas (BWV 36, 61, and 62) confirms this significance, as well as the two additional organ settings, BWV 599 and BWV 699. The First Sunday of Advent was not only important as the opening of the church year, it was also the last time that concerted music was heard in Leipzig before Christmas. Further, the Sundays leading up to the First Sunday of Advent concentrated increasingly on eschatology, and this new beginning on the First Sunday of Advent also has important eschatological implications, which accounts for the prominence of the three "Nun komm" settings in the "Leipzig" chorales. Advent heralds the coming of Christ. Christ is also met in death; thus, the meeting of Christ with humanity can also be understood in a purely eschatological way.

Nun komm, der Heiden Heiland (BWV 599)

The final part of this chapter concerns itself with Bach's two shorter settings of this chorale tune: BWV 599 from the *Orgelbüchlein* and BWV 699 from the individually transmitted chorales. BWV 599 is the first setting of Bach's *Orgelbüchlein*, in keeping with many of the hymnbooks of the time that opened with this hymn. This is a short setting of a mere ten bars, and, as with many of the *Orgelbüchlein* settings, the cantus firmus appears uninterrupted and almost unadorned in the top part (example 5.11). The free treatment of the five-part texture is almost unprecedented in the *Orgelbüchlein*.[67] Other striking features of the setting are the dotted rhythms of the pedal part, the sense of descent in the part writing, and the *suspirans* character of the accompanying parts.[68] When Bach embellishes the second note of lines 1 and 4 of the chorale melody, he adds yet another cross symbol to the one inherent in the chorale melody.

Example 5.11. BWV 599 (mm. 1–3)

There are many links to the various theological concepts relating to Advent discussed above. The cross symbol naturally links incarnation and atonement. This symbol also appears in the inner parts and sometimes between parts. The majestic dotted rhythm can be related to Christ as King and his triumphant entry into Jerusalem as told in the Gospel of the day.[69] The sense of descent created in the entry of the motivic writing from soprano to bass can refer to the incarnation. One may look no further than the "Et incarnatus est" of the *B-Minor Mass*, written many years later, to see how Bach uses *catabasis* as a means of portraying the incarnation.[70] The use of the *figura suspirans* in all but one measure of this composition is striking. This breathy figure helps to maintain an air of suspense or expectancy (this is similar to the same breathless portrayal of the text "Nun komm, der Heiden Heiland" in BWV 36.2). Bearing all this in mind, can one arrive at conclusions regarding text and music in BWV 599? Bach is laying emphasis on the incarnation and Christ as Savior. This logically leads one to verse 1 of the hymn text. It is the only verse that is so specific regarding Christ's role as Savior. This setting cannot be regarded as a line-by-line portrayal of the text, but more a general depiction of the aspects of Advent summed up in the opening verse—majesty, incarnation, descent to earth, and the world marveling at the miracle of the birth of Christ.

Nun komm, der Heiden Heiland (BWV 699)

The final setting to be discussed was probably Bach's first setting of Luther's hymn: BWV 699. This is a simple fughetta based on the opening line of the chorale. Peter Williams points out that comparison with BWV 659 shows how the countersubject in m. 4 may be derived from the chorale melody[71] (example 5.12). This means that absolutely every measure of this short sixteen-bar setting has a reference to the chorale. Bach uses the modal form of the chorale melody as a fugue subject while the countersubject has the sharpened leading note.

Williams has described this setting as possessing a "mystifyingly sad-winsome quality."[72] This atmosphere is maintained by the many suspensions and enhanced by the insertion of a passing A-flat in the pedal at beat 4 of

Example 5.12. BWV 699 (mm. 1–5)

m. 11, creating a Phrygian cadence. Due to the very simple motivic development, one cannot say that Bach is making any grand gestures with regard to text-music relationships. However, the marked repetition of the opening line of the chorale and its associated countersubject leads one to believe that Bach was portraying verse 1 here, and particularly the text "Nun komm, der Heiden Heiland," which sums up much of the soteriological message of Advent.

CONCLUSION

Thus, it is clear that although Bach set verses from Luther's "Nun komm, der Heiden Heiland" nine times, many of the same Advent themes run through all the settings. Subtle nuances and theological allusions point to various verses of the chorale text, and the cantatas remain a starting point for the interpretation of the organ works. No one isolated musical element alone can point to a particular verse, but the consistent combinations of musical aspects such as those seen above help to confirm and consolidate the theological context and meaning.

NOTES

1. Philipp Wackernagel, *Das deutsche Kirchenlied von der ältesten Zeit bis zu Anfang des XVII. Jahrhunderts*, 5 vols. (1864–1877, repr. Hildesheim: Olms, 1964), 1:16; Johannes Kulp, *Die Lieder unserer Kirche*, Handbuch zum Evangelischen Kirchengesangbuch, Sonderband, ed. Arno Büchner and Siegfried Fornaçon (Göttingen: Vandenhoeck und Ruprecht, 1958), 7.

2. Martin Luther, *D. Martin Luthers Werke: Kritische Gesamtausgabe* [Weimarer Ausgabe] (Weimar: H. Böhlau, 1883–   ), 35:149 [subsequently cited as *WA*]; Kulp, 9.

3. Kulp, 8.

4. Ibid., 10.

5. Markus Jenny, *Luthers geistliche Lieder und Kirchengesänge: Vollständige Neuedition in Ergänzung zu Band 35 der Weimarer Ausgabe*, Archiv zur Weimarer Ausgabe der Werke Martin Luthers, 4 (Cologne: Böhlau, 1985), 72–73.

6. *WA* 35:150; Martin Luther, *Liturgy and Hymns*, ed. Ulrich S. Leupold, Luther's Works, 53 (Philadelphia: Fortress Press, 1965), 235–36; and Jenny, 72.

7. Jenny, 72–73.

8. *Schuldiges Lob Gottes oder Geistreiches Gesangbuch* (Weimar: Mumbach, 1713), 2.

9. Translation based on Mark Bighley, *The Lutheran Chorales in the Organ Works of J. S. Bach* (St. Louis: Concordia Publishing House, 1986), 185 ff.

10. Detlef Gojowy, "Kirchenlieder im Umkreis von J. S. Bach," *Jahrbuch für Liturgik und Hymnologie* 22 (1978): 90–92 lists "Nun komm, der Heiden Heiland" for the First, Third, and Fourth Sundays of Advent; the 1693 Leipzig hymnal of Gottfried Vopelius lists it as a hymn for all four Sundays of Advent. See also Günther Stiller, *Johann Sebastian Bach und das Leipziger gottesdienstliche Leben seiner Zeit* (Kassel: Bärenreiter, 1970), 220; Günther Stiller, *Johann Sebastian Bach and Liturgical Life in Leipzig*, ed. Robin A. Leaver (St. Louis: Concordia Publishing House, 1984), 233.

11. For further discussion of the opening of this hymn text see Robin A. Leaver, "Eschatology, Theology and Music: Death and Beyond in Bach's Vocal Music," in *Bach Studies from Dublin*, Irish Musical Studies, 8, ed. Anne Leahy and Yo Tomita (Dublin: Four Courts Press, 2004), 138.

12. Bach himself wrote the order of service for the first Sunday of Advent at Leipzig inside the covers of the scores of his two Advent cantatas BWV 61 and 62; see *Bach-Dokumente*, vol. I, ed. Werner Neumann and Hans-Joachim Schulze (Kassel: Bärenreiter, 1964), no. 178, p. 248 and no. 181, p. 251.

13. Martin Petzoldt, "Zur Frage der Textvorlagen von BWV 62, 'Nun komm der Heiden Heiland,'" *Musik und Kirche* 60 (1990): 303.

14. Kulp, 11.

15. Petzoldt, 308. He cites the following biblical sources: Ps 80:2–3, Is 7:14, Ez 44:2, Ps 19, Ps 45, Mt 20:28, Lk 2:18, Jn 1:13–4, Mt 1:25, Jn 16:28, 2 Cor 12:9, Lk 2:8–12, and 2 Cor 4:6.

16. All German biblical citations from *Die Bibel oder die ganze heilige Schrift des alten und neuen Testaments nach der deutschen Übersetzung Martin Luthers mit erklärenden Anmerkungen* (Stuttgart: Deutsche Bibel Gesellschaft, 1912).

17. All English biblical citations from the King James translation of the Bible.

18. *WA* 10[1b]:10.

19. *The Sermons of Martin Luther: The Church Postils*, ed. John Nicholas Lenker (Grand Rapids, Mich.: Baker Books, 1983), 6:17 (subsequently cited as *Church Postils*).

20. Robin A. Leaver, "Bach's Understanding and Use of the Epistles and Gospels of the Church Year," *Bach: The Quarterly Journal of the Riemenschneider Bach Institute* 6 (October 1975): 8; Albert Clement, "De orgelkoraalbewerkingen van J.S. Bach in het kerkelijk jaar," *Het Orgel* 86 (1990): 323.

21. *WA* 10[1b]:12.

22. *Church Postils*, 6:19.

23. This notion of light representing good and darkness evil is, of course, a well-established biblical theme. Light is also associated with the prophecy of the birth of

Christ, as seen in Isaiah 9:1: "The people that walked in darkness have seen a great light; they that dwell in the land of the shadow of death, upon them hath the light shined." Luke 1:79 is also concerned with the Savior: "to give light to them that sit in darkness and in the shadow of death, to guide our feet into the way of peace."

24. Clark Kelly, "Johann Sebastian Bach's 'Eighteen' Chorales BWV 651–668: Perspectives on Editions and Hymnology" (DMA diss., University of Rochester, Eastman School of Music, 1988), 171.

25. Gojowy, 86–89, 90–92.

26. Stiller (1970), 220; Stiller (1984), 233.

27. See Robin A. Leaver, "Bach and Hymnody: The Evidence of the Orgelbüchlein," *Early Music* 13 (May 1985): 235.

28. Bach also employed this form with chorale in the cantata *O Ewigkeit, du Donnerwort* (BWV 20), composed for the First Sunday after Trinity and first performed on 11 June 1724. In this case the French overture was a metaphor for the beginning of Bach's second *Jahrgang*, as BWV 20 was the first cantata of this series.

29. Hans-Joachim Schulze and Christoph Wolff, *Bach Compendium* (Leipzig: Peters, 1985), 1:53 (subsequently cited as *BC*).

30. Ibid., 231. I am grateful to Szymon Paczkowski for reminding me of this connection.

31. As Robin A. Leaver has pointed out, this is why the first chorale we hear in the *Christmas Oratorio* is a verse of Paul Gerhardt's "Wie soll ich dich empfangen," sung to the melody of the so-called passion chorale "Herzlich tut mich verlangen." Therefore, by means of a melody so inextricably linked with the passion, Bach is making a subtle theological point by linking incarnation and atonement in the *Christmas Oratorio*. See Robin A. Leaver, "The Mature Vocal Works and Their Theological and Liturgical Context," in *The Cambridge Companion to Bach*, ed. John Butt (Cambridge: Cambridge University Press, 1997), 98.

32. It is interesting to note another possible allusion to the Sanctus text in movement 1 of Bach's latest Advent cantata, BWV 36 ("der Herr der Herrlichkeit" [the Lord of Glory]; see Melvin P. Unger, *Handbook to Bach's Sacred Cantata Texts: An Interlinear Translation with Reference Guide to Biblical Quotations and Allusions* [Lanham, Md.: Scarecrow Press, 1996], 129). The prominence of triplets in this movement is reminiscent of Bach's use of triplets in the Sanctus of the *B-Minor Mass*, where it is certainly connected with the symbolism of the number 6.

33. The use of *catabasis* to portray incarnation can been seen very clearly in Bach's much later setting of the "Et incarnatus est" of the *B-Minor Mass*. I have commented elsewhere ("Text-Music Relationships in the 'Leipzig' Chorales of Johann Sebastian Bach," [PhD diss., Utrecht University, 2002], 78) on the progression of the cantus firmus from soprano to bass in the chorale prelude *O Lamm Gottes unschuldig* (BWV 656) and how this may depict the journey of the Lamb of God from heaven to earth. The treatment of the cantus firmus in BWV 61.1 is analogous.

34. This is a frequent technique employed by Bach. See, for example, his setting of the word "alle" in the motet *Lobet den Herrn, alle Heiden* (BWV 230) both at the phrase "alle Heiden" and "und preiset ihn, alle Völker." Each time he sets verse 1 of "Nun komm, der Heiden Heiland" in either a cantata movement or a chorale prelude,

he employs circular movement to depict all the world. This kind of circular motion depicting the rejoicing world is also a common feature of settings of "Nun komm, der Heiden Heiland" by other seventeenth-century composers such as Michael Praetorius and Samuel Scheidt. It is also interesting to examine Heinrich Schütz's setting of "Nun komm, der Heiden Heiland" (SWV 301) from Part I of *Kleine geistliche Konzerte*. When Schütz gets to line 3 of the text, he also breaks out into circular motion and melismatic writing. It is possible that Bach knew this setting; if not, he would at least have been familiar with the kind of writing that Schütz and his contemporaries had learned from such Italian composers as Giovanni Gabrieli and Claudio Monteverdi. We know that there were copies of thirty works by Schütz in the choral library at St Michael's in Lüneberg where Bach spent some time from 1700 to 1702. See Christoph Wolff, *Johann Sebastian Bach: The Learned Musician* (New York: W.W. Norton, 2000), 58. At the time of writing, scholars at the Bach-Archiv, Leipzig are compiling a complete catalogue of the music in the library of the Thomasschule. This catalogue will offer invaluable information regarding the music that Bach used on a daily basis.

35. This kind of strong triadic writing is frequently associated by Bach with God's power, e.g., the opening movement of *Gelobet sei der Herr, mein Gott* (BWV 129), whose entire movement is an outpouring of joy in praise of God the Father, who is extolled by means of trumpet fanfares and emphatic triadic writing.

36. Leaver, "Eschatology and Beyond," 138. I have also discussed the role of the Trinity with regard to salvation in my PhD dissertation (163 f.).

37. This is also true of the third section of BWV 659 (m. 21 onward).

38. One might argue that this is just a repetition of a "Hauptthema," but it is more usual in Bach's chorale fantasia-type works for him to anticipate each line of the chorale rather than reiterate one line consistently. If Bach does reiterate an opening line, it is usually to make a theological point, as in his many settings of "Nun komm." He employs a similar procedure in the opening line of the *Estomihi* cantata *Herr Jesu Christ, wahr' Mensch und Gott* (BWV 127), where the first line of the chorale is reiterated in diminution throughout the movement to emphasize Christ as true man and God.

39. For the precise history see *BC* 1:55 f.; and Nicholas Anderson, "Schwingt freudig euch empor," in *J. S. Bach*, ed. Malcolm Boyd, Oxford Composer Companions (Oxford: Oxford University Press, 1999), 444–45.

40. Bach frequently used chromaticism to portray Christ's sacrifice, a most striking example being the chorale prelude for organ *Jesus Christus unser Heiland* (BWV 665) in the line "durch das bitter Leiden sein" (mm. 27–38).

41. For a discussion of number symbolism in the Credo of the *B-Minor Mass*, see Robin A. Leaver, "Number Associations in the Structure of Bach's *Credo, BWV 232*," *Bach: The Quarterly Journal of the Riemenschneider Bach Institute* 7 (July 1976): 17–24.

42. *Dies sind die heil'gen zehn Gebot* (BWV 678) and *Vater unser im Himmelreich* (BWV 682) are both canonic pieces where the canon could refer to the law or will of God. In the latter case, Christ is fulfilling the will of the Father. See Albert Clement, *Der dritte Teil der Clavierübung von Johann Sebastian Bach: Musik - Text -*

Theologie (Middelburg: AlmaRes, 1999), 194, where he has shown this to be relevant to verse 4 of this hymn.

43. Albert Clement, "'O Jesu, du edle Gabe.' Studien zum Verhältnis von Text und Musik in den Choralpartiten und den Kanonischen Veränderungen von Johann Sebastian Bach" (PhD diss., Utrecht University, 1989), 179 and 185. He cites *O Lamm Gottes unschuldig* (BWV 618) and *Christe, du Lamm Gottes* (BWV 619) as examples of canonic treatment reflecting Christ fulfilling the will of the Father. On page 63 he also points out that early Dutch composers used canon as a means of reflecting the text when it was required. Bach would have been acquainted with this idea. David Yearsley has shown how German composers of the seventeenth and eighteenth centuries used canon in the context of approaching death: David Yearsley, *Bach and the Meanings of Counterpoint* (Cambridge: Cambridge University Press, 2002), 1–41.

44. Helene Werthemann, "Johann Sebastian Bachs Orgelchoral 'Nun komm, der Heiden Heiland,' a due bassi e canto fermo," *Musik und Gottesdienst* 13 (Nov./Dec. 1959): 165.

45. Philipp Spitta, *Johann Sebastian Bach*, trans. Clara Bell and J. A. Fuller-Maitland, (1889, repr. New York: Dover, 1992), 3:51.

46. *WA* 41:83. I am very grateful to Mary Greer for pointing out this connection to me.

47. Martin Luther, *Selected Psalms II*, ed. Jaroslav Pelikan, Luther's Works, 13 (St. Louis: Concordia Publishing House, 1956), 233.

48. See also Philippians 2:6; "His state was divine, yet he did not cling to his equality with God." In his Bible commentary Luther deals with this passage in detail: "Göttliche Gestalt und Gewalt (Gott gleich sein) hatte Christus bei dem Vater von Ewigkeit her . . . im Gehorsam gegen seines Vaters Gegenwillen und aus liebe zu uns erniedrigte er sich selbst sogar bis zum Verbrechertod am Kreuz" (*Luther Bibel*, New Testament, 320). [Divine form and power (as one with God) was possessed by Christ with the Father since eternity . . . in fulfilling his Father's wishes and out of love for us he humbled himself to a criminal's death on the cross.] Luther is clearly also stressing Christ's equality with the Father, while also pointing to his independence as a human being.

49. For more on the polonaise see Meredith Little and Natalie Jenne, *Dance and the Music of J. S. Bach*, expanded ed. (Bloomington: Indiana University Press, 2001), 194 ff.

50. This is the subject of ongoing research by Paczkowski.

51. See Szymon Paczkowski, "Über die Funktionen der Polonaise und des polnischen Stils am Beispiel der Arie 'Glück und Segen sind bereit' aus der Kantate 'Erwünschtes Freudenlicht' BWV 148 von Johann Sebastian Bach," in *Johann Adolf Hasse in seiner Epoche und in der Gegenwart: Studien zur Stil- und Quellenproblematik*, ed. Szymon Paczkowski and Alina Zórawska-Witkowska (Warsaw: Instytut Muzykologii Uniwersytetu Warszawskiego 2002), 209–11. He explains how the polonaise, as a king's dance, opened every court ball in the time of August II and August III, and consequently the dance became associated with kingship. Paczkowski's research has shown how the dance then became associated in the music of Bach with the King of Heaven (e.g., the "Et resurrexit" of the *B-Minor Mass*) [Paper read at the

10th Biennial International Conference on Baroque Music, University of La Rioja, Logrono, Spain, July 2002]. Paczkowski also cites Johann Mattheson regarding the setting of a chorale melody in a polonaise style (Ibid., 210 f.).

52. Russell Stinson has suggested that BWV 660a may have been composed as late as 1717, given the clear Vivaldian influence on the ritornello structure; see Russell Stinson, "New Perspectives on Bach's Great Eighteen Chorales," *Historical Musicology: Sources, Methods, Interpretation*, ed. Stephen A. Crist and Roberta Montemorra Marvin (Rochester: University of Rochester Press, 2004), 43. See also Stinson, *J. S. Bach's Great Eighteen Chorales* (New York: Oxford University Press, 2001), 11, 24 f., 19 for dating of BWV 659–61. Peter Williams places these settings in the same period; see *The Organ Music of J. S. Bach*, 2d ed. (Cambridge: Cambridge University Press, 2003), 363 ff.

53. Hans Klotz maintained that the "Siebzehn Chorälen" belonged to Bach's last decade and perhaps were entered into P271 as late as 1749; see Klotz, *Die Orgelchoräle aus der Leipziger Originalhandschrift: Kritischer Bericht*, Johann Sebastian Bach, Neue Ausgabe sämtlicher Werke, series 4, vol. 2 (Kassel: Bärenreiter, 1957), 13. In the 1950s, in his important work on Bach chronology, Georg van Dadelsen had dated the works in this manuscript to the period 1744–1748. More recently, Yoshitake Kobayashi gained access to further documents that were unavailable to Dadelsen and has shown that the first thirteen entries date from 1739–1742, and the fourteenth and fifteenth from 1746–1747 (Stinson, 2001, 30; Kobayashi, "Zur Chronologie der Spätwerke Johann Sebastian Bachs: Kompositions- und Aufführungstätigkeit von 1736 bis 1750," *Bach-Jahrbuch* 74 [1988]: 45, 56–57; Kobayashi: *Die Notenschrift Johann Sebastian Bachs: Dokumentation ihrer Entwicklung*, Johann Sebastian Bach, Neue Ausgabe sämtlicher Werke, series 9, vol. 2 [Kassel: Bärenreiter, 1989], 207).

54. See *The New Bach Reader*, ed. Hans T. David and Arthur Mendel, rev. Christoph Wolff (New York: W. W. Norton, 1998), no. 20, pp. 46–47 (subsequently cited as *NBR*); and *Bach-Dokumente*, vol. II, ed. Werner Neumann and Hans-Joachim Schulze (Kassel: Bärenreiter, 1969), no. 16, pp. 19–21.

55. Another example is the chorale prelude *O Lamm Gottes unschuldig* (BWV 618), where the text is also clearly related to Christ's cross and passion.

56. Stinson, *J. S. Bach's Great Eighteen Chorales*, 87.

57. Roswitha Bruggaier, "Das Urbild von Johann Sebastian Bachs Choralbearbeitung 'Nun komm der Heiden Heiland' (BWV 660)—eine Komposition mit Viola da Gamba?" *Bach-Jahrbuch* 73 (1987): 165–68. Albert Schweitzer suggested that BWV 660 might be an arrangement of the Schübler variety; see Albert Schweitzer, *J. S. Bach*, trans. Ernest Newman (New York: Dover, 1966), 1:292. Wilhelm Rust also suggests this under the title of this trio in the preface to the Bach-Gesellschaft edition, vol. 25, pt. 2, p. xxiii. Rust arpeggiated the chords in m. 15 and m. 42, since he suspected that this voice was originally an obbligato cello part. We know that Bach rearranged much music for organ (concertos and the Schübler Chorales). A more analogous example might be the sinfonia that opens Part 2 of the cantata *Die Himmel erzählen die Ehre Gottes* (BWV 76). This movement is scored for oboe d'amore, viola da gamba, and continuo and was rearranged by Bach a few years later to become the opening movement of the Trio Sonata in E Minor (BWV 528). This shows Bach transferring a similar texture to the organ, although this time there is no chorale involved.

58. Although much work has been done regarding the theological significance of the sacred and chorale-based music of Bach, there has been little attention given to the possible theological significance of the so-called free instrumental works. See Anne Leahy, "Bach's Prelude, Fugue and Allegro for Lute (BWV 998): A Trinitarian Statement of Faith?" *Journal of the Society for Musicology in Ireland* 1(2005): 33–51.

59. One is reminded of the opening of Felice Anerio's (ca. 1560–1614) four-part motet "Christus factus est" where similar dissonances occur. The opening four notes of the soprano part in the motet correspond to that of "Nun komm, der Heiden Heiland." Anerio sets the alto part with a semitone dissonance against the soprano. Here Anerio has shaped his soprano line in the sign of the cross at the word "Christus." There is no evidence that Bach had a copy of Anerio's "Christus factus est" in his collection. Even though it seems that Bach did not own a copy of this motet, it is interesting to note that this kind of writing was not uncommon in the Renaissance. (Anerio is not one of the composers mentioned by Kirsten Beißwenger in her book on Bach's collection of Latin church music: *Johann Sebastian Bachs Notenbibliothek*, Catalogus Musicus, 13 [Kassel: Bärenreiter, 1992].)

60. This figure appears at m. 1 (twice), m. 9, m.10 (twice), m.15 (twice), m.18, m. 20 (twice), m. 21, m. 22, m. 26, m. 27, m. 33, m. 34, m. 35, and m. 36 (twice).

61. Similar crossings in the same tortured manner can be related to Christ and his passion in the opening chorus of the *St. John Passion*.

62. This is not the same as the additional voices added at the end of BWV 651, 652, 655, and 664, where it seems to be more associated with exuberant joy.

63. Leahy, PhD diss., 8.

64. *WA* 10[1b]:11; *Church Postils*, 6:17.

65. In *Herr Jesu Christ, dich zu uns wend* (BWV 655) and in *Allein Gott in der Höh sei Ehr* (BWV 664) Bach changed from 2/2 in the Weimar version of both settings to 4/4 in the Leipzig settings.

66. See *NBR*, pp. 19–20 f. The editors discuss Bach's use of inversion in the puzzle canon of 1747: "The canon is an occasional and unpretentious composition, without text, but it reveals to us how strongly Bach felt the change of *Affect* accomplished solely by inversion, trusting the mere indication of a similar contrast in words to tell any able musician the puzzle's solution" (p. 20). The reference is to the puzzle canon but the implication is that Bach's use of inversion would automatically have been understood as having a relationship to the text.

67. Russell Stinson also comments on this aspect of the compositional style: *The Orgelbüchlein* (Oxford: Oxford University Press, 1999), 101.

68. See also Williams, *The Organ Music of J. S. Bach*, 2d ed., 239 f.

69. This is not to say that this is in the French overture style as BWV 61 where the overture is a clear portrayal of the start of the church year and Christ's entry into Jerusalem. However, the majestic rhythm can still be easily related to Christ as King (See also Williams, 239).

70. Williams also makes this point; see *The Organ Music of J. S. Bach*, 2d ed., 240.

71. Ibid., 438.

72. Ibid.

6

Historically Informed Rendering of the Librettos from Bach's Church Cantatas

Michael Marissen

Neither traditional Bach scholarship nor historically informed performance have generally given enough attention to an essential problem: what do the German texts Bach set in his church cantatas actually mean? When preparing English translations, of course, this question cannot be ignored, and historical work in religion, Bible, and language can provide sound answers. I will propose new findings in five categories: 1) where the text seems straightforward but has a different meaning when viewed biblically, 2) where the text assumes specific biblical knowledge on the part of the listener to complete its thought, 3) where the text assumes specific knowledge of Lutheran theology, 4) where the text contains archaic language, and 5) where the text may on the face of it seem well nigh unto impossible to understand.

MEANINGS MADE CLEAR BY BIBLICAL REFERENCES

For a first example, consider the following italicized passage in the bass recitative from Bach's Cantata 122, *Das neugeborne Kindelein*:

Dies ist ein Tag, den selbst der Herr gemacht,
Der seinen Sohn in diese Welt gebracht.
O selge Zeit, die nun erfüllt!
O gläubigs Warten, das nunmehr gestillt!
O Glaube, der sein Ende sieht!
O Liebe, die Gott zu sich zieht!
O Freudigkeit, so durch die Trübsal dringt
Und Gott der Lippen Opfer bringt!

TERRY[1] (1926)
O love, enter in God's light!

UNGER[5] (1996)
O love, which God to itself draws!

DRINKER[2] (1942)
Oh staunchness, to God and His will!

HERREWEGHE cd[6] (1996)
O love, that God has accepted!

HARNONCOURT cd[3] (1982)
Oh staunchness, to God and His will!

STOKES[7] (1999)
O Love, that draws God to itself!

AMBROSE[4] (1984)
O love here, which doth draw God nigh!

KOOPMAN cd[8] (2003)
O love here, which doth draw God
nigh!

For Cantata 122 all our translators agree that the bass recitative speaks of love that draws God to itself. On solely grammatical grounds, however, the thought could just as easily be that the "drawing" is being performed by "God," not by "love." From a Lutheran theological perspective—where God initiates, people respond—this is more likely to be the intended reading, as the biblical passage it presumably alludes to, Jeremiah 31:3, says in the Luther Bibles of Bach's day[9]:

> Der HErr ist mir erschienen von fernen: Ich [*Gott*] habe dich je und je *geliebet,* darum hab ich dich *zu mir gezogen* aus lauter Güte.
>
> ("The LORD has appeared to me from afar: 'I [i.e., *God*] have *loved* you for-ever and ever; therefore have I *drawn* you *to me* out of pure kindness.'")

Thus, the Cantata 122 passage should probably best be rendered, "O love which God draws to himself."

As a second, more involved example consider the alto aria from Cantata 12, *Weinen, Klagen, Sorgen, Zagen*:

> *Kreuz und Krone sind verbunden,*
> *Kampf und Kleinod sind vereint.*
> Christen haben alle Stunden
> Ihre Qual und ihren Feind,
> Doch ihr Trost sind Christi Wunden.

TERRY (1926)
Cross and crown are one together,
Only striving victory gives.

SUZUKI cd[12] (1996)
Cross and crown are linked to
gether,
Struggle and jewel are united.

DRINKER (1942)
Cross and Crown are bound together,
Palm and war together go.
(*or,* Palm and battle gether go.)

UNGER (1996)
Cross and crown are tied together,
Battle and treasure are united.

LEONHARDT cd[10] (1971)
Cross and crown are joined together,
Struggle and gem are united.

STOKES (1999)
Cross and crown are bound
together,
Conflict and jewel are united.

AMBROSE (1984)
Cross and crown are joined together,
Gem and conflict are made one.

JUNGHÄNEL cd[13] (2000)
Cross and crown are joined
together,
Struggle and gem are united.

KOOPMAN cd[11] (1995)
Cross and crown are joined together,
Struggle and gem are united.

RIFKIN cd[14] (2001)
Cross and crown are bound
together,
Struggle and the jewel are one.

Each translation makes good Lutheran sense of the first line, but what does it mean to say that "conflict and jewel are united"? That one can win valuable booty in war? To get a better sense of the meaning of the second line we can turn to Luther's rendering of 1 Corinthians 9:24–25's[15]:

> Wisset ihr nicht, daß die, so in den Schranken laufen, die laufen alle, aber Einer erlanget das *Kleinod*? Laufet nun also, daß ihr es ergreifet. Ein jeglicher aber, der da *kämpfet*, enthält sich alles Dinges: jene also, daß sie eine vergängliche *Krone* empfangen; Wir aber eine unvergängliche.
>
> ("Do you not know that they who run in the course, run all; but one gets the *[prize] medal*? Now then, run, that you may obtain it. But each man who *competes*, abstains from all things: those men [will exercise this self-control], then, that they may receive a perishable *crown* [i.e., a victory wreath]; but we [abstain so that we may receive] an imperishable one.")

In light of this passage, then, the *Kleinod* of Cantata 12 would be not a jewel or gem but the bronze, silver, or gold medal a winner receives in a sports contest. (In other contexts, however, such as in the bass aria from Cantata 197a, *Kleinod* can indeed mean "jewel" or "gem.") Likewise, the *Kampf* in line 2 is not primarily a battle, struggle, or conflict but a contest or competition, i.e., a *Wettkampf*. And the *Krone* is not primarily a regal, diamond-studded crown of metal but a crown of victory, a wreath whose leaves would be expected eventually to decay.[16] (Yet note that the aria does go on to speak of the Christian's everlasting "enemy," just as 1 Corinthians 9:26 goes on to speak of "fighting" [Luther: *fechten,* literally "fencing"].) Thus, a historically informed rendering of these lines would read, "Cross and victory wreath are bound together, / Contest and prize medal are united."

This reading would jibe well with Bach's musical setting too. For a start, in this aria the first vocal solo is accompanied by the whole of the oboe line that had preceded it—thus ritornello and episode, too, are "*vereint*."[17] Furthermore, a longstanding editorial quandary becomes unperplexing when the libretto is understood biblically. The great music historian Arnold Schering could not believe that Bach intended the alto to continue singing at the fourth eighth-note of bar 16 and for the oboe to follow with its canon at the second eighth-note of bar 17.[18] Schering emended the passage so that the oboe takes the reading of the alto entry at bar 16, and the alto follows in canon not at the second but at the *fourth* eighth-note of bar 17. (Incidentally, Junghänel's recording adopts Schering's contrapuntal emendation but switches his scoring around so that the oboe follows the alto.) But in Bach's notation, the alto and oboe engage in a brief canonic chase where they end together, "*vereint*," on the third quarter note of bar 17.

MEANINGS MADE CLEAR BY IMPLIED BIBLICAL PHRASES

This category involves passages that are verbally incomplete (knowingly) and thus can easily be misunderstood. Consider the first bass recitative from Cantata 152, *Tritt auf die Glaubensbahn*:

> *Der Heiland ist gesetzt*
> *In Israel zum Fall und Auferstehen.*
> Der edle Stein ist sonder Schuld,
> Wenn sich die böse Welt
> So hart an ihm verletzt,
> Ja, über ihn zur Höllen fällt,
> Weil sie boshaftig an ihn rennet
> Und Gottes Huld
> Und Gnade nicht erkennet!
> Doch selig ist
> Ein auserwählter Christ,
> Der seinen Glaubensgrund auf diesen Eckstein leget,
> Weil er dadurch Heil und Erlösung findet.

TERRY (1926)
The Saviour now is set
in Israel for fall and rise of many.

KOOPMAN cd[21] (1995)
A symbol is this child
In Israel, of death and
Resurrection!

DRINKER (1942)
A symbol is this child
in Israel, of death and Resurrection!

UNGER (1996)
The Savior has been established
In Israel for falling and rising.

AMBROSE (1984)
The Savior is in charge
In Israel o'er fall and resurrection.

SUZUKI cd[22] (1997)
The saviour is sent
To Israel, to fall and be
resurrected!

HARNONCOURT cd[19] (1985)
A symbol is this child
in Israel, of death and Resurrection!

STOKES (1999)
The Saviour has been placed in
Israel
For the fall and resurrection.

RICERCAR cd[20] (1989)
The saviour was condemned to death in
Israel, and there also to be resurrected!

TAYLOR cd[23] (2002)
A symbol is this child
In Israel, of death and
Resurrection!

Here our translators give a striking variety of readings for the opening lines. Nonetheless, this movement is most likely neither about Jesus' falling and rising, nor his being placed or set in Israel (as opposed to, say, in Egypt), nor his being a symbol, nor his being condemned in Israel. Bach's congregations would have just heard a pericope from Luke 2 chanted in the liturgy,[24] which at verse 34b reads:

Siehe, dieser wird gesetzt zu einem Fall und Auferstehen vieler in Israel; . . .
("Look, this one is set for a fall and rising again of many in Israel; . . .")

That is to say, according to the Gospel of Luke, Jesus was placed by God for the fall and rising again of *many people in Israel*. The recitative lines from Cantata 152 would thus be best rendered, "The Savior is set / For the fall and rising again [of many] in Israel!," in recognition of the scriptural passage it is meant to echo.

For a second example, consider the bass aria from Cantata 98, *Was Gott tut, das ist wohlgetan*:

Meinen Jesum laß ich nicht,
Bis mich erst sein Angesicht
Wird erhören oder segnen.
Er allein
Soll mein Schutz in allem sein,
Was mir Übels kann begegnen.

TERRY (1926)
Never Jesus will I leave
Till He shall upon me breathe
Words of comfort and His blessing.

UNGER (1996)
I will not my Jesus go,
Until his countenance
Will grant favorable hearing (to
me) or bless (me).

DRINKER (1942)
Jesus will I never leave
'til His blessing I receive,
He will aid me and abet me.

STOKES (1999)
I shall not forsake my Jesus,
Until He
Hear me and bless me.

LEONHARDT cd[25] (1979)
Jesus will I never leave
'til His blessing I receive,
He will aid me and abet me.

GARDINER cd[26] (2000)
I shall not let my Jesus go
until His face
shall hear my prayer or bless me.

AMBROSE (1984)
I my Jesus shall not leave
Till me first his countenance
Shall give favor or its blessing.

Only the rendering in the Gardiner cd catches fully the apparent allusion to Genesis 32:26, with both the verb "to go" and its auxiliary "let."

> Und er sprach: *Laß* mich *gehen,* denn die Morgenröte bricht an. Aber er antwortete: Ich *lasse* dich nicht *[gehen],* du segnest mich denn.
> ("And he [the man/angel/God] said: '*Let* me *go,* for the rubescence of the morning [sky] is breaking in.' But he [Jacob] answered: 'I will not *let* you *[go],* unless you bless me.'")

In Cantata 98, then, the text does not speak of "leaving" Jesus, much less of "forsaking" him. It suggests rather that followers of Jesus metaphorically re-live the experience of Jacob: they are in a profound spiritual struggle, and they will not let go in this wrestling match until they are blessed. (According to Luther's radically Christocentric reading of the Hebrew Scriptures, it was actually Christ himself whom Jacob wrestled with at Peniel.[27]) An informed translation would thus read, "I shall not let my Jesus [go], until his face gives heed to me or blesses me."

MEANINGS MADE CLEAR FROM
BIBLICAL/THEOLOGICAL REFERENCES

The soprano aria from Cantata 80, *Ein feste Burg ist unser Gott*, seems straightforwardly to affirm that God's image should "shine once again in me," and most translators appear to agree.

> Komm in mein Herzenshaus,
> Herr Jesu, mein Verlangen!

Treib Welt und Satan aus
Und laß dein Bild in mir erneuert prangen!
Weg, schnöder Sündengraus!

TERRY (1926)
And make my soul Thine own new
garnished dwelling!

RIFKIN cd[29] (1987)
And let thy image shine renewed
within me.

DRINKER (1942)
and let Thine image ever shine before me.

HERREWHEGE cd[30] (1990)
And let your image shine again
within me!

HARNONCOURT cd[28] (1978)
and let Thine image ever shine before me.

UNGER (1996)
And let thine image be resplendent
anew in me!

AMBROSE (1984)
And let thine image find in me new glory!

STOKES (1999)
And let your image gleam in me
anew!

But with its use of *erneuert*, however, the text more likely projects a somewhat different sense, namely: "let your image shine forth in a renewed me." This reading reflects Luther's subtle but theologically significant understanding of Colossians 3:9–11[31]:

Lüget nicht untereinander; ziehet den alten Menschen mit seinen Werken aus und ziehet den neuen an, der da *erneuert*[32] wird zu der Erkenntnis, nach dem Eben*bilde* des, der ihn geschaffen hat: da nicht ist Grieche, Jude, Beschneidung, Vorhaut, Ungrieche, Scythe, Knecht, Freier; sondern alles und in allen Christus.

("Do not lie to one another; put off the old man [i.e., the fallen Adam] and his works and and put on the new [i.e., the sinless Christ, who is the new man], which is being *renewed* in knowledge according to the *image* of him who has created him: where there is no Greek, Jew, circumcision, foreskin, non-Greek, Scythian, servant, free man; rather all, and in all, is Christ.")

In this reading of Paul's letter, a person who has put on the New Man (Christ) is renewed according to the image of God (i.e., a person's whole being as the "image of God" is restored by union with Christ, who is the very "image of the invisible God," according to Colossians 1:15—it is not God's image itself that is renovated: rather, fallen human beings are made new into God's image[33]). The text from Bach's cantata, then, would be speaking of a renewed person, not of a radiance anew or of God's image being made new. A meticulous translation would thus be, "And let your image shine in me [who is being] renewed [in knowledge after the image of the creator]."

A second example: In the closing chorale from Cantata 190, *Singet dem Herrn ein neues Lied*, there is some confusion among translators about the sense of the third line from the end.

Laß uns das Jahr vollbringen
Zu Lob dem Namen dein,
Daß wir demselben singen
In der Christen Gemein;
Wollst uns das Leben fristen
Durch dein allmächtig Hand,
Erhalt deine lieben Christen
Und unser Vaterland.
Dein Segen zu uns wende,
Gib Fried an allem Ende;
Gib unverfälscht im Lande
Dein seligmachend Wort.
Die Heuchler[34] *mach zuschanden*
Hier und an allem Ort!

TERRY (1926)
Stablish among believers
Thine own Almighty realm,
And all earth's vain deceivers
Right utterly o'erwhelm!

DRINKER (1942)
let truth and simple candor
to honor be restored,
hypocrisy and slander
be ev'rywhere abhorred.

AMBROSE (1984)
Give unalloyed this country
Thy grace-inspiring word.
To hypocrites bring ruin
Both here and ev'rywhere!

UNGER (1996)
Grant unadulterated in this land
Thy beatific Word.
Confound all hypocrites
Here and in every place!

KOOPMAN cd[35] (1998)
Spread thy beatific word
unadulterated throughout the land.
Confound the hypocrites
here and everywhere!

STOKES (1999)
Give throughout the land
Thy pure and joy-inspiring Word.
Destroy all the hypocrites
Here and everywhere!

SUZUKI cd[36] (2003)
Give unfalsified to the world
Your blessed word.
Destroy the devil
Here and throughout the world.

Is God's *seligmachend* Word grace-inspiring, pure, joy-inspiring, blessed, or beatific? Only the rendition "beatific" (whose precise meaning is, "*making* blessed") approaches the right idea, but even it is probably not quite correct. Bach's librettist most likely alludes to a notion of God's Word as *salvific* (i.e., *selig* in the sense of *"eternally* blessed," though this would be, of course, a heavenly blessedness experienced proleptically in the services in Bach's Leipzig churches), something proclaimed at James 1:21:[37]

> Darum so leget ab alle Unsauberkeit und alle Bosheit und nehmet das Wort an mit Sanftmut, das in euch gepflanzet ist, welches kann eure Seelen selig machen.
> ("Therefore lay aside all filthiness and all evil, and accept with meekness the Word that is planted in you, which is able to make your souls blessed [i.e., which is able to save your souls].")

The Cantata 190 passage is thus best translated as "Grant uncorrupted in the land / Your saving Word. / Put the hypocrites to shame / Here and in every place!"[38]

As a final, more involved example of questions of theological understanding, consider the tenor recitative from Cantata 31, *Der Himmel lacht! die Erde jubilieret*, which presents the additional problem of having several different readings of the German text in modern editions. Bach's own score does not survive; the earliest source is the set of vocal parts that Samuel Gottlieb Heder, a student at the Thomasschule, copied in 1731.[39] Heder was evidently confused by Bach's score (from which he apparently copied), and modern editors have sometimes ventured further improvements on Heder's solutions to the problems in his model. Here is the German text as it most likely should read, along with various translations (and their German sources, if different from the italicized lines 4–6).

So stehe dann, du gottergebne Seele,
Mit Christo geistlich auf!
Tritt an den neuen Lebenslauf!
Auf! von den toten Werken!
Laß, daß dein Heiland in dir lebt,
An deinem Leben merken!
Der Weinstock, der jetzt blüht,
Trägt keine tote Reben!
Der Lebensbaum läßt seine Zweige leben!
Ein Christe flieht
Ganz eilend von dem Grabe!
Er läßt den Stein,
Er läßt das Tuch der Sünden
Dahinten
Und will mit Christo lebend sein.

TERRY (1926)
Flee all the works of darkness!
Soul, let thy Saviour now above
remark thy love and goodness!

KOOPMAN cd[41] (1995)
Up! follow now thy Saviour.
Stay, let Him ever live in thee,
And mark well thy behaviour!
booklet:
Auf! von des Todes Werken!
Laß, daß dein Heiland in der
Welt, an deinem Leben
merken!
performance:
. . . in dir weiht [?], . . .

DRINKER (1942)
Up! follow now thy Saviour.
Stay, let Him ever live in thee,
and mark well thy behaviour!
Auf! von den toten (*or,* Todes)
Werken!
Lass, lass [*sic*] dein Heiland in dir
[*sic*] Welt,
an deinem Leben merken!

UNGER (1996)
Up from thy dead works!
Allow thy Savior to live in thee,
To be observed in thy life!
Auf! von den toten Werken!
Laß, daß dein Heiland in dir lebt,
An deinem Leben merken!

HARNONCOURT cd[40] (1974)
Up! follow now thy Saviour.
Stay, let Him ever live in thee,
and mark well thy behaviour!
booklet and performance:
Auf! von des Todes Werken!
Laß, daß dein Heiland in der Welt,
An deinem Leben merken!

SUZUKI cd[42] (1998)
Up, from the works of death.
May the saviour in the world
regard your life.
booklet:
Auf! von des Todes Werken!
Laß, daß dein Heiland in der
Welt,
an deinem Leben merken!
performance:
. . . von den toten Werken!
. . . in dir lebt, . . .

AMBROSE (1984)
Rise, leave the works of dying!

Make thine own Savior in the world

Be in thy life reflected!
Auf! von den toten Werken!
Laß, daß dein Heiland in der Welt,
An deinem Leben merken!

STOKES (1999)
Rise! Abandon the pursuit of
death!
Let the existence of the Saviour in
this world
Be reflected in your life!
Auf! von des Todes Werken!
Laß, daß dein Heiland in der
Welt,
An deinem Leben merken!

The libretto booklets distributed in Bach's churches for renderings of the cantata in 1724 and 1731 both provide the surely correct reading "von den toten Werken," a phrase presumably alluding to Luther's translation of Hebrews 9:14[43]:

> Denn so der Ochsen und der Böcke Blut, und die Asche, von der Kuhe gesprenget, heiliget die Unreinen zu der leiblichen Reinigkeit, wie vielmehr wird das Blut Christi, der sich selbst ohne allen Wandel durch den Heiligen Geist GOtt geopfert hat, unser Gewissen reinigen *von den toten Werken,* zu dienen dem lebendigen GOtt!
>
> ("For if the blood of oxen and goats and the sprinkled ashes of the heifer sanctifies the impure person unto bodily purity, how much more will the blood of Christ, who through the Holy Spirit offered himself immutable to God, purge our conscience *from dead works,* to serve the living God?")

Cantata 31, then, speaks not of the "works of darkness," the "works of dying," the "works of death," a "pursuit of death," or of "*your* dead works" but rather of "works that are [per se] dead." Luther's notion here is that works are "dead" because they can do nothing to justify a person in the face of God's wrath. According to Luther, persons can be justified before God only by having Christ's righteousness imputed to them, as appropriated through the unmerited gift of faith. Good works are the *fruit* of right faith; they are of no help in justification.[44]

The more likely reading of line 5, "Laß, daß dein Heiland *in dir lebt*"[45] (not ". . . *in der Welt*"), advocates humans' focusing only on Christ's imputed righteousness (i.e., because the Saviour "lives in you"). The passage from Cantata 31—best translated as "Up, from dead works! / Let [the fact] that your Saviour lives in you / be observed in your life!"—in true Lutheran fashion does not advocate reward for good works or for any ritual acts of purification.

PASSAGES OBSCURED BY ARCHAIC LANGUAGE

For the bass recitative from Cantata 39, many translators render *milde* as "gentle."

Der reiche Gott wirft seinen Überfluß
Auf uns, die wir ohn ihn auch nicht den Odem haben.
Sein ist es, was wir sind; er gibt nur den Genuß,
Doch nicht, daß uns allein
Nur seine Schätze laben.
Sie sind der Probestein,

Wodurch er macht bekannt,
Daß er der Armut auch die Notdurft ausgespendet,
Als er mit milder Hand,
Was jener nötig ist, uns reichlich zugewendet.
Wir sollen ihm für sein gelehntes Gut
Die Zinse nicht in seine Scheuren bringen;
Barmherzigkeit, die auf dem Nächsten ruht,
Kann mehr als alle Gab ihm an das Herze dringen.

TERRY (1926)
They are a trust, indeed,
in that He asks our care
to give from out our plenty where our help
is needed,
as He, with favour rare,
to meet our daily need
with lavish hand's provided.

HERREWEGHE cd[47] (1993)
They are the touchstone
by which he makes known
that he alleviates poverty as well
as necessity,
since he richly bestows whatever
is necessary
with gentle hand.

DRINKER (1942)
they are the touchstones, too,
by which He tells to you
that what He gives is not alone to fill
your need,
but that for poorer folk you have the
wherewithal
their hungry mouths to feed.

UNGER (1996)
They are the touchstone,
by which he makes known
That he has also provided the poor
with their necessities,
When he with liberal hand,
Richly bestows on us what is
needful to them.

LEONHARDT cd[46] (1975)
they are the touchstones, too,
by which He tells to you
that what He gives is not alone to fill
your need,
but that for poorer folk you have the
wherewithal
their hungry mouths to feed.

STOKES (1999)
They are the touchstone,
By which He reveals
That He provides the bare necessi-
ties even for the poor,
When He with gentle hand
Showers upon us all that they need.

AMBROSE (1984)
They as a touchstone serve,
By which he hath revealed
That he to poor men also need hath freely
given,
And hath with open hand,
Whate'er the poor require, to us so richly
proffered.

KOOPMAN cd[48] (2004)
They as a touchstone serve
By which he hath revealed
That he to poor men also need
hath freely given,
And hath with open hand,
Whate'er the poor require, to us so
richly proffered.

In the eighteenth century, however, this word had several meanings, including *freigebig* ("generous"). This is the understanding readers in Bach's day would have brought to such passages as Psalm 37:21 (which speaks of the righteous person, who is generous[49]), Ecclesiastes 7:7 (which speaks of corrupting a generous heart[50]), and Ezekiel 16:36–37 (which speaks of the wanton [i.e., an ironic "generous"] outpouring of one's wealth[51]). In Cantata 39 *milde* as "generous" makes a great deal more sense than as "gentle."

For a second example: Even in Bach's day *mildiglich* was an archaism, an older form for *milde*. Thus the last line of the closing chorale from Cantata 28, *Gottlob! nun geht das Jahr zu Ende*, should most likely be translated, "And feed us *generously*" rather than "gently" or "tenderly."

All solch dein Güt wir preisen,
Vater ins Himmels Thron,
Die du uns tust beweisen
Durch Christum, deinen Sohn,
Und bitten ferner dich:
Gib uns ein friedsam Jahre,
Für allem Leid bewahre
Und nähr uns mildiglich.

TERRY (1926)
We beg a further prayer:
"Peace with the New Year send us,
From every ill defend us,
And hold us in Thy care!"

DRINKER (1942)
do Thou our prayer hear:
"In paths of peace direct us,
from ev'ry ill protect us,
thruout this coming year."

HARNONCOURT cd[52] (1974)
do Thou our prayer hear:
In paths of peace direct us,
from ev'ry ill protect us,
thruout this coming year.

AMBROSE (1984)
And further ask of thee:
Give us a peaceful year now,
From ev'ry woe defend us
And us with kindness feed.

UNGER (1996)
And ask furthermore of thee:
Give us a peaceful year;
From all harm protect
And feed us tenderly.

STOKES (1999)
And beseech Thee now as well
To grant us a peaceful year,
To protect us from all sorrow
And gently to sustain us.

KOOPMAN cd[53] (2004)
And further ask of thee:
Give us a peaceful year now,
From ev'ry woe defend us
And us with kindness feed.

PASSAGES THAT ARE SIMPLY DIFFICULT

Some passages in the librettos from Bach's church cantatas are on the face of it simply difficult.[54] One notorious line that has plagued many readers appears in the closing movement from Cantata 60, *O Ewigkeit, du Donnerwort*, a four-part chorale inevitably encountered in undergraduate harmony and counterpoint classes. What does it mean to exclaim, as this text does, "Herr, wenn es dir gefällt, *so spanne mich doch aus*"?

Es ist genung;
Herr, wenn es dir gefällt,
So spanne mich doch aus!
Mein Jesu kömmt;
Nun gute Nacht, o Welt!
Ich fahr ins Himmelshaus,
Ich fahre sicher hin mit Frieden,
Mein großer Jammer bleibt danieden.
Es ist genung.

TERRY (1926)
It is enough!
Lord, brace me to the test
When toward me Death shall nod!

DRINKER (1942)
It is enough:
Lord, when it pleases Thee
do Thou unshackle me.

HARNONCOURT cd[55] (1976)
It is enough;
Lord, when it pleases Thee
do Thou unshackle me.

AMBROSE (1984)
It is enough;
Lord, if it be thy will,
Then let me rest in peace!

UNGER (1996)
It is enough;
Lord, if it pleases thee,
Then indeed put me to rest!

KOOPMAN cd[56] (1999)
It is enough,
Lord, when it pleases Thee
Do Thou unshackle me.

STOKES (1999)
It is enough:
Lord, if it be Thy will,
Free me from my burden!

SUZUKI cd[57] (2001)
It is enough:
Lord, if it pleases you
Let me relax.

I suspect that Drinker and Stokes are closest to the sense of this passage and its use of the word *ausspannen*. Luther's translation of Job 30:11 may provide a helpful clue:

Sie haben mein Seil ausgespannet, und mich zunichte gemacht, und das Meine abgezäumet.

("They have unharnessed my rope, and ruined me, and unbridled what is mine.")

Ausspannen otherwise appears in the Old Testament of the Luther Bibles of Bach's day only at Ezekiel 26:4, 5, 14 and Hosea 5:1, each time having to do with the spreading out of fishnets; the verb does not show up in Luther's New Testament.

Considering Luther's use in Job 30:11 of *abgezäumet* ("unbridled"), and considering the standard German expression *Die Pferde ausspannen* ("unharness the horses"), I would offer as a best construal for Cantata 60's vexing *So spanne mich doch aus* the rendering: "Then do unharness me [of the world's "trappings," and from the yoke of the world's endless sorrows, trials, and burdens[58]]." These sentiments were certainly explored fully in many Lutheran sermons of Bach's day and earlier. For example, in a late seventeenth-century collection of funeral sermons Heinrich Müller writes:

> Simeon nennet den Tod eine Außspannung. [In marg. Luc 2/29.] Hie sind wir eingespannet in das Joch der Mühe / deß Jammers und Leidens. Der Tod spannet uns auß aus dem Leidens= und Angst=Joch.[59]
>
> ("Simeon calls death an unharnessing [margin: "Luke 2:29"[60]]. Here [in the present world] we are harnessed in the yoke of trouble, misery, and suffering. Death unharnesses us out from the yoke of suffering and fear.")

Each of these new suggested renderings for the librettos from Bach's cantatas works out of insights that are likely to occur to us only with a knowledge of the broader religious contexts of Bach's music and poetry. Unlike us, Bach lived and worked in a biblically literate culture. We cannot hope adequately to understand his output unless we work to become historically informed about his religious *Sitz im Leben*, whatever our own predilections might be.

NOTES

1. Charles Sanford Terry, *Joh. Seb. Bach: Cantata Texts, Sacred and Secular; with a Reconstruction of the Leipzig Liturgy of His Period* (London: Constable, 1926).

2. Henry S. Drinker, *Texts of the Choral Works of Johann Sebastian Bach in English Translation*, 2 vols. (New York: Association of American Colleges, Arts Program; 1942–1943). On the whole, neither Terry's nor Drinker's translation promotes historically informed understanding of the librettos Bach set to music. Drinker's intent was to make acceptable singing translations, not to convey essentially literal meanings to listeners following the German; nonetheless, many early-music recordings have adopted his readings for their cd booklets.

3. Teldec 242609.

4. *The Texts to Johann Sebastian Bach's Church Cantatas*, trans. Z. Philip Ambrose (Hänssler: Neuhausen-Stuttgart, 1984).

5. Melvin P. Unger, *Handbook to Bach's Sacred Cantata Texts* (Lanham, Md.: Scarecrow Press, 1996). This is by far the best translation of the librettos from Bach's cantatas.

6. Harmonia mundi France 901594. Record companies often claim historical "authenticity" for their productions. For convenience I have identified recordings by their conductors, but this is not meant to suggest that conductors always have control over all aspects of their recordings, including the libretto translations.

7. *Johann Sebastian Bach: The Complete Church and Secular Cantatas*, trans. Richard Stokes (Ebrington, Gloucestershire: Long Barn Books, 1999).

8. Challenge Classics 72213.

9. Allusion noted in Ulrich Meyer, *Biblical Quotation and Allusion in the Cantata Libretti of Johann Sebastian Bach* (Lanham, Md.: Scarecrow Press, 1997), 15. See also John 6:44. This does not, however, make for good poetry: in the surrounding lines it is the noun at the beginning of the line that initiates the action.

10. Teldec 2425000.

11. Erato 0630-12598.

12. BIS 791.

13. Harmonia mundi France 901694.

14. Dorian 93231.

15. The allusion is noted in Meyer, 56; also in Unger, 43.

16. Cf. Revelation 2:10, where suffering and the "crown of life" are linked. Compare also, e.g., the early eighteenth-century picture of God holding out a crown and cross for the follower of Christ in Lucia Haselböck, *Bach Textlexikon: Ein Wörterbuch der religiösen Sprachbilder im Vokalwerk von Johann Sebastian Bach* (Kassel: Bärenreiter, 2004), 127.

17. See the either/or analysis of ritornellos and episodes in Laurence Dreyfus, *Bach and the Patterns of Invention* (Cambridge, Mass.: Harvard University Press, 1996), 59–102. Perhaps Dreyfus is too rigid in saying that segments of Bach's concerto-style music belong to one or the other category. Are not, e.g., bars 46–47 of the first movement from Bach's Second Brandenburg Concerto working simultaneously as the final segment of an episode (see the sequence from D–g–C–F at bars 40–47) *and* as the first segment of the ensuing ritornello (see the ritornello segments 1 and 2 at bars 46–50)?

18. Johann Sebastian Bach, *Kantate 12: Weinen, Klagen*, ed. Arnold Schering (Zürich: Eulenberg, 1926).

19. Teldec 242632.

20. Ricercar 061041.

21. Erato 0630-12598.

22. BIS 841.

23. Atma 2-2279.

24. Noted in Terry, 101; Meyer, 13; and Unger, 521.

25. Teldec 2292-42583.

26. Archiv 463586.

27. Martin Luther, *Lectures on Genesis: Chapters 31–37*, trans. Paul D. Pahl, ed. Jaroslav Pelikan, Luther's Works, vol. 6 (St. Louis: Concordia Publishing House, 1970), 144, where Luther states, "Without any controversy we shall say that this man [with whom Jacob wrestled] was not an angel but our Lord Jesus Christ, eternal God and future Man, to be crucified by the Jews."

28. Teldec 242577.

29. Editions de l'Oiseau-Lyre 417250.

30. Harmonia mundi France 901326.

31. This allusion noted in Meyer, 159.

32. In other Luther Bibles of Bach's day, *verneuert.*

33. Also, Paul's word "renew" [Greek, *anakainoo*] means "made new in [something's] *nature,*" as opposed to "new in time" [*neos*]; see Gerhard Kittel and Gerhard Friedrich, eds., *Theological Dictionary of the New Testamemt, Abridged in One Volume,* trans. and abridged by Geoffrey W. Bromiley (Grand Rapids, Mich.: Eerdmans, 1985), 388. Hence Luther's rendering as *"[v]erneuert."*

34. In most contemporary hymnbooks, not *Heuchler* but *Teufel* (Werner Neumann, ed., *Sämtliche von Johann Sebastian Bach vertonte Texte* [Leipzig: Deutscher Verlag für Musik, 1974], 40).

35. Erato 3984-21629.

36. BIS 1311.

37. The allusion is noted in Meyer, 17.

38. For *unverfälscht*, see the "uncorrupted doctrine" (Luther, "unverfälschte Lehre") of Titus 2:7.

39. For the details, see Alfred Dürr, *Kantaten zum 1. Ostertag: Kritischer Bericht,* Johann Sebastian Bach, Neue Ausgabe sämtlicher Werke, series 1, vol. 9 (Kassel: Bärenreiter, 1986), 37–39.

40. Teldec 242505.

41. Erato 4509-98536.

42. BIS 851.

43. The allusion is noted in Dürr, 52; Unger, 112; and Meyer, 47.

44. For a full discussion, see Robin A. Leaver, *Luther on Justification* (St. Louis: Concordia Publishing House, 1975), and Alister E. McGrath, *Iustitia Dei: A History of the Christian Doctrine of Justification*, rev. and expanded ed. (Cambridge: Cambridge University Press, 1998).

45. See also Galatians 2:20, . . . *Christus lebet in mir* ("Christ lives in me"); noted in Meyer, 47.

46. Teldec 8.35269.

47. Virgin Classics 7-59320.

48. Challenge Classics 72216.

49. Luther, "Der Gottlose borget und bezahlet nicht; der Gerechte aber ist barmherzig und milde."

50. Luther (verse 8 in the Bibles of Bach's day), "Ein Widerspenstiger machet einen Weisen unwillig und verderbet ein mild Herz."

51. Luther, "So spricht der HERR HERR: Weil du denn so milde Geld zugibst, und deine Scham durch deine Hurerey gegen deine Bulen entblößest und gegen alle

Götzen deiner Greuel; und vergeußest das Blut deiner Kinder, welche du ihnen opferst; darum siehe, will ich sammeln alle deine Bulen, mit welchen du Wohllust getrieben hast, samt allen, die du für Freunde hieltest, zu deinen Feinden; und will sie beyde wider dich samlen allenthalben und will ihnen deine Scham blößen, daß sie deine Scham gar sehen sollen." In other Bibles, not "wealth" (Luther, "Geld") but "lust."

52. Teldec 242504.

53. Challenge Classics 72215.

54. For example, even Werner Neumann, a German specialist on the librettos Bach set, says of the poetry in the thirteenth movement from Cantata 76: "it is hard to understand." Neumann, 100.

55. Teldec 8.43745.

56. Erato 3984-25488.

57. BIS 1111.

58. See the penultimate line of the chorale stanza, "Mein großer Jammer bleibt danieden."

59. Heinrich Müller, *Gräber der Heiligen / Mit Christlichen Leich=Predigten*, ed. Johannes Caspar Heinsius (Frankfurt am Main, 1685), 478–79; quoted in Renate Steiger, *Gnadengegenwart: Johann Sebastian Bach im Kontext lutherischer Orthodoxie und Frommigkeit* (Stuttgart-Bad Cannstatt: Frommann-Holzboog, 2002), 113. In Dietrich Buxtehude's cantata *Ich habe Lust abzuscheiden*, BuxWV 47, "ausspannen" is employed to express these same sentiments.

60. That is, referring to the Greek word *apolyo*, "dismiss" or "set free." Note, too, that the line "Ich fahre sicher hin mit Frieden" at the end of the chorale from Cantata 60 alludes to Luther's translation of Luke 2:29 ("HErr, nun lässest du deinen Diener im Frieden fahren").

7

The Role of the "Actus Structure" in the Libretto of J. S. Bach's Matthew Passion

Don O. Franklin

My purpose in this chapter is to view the libretto of the Matthew Passion of J. S. Bach from a new perspective, namely, as a series of six successive "acts" that correspond to the primary events of the passion as defined by Lutheran tradition. The six acts include: 1) the Preparation (Vorbereitung), consisting of the events that precede the passion, including the anointing of Jesus' feet by Mary Magdalene, and the Last Supper; 2) Act I (Hortus), the Garden of Gethsemane; 3) Act II (Pontifices), the Trial before Caiaphas; 4) Act III (Pilatus), the Trial before Pilate; 5) Act IV (Crux), the Crucifixion; and 6) Act V (Sepulchrum), the Burial. In his 1985 study of Bach's Matthew Passion, Martin Petzoldt pointed out the ways in which Bach's libretto reflects these six divisions, including the placement of a chorale or chorus at the end of each act.[1] But, to date, the implications of what I will call the Actus structure for the design and compilation of the Matthew Passion libretto have not been systematically explored.

To do so reveals the extent to which Bach and Picander modeled their libretto on the Actus structure not as set forth by Martin Luther, but by the late seventeenth-century theologian Johannes Olearius, whose divisions of Matthew's narrative, as will be shown, deviate at several key points from those of Luther. To view the Matthew Passion libretto as a series of six acts also reveals a schematic structure that, while standing in contrast to the two-part liturgical structure by which we traditionally have viewed the work, can also be seen to serve as its foundation and skeletal framework. The first part of the chapter focuses on the extent to which Bach's Matthew Passion is modeled on the commentary of Olearius, the second part on the libretto's schematic structure. A final section is devoted to surveying the role of the Actus structure in the so-called "Keiser" Mark Passion scores that Bach performed in Weimar and Leipzig.

For Bach to structure his passion libretto to correspond to the series of six acts described above is understandable in light of the key role it plays in Luther's writings and, subsequently, in Lutheran practice. In his 1546 trans lation of the New Testament, Luther divides Matthew's narrative into six acts in the manner shown in table 7.1, numbering them consecutively as Acts I–VI. (For the purposes of this chapter, I refer to the six sections as they more commonly are described by late sixteenth- and early seventeenth-century writers, that is, as shown in the far right column of table 7.1.) Following the Reformation, the Actus structure became an integral part of the biblical com mentaries and collections of passion sermons that proliferated in the late sev enteenth and early eighteenth centuries. Available to Bach and Picander in preparing the Matthew Passion libretto would have been not only the several editions of Luther's works found in Bach's library, but also a number of seventeenth-century publications. One of these, *Aurifodina Theologica*, a commentary by Christoph Scheibler published in 1673, was issued in a new edition in 1727 likely known to Bach.[2] He also undoubtedly was familiar with the commentary of Abraham Calov, known today as "Bach's Bible," though it did not became part of his library until 1733.[3] Still another volume acces sible to Bach and Picander was the Dresden Gesangbuch, the hymnal in use in Leipzig during Bach's tenure. An appendix to the hymnal titled "Historia des Leidens" included a complete text of the passion narrative based on the accounts in the four Gospels.[4] In each of these publications, the Actus struc ture appeared in the form described by Luther.

However, as seen in table 7.1, it was not to any of the above volumes that Bach and Picander turned when designing their libretto, but, rather, to the bib lical commentary of Johannes Olearius.[5] That Bach and Picander chose to model their libretto on Olearius's divisions is doubtless due in part to Bach's familiarity with the commentary, and what I described in an earlier study of the libretto of Cantata 67 as its "user-friendly" qualities.[6] (In that study I il lustrated how Bach and his unknown librettist were able, by consulting the commentary, along with its references to other publications of Olearius, to de rive with minimal effort the main themes and biblical verses used in the li bretto.) In particular, it is the clear and systematic organization of Olearius's commentary, along with his outline of the individual episodes within each of the acts, that provided a useful guide to a composer and librettist seeking to establish the framework for their libretto. These qualities are readily apparent in the portion of Olearius's commentary shown in table 7.2. Serving as an in troduction to the biblical narrative that follows, it includes: 1) a heading that ascribes a didactic or instructional purpose to each chapter, 2) an overall out line of the primary events that take place in the chapter, and 3) a list of the episodes that take place within each of the acts, each with its own set of

Table 7.1. Division of Biblical Narrative According to Actus Structure in Luther, Olearius, and Matthew Passion Libretto

Luther, 1546	Verse division	Olearius, 1678–1681	Verse division	JSB/Picander Verse division	Actus Structure
Chapter 26		Das Leiden: fordert Danckbarkeit			
I. Alte Osterlamm. Abendmal	17–25 26–29	Die Vorbereitung	1–35	1–35	Vorbereitung
II. Oleberg	30–56	Die Beschreibung I. Im Garten	36–56	36–56	Act I, Hortus
III. Caiphas Hause	57–75	II. In Caiphas Pallast	57–75	57–75	Act II, Pontifices
Chapter 27		Die Creutzigung			
IIII. Christus [vor] Pilatum gefüret	1–31	I. Was vorhergegangen/ nehmlich . . .	1–26a	1–30	Act III, Pilatus
		II. Wie es mit der Creutzigung ergangen/nehmlich . . .	26b–35a		
V. Leiden	32–56	III. Was auf die Creutzigung ferner ergangen/nehmlich . . .	35b–50	31–50	Act IV, Crux
VI. Christus begraben	57–66	[Sepulchrum]	51–66	51–66	Act V, Sepulchrum

verses, a list far more detailed and comprehensive than those found in the volumes cited above.[7]

As shown in table 7.2, Olearius divides the narrative in Matthew, chapter 26 into three primary divisions that correspond to the first three acts described above: "Die Vorbereitung," "Im Garten," and "In Caiphas Pallast." The latter two he lists under the general title: "Die Beschreibung/was vorgegangen;" that is, a description of the events that precede the Crucifixion. In contrast to Luther, Olearius places the division between the Vorbereitung and Act I not after the Last Supper (vs. 29, see table 7.1), but, rather, six verses later, after the scene in which Jesus informs Peter that he will betray him, to which Peter and then the disciples respond: "Und wenn ich mit dir sterben müsste, so will ich dich nicht verleugnen. Desgleichen sagten auch alle Jünger." vs. 36 (And should I have to die with you, I will not disavow you even then. All the disciples said similar things.).[8] The chorale verse with which Bach then ends the act speaks for the believer when it states: "Ich will hier bei dir stehen, Verachte mich doch nicht!" (I will stand here beside you; please do not despise me!).

As his heading for chapter 27 indicates, Olearius gives prominence to "Die Creutzigung" (The Crucifixion). However, rather than divide the first fifty verses of the narrative in the traditional manner between Act III (Pilatus) and Act IV (Crux), he conflates the two acts into a larger unit, which he then divides into three subdivisions that include: 1) the trial before Pilate to the point where the crowd demands the release of Barrabas and Jesus is given over to be crucified (vs. 1–26a), 2) the scourging ("Geisselung") of Jesus and the procession to Golgotha that ends with Jesus being nailed to the cross (vs. 26b–35a), and 3) the division of clothes by the soldiers (table 7.2, III. 1. "Der Theilung der Kleider," vs. 35b–50).

In this case, Bach and Picander do not observe Olearius's tripartite division, but, instead, follow the Actus structure shown in the far right column of table 7.1. However, in dividing Act IV (Crux) from Act V (Sepulchrum), they again adhere to Olearius's division of the narrative. Rather than following Luther in concluding Act IV after the earthquake scene and the rending of the veil of the temple (vs. 56), they follow Olearius in concluding the act after verse 50, which describes Jesus' death, preceded by his crying out to his father in response to the taunts of the crowed: "Halt! lass sehen, ob Elias komme und ihn helfe? Aber Jesus schriee abermal laut, und verschied." (Wait! Let us see: might Elijah come and save him? But Jesus again shouted loudly and departed this life.) Here the chorale verse Bach inserts into the narrative to mark the end of the act, "Wenn ich einmal soll scheiden. So scheide nicht von mir!" (When some day I am to part [from this world], then do not part from me), once again speaks of the significance of Jesus' death for the

Table 7.2. Division of Biblical Narrative in Olearius's Commentary and Matthew Passion Libretto.

Olearius: Biblische Erklärung		Libretto of Matthew Passion		
Actus structure	Olearius's chapter headings and subdivisions of the narrative	Verse division	Titles ascribed to interpolations by Picander	Interpolated chorale and poetic texts
Chapter 26	Das Leiden. Das Leiden fordert Danckbarkeit.		Die Tochter Zion und die Gläubigen	Kommt, ihr Töchter
Vorbereitung	Das Leiden unsers HERRN JEsu Christi weiset:	Vorbereit		
Mt. 26: 1–35	I. Die Vorbereitung			
	1. Christ verfas[sen]. v.1–2	1–2		
	2. Seiner Feinde. v.3–5	3–		Cl: Herzliebster
	3. Deß *Weibes* durch die *Salbung*, v. 6–13			Du Lieber/Buß und Reu
		13	Als das *Weib* Jesus *gesalbet* hatte	
	4. Deß Verräthers. v. 14–16	14–16	Als Judas die Silberlinge genommen	Blute nur
	5. Deß Osterlamms. v.17–20	17–		
	6. Der Jünger (1) durch die Errinerung von Verrät. v.22–23. (2) durch die Einsetzung deß heiligen *Abendmahls*, v. 26–29.	22– 23–		Cl: Ich bins
		29	Als Jesus das *Abendmahl* gehalten	Wiewohl/Ich will dir mein
	7. Deß HERRN Christi durch singen des Lobgesangs und das Hinausgehen an den Oelberge, v. 30	30–		
	8. Deß Petri nechst den andern insonderheit: durch Verkündigung seines Falls, v.31–35	32		Cl: Erkenne mich
		33–		Cl: Ich will hier bei dir
		35		

Table 7.2. (Continued).

Hortus Mt. 26: 36–56	II. Die Beschreibungen/Was vorgegangen	Act I		
	I. Im Garten			
	(1) *Am Oelberge*, v. 36. da bey entstandener *Todes=Angst*, v. 37. 38.	36–38	*Als Jesus am Oelberge zagt*	O Schmerz/Ich will
	das Gebet zum drittenmal wiederholet v. 39–44. und die Jünger ermuntert	39	*Nach dem Worten:* Mein Vater ist's möglich	Der Heiland/Gerne will ich
		40–42		Cl: Was mein Gott
	worden v. 45–46	43–		
	(2) Bey deß Verräthers Ankunft und Kuß. v. 47–49. darauf der HERR *gefangen* v. 50. Petrus als er Malcho das Ohr abgehauen verwarnet. v. 51–54, die That bestraft. v.55. und alle Jünger geflohen. v.56.	50	*Als Jesus gefangen worden*	So ist mein Jesus: Sind Blitze
		51–		Cl: O Mensch (concerted)
		56		
			Die Gläubigen und Zion	Ach, nun
Pontifices Mt. 26: 57–75	II. In Caiphas Pallast v. 57, wohin Petrus gefolget, v. 58. da	Act II 57–		
	1. Falschen Zeugen abgehöret, v. 59–61	60a 60b–		Cl: Mir hat die Welt
	2. der HERR befraget, v. 62–63 und geantwortet, v.64	63a 63b–	*Nach dem Worten:* Aber Jesus schweig	Mein Jesus schweigt/Geduld

Table 7.2. (Continued).

	3. darauf als in Gotteslästerer v. 65 (1) des Todes schuldig erkant, v. 66 (2) verspeyet und *geschlagen* worden, v. 67–68	68		Cl: Wer hat dich geschlagen
	(3) bis ihn endlich Petrus dreymal verläugnet, v. 69–74 durch das Han-Krehen erinnert/und *seine Sünde bitterlich beweinet, v. 75.*	69–		Erbarme dich / Cl: Bin ich gleich
		75	*Als Petrus weinete*	
Chapter 27	Die Creutzigung. Die Creutzigung bringt Schmertz und Leid.			
Pilatus/Crux Mt. 27: 1–26[a]	Die Creutzigung JESU CHRISTI weiset I. Was vorhergegangen/nemlich 1. Der Blut-Rath/und die beschlossene Uberantwortung,und das Hinführen zu Pilato v. 1. 2.	Act III		
		1–		
	2. Die Verzweyfelung deß Verräthers v. 3–5. und *Anwendung deß Blut-Geldes,*verf. 6–10.	6	Nach den Worten: Es taugt nicht . . . denn es ist *Blut-Geld*	Gebt mir meinem Jesus wieder
	3. Die Handlung vor dem Landpfleger v.11–18. ungeachtet der Warnung seines Weibes v. 19. Da endlich der Mörder Barabas loß gegeben/der unschuldige Christus über zum Creutz-Tode übergeben verf. 26[a]	7–		
		14		Cl: Befiehl du
		15–		Cl: Wie wunderbarlich
		22		Er hat uns allen/Aus Liebe
		23a		
		23b–	Nach den Worten Pilati: Was hat er denn übels getan?	
Mt. 27: 26[b]–35[a]	II. Wie es mit der Creutzigung ergangen/nemlich auf erfolgte Geisselung v. 26[b]	26[b]	Als Jesus *gegeißelt* würde	Erbarm es/Können Tränen
	Crönung v. 27–29, Verspeyung/Schlagen v. 29–30	27–		Cl: O Haupt voll Blut
		30		

Table 7.2. (Continued).

	Act IV		
und Ausführung v. 31. da *Simon das Creutz tragen* helffen v. 32 ist der liebe Heyland mit Gallen geträncket v. 34. und ans Creutz gebracht und angenagelt worden v. 35[a]	31–32 33–	*Als Simon von Kyrene das Kreuz*	*Ja freilich/Komm, Süsses Kreuz*
Mt. 27: 35[b]–50	III. Was auf die Creutzigung ferner ergangen/nemlich 1. Die Theilung der Kleider deß Herrn/verf. 35[b] 2. Die Bewahrung deß Herrn durch die Kreigs-Knechte/ v. 36 3. Die Anbettung deß Creutz-Tituls v. 37. 4. Die schimpfliche Stellung des Creutzes zwischen zweyen Mördern/ v.38		
	5. Die schändliche Lästerung/v. 39–44. 6. Die schreckliche Verfinsterung v. 45. 7. Die erbärmliche Anzeigung der Jammer=klage/Eli/Eli/ v. 46. 8. Die boßhaffte Verspottung v. 47 9. Die nochmahlige Tränckung mit Essig/v.48	44 45–	Als Jesus gekreuziget worden	Ach Golgotha/Sehe-, Jesus hat

Table 7.2. (Continued).

	10. Die erneuerte Verspottung v. 49			
	11. Die klägliche Wiederholung deß Jammer-Schreyes v. 50			
	12. Die denckwürdige Vollendung alles Leydens durch den Todt Jesu Christi v. 50–auf welchen Todt	50		Cl: Wenn ich einmal
Sepulchrum Mat. 27: 51–66	I. Sehr grosse Wunder gefolget. Denn	Act V		
	1. Der Fürhang deß Tempels ist zurissen/v. 51	51–		
	2. Die Erde ist erbebet/			
	3. Die Felsen zurissen v. 51			
	4. Die Gräber eröffnet v. 52–53			
	II. Der Hauptmann sammt andern hats bezeuget/daß Gottes Sohn am Creutz gestorben/ v. 54.			
	III. Die Weiber sind beym Creutz beharret/v. 55. 56			
	IV. Das Begräbnis ist durch Joseph bestellet v. 57–61	58	Als Jesus vom Kreuze genommen worden	Am Abend/Mache dich
	V. Das Grab versiegelt worden/ v. 62–66.	59–66	Nach den Worten: Und versiegelten den Stein.	Nun ist der Herr zur Ruh/ Wir setzen uns mit Tränen

believer. Act V then begins with the text that describes the earthquake scene, to which Olearius refers in his commentary as a "Sehr grosse Wunder" (table 7.2, Sepulchrum, I–II, vs. 51–54).

Table 7.2 also reveals the extent to which the Matthew Passion libretto adheres to Olearius's subdivision of the six acts as individual episodes, each with its own group of verses. (Not discussed in this chapter are the origins of Picander's texts, which are discussed in detail by Elke Axmacher.[9]) Looking in detail at the libretto's division of the narrative in chapter 26: in the Vorbereitung section, Bach and Picander interpolate poetic texts after three of the eight episodes described by Olearius. They insert the first set of texts, "Du lieber Heiland du" and "Buß und Reu," after vs. 6–13 (I.3. "Deß Weibes durch die Salbung"); the second, a single aria text, "Blute nur," after vs. 14–16 (Nr. 4, "Deß Verräthers"); and the third, another set of texts, "Wiewohl mein Herz" and the aria, "Ich will dir mein Herze schenken," after verse 29 (Nr. I. 6 , ". . . durch die Einsetzung deß heiligen Abendmahls"). The titles that Picander assigns to each interpolation, such as "Als Jesus das Weib Jesus gesalbet hatte," correspond directly to the description ascribed to the episode by Olearius.

In Act I (Hortus), Bach and Picander interpolate three pairs of texts in the narrative, with two of the three corresponding directly to the divisions noted by Olearius. The first (in the form of a dialogue) is the accompanied recitative and aria, "O Schmerz!" and "Ich will bei meinem Jesu wachen" (table 7.2, II I (1) "Am Oelberge, vs. 36–38), and the second, another dialogue, "So ist mein Jesus" and chorus "Sind Blitze," the latter pair inserted after the scene in which Judas betrays Jesus with a kiss, resulting in Jesus' arrest (vs. 50). However, the third set of texts, "Der Heiland" and "Gerne will ich," is inserted after the first of the three prayers ("dreymal Gebet") mentioned by Olearius, in which Jesus asks that "this cup pass from him." Because the placement of this set of texts does not occur at the end of, but rather within, an episode, Picander adds the rubric: "Nach dem Worten," followed by the first line of the appropriate verse, "Mein Vater's ist's möglich."[10] We see the same rubric in Act II (Pontifices) where Bach and Picander insert another set of poetic texts ("Mein Jesus schweigt" and "Geduld"), this time again within, rather than at the end of, an episode (II. 2). In Act II, they, in addition, place another aria text, "Erbarme dich," at the end of the scene in which Peter denies Jesus, followed by a chorale verse that concludes the act. As is shown later, the interpolation of poetic texts in the remaining three acts of the narrative reflects a similar pattern.

Looking at the disposition of the poetic texts in the libretto as a whole (see table 7.3), reveals that each of the acts, except for Act II (Pontifices), includes two interpolations consisting of a pair of poetic texts, the first of which is des-

Table 7.3. Disposition of Poetic Texts by Act in Matthew Passion Libretto

Actus structure	Incipits of core movements consisting of an accompanied recitative and aria	Incipit of additional movement	Total Nr
Part 1		Dialogue: Kommt, ihr	1
Vorbereitung Mt 26: 1–35	Du Lieber/Buß und Reu Wiewohl, Ich will dir	Aria: Blute nur	3
Act I Hortus Mt 26: 36–56	O Schmerz, Ich will Der Heiland, Gerne will ich	Duet/Cs: So ist mein Jesus/Sind Blitze	3
Part 2		Dialogue: Ach, nun	1+
Act II Pontifices Mt 26: 57–75	Mein Jesus schweigt, Geduld	Aria: Erbarme dich	2=3
Act III Pilatus Mt 27: 1–30	Er hat uns allen, Aus Liebe Erbarm es, Können Tränen	Aria: Gebt mir meinem Jesus	3
Act IV Crux Mt 27: 31–50	Ja freilich, Komm, süsses Kreuz Ach Golgotha, Sehet		2
Act V Sepulchrum Mt 27: 51–66	Am Abend, Mache dich Nun ist der Herr, Wir setzen		2

ignated as an accompanied recitative and the second as an aria. Furthermore, four of the acts also include an additional text in the form of an aria, or (in Act I) a duet with chorus. As shown in the far right column of table 7.3, the number of poetic texts interpolated in four of the acts totals three (if we include the dialogue, "Ach, nun," added at the beginning of Act III), and includes a total of two in the remaining two acts. Viewed in this light, each of the six acts can be seen to be derived from what could be described as a precompositional pattern or template that is comprised of two poetic texts plus an additional poetic text and a concluding chorale verse.

Before looking in detail at the schematic structure of the Matthew libretto, we examine briefly Bach's disposition of poetic verses and chorales in the libretto of his first passion, the 1724 setting of John's narrative. In designing the libretto, Bach and his unknown librettist faced the same issues described above but addressed them in a far less systematic and comprehensive manner. Furthermore, the libretto of the passion differed in two respects: 1) John's account began with Act I, the Garden scene, with no mention of the Preparation, and therefore included only Acts I–V; and 2) added to John's account were two passages (cited in the table) taken from the Matthew and Mark passion narratives. However, as he did with the Matthew libretto, Bach divides the narrative to correspond to the Actus structure, again using Olearius's commentary as his model, but in a far less consistent manner.[11] Moreover, as shown in table 7.4, he interpolates far fewer poetic texts than he does in the Matthew libretto, though their disposition reflects a similar pattern: that is, Acts II, III, and IV include a core of two interpolations that take the form of N+Aria, N+Aria+C1, N+Aria/C1, or N+Arioso+Aria, with a third interpolation added in Acts II and IV. By far the greatest number of schematic units include chorales (N+Cl).

The schematic outline of the Matthew Passion, shown in table 7.5, reveals a design more complex as well as more comprehensive. While units comprised of narrative and chorale (N+Cl) are proportionately less frequent in the Matthew libretto, units comprised of sections of narrative followed by accompanied recitative and aria (N+AccR+Aria) predominate. Of the fifteen poetic texts interpolated into the narrative (as opposed to the nine in the John Passion), eleven take the form of N+AccR+Aria, a schematic unit that functions as a core module within each of the six acts. (Not considered in this context are the turba choruses, the number of which varies in each act, that comprise an integral part of Bach's setting of the passion narrative.)

To view the schematic structure from this perspective illustrates how Bach could have easily converted the series of six individual sections into the two-part liturgical form required for performance in Leipzig in the Good Friday Vesper service; namely, by designating the Vorbereitung section and Act I as

Table 7.4. Schematic Outline of John Passion Libretto

Nr of units	1	2	3	4	5
Exordium					
Act I Hortus Jn 18:1–11	N+Cl	N+Cl			
Act II Pontifices Jn 18:12–27 Mt 26:75	N+Aria	N+Aria	N+Cl	N+Aria+Cl	
Exordium					
Act III Pilatus Jn 18:28–19:22	N+Cl	N+Arioso +Aria	N+Cl	N+Aria	N+Cl
Act IV Crux Jn 19:23–37 Mk 15:38	N+Cl	N+Aria	N+Aria/Cl	N+Arioso+ Aria	N+Cl
Act V Sepulchrum Jn 19:38–42	N+Cs+Cl				

Part 1 and the remaining four sections, Acts II–V, as Part 2. To further artic-ulate this two-part structure, Bach begins Part 1 in his early score with the chorale-chorus "Kommt, ihr Töchter" and concludes with the four-part chorale "Jesum laß ich nicht von mir." In copying out his autograph, and fi-nal, score in 1736, Bach, in addition to making minor changes in voicing and instrumentation, replaced the four-part chorale at the end of Part 1 with his concerted setting of the chorale verse, "O Mensch bewein," a movement he used earlier in his 1725 score of the John Passion. As a result of this substi-tution, the opening exordium and concluding concerted chorale serve as the outer structural pillars of Part 1. To mark off Part 2 of the liturgical structure, Bach follows a similar process, once again adding an exordium and conclud-ing with a final chorus rather than a four-part chorale.

Warranting brief mention in this context is the libretto of the Mark Passion, also compiled by Bach and Picander. Although composer and librettist again divide the narrative to correspond to the Actus structure,[12] the schematic de-sign of the Mark libretto includes only one aria text in each act and no

Table 7.5. Schematic outline of Matthew Passion Libretto

Nr of units	1	2	3	4	5	6	7
Exordium							
Vorbereitung Mt 26: 1–35	N+Cl	N+Acc R+ Aria	N+Aria	N+Cl	N+Acc R +Aria	N+Cl	N+Cl
Act I Hortus Mt 26: 36–56	N+Acc R +Aria	N+Acc R +Aria	N+Cl	N+Aria+Cs	N+Cl		
Exordium							
Act II Pontifices Mt 26: 57–75	N+Cl	N+Acc R +Aria	N+Cl	N+Aria+Cl			
Act III Pilatus Mt 27: 1–30	N+Aria	N+Cl	N+Cl	N+AccR +Aria	N+AccR +Aria	N+Cl	
Act IV Crux Mt 27: 31–50	N+Acc R +Aria	N+Acc R +Aria	N+Cl				
Act V Sepulchrum Mt 27: 51–66	N+Acc R +Aria	N+Acc R +Cs					

accompanied recitatives. The absence of the latter may be due to Bach's use of parody procedures, that is, by his choosing arias composed earlier to be given new texts by Picander. Furthermore, Bach limits his schematic units to two types, namely, N+Aria, and N+Cl. Of the 24 interpolations, 16 are chorale verses.[13] In short, for Bach's third, and only, parody passion setting, he and Picander designed a libretto based on the same principles as the Matthew libretto, but in a simplified and drastically reduced form.

Finally, we consider the role of the Actus structure in the so-called "Keiser" Mark Passion, a score Bach first performed in Weimar between 1711 and 1714, and then reperformed as a two-part work in 1726 in Leipzig. Yet another pasticcio version of the passion with movements drawn from Handel's Brockes Passion was performed by Bach in the 1740s. But before turning to these works, we look first at a text that I propose was central to Bach's use of the Actus structure, namely, Barthold Brockes's "Die für die Sünde der Welt leidende und sterbende Jesus." Published in 1712, the libretto takes the form not of a liturgical passion whose narrative is based directly on the biblical text, such as the John and Matthew librettos. Rather, Brockes's narrative, as is typical of an oratorio-type passion, takes the form of a poetic paraphrase of the biblical texts, based primarily on Matthew's account. Although its sequence of secco recitatives, accompanied recitatives, arias, and choruses, does not follow as schematic a structure as Bach's settings, Brockes's "poetic" narrative uses as its overall framework the Actus structure, albeit in the form of Luther (see table 7.1), beginning with the Abendmal (vs. 17), but ending with the Crucifixion. Further, he adds at the end of each act a chorale verse that he describes as a "Choral der Christlichen Kirche" (Chorale of the Christian church). In short: in Brockes's structuring of his libretto to correspond to the Actus structure and his inclusion of a chorale to mark the end of each act, we see evidence of the procedures that Bach will employ in designing the libretti of his own liturgical passions, as well as in his performances of the "Keiser" Mark Passion.[14]

As Daniel Melamed points out, the libretto of the Mark Passion that Bach had at his disposal in Weimar included several additions to the original 1707 text, set by a composer whose identity remains unknown.[15] As shown in table 7.6, the post-1707 additions included three Sinfonias that separate the four main sections of the text from one another, namely Acts I–II and Act III (the Vorbereitung portion of Mark's narrative is omitted), Acts III and IV, and Acts IV and V. Also added at the end of Act IV is a chorale verse ("Wenn ich einmal") set not in four parts but for a solo voice and obbligato continuo. To these additions, Bach adds two four-part chorales, whose purpose, I propose, is to bring the libretto into greater conformity with the Actus structure shown in table 7.6. Bach appears to have been content to follow conventional practice

Table 7.6. Division of Narrative in 1707 Text of Mark Passion and in Weimar and Leipzig Performances by Bach

Division	1707 interpolations*	Post-1707 additions	Weimar additions	1726 Leipzig additions
Actus Structure				
Exordium				Part 1
Acts I–II.				
Hortus				
Pontifices				
Mk 14: 26–72	Aria: Wein, ach wein			Cl: So gehst du nun
		Sinfonia		Part 2
Act III				
Pilatus				
Mk 15: 1–14	[no interpolation]		Cl: O hilf, Christe	Cl: O hilf Christe
		Sinfonia		
Act IV				
Crux				
Mk 15: 15–37	Aria: Seht			
	Menschen Kinder	Cl: Wenn ich einmal		
		Sinfonia		
Act V				
Sepulchrum				
Mk 15: 38–47	Cs: O Seelig ist zu			
	dieser Frist		Cl: O Traurigkeit	Cl: O Traurigkeit

*Included are only the interpolations that appear at the end of each section of text

in allowing the aria portraying Peter's lament at his betrayal of Jesus, based on the chorale text ("Wein ach wein"), to conclude Acts I–II, and the solo chorale setting to conclude Act IV. But by adding "O hilf uns, Christe, Gottes Sohn" at the end of the narrative in Act III (Pilatus) and inserting the first verse of the chorale "O Traurigkeit" immediately after the narrative that ends Act V, he makes certain that four-part chorales mark the ends of the narratives in Acts III and V.

In reperforming the Mark score in 1726 and adapting it to the two-part liturgical form required for Leipzig practice, he retains the two chorales and, in addition, adds another chorale verse to the score, "So gehst du nun, mein Jesus hin" to conclude Part 1.[16] With the addition of this chorale, Bach's 1726 Mark performance score includes a four-part chorale setting at the end of each major division in the narrative, a pattern identical to those we saw in the Brockes libretto as well as in Bach's Matthew and John Passions. In the pasticcio version of the Keiser score Bach performed in Leipzig in the 1740s, with interpolations from Handel's *Brockes Passion*, Bach retains the chorales added for the Weimar, but not for the 1726 Leipzig, performance.[17]

In summary: To view the libretto of Bach's Matthew Passion in terms of its Actus structure reveals the presence of an "embedded" series of six acts. Identifying and describing each of the acts exposes a schematic design that sheds light on the process by which Bach compiled the librettos of his Leipzig liturgical passions, as well as the ways in which he adapted the "Keiser" Mark Passion for performance in Weimar and Leipzig. To what extent the Actus structure plays a role in the other passions Bach may have performed in the 1740s warrants further study. That Carl Phillip Emanuel employed the structure in his Hamburg Matthew settings in the form used by his father can be seen in his divisions of the narrative as well as in his placement of the chorales and interpolated poetic texts.[18]

NOTES

1. Martin Petzoldt, "Passionspredigt und Passionsmusik der Bachzeit," in *Johann Sebastian Bach, Matthäus Passion, BWV 244: Vorträge der Sommerakademie J. S. Bach 1985*, ed. Ulrich Prinz (Kassel: Bärenreiter, 1990), 8–23. In his text, Petzoldt outlines the Actus structure for each of Bach's three passions, including his placement of a chorale (or chorus) at the end of each act.

2. Christoph Scheibler, *Aurifodina Theologica: Oder, Theologische und geistliche Goldgrube/Das ist/Teutsche Theologica Practica* (Frankfurt am Main, 1664). A second edition of the volume was published in Leipzig in 1727, with a preface by Johann Gottlob Pfeiffer, professor of theology at the University of Leipzig. It is likely that Bach was aware of the new edition, as the Leipzig Superintendent made a point of recommending it to his congregations.

3. Abraham Calov, *Die heilige Bibel nach S. Herrn D. Martini Lutheri Deutscher Dolmetschung und Erklärung*, 3 vols. (Wittenberg, 1681–1682).

4. The text of the passion narrative in the "Historia des Leidens," the appendix to the Dresden Gesangbuch, adheres to the divisions noted by Luther: chapter 26: Vorbereitung, vs. 1–29; Act I, vs. 30–56; Act II, vs. 57–75; chapter 27: Act III, vs. 1–31; and the final section, vs. 32–66. It also includes references to the comparable passages in the passion narratives of the other three Gospels. This "composite" version of the passion story dates to the *Passions-Harmonie* of Johannes Bugenhagen, a colleague and student of Luther.

5. Johannes Olearius, *Biblische Erklärung: Darinnen, nechst dem allgemeinen Haupt-Schlüssel der gantzen heiligen Schrifft*, 5 vols. (Leipzig, 1678–1681).

6. For a discussion of the procedures by which Bach compiled his libretto for Cantata 67, see Don O. Franklin, "'Recht Glauben, Christlich Leben, Seelig Sterben:' Johann Olearius and Johann Sebastian Bach," in *Die Quellen Johann Sebastian Bachs: Bachs Musik im Gottesdienst; Bericht über das Symposium 4.–8. Oktober 1995 in der Internationalen Bachakademie Stuttgart* (Heidelberg: Manutius Verlag, 1998), 229–48.

7. Calov's list of episodes for chapter 26, for example, lists only the three major divisions shown in table 7.1: "(I.) Was vor dem Leiden Christi hergegangen, als wie er dasselbe verkündiget . . . v. 29; (II.) Bey dem Ausgang an den Oelberg wider der Jünger Aergernis/ . . . v. 45; (III.) Drauff kömpt Judas mit der Schar . . . v. 75."

8. My thanks to Michael Marissen for permission to use his English translation of the German text from his forthcoming publication: "The Parallel German-English Texts of Bach's Oratorios, with Annotations." Also see his contribution to this volume titled "Historically Informed Rendering of the Librettos from Bach's Church Cantatas."

9. Elke Axmacher, *"Aus Liebe will mein Heyland sterben," Untersuchungen zum Wandel des Passionsverständnisses im frühen 18. Jahrhundert*, Beiträge zur theologischen Bachforschung, 2 (Neuhausen-Stuttgart: Hänssler-Verlag, 1984), 53–56.

10. The interpolation comes not at the end of the episode described by Olearius (I.1. (1) "das Gebete zum drittenmal wiederholet," v. 39–44), but after the first time that Jesus prays (vs. 41): ". . . so gehe dieser Kelch von mir; doch nicht wie ich will, sondern wie du willst."

11. For a discussion of the ways in which Bach derives several of his themes and divisions of his libretto from Olearius, see Don O. Franklin, "The Libretto of Bach's John Passion and the 'Doctrine of Reconciliation': An Historical Perspective," in *Proceedings of the Royal Netherlands Academy of Arts and Sciences*, ed. A. A. Clement, vol. 143 (1995), 179–203.

12. For an outline of the division of Mark's narrative into six acts, see Petzoldt, 17.

13. The schematic outline of Bach's Mark Passion, excluding the opening chorus and aria that function as the exordia for Parts 1 and 2, can be summarized as follows: Vorbereitung: N+Cl, N+Cl, N+Cl, N+Aria; Act I: N+Cl, N+Cl, N+Cl, N+Aria, N+Aria, N+Cl, N+Cl; Act II: N+Cl, N+Cl, N+Cl, N+Cl; Act III: N+Aria, N+Cl; Act IV: N+Cl, N+Cl, N+Aria, N+Cl; Act V: N+Cs.

14. The setting of the Brockes text most likely familiar to Bach was that of Reinhard Keiser, published in 1712. That Bach retained an interest in the Brockes text throughout his lifetime can be seen by his drawing on the libretto as the source for his poetic texts in both the John and Matthew Passions and, at the end of his life, copying out Handel's setting of the libretto, a score on which he drew in compiling his 1740s pasticcio score. See note 16.

15. See Daniel R. Melamed, *Hearing Bach's Passions* (New York: Oxford University Press, 2005), 78–87, and table 5.1. See also Daniel R. Melamed and Reginald L. Sanders, "Zum Text und Kontext der 'Keiser'-Markuspassion," *Bach-Jahrbuch* 85 (1999): 35–50.

16. For a discussion of Bach's addition of chorales to the two scores, see Kirsten Beißwenger, *Johann Sebastian Bachs Notenbibliothek*, Catalogus Musicus, 13 (Kassel: Bärenreiter, 1992), 170–78. See also Melamed, *Hearing*, 87–91.

17. In the pasticcio, Bach substituted Handel's aria "Wisch ab der Tränen" for the chorale verse "O Traurigkeit." For a discussion of Bach's pasticcio passion, see Beißwenger, 178–90. See also her essay "Markus-Passion. Passions-Pasticcio nach Reinhard Keiser und Georg Friedrich Handel," *69. Bach-Fest Leipzig, 30. März bis 5. April 1994*, 110–15 [Bach-Fest-Buch], and Melamed, *Hearing*, 91–94.

18. See Don O. Franklin, "Carl Philipp Emanuel Bach's 1789 Matthew Passion as Pasticcio and Parody," in *Passion, Affekt und Leidenschaft in der frühen Neuzeit*, Wolfenbütteler Arbeiten zu Barockforschung, 43, ed. J. A. Steiger, in collaboration with Ralf Georg Bogner, Ulrich Heinen, Renate Steiger, Melvin Unger, and Helen

Watanabe-O'Kelly (Wiesbaden: Harrassowitz, 2005), 637–54. Because Hamburg restricted the scope of its Matthew Passion settings to the portion of the narrative that begins after the Vorbereitung and concludes before Act V, Emanuel's libretto commences with Act I. But in contrast to his predecessor, Georg Philipp Telemann, the narrative begins not with vs. 30, as Luther, but, following Olearius's division, with vs. 36. Unlike the libretti of Sebastian and Emanuel, Telemann's passion texts give little indication of conforming to the Actus structure.

8

Two Unusual Cues in J. S. Bach's Performing Parts

Daniel R. Melamed

J. S. Bach's contact with an anonymous *St. Mark Passion*—a work he attributed to Reinhard Keiser but whose authorship is open to question—spanned more than thirty years.[1] Bach's performance of the piece is documented in three sets of parts that tell us a great deal about his practices in presenting passion music and about his adaptation of a borrowed work to fit local requirements.[2] But these parts also offer evidence of two kinds we rarely find in the surviving Bach materials: cues evidently entered by a performer in the course of the parts' practical use, and instructions within one part that its user should refer to another part for necessary music.

PITCH CUES

The oldest layer of material for the *St. Mark Passion* is a nearly complete set of performing parts dating from the years Bach worked in Weimar. The vocal material in this set consists of four vocal parts, one in each range, that contain all the sung music in the passion. The alto part contains pitch cues at the beginning of almost every movement in which that voice participates. The cues supply the tonic of the movement or the local cadence point in a recitative, and were presumably meant to help the singer find his starting note (see figure 8.1 and table 8.1).

There is no cue for the chorale "O hilf, Christe" that Bach evidently added to the passion setting. This movement may not have been clearly represented in the material from which the annotator worked. There is a cue, though, for the other chorale evidently added by Bach, "O Traurigkeit"; this cue also

**Figure 8.1. J. S. Bach's Weimar-era alto part for the anony-
mous *St. Mark Passion* with inserted pitch cues at the beginning of each movement. D-B Mus. ms. 11471/1**

serves for the original setting of its last two stanzas, "O selig ist" that immediately follows it. It is not clear why there is no cue for the alto aria "Was seh
ich hier?" unless the annotator simply could not believe that the movement is
really in B♭ minor.

The cues appear to be in a different hand from the rest of the part, the first
portion of which was copied by the scribe known as Anon. Weimar 1 and the
remainder by J. S. Bach. The hand that entered the cues is not identifiable but
does not appear to be Bach's. The placement of the cues suggests that they
were entered after the part was copied; the harmonic information they supply
implies that the person who entered them had access to a score or at least a
basso continuo part.

There are no pitch cues in any of the other vocal parts; taken together, the
evidence hints that the cues were added by the alto himself, whoever he was.
Three altos from the Weimar chapel during Bach's tenure are known by name
and little else—Bluhnitz, Graf, and Bernhardi—and each is presumably a
candidate for having entered the cues.[3] But it is worth remembering that we
do not know when or where Bach performed this passion setting or whether
his regular court singers participated.

It is not difficult to see why a singer might add cues, especially in a complex work like a passion with its many vocal entrances. It does not appear to

**Table 8.1. Pitch Cues in J. S. Bach's Weimar-Era Alto Part
for an Anonymous *St. Mark Passion***

Alto entrance point	Cue in part	Key of movement/cadence
Sinfonia/Chorus "Jesus Christus ist um unser Missetat willen verwundet"	G	g
Chorale "Was mein Gott will"	A	a
"Welchen ich küssen werde"	F	F (recit cadence)
"Wir haben gehöret, daß er saget"	G	G/B♭
"Antwortest du nichts zu dem"	D	D (recit cadence)
"Bist du Christus"	C	C (recit cadence)
"Was dürfen wir weiter Zeugnis"	D	D (recit cadence)
"Weissage uns"	C	C
"Wahrlich du bist einer"	B	B♭
Aria "Klaget nur"	dis	E♭
"Kreuzige ihn"	B	B♭
"Kreuzige ihn"	D	d
Chorale "O hilf, Christe"	[ ]	D
"Gegrüßet seist du"	F	F
Aria "Was seh ich hier?"	[ ]	b♭
"Pfui dich"	B	B♭
"Et hat andern geholfen"	A	a
"Siehe, er rufet den Elias"	G	g
"Halt! Lasst sehen"	A	A
Chorale "Wenn ich einmal soll scheiden"	B	B♭
"Wahrlich dieser ist Gottes Sohn gewesen"	G	G
Aria "Dein Jesus hat das Haupt geneiget"	G	g
Chorale "O Traurigkeit"/"O selig ist"	G	g

have been the practice—or indeed the prerogative—of singers in Bach's time to mark parts with pitch cues or anything else. The unknown alto singer who used this part under Bach in the 1710s nonetheless apparently felt he needed them, and left us rare documentation of a part's practical use.

A CUE TO REFER TO ANOTHER PART

When Bach performed the *St. Mark Passion* in 1726 in Leipzig he prepared a new set of vocal and instrumental parts. Only a few survive from this performance but the others must have existed because Bach's revisions to the work made the older ones unusable. Bach changed relatively few movements compared to the version he had performed in his Weimar years, but he did redistribute vocal duties. In Bach's Weimar-era material, the four vocal parts account for all the dramatic roles: the soprano includes the part for the maid; the alto includes Judas, the High Priest, a soldier, and a centurion; the tenor

**Table 8.2.   J. S. Bach's Distribution of Roles
in Two Sets of Parts for the *St. Mark Passion***

Part	Roles included
c. 1711–1714	
Soprano	Maid
Alto	Judas, High Priest, captain, soldier
Tenore Evangelista	Evangelist, Peter, Pilate
Bassus Jesus	Jesus
1726	
Soprano	Maid
Alto	captain, soldier
Tenore Evang	Evangelist
Basso Jesus	Jesus
Tenore Petrus et Pilatus	Peter, Pilate
[Alto	Judas, Caiphas] (missing)

includes the Evangelist, Peter, and Pilate; and the bass part includes the music for Jesus (see table 8.2). It is thus likely that the work was performed in those years by exactly four singers.

In Leipzig Bach could evidently count on more singers for the annual passion performance and so distributed the roles among more than four people. The surviving material from 1726 includes four principal vocal parts copied by Johann Heinrich Bach with text entered by Johann Sebastian himself. As in the Weimar-era parts, the soprano part includes the maid, and the bass part contains Jesus. Bach removed the music for Peter and Pilate (along with one aria for Peter) from the principal tenor part to an additional part marked "Tenore Petrus et Pilatus." The situation is complicated because some of this material was also entered in the main part but then bracketed. We cannot be certain whether this was the result of a misunderstanding between Bach and his copyist that was fixed immediately, or whether it represents two stages (and perhaps two performances). But either in 1726 or shortly thereafter, Bach assigned the tenor-range music to two distinct singers by dividing it between two parts.

Something similar must have happened with the alto-range music. The 1726 principal alto part includes the centurion's and the soldier's music, as did the Weimar-era part, but lacks the larger roles of Judas and Caiphas. This music was presumably extracted to another part now lost, either to one dedicated to these roles (perhaps called something like "Alto Judas et Caiphas" by analogy to the extra tenor part) or to a hypothetical alto ripieno part if Bach employed ripieno singers, as seems likely. In 1726 the music of Judas and Caiphas was thus sung by some singer other than the alto concertist who used the principal part.

But there is a curious feature of that part not found anywhere else in the Bach materials. During one long rest and one movement marked "tacet" for this singer there are clear references, evidently in Bach's hand, identifying the characters Judas and Caiphas who sing in these places (see figure 8.2). This is puzzling because the music for these roles is *not* present in the part, as we have seen, and there is no reason why the singer using the part would need to know about these roles sung by someone else. There are no other such entries in any of Bach's other passion parts—that is, no cues for small roles whose music is not present.

Why did Bach do this? If the principal alto part was intended for one person, as seems likely, it is hard to see why its singer would need to know that the small roles, which were not his responsibility, were to be sung at these moments. If the part had been intended for use by more than one singer (as has sometimes been proposed) there would have been little point in removing the music for Judas and for Caiphas in the first place. The best explanation is that the entries, evidently made after the part was copied, represent instructions to its user to refer to another part and to sing the roles of Judas and Caiphas in addition to the material in the principal part.

Figure 8.2. J. S. Bach's 1726 alto part for the anonymous *St. Mark Passion* showing Bach's inserted cues for "Judas" (3rd staff) and for "Caiphas" (bottom staff). D-B Mus. ms. 11471/1

We do not know exactly when this took place. The four principal vocal parts for the *St. Mark Passion* date from 1726, but because the set is incomplete and because it is not possible to date some features (like these cues) exactly, it is possible that they were reused sometime in the 1730s. That could mean, for example, that Bach separated the roles of Judas and Caiphas in 1726 but in some later performance required the alto concertist to sing both from the principal part and from that for Judas and Caiphas, which functioned as an insert in the main part.

In any event we have a rare documented performance under Bach in which we probably have to reckon with *fewer* singers than the total number of performing parts. We also have apparently unique cues in Bach's performing parts that refer a singer to another part for music for which he was responsible. Bach was clearly capable of indicating this in exceptional situations that required it.

NOTES

1. The most important studies of the *St. Mark Passion* are Alfred Dürr, "Zu den verschollenen Passionen Bachs," *Bach-Jahrbuch* 38 (1949/50): 81–99; Andreas Glöckner, "Johann Sebastian Bachs Aufführungen zeitgenössischer Passionsmusiken," *Bach-Jahrbuch* 63 (1977): 75–119; and Kirsten Beißwenger, *Johann Sebastian Bachs Notenbibliothek*, Catalogus Musicus, 13 (Kassel: Bärenreiter, 1992). Some new information on the origin of the work can be found in Daniel R. Melamed and Reginald L. Sanders, "Zum Text und Kontext der 'Keiser'-Markuspassion," *Bach-Jahrbuch* 85 (1999): 35–50, and a study of his latest performance of the work in Daniel R. Melamed, "Bachs Aufführung der Hamburger Markus-Passion in den 1740er Jahren," in *Bach in Leipzig—Bach und Leipzig. Konferenzbericht Leipzig 2000*, ed. Ulrich Leisinger, Leipziger Beiträge zur Bach-Forschung, 5 (Hildesheim: Olms, 2002), 289–308.

2. Bach's performing materials are held by the Staatsbibliothek zu Berlin/Stiftung Preußischer Kulturbesitz, Musikabteilung mit Mendelssohn-Archiv, Mus. ms. 11471/1 and N. Mus. ms. 468, and some material in private possession. Modern editions are Felix Schroeder's (Stuttgart: Hänssler-Verlag, 1967), a problematic mixture of Bach's Weimar-era and 1726 versions; and Hans Bergmann's (Stuttgart: Carus-Verlag, 1997), which presents the Weimar-era version.

3. *Bach-Dokumente*, vol. II, ed. Werner Neumann and Hans-Joachim Schulze (Kassel: Bärenreiter, 1969), pp. 55, 63.

9

Johann Sebastian Bach and the Praise of God: Some Thoughts on the *Canon Triplex* (BWV 1076)[1]

Albert Clement

> But the things theologians and musicians learned on earth they will also practice in heaven, that is, to praise God.[2]

THE IMAGE OF BACH

It is with good reason that Robin A. Leaver quotes the words above, by the influential German music theorist Johann Mattheson, at the beginning of his fine study *Music as Preaching: Bach, Passions and Music in Worship*, for Mattheson's statement summarizes a principal thought that was generally shared by German musicians of his time. This is especially true of Bach. While the influential twentieth-century musicologist Friedrich Blume tried to convince his audience in the sixties that the image of Bach, "der schöpferische Diener am Wort, der eherne Bekenner des Luthertums" (the creative servant of the Word, the former confessor of Lutheranism), actually had to be considered as a legend,[3] we now know that the opposite is true. Clear evidence is supplied by the rediscovered Bible commentary once owned by Bach: *J.N.J. Die Heilige Bibel nach S. Herrn D. MARTINI LUTHERI*, edited in three large volumes by the Wittenberg theologian Abraham Calov. These volumes contain, among other things, marginal comments in Bach's hand, and their rediscovery is, therefore, of immense importance to Bach scholars to the present day.

The evidence concerning Bach's faith as contained in the Calov Bible commentary was made widely available in the "Bach year" 1985 by Robin A. Leaver, who published an edition containing facsimiles of many of the comments and other markings in the volumes.[4] It was not clear by that time—the preface of Leaver's edition is dated 25 January 1985—whether *all* underlinings and markings in the three volumes were made by Bach. In the same year, however, Howard H. Cox argued that all comments, corrections, underlinings, and other markings in the volumes were indeed made by one and the same person, namely Bach.[5]

The rediscovered Bible commentary provided additional proof regarding Bach's faith and his position concerning music. Christoph Trautmann was one of the first authors who, by specifically referring to the Calov commentary, pointed out that Blume's image of Bach was wrong.[6] However, even if the number of explicit theological utterances by Bach found in other sources may be modest,[7] there are still very well-known examples today—of which some should, in fact, also have been clear to Blume—of Bach testifying to the aim "he pursued throughout his life, as can be documented from his own writing."[8] Leaver summarizes a number of such examples, including the following ones, making clear that this aim was to dedicate his creative work—both composition and performance—"to the greater glory of God":[9]

- At the end of many of Bach's manuscripts, including copies he made of other composers' works, we find the abbreviation *S.D.G.* (*Soli Deo Gloria*) or similar ascriptions (such as *S.D.Gl.*, *D.S.G.*, *D.S.Gl.*);[10]
- Bach's request, dated 25 June 1708, for dismissal from his post as organist of the Blasiuskirche in Mühlhausen made it clear that his "Endzweck" (ultimate goal) was "eine *regulirte* kirchen *music* zu Gottes Ehren" (a well-regulated church music to the glory of God);[11]
- The title page (perhaps dating from sometime after 1720) of Bach's *Orgelbüchlein* contains the dedication:

  Dem Höchsten Gott allein zu Ehren, Dem Nechsten, draus sich zu belehren.[12]

  [To the glory of God on high alone and for my fellow man to learn from it.]

- Alongside Calov's comments on Exodus 15:20, Bach wrote the marginal note "NB. Erstes Vorspiel auf 2 Chören zur Ehre Gottes zu musiciren" (NB. First prelude for 2 choirs to be performed for the glory of God). Calov's comments read as follows:

  Es haben hier aber Mirjam und die andern Israelitischen Weiber nicht ein neues Lied angestimmet und gesungen / sondern was Moses mit den Israelitischen Männern ihnen vorgesungen / gleich als in einen *Echo* nachgesungen / wie aus ihrem *Responsorio* im Anfang des Danckliedes zu sehen;

und muß eine gewaltige Weise / und mächtiger Schall und Wiederschall von diesen zweyen Choren gewesen seyn / da so viel hunderttausend Männer / und nicht minder an der Zahl Weiber und Kinder zusammen gesetzt / und gesungen haben. Wird auch wol nicht leicht jemals ein solcher starcker Freuden=Gesang erschollen seyn / auff Erden / ohne von den Engeln GOttes bey der Geburth Meßiae unsers Heylandes Luc. II.13.

[However, Miriam and the other Israelite women did not intone and sing a new song here, but they performed an immediate *echo* of what Moses and the men of Israel had sung to them, which is evident from the *response* at the beginning of their song; and a mighty melody and a tremendous resonance and reverberation there must have been between these two choruses, where so many hundred thousand men, and no fewer women and children, joined in song. It is also, indeed, not insignificant that such a powerful song of joy resounded on earth from the angels of God at the birth of the Messiah, our Savior Luke 2:13.]

Leaver suggests that the reference to the music of the Christmas angels might imply that Bach's marginal note refers to (settings of) the *Gloria in excelsis Deo*, and he refers to Trautmann, who thought that Bach probably used the word "Vorspiel" in the sense of antiphonal, multichoral performance.[13] Leaver carefully concludes his discussion of Bach's marginal note by indicating that it also may simply be a general comment on the beginning of antiphonal music.[14]

As a teacher, Bach endorsed the following definition by Friedrich Erhardt Niedt:

Der General Bass ist das vollkommste *Fundament* der *Music* welcher mit beyden Händen gespielet wird dergestalt . . . damit dieses eine wohlklingende *Harmonie* gebe zur Ehre Gottes und zulässiger Ergötzung des Gemüths und soll wie aller *Music*, also auch des General *Basses Finis* und End Uhrsache anders nicht, als nur zu Gottes Ehre und *Recreation* des Gemüths seyn. Wo dieses nicht in Acht genommen wird da ists keine eigentliche *Music* sondern ein Teuflisches Geplerr und Geleyer.[15]

[The figured bass is the most complete foundation of music which is played with both hands in such a way . . . that the result is a well-sounding harmony to the glory of God and justifiable gratification of the senses; for the sole end and aim of all music, as well as that of the figured bass, should be nothing else than for the glory of God and pleasant recreation of the mind. Where this is not kept in view, there can be no true music but only a devilish scraping and bawling.]

This overview could easily be extended by much other written evidence— such as Bach's practice to head manuscripts with "*J.J.*" (*Jesu* Juva—Jesus, help me) demonstrating his "specifically Christian understanding of human creativity under the grace of God,"[16] as well as biographical facts—such as Bach receiving the Lord's Supper at home, shortly before his death,[17] from the Leipzig minister Christoph Wolle—but it may be sufficient to demonstrate Bach's attitude as a musician. It is clear that Bach testified again and again to the dedication of his work to the glory of God and that *Soli Deo Gloria* was his lifelong motto.

HAUßMANN'S IMAGE OF BACH

Being aware of the fact that Bach's music, writings, and biographical circumstances all lead to one and the same conclusion, namely that he pursued praise and thanksgiving to God throughout his life—also apparent from the fact that the Psalms were a constant source of inspiration to him,[18] the question arises whether this image of Bach coincides with the image that Bach actually wanted to portray to his audience, i.e., the tangible image of Bach depicted in his official capacity as a musician. Such an image exists: it is the famous oil painting by the Leipzig portraitist Elias Gottlob Haußmann (1695–1774), of which two versions survived: one dating from 1746 (Historisches Museum der Stadt Leipzig) and one from 1748 (William H. Scheide Library, Princeton). On the excellently preserved replica of 1748 the countenance is more expressive and the music on the sheet in Bach's hand clearer than on the portrait of 1746.[19]

The early history of the painting is unknown. It has been repeatedly suggested that there might be some connection with Bach joining Mizler's *Correspondirende Societät der musikalischen Wissenschaften* as its fourteenth member in June 1747 (see below). In 1746 the society's statute decrees (article XXI):

> Auch soll ein iedes Mitglied sein Bildniß, gut auf Leinwand gemalet, nach seiner Bequemlichkeit, zur Bibliothek einschicken, woselbst es zum Andenken wohl aufbehalten, und seinem Lebenslaufe, wenn solcher in den Schriften der Societät erzählet wird, in Kupfer gestochen vorgesetzet werden.[20]

> [Also, every member should, whenever possible, send a picture of himself— well painted on canvas—to the library, where it will be well kept in his memory and will be added as an engraving to his biography when this is related in the society's publications.]

This is a likely connection, since the triple canon shown to the onlooker is identical with the "dreyfache Kreisfuge mit sechs Stimmen" (threefold circular fugue in six parts),[21] which Bach submitted to the Society in 1747. There is nothing, however, to prove the theory that the portrait was painted for Bach's joining Mizler's Society; there are no portraits of other members available for comparison, and nothing is known about the fate of such paintings after the Society's dissolution.[22] Yet it is certain that the portrait belongs to the iconographic *Amtsbild* genre.[23] Already in 1976, Christoph Wolff noted:

> Zahlreiche Komponisten wurden in ähnlicher Weise dargestellt mit den Insignien ihres Amtes, einer Notenrolle oder einem Notenblatt (sehr häufig einen Kanon enthaltend, so etwa Scheidt auf dem Titelblatt seiner *Tabulatura Nova*, Hamburg 1624, oder Spieß auf dem Titelblatt seines *Tractatus Musicus Compositorio-practicus*, Augsburg 1745).[24]

> [Many composers were portrayed in a similar way, with the tools of their trade, a roll or sheet of music (often showing a canon; e.g., Scheidt on the frontispiece of his *Tabulatura Nova*, Hamburg 1624, or Spieß on the title page of his *Tractatus Musicus Compositorio-practicus*, Augsburg 1745).]

Bach is also represented as a "learned" musician, showing the spectator an enigmatic canon. If this piece was to demonstrate his status, then the obvious question is: of all the compositions Bach could have chosen, why did he select this one? In order to answer this question, it is necessary to focus on the canon.

THE *CANON TRIPLEX* IN MODERN LITERATURE

Apart from the fact that Bach chose the *Canon triplex à 6 Voc.* (BWV 1076) to show to the spectator of the Haußmann painting, the piece occupies a very special place in his canonic œuvre: it is the only triple canon he ever wrote. Moreover, together with his canonic organ composition *Einige canonische Veränderungen über das Weynacht-Lied: Vom Himmel hoch da komm ich her* (BWV 769), it is the only piece that Bach submitted to Mizler's Society (see above), as is testified in the *Denkmal* that appeared in vol. 4 of Mizler's *Musikalische Bibliothek*:

> Unser seel. Bach ließ sich zwar nicht in tiefe theoretische Betrachtungen der Musik ein, war aber desto stärcker in der Ausübung. Zur Societät hat er den Choral geliefert: Von Himmel hoch da komm' ich her, vollständig ausgearbeitet, der hernach in Kupfer gestochen worden. Er hat auch den Tab. IV.f.16. abgestochenen Canon, solcher gleichfalls vorgeleget, und würde offenbar noch viel mehr gethan haben, wenn ihn nicht die kurze Zeit, indem er nur drey Jahre in solcher gewesen, davon abgehalten hätte.[25]

> [Although our late Bach did not enter into deep theoretical reflections on music, he was all the stronger in its practical application. For the society he supplied the

chorale Vom Himmel hoch da komm' ich her, completely worked out, which
was subsequently engraved. He also submitted the canon shown in Tab, IV,f,16,,
and would obviously have done tar more still, if not the shortness of time—he
was only a member for three years—would have prevented him from doing so.]

Bach scholars have tried to explain the enigmatic character of the canon in
several ways. In 1950, Friedrich Smend devoted a study to BWV 1076 in
which he interpreted the canon using *gematria*. It was, in fact, the Dutch pi-
anist Henk Dieben who had drawn Smend's attention to *gematria* relating to
Bach in 1942, but this was never mentioned by Smend.[26] In his study, *Johann
Sebastian Bach bei seinem Namen gerufen*,[27] Smend suggested that certain
groups of notes (according to his own resolution of the canon) corresponded
with the names of "J. S. BACH" and "G. F. HAENDEL," which were "hidden" in the enigmatic composition.[28] However, Smend's interpretations were
with good reason dismissed by later scholars, and his resolution of the canon
was rejected.[29]

After Smend's publication some new facts on the history of BWV 1076
were revealed. In 1966 Leopold Nowak announced the discovery of a second
copy of the original print.[30] This was the sheet that Meinrad Spieß took from
the Society's fifth circular.[31] The 1747 print was most likely intended, in the
first place, for the members of the learned Society.[32]

When in 1974 the fourteen canons BWV 1087 were discovered in Bach's
own copy of the *Goldberg Variations*, there called "Verschiedene *Canones*
über die ersteren acht *Fundamental=Noten* vorheriger Arie" (Various canons
on the first eight fundamental notes of the preceding aria), BWV 1076 appeared in a new light.[33] There is speculation that the fourteen canons might
have been originally intended as a contribution for the Society, but that Bach
then replaced them with the masterly *Canonic Variations*.[34] Wolff, for instance, wrote in 1976: "Actually, the thematic relationship between the two
works suggests that the idea to elaborate the Christmas cantus firmus originated as an afterthought in connection with the fourteen canons."[35] The fact
that the number 14 ($14 = 2 + 1 + 3 + 8 = B + A + C + H$) represents Bach's
name within this context has not escaped scholarly attention.[36]

More recently, Matthias Wendt published a short study on BWV 1076, in
which he also mentions that the number of the fourteen canons is the equiva-
lent of B+A+C+H, and that Bach also was—thus not coincidentally—the
fourteenth member to join Mizler's Society.[37] Those suggestions are not new,
nor is his idea that Bach may originally have intended BWV 1087 for the Society, but his own statement that Bach would have depicted his own name "J.
S. BACH" as well as that of "C. H. GRAUN" is even weaker than Smend's

(and to some extent based on incorrect and inconsistent premises) and therefore not solid.[38]

TOWARD BACH'S IMAGE OF THE *CANON TRIPLEX*

Although the hypothesis that the fourteen canons BWV 1087 may have been meant for Mizler's Society first but were then replaced by the *Canonic Variations* (BWV 769) is conceivable, it remains unexplained why aferwards Bach still handed in one of these fourteen canons along with BWV 769. The question also arises: why specifically this canon?

There is another canon from the group of BWV 1087 that Bach later used for a special occasion. He wrote canon no. 11 in a slightly different form (BWV 1077) in the *Stammbuch* of the theology student Johann Gottfried Fulde. Bach's choice of that canon is no coincidence, for it lends itself to conveying theological significance. As a hint, the composer added the device "*Symbolum. Christus Coronabit Crucigeros.*"[39]

If Bach submitted BWV 1076 to the Societät, and, moreover, chose it for his portrait, it seems obvious that he associated a certain significance with this canon too. This significance, however, can only be uncovered if one considers the context.[40]

First, it seems important that besides BWV 1076 Bach offered a second composition to Mizler's Society: the *Canonic Variations on "Vom Himmel hoch da komm ich her"* (BWV 769). This fact is important because it connects the two compositions closely. But there are further connecting elements. A second factor is their striking thematic resemblance, also pointed out by Wolff. His idea that Bach's decision to elaborate the Christmas cantus firmus may have originated as an afterthought in connection with the fourteen canons (on the basis of their thematic relationship) must remain hypothetical; yet, the thematic resemblance between the bass line of BWV 1076 and the first line of Martin Luther's Christmas hymn is a fact (example 9.1).[41]

Example 9.1. BWV 769, Incipit of the cantus firmus; BWV 1076, Bass line

A third connecting element is that both BWV 1076 and 769 are canonic compositions. Fourth, they both have an enigmatic structure: not only BWV 1076 had to be resolved, but this is also true of BWV 769. The words "vollständig ausgearbeitet" (see quotation above) in Mizler's *Musikalische Bibliothek* have caused many misunderstandings in modern literature. They certainly do not mean that Bach resolved the canons himself, because he presented them in the way that they consequently appeared in print ("der hernach in Kupfer gestochen worden"), i.e., not in a notation ready to be used by the organist who wanted to play the variations, but with only the incipit of the *comes* in variations 1, 2, and 3, and with variation 4 printed in score (4 staves).

Still in 1787, Daniel Gottlob Türk mentioned the following ways of treating a chorale: "bald in dieser, bald in jener Stimme, bald kanonartig, per augmentationem, diminutionem, alla stretta, oder all' roverscio" (sometimes in one part, sometimes in the other, sometimes as a canon, per augmentationem, diminutionem, alla stretta, or all' roverscio), with reference to Bach's *Canonic Variations*.[42] It is clear that the author of the above-quoted remark ("der hernach . . .") in the *Musikalische Bibliothek*, Mizler himself, was thinking along the same lines as Türk and others,[43] and simply meant that Bach had completely worked out "den Choral" (the chorale) *compositionally*.[44]

Many features of BWV 769 that were of interest to Mizler's Society remained to be noticed and/or revealed by its members, including a) its plan; b) the symmetrical structure of the four canons in variations 1–4 on the one hand, and the four cantus firmus canons in variation 5 (numbered 1–4 in the orginal print!) on the other; c) the fact that all intervals from second to ninth are represented by the distances of the canonic entries if the fifth below is counted as fourth; and d) last but not least, that a relationship between music and text existed.[45] The *Correspondirende Societät* was highly interested in the relationship between language and music.[46] As I pointed out earlier, it appears that

- the first four strophes of Luther's hymn are depicted by Bach in the first four variations of BWV 769 with the free canons,
- strophes 5–12 are depicted in variation 5 by the four two-part cantus firmus canons (each part being related to one verse),
- strophe 13 is depicted by the *diminutio*, and
- strophe 14 by the *alla stretta*.[47]

In doing so, Bach was setting *14* verses (a number corresponding to the number of canons in BWV 1087 *as well as* to his membership in Mizler's Society *and* to B+A+C+H) of Luther's Christmas hymn, leaving out the 15th, final strophe, which is a doxology. Is it possible that Bach gave musical expression to the doxology with the other work he presented to the Society, namely the *Canon triplex* (figure 9.1)?

There appear to be a number of arguments in support of this suggestion. First of all, being a doxology, strophe 15 of Luther's Christmas hymn stands somewhat apart from the preceding 14 strophes (for the complete text of "Vom Himmel hoch da komm ich her," see appendix). It is, therefore, conceivable that Bach would allude to the doxology in a separate composition. Furthermore, it has already been noted that there is a striking melodic resemblance between the *soggetto* of the canon and the first melodic line of the Christmas hymn tune, that both BWV 769 and 1076 are canonic compositions, and that they both have an enigmatic structure.

However, even if BWV 1076 is related to Bach's Christmas canons from a compositional point of view (especially with the cantus firmus canons and their answer *in retrograde*), this does not explain why Bach would have chosen this very canon out of 14 in order to give it—after slight adaptation—to the Society. A comparison with the 13 other canons makes it clear that the

Figure 9.1. BWV 1076 as engraved in Mizler's *Musikalische Bibliothek,* Vol. IV/1, p. 185

canon under concern is unique in two ways: it is the only *Canon triplex*, and
at the same time also the only canon in six voices. For Bach this may have
provided the connection to strophe 15 of Luther's Christmas hymn, since the
doxology is a song of praise to the Triune God. A three-part canon is well
suited for alluding to the Trinity. Also in the works of several Renaissance
composers one finds "Trinity canons" in three parts.[48] The number of bars
noted down (printed as well as painted)—namely 3—may also point to the
Trinity, while the number of notes is *30*, and therefore an enhancement of 3.
The fugal answer in consonant intervals leads to a six-part polyphonic texture. In a sense, one might see here a connection to the six-part ending of
BWV 769, which is also a song of praise. Particularly enlightening, however,
is a comparison with another of Bach's works.

In an altogether different context Smend remarked about BWV 1076: "Die
Gruppierung ihrer sechs Stimmen finden wir nur ein einziges Mal in Bachs
Vokalwerk, da nämlich, wo die Kirche 'cum Angelis et Archangelis, cum
Thronis et Dominationibus cumque omni militia coelestis exercitus' den
Hymnus göttlicher Glorie anstimmt: *Sanctus, Sanctus, Sanctus Dominus
Deus Sabaoth. Pleni sunt coeli et terra gloria Eius*" (the grouping of its six
parts we find but once in Bach's vocal work, namely there, where the church
intones 'cum Angelis et Archangelis, cum Thronis et Dominationibus cumque
omni militia coelestis exercitus' the hymn of divine glory: *Sanctus, Sanctus,
Sanctus Dominus Deus Sabaoth. Pleni sunt coeli et terra gloria Eius*).[49] Indeed, in the *B-Minor Mass* (BWV 232) we find a remarkable resemblance in
the distribution of voices: see music example 9.2. The content of the text
shows a stunning similarity with that of strophe 15 of "Vom Himmel hoch."

Although a song of praise lends itself to a rich setting in multiple parts,[50]
the question arises whether there might be some further significance to the
six-part setting of the two above-mentioned works. Not only do they show
possible similarities in their texture and in the content of their texts, but also
both hold a special place in Bach's œuvre. The passage "Pleni sunt *coeli et
terra* gloria eius" from the Sanctus might indicate this idea. The number six
plays an important role in musical numerology. Following theorists such as
Gioseffo Zarlino and Johannes Lippius, composers of Bach's times saw the
figure six as a *signum perfectionis* in accordance with the six days of God's
perfect creation.[51] It is conceivable that also BWV 1076 refers to the praise
of God. In strophe 15 of Luther's chorale, mankind gives praise to God (lines
1 and 2) and in so doing joins the angels in their joy (lines 3 and 4)—see the
text of this strophe in the appendix. In other words, God is honored in heaven
and on earth, i.e., by his whole creation.

These thoughts on BWV 1076 do not only explain a further connection between the *Canon triplex* (BWV 1076) and the other composition presented to

Example 9.2. BWV 232, *Sanctus*, Incipit of the Vocal Parts

Mizler's Society by Bach, the *Canonic Variations* (BWV 769), but if the *Canon triplex* is indeed to express the doxology of Luther's Christmas hymn, this would make sense from other points of view as well.

First, the doxology of Luther's Christmas hymn corresponds with the motto preceding the Society's statute in 1746: "Gott allein die Ehre" (Honor to God alone). Mizler's learned Society saw it as the foremost task of music, that "Gott der Allmächtige damit gelobet und gepreißet wird" (the almighty God is being praised and worshipped in it).[52] Its first and foremost rule (out of thirty-two) reads as follows:

> I. Im Namen des dreyeinigen Gottes verbindet sich iedes Mitglied zu allen nach-folgenden Gesetzen, auch die musikalischen Wissenschaften, nach seinen Kräften und Umständen, bestmöglichst zur Ehre Gottes und zum Nutzen und Vergnügen des Nächsten befördern zu helfen.[53]

> [I. In the name of the Triune God, each member subscribes to the following rules and also to help the promotion of musical science as much as possible, accord-ing to one's means and circumstances, for God's honor and the benefit and en-tertainment of one's fellow man.]

It seems that if Bach wanted to apply this rule to a piece with an implied text in order to honor the Triune God, he could not have chosen a better composition than a three-fold canon (the word "canon" meaning law/rule[54]) with a text expressing glory to God as in strophe 15 of Luther's "Vom Himmel hoch."

Second, if BWV 1076 indeed refers to the above-mentioned text, it also becomes apparent why Bach chose to be depicted with it on the Haußmann portrait. Following Walter Blankenburg, Werner Braun has remarked that the canon in Bach's œuvre—although in the first place, certainly a sign of his musical genius—points beyond itself: "als Sinnbild der Unendlichkeit oder Vollkommenheit etwa wird sie [= die "gebundene Fuge"] zum theologischen Symbol" (as image of e.g., eternity or perfection it [the strict fugue] becomes a theological symbol).[55] A survey of the numerous canons found on portraits from the seventeenth and early eighteenth centuries shows that these are mostly canons with religious mottos.

An example is the engraving of Samuel Scheidt (1587–1654) mentioned above by Wolff, which was added in 1624 to the first part of his *Tabulatura nova*. The legend of Isach Caesar praises the court *Kapellmeister* as the prince of music. In front of the composer lies a four-part *Canon contrarius* with the text "*In te Domine speravi, non confundar in aeternum*" (In you, Lord, I take refuge. Let me never be put to shame)—Psalm 31:2a. Incidentally, this is the final line of the *Te Deum*, which Luther valued so highly that he saw it as a third creed besides the Apostles' and the Athanasian Creed.[56]

More interesting in this context, however, is an engraved portrait of the Württemberg court *Kapellmeister* Samuel Friedrich Capricornus [Bockshorn] (1628–1665)—see figure 9.2. It was first published in *Ander Theil geistlicher Harmonien mit 2. und 3. Stimmen wie auch 2. Violinen* (Stuttgart, 1660).[57] It shows the composer with a *Canon perpetuus à 6 Voci* on the words "*Sanctus [sanctus, sanctus,] Dominus Deus Sabbaoth.*" Capricornus was one of the most renowned Protestant South German church composers. He was the son of a Lutheran pastor and had also studied theology himself. Remarkably, the canon underneath his portrait is in six parts. It may be safely assumed that Bach, whose son Carl Philipp Emanuel famously possessed an extensive collection of paintings—Capricornus's portrait among them—was familiar with this tradition of portrait canons with religious mottos.[58] Would it not make sense, then, if in line with this tradition, the canon on the Haußmann painting would also bear a religious motto, namely an allusion to strophe 15 of Luther's Christmas hymn? In this context, one might underlie the *soggetto* with the text of the (almost identical—see above) line: "Lob, Ehr sei Gott im höchsten Thron" (Praise and glory be to God in the highest throne).

Bach could hardly have chosen a better device to be depicted with on a portrait, for this text summarizes the heart of his faith: one has to praise God in the highest throne, who gave his only son (strophe 15). The last two phrases of the doxology have to be understood in a wider meaning: the "new year"

Figure 9.2. Engraving of S. F. Capricornus by Ph. Kilian after a painting by G. N. List

signifies the new era that has begun with Christ's birth. In this light, the *Canon triplex* is, in its form as *Canon perpetuus*, an adequate allusion to eternity and to eternal worship (cf. Capricornus's canon above).[59]

In addition, it finally seems appropriate to refer to the description of the medal that was designed on the occasion of the foundation of Mizler's Society. In the *Musikalische Bibliothek*, this medal is descibed as follows:

> Ein solcher merkwürdiger Umstand in der Historie der Music hat billig verdienet mit einer Medaille verewiget zu werden, in dem zu unsern Zeiten ein neuer *periodus* der Music sich angefangen, worauf die Medaille zielet. Nemlich das nackende Kind so gegen Morgen zu hoch flieget, auf den Kopf einen klarleuchtenden Stern und in der rechten Hand eine umgekehrte brennende Fackel hat, neben welcher eine Schwalbe flieget, zeiget das Anbrechen des Tages in der Music an. Der Cirkel der durch die drey Winckel eines gleichseitigen Dreyecks gehet und die musikalischen Zahlen 1. 2. 3. 4. 5. 6. in sich hält, und um welchen Bienen fliegen, ist das Siegel der Societät der musicalischen Wissenschafften, welches den Fleis der Societät, die Musik durch die Mathematic und Weltweißheit zu verbessern, vorstellet.[60]

> [Such a remarkable circumstance in the history of music has easily deserved to be immortalized by means of a medal, as in our times a new period of music has begun, to which the medal refers. Namely, the naked child flying too high at dawn, on its head a bright shining star and in its right hand a burning torch upside down, next to which a swallow flies, indicates the beginning of the day in music. The circle that crosses the three angles of an equilateral triangle and contains the musical numbers 1, 2, 3, 4, 5, 6, with bees flying around it, is the seal of the *Societät der musicalischen Wissenschaften*, symbolizing the society's diligence in order to improve music by mathematics and common knowledge.]

A comparison of this description with the structure of the *Canon triplex* and the contents of the doxology may lead to a number of tempting analogies, such as the naked child (the child Jesus), the new period (the new year), the star (the Christmas star/the morning star), the burning torch (the light of the world), the circle (the circular canon), *three* angles/an equilateral *triangle* (the canon *triplex*), the musical numbers 1–6 (the six parts of the canon), mathematics (the extraordinary mathematical structure of BWV 1076), etc. Being aware of the fact that Bach also had a special interest in coins and medals,[61] it may seem conceivable that the combination of the *Canon triplex* with the doxology of Luther's Christmas hymn served at the same time as a tribute to the Society's principles as represented by its medal.

Walter Blankenburg wrote about Bach: "Die Devise *Soli Deo gloria* steht ausgesprochen oder unausgesprochen [!] unter allen seinen Schöpfungen" (the motto *Soli Deo gloria* stands explicitly or implicitly [!] underneath all his creations).[62] If this last suggestion is true of his *Canon triplex* BWV 1076, representing his motto *Soli Deo Gloria* in Luther's words, then this explains a) why this piece was especially apt for Mizler's Society, underlining the Society's first and foremost rule, namely to honor God in music; b) why Bach presented it together with BWV 769, proving his craftsmanship as well as his ability to give expression to words in music, and finally c) why Bach chose to be depicted with it on the Haußmann portrait: in its new version the unique *Canon triplex* BWV 1076 had become Bach's unique *Representations-Kanon*, teaching others to join him in giving praise to God, as the angels do in heaven.

APPENDIX: VOM HIMMEL HOCH DA KOMM ICH HER[63]

1. Vom himmel hoch da komm ich her,
ich bring euch gute neue mähr,
der guten mähr bring ich so viel,
davon ich singen und sagen will.

1. I come here from heaven on high
and bring you good, new tidings.
I bring so many good tidings,
of which I will sing and speak.

2. Euch ist ein kindlein heut gebohrn,
von einer jungfrau auserkohrn,
ein kindelein so zart und fein,
das soll eur freud und wonne seyn.

2. A child is born to you today
of a chosen virgin;
a baby so tender and good,
who shall be your joy and delight.

3. Es ist der Herr Christ, unser Gott,
der will euch führn aus aller noth,
er will eur Heyland selber seyn,
von allen sünden machen rein.

3. He is the Lord Christ, our God,
who wants to lead you from all misery.
He himself wants to be your Savior
to make you free from all sins.

4. Er bringt euch alle seligkeit,
die Gott der Vater hat bereit,
daß ihr mit uns im himmelreich
sollt leben nun und ewiglich.

4. He brings the salvation
which God the Father has prepared
for you all
so that you may live with us
now and forever in the kingdom of
heaven.

5. So merket nun das zeichen recht,
die krippen, windelein so schlecht,
da findet ihr das Kind gelegt,
das alle welt erhält und trägt.

5. This is the sign that you should note:
the manger and rough clothing.
There you will find the child laid,
who saves and bears the world.

6. Des laßt uns alle fröhlich seyn,
und mit den hirten gehn hinein,
zu sehen was Gott hat beschert,
und mit seinm lieben sohn verehrt.

6. Therefore let us be glad
and enter with the shepherds
to see what God has given us
in his dear, honoured Son.

7. Merk auf mein herz, und sieh
dort hin,
was liegt dort in dem krippelein?
Wes ist das schöne kindelein?
Es ist das liebe Jesulein.

7. Attend my heart and look in there.
What lies in the little manger?
Whose is the beautiful child?
It is the dear baby Jesus.

8. Bis willkommen du edler gast,
den sünder nicht verschmähet hast,
und kömmst ins elend her zu mir,
wie soll ich immer danken dir?

8. Welcome, you precious guest!
You have not despised the sinner
and come to me here in this misery.
How will I ever be able to thank
you?

9. Ach Herr, du schöpfer aller ding,
wie bist du worden so gering,
daß du da liegst auf dürrem gras,
davon ein rind und esel aß?

9. Lord, you creator of all things,
how humble you have become
that you lie there on dry grass
from which an ox and donkey have
eaten?

10. Und wär die welt vielmal so weit,
von edelstein und gold bereit,
so wär sie dir doch viel zu klein,
zu seyn ein enges wiegelein.

10. And were the world many times
as wide,
beset with precious gems and gold,
it would still be much to small
to be a narrow little crib for you.

11. Der sammet und die seiden dein
das ist grob heu und windelein,
darauf du könig so groß und reich
herprangst, als wärs dein himmelreich.

11. Coarse hay and swaddling cloths
are your velvet and silk
on which you, king so great and rich,
show off, as if it were your heavenly
kingdom.

12. Das hat also gefallen dir,
die wahrheit anzuzeigen mir,
wie aller welt macht, ehr und gut
für dir nichts gilt, nichts hilft,
noch thut.

12. You have chosen this way
to show me the truth,
that none of the world's power, glory
and goods have value before you,
and help and do nothing.

13. Ach! mein herzliebstes Jesulein,
mach dir ein rein sanft bettelein,
zu ruhn in meines herzens schrein,
daß ich nimmer vergesse dein.

14. Davon ich allzeit frölich sey,
zu springen, singen immer frey,
das rechte Susaninne schon,
mit herzenslust den süssen ton.

15. Lob, ehr sey Gott im höchsten
thron,
der uns schenkt seinen eingen Sohn,
des freuen sich der engelschaar,
und singen uns solch neues jahr.

13. O my heart's dearest baby Jesus!
Make yourself a pure, soft little bed
to rest in my heart's chamber
so that I never forget you.

14. For this I am always happy,
jumping and singing the beautiful,
true lullaby ever free,
the sweet tones with heart's desire.

15. Praise and glory be to God in the
highest throne,
who gives us his only Son.
Therefore the angel host rejoices
and sings us such a new year.

NOTES

1. This chapter is the largely extended, updated, and translated version of a notion originally expressed in my PhD dissertation (Utrecht University, 1989). I am most grateful to Sally Holman, Tassilo Erhardt, and Hans Clement (Middelburg), as well as the editor of this Festschrift, for all their help and valuable suggestions.

2. Cf. Robin A. Leaver, *Music as Preaching: Bach, Passions, and Music in Worship*, Latimer Studies, 13 (Oxford: Latimer House, 1982), 3. In his writings, Mattheson repeatedly stresses that the ultimate aim of music is the praise of God.

3. Friedrich Blume's lecture entitled "Umrisse eines neuen Bach-Bildes" was delivered at the Bachfest of the *Internationale Bach-Gesellschaft* in Mainz on 1 June 1962. It was published in *Musica* 16 (July–August 1962): 169–76, and it also appeared autonomously as *Jahresgabe 1961* [*sic*] of the *Societas Bach Internationalis* (Kassel, 1962). A reprint followed in Friedrich Blume, *Syntagma Musicologicum: Gesammelte Reden und Schriften*, ed. Martin Ruhnke (Kassel: Bärenreiter, 1963), 466–79, with a postscript by Blume (pp. 898–99).

4. Robin A. Leaver, *J. S. Bach and Scripture: Glosses from the Calov Bible Commentary* (St. Louis: Concordia Publishing House, 1985).

5. Howard H. Cox, "Tintenanalyse als neues Mittel der Bachforschung: Schrieb Bach alles, was an Eintragungen in der Calov-Bibel enthalten ist?" in *Bericht über die Wissenschaftliche Konferenz zum V. Internationale Bachfest der DDR in Verbindung mit dem 60. Bachfest der Neuen Bachgesellschaft, Leipzig, 25. bis 27. März 1985*, ed. Winfried Hoffmann and Armin Schneiderheinze (Leipzig: VEB Deutscher Verlag für Musik, 1988), 291–94.

6. Christoph Trautmann, "'Calovii Schrifften. 3. Bände' aus Johann Sebastian Bachs Nachlaß und ihre Bedeutung für das Bild des lutherischen Kantors Bach," *Musik und Kirche* 39 (1969): 145–60.

7. Ulrich Meyer, "Johann Sebastian Bachs theologische Äußerungen," *Musik und Kirche* 47 (1977): 112–18.

8. Leaver, *J. S. Bach and Scripture*, 107.

9. Ibid., 106.

10. Cf. the list given by Leaver.

11. *Bach-Dokumente*, vol. I, ed. Werner Neumann and Hans-Joachim Schulze (Kassel: Bärenreiter, 1963), no. 1, p. 19.

12. See e.g., the facsimile edition of Johann Sebastian Bach, *Orgelbüchlein, BWV 599–644: Faksimile der autographen Partitur*, ed. Heinz-Harald Löhlein, Documenta Musicologica, Zweite Reihe: Handschriften-Faksimiles, 11 (Kassel: Bärenreiter, 1981).

13. Leaver, *J. S. Bach and Scripture*, 71.

14. Ibid., 72.

15. Philipp Spitta, *Joh. Seb. Bach*, 3d ed. (Leipzig: Breitkopf und Härtel, 1921), 2:915f.

16. Leaver, *J. S. Bach and Scripture*, 53.

17. About Wolle, see, for instance, Martin Petzoldt, "Christian Weise d.Ä. und Christoph Wolle—zwei Leipziger Beichtväter Bachs," in *Bach als Ausleger der Bibel: Theologische und musikwissenschaftliche Studien zum Werk Johann Sebastian Bachs*, ed. Martin Petzoldt (Göttingen: Vandenhoeck und Ruprecht, 1985), 109–29.

18. Leaver, *J. S. Bach and Scripture*, 99.

19. Other portraits allegedly of Bach are considered doubtful. Besides the two known paintings of Bach by Haußmann, presumably there existed a third portrait of the same type, painted for Wilhelm Friedemann Bach, in possession of Johann Friedrich Reichardt in 1780 and lost since the latter's death in 1814. Whether or not the painting discovered by Teri Noel Towe in 2000 has anything to do with the third portrait by Haußmann will be a subject of further research (see Teri Noel Towe, "The Portrait of Bach that belonged to Kittel," *Tracker* 46 [October 2002]: 14–18).

20. Lorenz Christoph Mizler, *Musikalische Bibliothek*, vol. III/2 (Leipzig, 1746), 353.

21. Ibid., vol. IV/1 (Leipzig, 1754), 108.

22. See e.g., Christoph Wolff, *Kanons, Musikalisches Opfer: Kritischer Bericht*, Johann Sebastian Bach, Neue Ausgabe sämtlicher Werke, series 8, vol.1 (Kassel: Bärenreiter, 1976), 20 (subsequently cited as Wolff, NBA VIII/1, KB).

23. Cf. Walter Blankenburg, "Die Bedeutung des Kanons in Bachs Werk," in *Bericht über die wissenschaftliche Bachtagung der Gesellschaft für Musikforschung, Leipzig 23. bis 26. Juli 1950* (Leipzig: C. F. Peters, 1951), 250–58, here p. 257; Hans Joachim Moser, "Die Symbolbeigaben des Musikerbildes," in *Musik und Bild: Festschrift Max Seiffert zum siebsigster Geburtstag* (Kassel: Bärenreiter, 1938), 35–52, here p. 43ff.

24. Wolff, NBA VIII/1, KB, 21.

25. Mizler, *Musikalische Bibliothek*, vol. IV/1, 173.

26. A most revealing survey about this matter is given in the Utrecht University PhD dissertation of Thijs Kramer, *Zahlenfiguren im Werk Johann Sebastian Bachs* (Hilversum, 2000), esp. chapter 1.

27. Friedrich Smend, *Johann Sebastian Bach bei seinem Namen gerufen: Eine Notenschrift und ihre Deutung* (Kassel: Bärenreiter, 1950); reprinted in Friedrich Smend, *Bach-Studien: Gesammelte Reden und Aufsätze*, ed. Christoph Wolff (Kassel: Bärenreiter, 1969).

28. Smend, *Bach-Studien*, 190ff.

29. Cf. Hans Theodore David and Arthur Mendel, *The Bach Reader*, rev. ed. (London: J. M. Dent, 1966), 461f.; Wolff, NBA VIII/1, KB, 40.

30. Leopold Nowak, "Ein Bach-Fund," *Fontes Artis Musicae* 13 (January–April 1966): 95–98.

31. Wolff, NBA VIII/1, KB, 20.

32. Ibid., 24, 33.

33. For an overview of all literature published shortly after the recovered *Handexemplar*, see Robin A. Leaver, "A New Bach Source," *The Bach Society Bulletin* 1 (February 1977): 27–28.

Here we find BWV 1076 as canon no. 13 in the older version. Bar 1 of the top part reads a minim (time signature: alla breve); the later version (original print and portrait; time signature: 4/4) replaces this with a crotchet and a crotchet rest. This appears to be a change for the better and BWV 1076 can be seen as an improvement of the earlier version. Cf. Walter Emery and Christoph Wolff, *Zweiter Teil der Klavierübung, Vierter Teil der Klavierübung, Vierzehn Kanons BWV 1087: Kritischer Bericht*, Johann Sebastian Bach, Neue Ausgabe sämtlicher Werke, series 5, vol. 2 (Kassel: Bärenreiter, 1981), 120f (subsequently cited as Emery and Wolff, NBA V/2, KB). Supposedly, Bach wrote the fourteen canons in his *Handexemplar* of the *Goldberg Variations* between 1741/42 and 1746. Yoshitake Kobayashi, however, in his essay "Zur Chronologie der Spätwerke Johann Sebastian Bachs Kompositions und Aufführungstätigkeit von 1736 bis 1750," *Bach-Jahrbuch* 74 (1988): 7–72, here p. 60, mentions the period from ca. 1747 until August 1748. According to him, the Parisian source probably represents a later clean copy of the early versions.

34. See e.g., Randolph N. Currie, "Bach's Newly Discovered Canons in a First Edition: Some Observations: Part II," *Bach: The Quarterly Journal of the Riemenschneider Bach Institute* 8 (July 1977): 3–12, here p. 5; Nicholas Kenyon, "A Newly Discovered Group of Canons by Bach," *The Musical Times* 117 (May 1976): 391–93, here 393.

35. Christoph Wolff, "Bach's *Handexemplar* of the Goldberg Variations: A New Source," *Journal of the American Musicological Society* 29 (Summer 1976): 224–41, here p. 240. Peter Williams, *The Organ Music of J. S. Bach* (Cambridge: Cambridge University Press, 1980), 2:316, commented on this remark by Wolff: "However it should be remembered (*a*) that this chorale melody must have loomed large in the composer's thoughts for over half a century, and (*b*) that he had already attempted several contrapuntal devices with it in BWV 700." In my opinion, this does not render Wolff's theory any less likely. Furthermore, Williams writes consistently, but erroneously "BWV 1081" instead of "BWV 1087."

36. See e.g., Leaver, "A New Bach Source"; Wolff, "Bach's *Handexemplar*," 229–31; Kenyon, "A Newly Discovered Group," 393; Currie, "Bach's Newly Discovered Canons in a First Edition: Some Observations," *Bach: The Quarterly Journal*

of the Riemenschneider Bach Institute 8 (April 1977): 15–22, here p. 18; Emery and Wolff, NBA Vol. V/2, KB, 122.

37 Matthias Wendt, "Bach und die Zahl 13 . . . Marginalien zu einem Randthema," in *Acht kleine Präludien und Studien über BACH: Georg von Dadelsen zum 70. Geburtstag*, ed. Kollegium des Johann-Sebastian-Bach-Instituts Göttingen (Wiesbaden: Breitkopf und Härtel, 1992), 86–93.

38. It appears, among other things, that a) Wendt did not thoroughly read the above-mentioned article by Kobayashi; b) his argument is inconsistent (e.g., the number 13 would represent GRAUN (G+R+A+U+N=7+17+1+20+13) because it is the "Quersumme" of 58, but he doesn't employ the same "method" for BACH, which would have resulted in the number 5); c) his "method" consists of adding up numbers etc. and therefore can be used to reach any result that is looked for; d) he does not hesitate to make the most peculiar assumptions, such as Bach misleading his contemporaries on purpose to keep it secret that he possessed an "übernatürliche Rechenbegabung" (supernatural mathematical talent—p. 90, note 6), etc. It is clear that this kind of reasoning has nothing to do with serious scholarship.

39. An extended essay on BWV 1077 was published by Heinrich Poos, "Christus Coronabit Crucigeros: Hermeneutischer Versuch über einen Kanon Johann Sebastian Bachs," in *Theologische Bach-Studien* I, ed. Walter Blankenburg and Renate Steiger (Neuhausen-Stuttgart: Hänssler, 1987), 67–97.

40. In this respect, the present study on BWV 1076 differs from others, which, among other things, leave its relationship with the *Canonic Variations* BWV 769 and the Haußmann painting out of consideration.

41. This is a very common theme in the baroque period (in G major). In 1950 Smend thought that this *soggetto* was by Handel (see *Bach-Studien*, 189). This erroneous view was still repeated ca. 25 years later (e.g., by Olivier Alain, "Un supplément inédit aux Variations Goldberg de J. S. Bach," *Revue de musicologie* 61/2 (1975): 244–94, and by Currie, "Bach's Newly Discovered Canons, Part II," p. 9, note 23). Already in 1967 Rudolf Flotzinger had shown that the theme had been used as early as 1640, but is certainly considerably older; see his article "Die Gagliarda Italiana: Zur Frage der barocken Thementypologie," *Acta Musicologica* 39 (1967): 92–100, here p. 94ff.

42. Cf. Albert Clement, *"O Jesu, du edle Gabe": Studien zum Verhältnis von Text und Musik in den Choralpartiten und den Kanonischen Veränderungen von Johann Sebastian Bach* (Utrecht, 1989), 158f; *Bach-Dokumente*, vol. III, ed. Hans-Joachim Schulze (Kassel: Bärenreiter, 1972), no. 919, pp. 432–34.

43. Those other authors include Johann Michael Schmidt (1754), Jacob Wilhelm Lustig (1756), Jacob Adlung (1758), and most explicitly Johann Georg Sulzer in his *Allgemeine Theorie der schönen Künste* (Leipzig, 1774), a work written in cooperation with the help of Bach's pupils Johann Philipp Kirnberger and Friedrich Agricola (see Clement).

44. For further discussion, see Clement, 159ff.

45. Ibid., 157, 173.

46. In the *Musikalische Bibliothek*, "musicalische retorica" is often mentioned in articles and reviews; several members also engaged intensively with this subject out-

side the society, e.g., Meinrad Spieß—his treatise of 1745, in which he discusses musical rhetoric, is reviewed in the *Musikalische Bibliothek*—and the versatile Heinrich Bokemeyer, who was also interested in cabbala (cf. Clement, 173).

47. See Clement, chapter 4.

48. Cf. Walter Blankenburg and Willem Elders, "Zahlensymbolik," *Die Musik in Geschichte und Gegenwart* (Kassel: Bärenreiter, 1976), vol. 16, col. 1974. In his monograph *Symbolic Scores: Studies in the Music of the Renaissance* (Leiden: E. J. Brill, 1994), Elders gives further examples. That allusions to the Trinity by the number 3 were commonplace is clearly demonstrated, e.g., in Bach's organ prelude *Allein Gott in der Höh sey Ehr* (BWV 675): see Albert Clement, *Der dritte Teil der Clavierübung von Johann Sebastian Bach: Musik - Text - Theologie* (Middelburg: AlmaRes, 1999), 91–93.

49. Smend, *Bach-Studien*, 192.

50. Cf. the final choruses and chorales of BWV 10, 36, 62, and 121, and the opening choruses of BWV 11 und 137.

51. Cf. Albert Clement, "On the Inner Correlation of the Six Chorales BWV 645–650 and Its Significance," *Bach: The Journal of the Riemenschneider Bach Institute* 34/2 (2003): 1–62, here p. 13f.

52. Mizler, *Musikalische Bibliothek*, vol. III/2, p. 348.

53. Ibid., p. 349.

54. Cf. Johann Gottfried Walther, *Musicalisches Lexicon, oder musicalische Bibliothec* (Leipzig, 1732), 132. See also Clement, *"O Jesu, du edle Gabe,"* especially 179 and 197ff.; and Clement, *Der dritte Teil der Clavierübung*, 99–101, 125, etc.

55. Werner Braun, "Bachs Stellung im Kanonstreit," in *Bach-Interpretationen*, ed. Martin Geck (Göttingen: Vandenhoeck und Ruprecht, 1969), 106–11 and 218–20, here p. 111.

56. Martin Luther, *Career of the Reformer IV*, ed. Lewis W. Spitz, Luther's Works, 34 (Philadelphia: Muhlenburg Press, 1960), 202.

57. In modern literature, a facsimile is provided by Walter Salmen, *Musiker im Porträt*, vol. 2: *Das 17. Jahrhundert* (Munich: C. H. Beck, 1983), 93.

58. Cf. *The Catalog of Carl Philipp Emanuel Bach's Estate: A Facsimile of the Edition by Schniebes, Hamburg, 1790*, ed. Rachel W. Wade (New York: Garland, 1981), 92–126.

59. The idea of eternity was expressed in many canons by other composers. Already in 1589, for instance, Jak. Paix sets the text "Ehre sei Gott in der Höhe" as a four-part canon "sine fine"; a secular application is, e.g., J. G. Walther's six-part *canon infinitus* on the words "Keuscheste Flammen, brennt ewiglich fort" (burn eternally, chaste flames). See Braun, "Bachs Stellung," 220, note 27.

Furthermore, if the canon parts (three themes and their answers *in retrograde*) of BWV 1076 are to depict the angels and mankind giving praise to God, the idea of the beginning of antiphonal performance as expressed by Leaver in regard of Bach's marginal note alongside Calov's comments (referring to the birth of Christ) on Exodus 15:20 comes to mind (see the introduction of this contribution).

60. Mizler, *Musikalische Bibliothek*, vol. IV/1, 106–7.

61. Cf. Leaver, *J. S. Bach and Scripture*, 78.

62. Walter Blankenburg, "Bach," *Theologische Realenzyklopädie* (Berlin: de Gruyter, 1980), 5:90–94, here 92.

63. German text according to Georg Christian Schemelli, *Musikalisches Gesang=Buch* (Leipzig 1736), 140–41. Translation after Mark S. Bighley, *The Lutheran Chorales in the Organ Works of J. S. Bach* (St. Louis: Concordia, 1986), 221–24.

10

Bach and Dresden: A New Hypothesis on the Origin of the *Goldberg Variations* (BWV 988)[1]

Yo Tomita

The last of Bach's *Clavierübung* series—presently known as the *Goldberg Variations* (BWV 988)—is a masterpiece surrounded by mysteries. According to Johann Nikolaus Forkel, this work was commissioned by Count Keyserlingk, a Russian ambassador to the electoral court of Dresden, who had been suffering from insomnia at the time, so that one of his servants named Goldberg could perform something "soft and somewhat lively" ("sanften und etwas muntern") on sleepless nights, hence deriving the famous nickname.[2] Meanwhile, recent scholarship concerning the biographical inquiries into the people behind this episode—Wilhelm Friedemann and Carl Philipp Emanuel, who reportedly supplied the information to Forkel, as well as Count Keyserlingk and Johann Gottlieb Goldberg (1727–1756), who were at the center of this anecdotal account—produced no fresh evidence either to support or to negate this question of the work's origin.[3] In this chapter, I am not pursuing this specific inquiry. Instead, I discuss the issue more broadly, in terms of how Bach may have collected ideas for this work, by posing the following hypothetical questions:

> Did Bach have a much broader vision of the composition than what we were told by Forkel?
>
> If it is the case, then what was his message for his audience?

When examining the *Goldberg Variations* from the context of Bach's long and productive career, one would notice a very striking period of a few years in which he managed to produce a series of monumental works for keyboard instruments: *Clavierübung III* (published in autumn 1739), the second part of the *Well-Tempered Clavier* (compiled between 1738 and 1742), and the *Goldberg Variations* (published in autumn 1741) that are not at all related to his official duties in Leipzig. In these works, one can find Bach's highly systematic approach to composition, actively exploring various styles and compositional techniques, both new and old, within a large but tightly-constructed structural boundary, as if to create a unique microcosm in each work.

It is significant that these works coincide in time with his rapidly changing social status and working environment, which are symbolically seen in the following incidents that immediately precede this period:

1. A prolonged dispute broke out in summer 1736 with the Rector of the St. Thomas School, Johann August Ernesti (1707–1781) over who had the right to appoint the general prefect, which made it difficult for Bach to carry out his daily duties as Cantor.[4] Although this dispute was settled eventually, Bach's dismay with the school as well as with the local authorities must have become ever stronger.[5]
2. Bach received the honorary title of "Compositeur to the Royal Court Orchestra" from the Dresden court in November 1736, which was the most significant development in his career to date. It was the title for which he had longed since 1733 or even earlier,[6] and was certainly a much needed morale boost for him domestically. We know, for example, that Bach used this connection to settle the above-mentioned dispute, which came in the form of the King's decree in December 1737.[7]
3. Bach's compositional style was criticized by a former pupil, Johann Adolph Scheibe (1708–1776). In an anonymous article published in *Der Critische Musicus* in May 1737, Scheibe mocked Bach's styles as "turgid and confused" ("schwülstiges und verworrenes"), labelling him as a man obsessed with artificial details, unable to appreciate the natural beauty that music can express.[8]

All of these three events could have had such a significant impact on Bach's life that they affected the way Bach composed his music from this point on, which resulted in what we now know about the outpouring of Bach's creative power.[9] If this observation is valid, then it is possible that this series of keyboard masterpieces received various forms of influence, particularly from Dresden, where Bach may have found a host of new ideas for writing these compositions.

Stylistically, the *Goldberg Variations* clearly shows features from both the French and Italian styles, two of the most fashionable national styles of the day. The opening aria is typically French: the abundant use of ornaments on an already richly embellished melody strongly alludes to the French *galant* style. In other movements we also find elements of the Italian style, such as

Variation 5, where the hand-crossing technique adds much brilliance to the texture. Yet Bach's exploration of these styles is not limited to those of modern, popular tastes of the day. The use of counterpoint—in this case, canons— is also a prominent feature of this work: they are positioned at every three variations, forming the structural pillars in the collection. Canon is the most strict, rule-bound type of composition—the type that Scheibe would have disapproved as archaic and artificial. It is tempting to think that Bach deliberately mixed the elements of both ancient and modern here so as to rebut Scheibe's accusations.[10]

One likely context from which all these stylistic elements were derived is the capital of Saxony, Dresden, with its rich musical life. Having received the honorary title of *Hof Compositeur* from the Dresden court, and having subsequently appeared in a public organ recital in the church of Our Lady, it is reasonable to assume that by the time Bach set about working on the *Goldberg Variations* he had already established different, much stronger ties with the musicians and patrons there. Thus, it is important to look beyond what Forkel actually mentions, namely that the *Goldberg Variations* was a commissioned work by one patron, and not assume naively that all the musical ideas Bach used to write the aria and thirty variations came solely from within Bach's creative imagination.

RECENT RESEARCH AND A NEW HYPOTHESIS

There is a recent trend in Bach scholarship to place greater importance on reevaluating what we already know from the wider context in which Bach worked—when and in what circumstances Bach met his fellow musicians and poets and their works—so that we can then in turn investigate what influences Bach may have received from them. In my opinion there are two very distinguished contributions in recent decades: the one is the study by Kirsten Beißwenger on Bach's music library,[11] and the other is Robin A. Leaver's study of Bach's theological library.[12] These two studies clarified what Bach actually—as well as most likely and possibly—owned, paving the way for further studies. Beyond this horizon of the so-called contextual Bach studies, there are also scholars working on hitherto neglected composers who had connections with Bach. The most important in our case are the composers whose works were performed regularly in Dresden.[13] There are several discussions along this line of inquiry from recent research that are worth mentioning:

- Jeanne Swack considers the possibility that Bach's Sonata in E-flat for flute and harpsichord (BWV 1031) was modelled on Quantz's QV2:18.[14]

- Ian Payne points out the possibility that Bach borrowed musical ideas for BWV 1056/2 from Telemann, TWV 51:G2.[15]
- Mary Oleskiewicz argues that the King's theme for the *Musical Offering* originated from Quantz, his flute teacher, which in turn found its origin in the works of Zelenka, who taught Quantz in Dresden, hinting that the Dresden court had a much more powerful influence on music making than hitherto believed.[16]

Yet, as far as the *Goldberg Variations* is concerned, I have not encountered an alternative theory to that of Forkel's claiming that the work has other roots in Dresden as well, although there are some notable discussions that examine a much broader historical background, seeking both the origin of its theme in the bass in the works of various authors[17] and the opening aria itself, for instance, in D'Anglebert's Menuet in the *Pièces de Clavecin* (1689) and Handel's Chaconne in the *Prelude and Chaconne* (1733).[18] They certainly show strong similarities to the stylistic features, harmonic progression, and texture of the Goldberg aria, but it has not been established whether Bach knew them, how Bach could have known them, or how he thought it appropriate to use them as his model for the *Goldberg Variations*.

My central hypothesis is clear by now: having became an iconic figure in the musical circles of Dresden, the Electoral capital of Saxony where many able musicians were recruited or attracted from other countries including France and Italy,[19] Bach attempted to show in the *Goldberg Variations* various ideas that he had encountered in Dresden. What is impressive is not only his encyclopaedic knowledge of the musical styles then current in Dresden, but also his abilities to digest and construct them in a unified composition. This theory at least makes sense in the historical context, for the *Goldberg Variations* was the first published "secular" work since he became the *Hof Compositeur* of the Dresden Court, which contrasts very well with the preceding work, the *Clavierübung III*, which was a "sacred" work. It is also worth pointing out a famous anecdote dating from this period that supports my argument: it describes the way Bach approached composition at the initial stage:

> [Bach] does not get into condition, as the expression goes, to delight others with the mingling of his tones until he has played something from the printed or written page, and has set his powers of imagination in motion. . . . The able man . . . has to play something from the page that is inferior to his own ideas. And yet his superior ideas are the consequences of those inferior ones.[20]

In order to prove my hypothesis, it is necessary to identify the ideas that Bach used in the *Goldberg Variations* in musical sources that originated in Dresden and could have been known to Bach. They must also contain the stylistic elements that represent the taste of the people of Dresden at that time. This study, however, does not extend to covering how Bach attempted to accommodate such a wide range of elements in this work. Rather, I shall focus my discussion in three specific areas of ongoing research that support my central hypothesis: melody, canons, and early drafts.

1. BACH'S MELODIES—ORIGINAL OR BORROWED?

First of all, let us consider the originality of Bach's melodies, about which Forkel writes so passionately in his biography of Bach, a topic to which he devotes an entire chapter. He describes Bach's melodies as "so open, clear, and intelligible that they, indeed, sound differently from the melodies of other composers."[21] In the next paragraph, where he makes specific reference to the melodies of the *Goldberg Variations*, he reiterates the individuality of Bach's melodies. He continues: "they are so new, so uncommon, and, at the same time, so brilliant and surprising that we do not find the like in any other composer."[22] Forkel then considers why Bach's melodies sound so original: he observes that "this particular nature of Bach's harmony and melody was also combined with very extensive and diversified use of rhythm."[23] To illustrate this point, let us examine the famous opening melody of the aria shown in example 10.1. If we look at it purely from the melodic shape of the right-hand part, by ignoring both its underlying harmony and rhythmic characterization, the melody loses all of its character; it is no longer unique. In fact, it becomes identical with that of the chorale melody "Freu dich sehr, o meine Seele," which is one of the most frequently used tunes in his cantatas—including BWV 30, which was performed around the time when Bach was engaged in composing the *Goldberg Variations*. Bach sets this melody in four metrically different ways in his cantatas, as shown in examples 10.2a–d. In terms of their musical character, I find little resemblance in them when comparing them to the melody of the Goldberg aria. But if we compare the Goldberg aria with the opening phrase of Telemann's melody from TWV 41:G8, as shown in example 10.3, we notice remarkable similarities between them, even though Telemann's melody does not contain all the notes of Bach's melody. This comparison serves to show that the character of melody depends very much on how it is set with both appropriate harmony and rhythm, and that the exactness of melodic shape is not an essential requirement.

Still, it also needs to be said that there is one aspect that Forkel overlooked in his observation of Bach's melody: the fact that Bach customarily borrowed musical ideas from the works of others and digested them as his own. In other

Example 10.1.   J. S. Bach, "Aria" (mm. 1–4) from *Goldberg Variations*, BWV 988/1

Example 10.2.   Chorale Tune "Freu dich sehr, o meine Seele," the opening phrase

Example 10.3.   G. P. Telemann, "Andante" (mm. 1–3) from *Sonata in G Major for Violin or Flute and Continuo*, TWV 41:G8

words, the issue is not only how Bach used them, but also what he used—how Bach chose them and why, which I shall pursue to further Forkel's original argument.

Perhaps the most interesting finding in this area of research comes from the work of Mary Oleskiewicz, who makes a fascinating observation on the way Bach used *coulé*.[24] It is certainly rare in Bach's works that this device was

Example 10.4. J. S. Bach, "Adagio ma non tanto" (mm. 1–2) from *Sonata in E Major for Flute and Continuo*, BWV 1035/1

used as an element of the theme, and, as she points out, the Flute Sonata in E major (BWV 1035, ca.1741, see example 10.4) may be the only other example in Bach's known works where this ornament is used in this manner.[25] She also points out a strong similarity between these melodies and that of Quantz's Flute Sonata, QV 1:159 (see example 10.5),[26] suggesting that Bach borrowed its idea from Quantz, who was then active in Dresden, where they presumably met. This is an interesting and plausible hypothesis, for all these examples date from roughly the same period, ca.1741.

Another example of melody is taken from the third variation (see example 10.6). This melody has a strong similarity to that of the second movement of his Harpsichord Concerto no. 5 in F minor (BWV 1056, see example 10.7), which Bach performed ca.1738. As Joshua Rifkin pointed out, this melody may have its roots in the lost Oboe Concerto in D minor.[27] Yet, as Ian Payne claims in his recent article, it is highly likely that Bach took this idea from Telemann's Oboe Concerto, TWV 51:G2 (see example 10.8),[28] which may in turn have been modelled on his earlier work, TWV 41:G9 (see example 10.9). Although no supporting evidence is found in the sources, it is quite likely that this hypothesis is correct, considering the fact that Telemann's instrumental music was frequently performed in Dresden in the 1730s.[29]

Having considered these few examples, it is clear that Forkel's view that Bach's melodies sound different from those of other composers should be taken with caution. Setting aside the well-known fact that Forkel was under the influence of then emerging German nationalism to propagate Bach to his fellow countrymen, his aesthetic judgement of "originality" appears to have been based on a very limited knowledge of other composers' music. Although

Example 10.5. J. J. Quantz, "Affettuoso" (mm. 1–4) from *Sonata for Flute and Continuo*, QV 1:159

Example 10.6. J. S. Bach, Variation 3 "Canone all Unisuono" (mm. 1–2) from *Goldberg Variations*, BWV 988/4

Example 10.7. J. S. Bach, "Largo" (mm. 1–3, transposed from A♭-major) from *Harpsichord Concerto in F Minor*, BWV 1056/2

Example 10.8. G. P. Telemann, *Concerto in G Major for Traversflute, Strings and Continuo*, TWV 51:G2/1

Example 10.9. G. P. Telemann, "Cantabile" (mm. 1–3) from *Sonata in G Major for Flute and Continuo*, TWV 41:G9/1

he is correct that the originality of melody depends on how the melody is set in musical context, we also need to consider the circumstances in which Bach approached his composition. The task of identifying the melodies that became Bach's models should be relatively straightforward, and there may be significant progress in research in the near future when we have at our disposal the huge corpus of musical works by the Dresden composers of the day. The real challenge will be the next process, namely to identify whether or not it is possible to prove that Bach knew these works.

2. INTERVAL CANONS

In the *Goldberg Variations* Bach employs interval canons from the unison to the ninth, the idea of which, as far as we know, he never used in his works before or after. From where did he take this idea? Again, there is a Dresden source that may have been Bach's model: Jan Dismas Zelenka's manuscript, now in the Sächsische Landesbibliothek, Dresden, shelfmark Mus. 1-B-98, volume 3. On pages 326–31 Zelenka copied eleven interval canons of Johann Joseph Fux, his composition teacher in Vienna, arranged in ascending order from the unison to the octave with some alternative settings. They are immediately followed by Zelenka's own nine canons entited "Sequuntur Canones J: D: Zelenka, quos idem ad imitationem Aestimatissimi sui Magistri supra eundem Cantum firmum sic posuit" (ZWV 191, ca. 1721). Zelenka starts with the canon at the ninth—as if he goes on a step further than his master—and proceeds in a descending order to the octave, sixth (i.e., skipping seventh), fifth, and so forth until he reaches the unison, as reproduced in example 10.10.[30] There are twenty canons in this series, with all of them built upon the same plain hexachord bass line; thus, there is little musical resemblance with Bach's canons, where each canon is built on a richly and uniquely decorated bass line (except Variation 27, canon at the ninth, which is written in two parts without the accompanying bass line). Yet the fact that Zelenka explores interval canons from the unison to the ninth (even though the seventh is omitted), as well as the manner in which these canons are presented in a three-part texture, strongly suggests that Bach took the idea from Zelenka. Furthermore, there is a sense of progression from Fux to Zelenka, and from Zelenka to Bach, an intellectual challenge to write more complex canons from their respective models, if indeed they were. The stylistic difference between Zelenka and Bach is, of course, very significant. But one must take into account the fact that Zelenka's canons were fairly straightforward compositional exercises, whereas Bach's were published keyboard pieces for "music lovers, to refresh their spirits,"[31] and between them there are almost twenty years, during which time the styles of canonic compositions went through great

[1] Canon ad Unisonum Del S: Fux.

[2] Canon ad 2^dam superiorem

[3] Canon ad 2 super. alio modo

Example 10.10. **Interval Canons of Fux and Zelenka in Manuscript Mus. 1-B-98 (vol. 3) in the Sächsische Landesbibliothek, Dresden**

[4] Canon ad 3^m superiorem

[5] Canon ad 4^{tam} superiorem

[6] Canon ad 5^m superiorem

Example 10.10. *(Continued).*

[7] Canon ad 6tam superiorem

[8] Canon ad 6 super. alio modo.

[9] Canon ad 7m superiorem

Example 10.10. *(Continued).*

[10] Canon ad 8 superiorem

[11] Canon ad 8 superiorem [alio modo]

[12] Canon ad Septimam inferiorem.

Example 10.10. *(Continued).*

[13] Canon in Octava inferiore.

[14] Canon in 6 inferiore.

[15] Canon in 5 inferiore.

Example 10.10. *(Continued).*

[16] Canon in 4 inferiore.

[17] Canon in 3 inferiore.

[18] Canon in 2da inferiore.

Example 10.10. *(Continued).*

[19 Canon in 2da inferiore] alio modo

Example 10.10. *(Continued).*

changes.[32] There are, in fact, some interesting similarities between their canons. Compare, for example, Zelenka's canons at the second (no. 19) and the third (no. 17) and the melodic ideas employed with their respective counterparts in Bach's Goldberg canons.

In future studies it will be necessary to examine whether or not Bach could have known this source in Dresden. At present, all I can say is that this seems likely, as Forkel reports that Bach knew Zelenka personally,[33] and around this time Christoph Mizler, one of Bach's pupils, was working on the German translation of Fux's *Gradus ad parnassum*, which was published in Leipzig in 1742.[34] There is some thought that Bach may have had some input into Fux's work. Bach also knew the Latin original of this work published in 1725.[35] Assessing its impact from a broader perspective, there is clear evidence in Bach's works from the late 1730s that he began to show greater interest in the *stile antico*.[36] It is possible that the friendship with Zelenka, who possessed a valuable collection of music, started from Bach's growing interest in older contrapuntal music.[37]

The implications of this hypothesis can be far reaching. First, the fact that Zelenka's canon included the one at the ninth, which can be seen as an unnecessary duplicate of the second, suggests that Bach planned to include this canon from the outset, thus providing evidence against Werner Breig's theory that Bach may have planned the *Goldberg Variations* initially as a set of twenty-four variations.[38] The lack of the canon at the tenth is likewise consistent with the evidence in Zelenka's source.

3. AN EARLY VERSION AND ITS IMPLICATION

We do not know the location of Bach's autograph manuscripts of the *Goldberg Variations*, which may have contained traces of how the work was compiled. While the recent discovery of Bach's personal copy of the first edition—which records Bach's later revisions fairly thoroughly—is undoubtedly a primary source for understanding Bach's final intention, it does not contain the kind of information that we need here.[39]

The only surviving manuscript known in the past that may have derived from the lost autograph is the copy of an opening aria that Anna Magdalena copied in her *Clavierbüchlein* of 1725.[40] The copy contains certain types of errors and minor variants hinting that it was copied from Bach's autograph before it was finalized for publication in 1741.[41]

Recently, however, another manuscript has come to my attention that is particularly relevant for this study. It is Go.S.19 of the Bach-Archiv, Leipzig, which is part of a large manuscript collection known as the "Bach-Sammlung Manfred Gorke."[42] The manuscript is a binio fascicle, and its contents are described briefly in table 10.1.

Table 10.1.   Contents of Go.S.19

folio	Contents	Description
1r	Title page	'PRELUDES. | pour le Clavecin | par Mr. | Jean Sebastien | Bach'
1v–2r	BWV 875a/1	Heading: 'Prelude I' An early 43-bar version of the prelude no. 6 of *WTC* II
2v–3r	BWV 884/1	Heading: 'Prelude II' An early version (same length) of the prelude no. 15 of *WTC* II
3v	BWV 988/6	Heading: 'Preludium III' An early version (same length) of Variation 5 of the *Goldberg Variations*.
4r	anon.	Heading: 'Polonoise' in G major.
4v		Blank

As I have discussed elsewhere in detail,[43] it is sufficient for the purpose of this article to say that all three Bach pieces are hitherto little known early versions of movements found in very well-known works, namely the *Well-Tempered Clavier* II (Preludes in D minor and G major respectively) and the *Goldberg Variations* (fifth variation). Because these works were compiled almost side-by-side in the late 1730s, it is quite possible to consider that all the pieces here are derived from a batch of drafts, now lost, dating back to the time when Bach worked on them.

Bach's pieces are followed by a dull, short, anonymous piece with a different title, "Polonoise." Based on the form and style of the preceding pieces by Bach, this may well be the work of the scribe, an issue that I shall explore later. As for the identity of the scribe, Ulrich Leisinger suggests the name Christoph Ernst Abraham Albrecht von Boineburg (1752–1840).[44] While Hans-Joachim Schulze's catalogue gives the date of this manuscript in the period of 1760–1770,[45] Leisinger comes up with more specific dates: all the pieces by Bach were copied ca. 1765–1770, whereas the last, unattributed piece was copied ca. 1775–1780.[46]

The implication of this find is three-fold and requires further studies in the future. First, all these movements—including the anonymous polonaise—could have originated from Bach's youthful days. It also supports the hypothesis that the *Goldberg Variations* once existed in an earlier form, possibly in a smaller cycle,[47] much earlier than we have previously believed, which is in line with many of Bach's keyboard works that are known in this way. It is true that the variation is the form that Bach explored most seriously in his last decade, the result of which is now known in his late works, such as the *Canonic Variations on "Vom Himmel hoch,"* the *Musical Offering*, and the *Art of Fugue*. However, there is a danger to exclude the possibility of an early origin, for there are at least two works in this genre that were composed much earlier, namely *Aria variata* (BWV 989), composed "before 1714,"[48] and the fragment of the C-minor Air with variation (BWV 991), contained in the *Clavierbüchlein* for Anna Magdalena Bach of 1722. This early version of the Goldberg fifth variation being extant, a further study should be carried out towards a new chronology of its origin and development.

Second, we must investigate the possibility that these pieces were brought together subsequently. For instance, Bach may have put these drafts in a folder that could be disposed of, or perhaps kept for use by his students. Likewise, many more opportunities could be anticipated once Bach's manuscripts left his house, for the pieces from different collections may still have been gathered together and labelled under the general title of "Bach's works."

Third and finally, it is worth considering the possibility—however remote and speculative it may be—that this polonaise was not Boineburg's composition, but a work by a Dresden composer—contemporary with Bach's *Goldberg Variations*—which Bach collected for composing the set in the late

Example 10.11. C. E. A. A. von Boineburg (?) 'Polonoise' in Manuscript Go. S. 19 in the Bach-Archiv, Leipzig

1730s. As mentioned above, Bach was apparently well known among his local circle to have "played something from the printed or written page, and has set his powers of imagination in motion."[49] This "Polonoise," shown in example 10.11, contains some features that are common with the first variation (which is also a polonaise) such as the continuing sixteenth-note pulse (which is uncommon in a polonaise movement), and the use of the bow-shaped melody with anapaest rhythm (which is perhaps more common as a character of this dance rhythm). In order to prove or disprove this theory, it would be necessary to find the real composer of this "Polonoise." Still, even if we find strong evidence suggesting that Boineburg was the composer,[50] a possibility still remains that he could have developed this piece from a sketch found in the same folder as the other Bach movements, thus entering a never-ending cycle requiring evidence.

To me it seems significant to ask why it was that a polonaise was chosen as the first variation in the *Goldberg Variations*. There is an unmistakable link to Dresden, the Royal capital of Saxony, where the Elector of Saxony and the King of Poland, Friedrich August II, resided. As Rolf Dammann claims, the choice of the polonaise, a polish dance, as the first variation had a political message.[51] Clearly, further research is required from both political and sociological angles.

As I have shown above, there are still many areas of research that could un-
veil still hidden truths. Whatever they may be, it is important that we do not
lose the context in which the musical work was created.[52]

NOTES

1. This article is a revised version of a paper presented in a colloquium entitled
"Bach and Dresden" at the 50th Annual Meeting of the Musicological Society of
Japan, held at the Tokyo National University of Music and Fine Arts in November
1999.

2. Johann Nikolaus Forkel, *Über Johann Sebastian Bachs Leben, Kunst und
Kunstwerke* (Leipzig: Hofmeister und Kühnel, 1802), 52. For an English translation
see *The New Bach Reader*, ed. Hans T. David and Arthur Mendel, rev. Christoph
Wolff (New York: W. W. Norton, 1998), p. 464 (subsequently cited as *NBR*).

3. See, for example, Rolf Dammann, *Johann Sebastian Bachs "Goldberg-
Variationen"* (Mainz: Schott, 1986), 11–18.

4. See *Bach-Dokumente*, vol. I, ed. Werner Neumann and Hans-Joachim Schulze
(Kassel: Bärenreiter, 1969), nos. 32–35, pp. 82–91; nos. 39–41, pp. 95–106; *Bach-
Dokumente*, vol. II, ed. Werner Neumann and Hans-Joachim Schulze (Kassel: Bärenreiter, 1969), nos. 382–83, pp. 268–76 (these sources subsequently cited as *BDok* I
and *BDok* II respectively). For English translations, see *NBR*, nos. 180–86, pp.
172–85 and nos. 192–96, pp. 189–96.

5. Bach's strikingly blunt response to the news that the Passion performance in
1739 was cancelled seems to illustrate this point most vividly. See *NBR*, no. 208, p.
204.

6. Bach's letter dated July 27, 1733 asking for such a title was lost during WWII, but
is reproduced in *BDok* I, no. 27, p. 74; English translation in *NBR*, no. 162, p. 158.

7. See *BDok* II, no. 406, p. 293; *NBR*, no. 196, pp. 195–96.

8. A series of exchanges and the contemporary commentaries are extracted in
BDok II, nos. 400, 409, 413, 420, 436, 442, and 552; English translation in *NBR*, nos.
343–48, pp. 338–53.

9. In his monograph *Bach* (London: Dent, 1983), 161, Malcolm Boyd states that
"the effect [of the dispute with Scheibe] on the music Bach was to write during the
last decade of his life was profound." It may be worth adding that Bach's resignation
in summer 1737 from the directorship of the Collegium Musicum may be seen in this
context as a necessary measure for him to focus on compositional activities.

10. It is indeed tempting to seek the possibility that Bach produced a "musical" re-
buttal of Scheibe's accusation with the *Goldberg Variations*, as Alan Street attempted
to demonstrate in his article "The Rhetorico-Musical Structure of the 'Goldberg' Variations: Bach's Clavierübung IV and the Institutio Oratoria of Quintilian," *Music
Analysis* 6 (1987): 89–131. His argument is unfortunately full of unfounded assumptions. In his monograph *Bach: The Goldberg Variations* (Cambridge: Cambridge University Press, 2001), 102, Peter Williams, for example, describes it as "naive and fan-
ciful."

11. Kirsten Beißwenger, *Johann Sebastian Bachs Notenbibliothek* (Kassel: Bärenreiter, 1992).

12. Robin A. Leaver, *Bachs theologische Bibliothek: Eine kritische Bibliographie* (Neuhausen-Stuttgart: Hänssler, 1983).

13. On liturgical music of the time in Dresden, see Wolfgang Horn, *Die Dresdner Hofkirchenmusik, 1720–1745: Studien zu ihren Voraussetzungen und ihrem Repertoire* (Kassel: Bärenreiter, 1987); *Zelenka-Studien* I (Kassel: Bärenreiter, 1993); Ortrun Landmann, *Die Telemann-Quellen der Sächsischen Landesbibliothek: Handschriften und zeitgenössische Druckausgaben seiner Werke* (Dresden: Sächsische Landesbibliothek, 1983); Janice B. Stockigt, *Jan Dismas Zelenka: A Bohemian Musician at the Court of Dresden* (Oxford: Oxford University Press, 2000).

14. Jeanne Swack, "Quantz and the Sonata in E-flat major for flute and cembalo, BWV 1031," *Early Music* 23 (February 1995): 31–54.

15. Ian Payne, "New Light on Telemann and Bach: Double Measures," *Musical Times* 139 (Winter 1998): 44–45; "Telemann's Musical Style c.1709–c.1730 and J. S. Bach: The Evidence of Borrowing," *Bach: Journal of the Riemenschneider Bach Institute* 30, no. 1 (1999): 42–64.

16. Mary Oleskiewicz, "The Trio Sonata in Bach's Musical Offering: A Salute to Frederick's Tastes and Quantz's Flutes?" *Bach Perspectives* 4 (1999), 79–110.

17. See, for example, Dammann, 23–35.

18. See Rudolf Flotzinger, "Die Gagliarda Italjana: Zur Frage der barocken Thementypologie," *Acta Musicologica* 39 (1967): 92–100, and Peter Elster, "Anmerkungen zur Aria der sogenannten Goldbergvariationen BWV 988: Bachs Bearbeitung eines französischen Menuetts," in *Bericht über die Wissenschaftliche Konferenz zum V. Internationalen Bachfest der DDR in Verbindung mit dem 60. Bachfest der Neuen Bachgesellschaft, Leipzig, 25. bis 27. März 1985* (Leipzig: VEB Deutscher Verlag für Musik, 1988), 259–67.

19. This hypothesis should be understood as the wider influences Bach received, e.g., new styles of music that he performed with his Leipzig collegium musicum as well as from his friends that are mentioned by Forkel, e.g., Hasse, his wife Faustina Bordoni, Sylvius Leopold Weiss, with whom Bach performed together as a guest musician. This tendency is considered to have became stronger when Wilhelm Friedemann Bach became the organist of the Sophienkirche in 1733.

20. Theodor Leberecht Pitschel, *Belustigungen des Verstandes und des Witzes* (Leipzig, 1741), 499 and 501. Extracted in *BDok* II, no. 499, p. 397; English translation in *NBR*, no. 336, pp. 333–34.

21. Forkel, 30: "so offen, klar und deutlich, daß sie zwar anders klingen als die Melodien anderer Componisten." English translation in *NBR*, p. 447.

22. Forkel, p. 31: "sie sind so neu, so ungewöhnlich und dabey so glänzend und überraschend, wie man sie bey keinem andern Componisten antrifft." English translation in *NBR*, p. 447.

23. *NBR*, p. 448.

24. Mary Oleskiewicz, "Bach, Quantz, and the Transverse Flute: Interrelationships and Influences," a paper read at the biennial meeting of the American Bach Society, Yale University, April 25, 1998. I am very grateful to her for making this unpublished paper available for my consultation.

25. The date of BWV 1035 is given by Robert L. Marshall, "J. S. Bach's Compositions for Solo Flute: A Reconsideration of Their Authenticity and Chronology," *Journal of the American Musicological Society* 32 (Fall 1979): 463–98. There is another instance of Bach's use of *coulé* in a similar melodic shape—but not as one of the main elements in the theme—in the B-major prelude of *WTC* II (BWV 892/1) in bars 24–25, a work that also dates from ca.1741.

26. Quoted by Oleskiewicz, "Bach, Quantz, and the Transverse Flute." See also Mary Oleskiewicz, "Quantz and the Flute at Dresden: His Instruments, His Repertory, and Their Significance for the *Versuch* and the Bach Circle" (PhD diss., Duke University, 1998), 430–34.

27. Joshua Rifkin, "Ein langsamer Konzertsatz Johann Sebastian Bachs," *Bach-Jahrbuch* 64 (1978): 140–47.

28. Payne, "New light on Telemann and Bach," 44–45; "Telemann's Musical Style," 58–59; also Steven Zohn and Ian Payne, "Bach, Telemann, and the Process of Transformative Imitation in BWV 1056/2 (156/1)," a paper read at the American Musicological Society meeting in Kansas City, Missouri, November 4–7, 1999.

29. Jeanne Swack, "On the Origins of the *Sonate auf Concertenart*," *Journal of the American Musicological Society* 46 (Fall 1993): 369–414, esp. 379.

30. See *Zelenka Dokumentation* (Wiesbaden: Breitkopf und Härtel, 1989), 1:78–81 for further details. I thank Janice Stockigt for pointing out this source in our private communication in 1999.

31. Lines 8–9 of the title-page of the original edition of 1741: "Denen Liebhabern zur Gemüths-Ergetzung."

32. It is worth adding that the writing of canons in *galant* style was apparently in vogue among a group of composers, including Telemann, in the late 1730s. See Denis Collins, "Bach and Approaches to Canonic Composition in Early Eighteenth-Century Theoretical and Chamber Music Sources," *Bach: Journal of the Riemenschneider Bach Institute* 30, no. 2 (1999): 27–48, at p. 38ff.

33. Forkel, 47; see *NBR*, p. 460.

34. Johann Joseph Fux, *Gradus ad parnassum oder Anführung zur regelmäßigen musikalischen Composition.* Auf eine neue, gewisse, und bishero noch niemahls in so deutlicher Ordnung an das Licht gebrachte Art ausgearbeitet (Leipzig: Mizler, 1742).

35. Bach's copy is now in the Staats- und Universitätsbibliothek Hamburg, shelfmark MS 202/2b.

36. Christoph Wolff, *Der stile antico in der Musik J. S. Bachs: Studien zu Bachs Spätwerk* (Wiesbaden: Franz Steiner, 1968).

37. Beißwenger, 22.

38. Werner Breig, "Bachs Goldberg-Variationen als zyklisches Werk," *Archiv für Musikwissenschaft* 32, no. 4 (1975): 243–65.

39. For the details of Bach's revisions in his personal copy, see Christoph Wolff, "Bach's *Handexemplar* of the Goldberg Variations: A New Source," *Journal of the American Musicological Society* 29 (Summer 1976): 224–41.

40. Mus. ms. Bach P 225 in Staatsbibliothek zu Berlin Preußischer Kulturbesitz. This aria is located on pages 76–77.

41. The date of publication has been ascertained by Gregory G. Butler, "Neues zur Datierung der Goldberg-Variationen," *Bach-Jahrbuch* 74 (1988): 219ff.

42. See *Katalog der Sammlung Manfred Gorke: Bachiana und andere Handschriften und Drucke des 18. und frühen 19. Jahrhunderts*, ed. Hans-Joachim Schulze (Leipzig: Musikbibliothek der Stadt Leipzig, 1977), 5ff.

43. Yo Tomita, "Bach and His Early Drafts: Some Observations on Little Known Early Versions of Well-Tempered Clavier II and the Goldberg Variations from the Manfred Gorke Collection," *Bach: Journal of the Riemenschneider Bach Institute* 30, no. 2 (1999): 49–72.

44. Ulrich Leisinger, *Die Bach-Quellen der Forschungs- und Landesbibliothek Gotha* (Gotha: Forschungs und Landesbibliothek, 1993), 87. For Boineburg, see Tomita, "Bach and His Early Drafts," 71; Hans-Joachim Schulze, *Studien zur Bach-Überlieferung im 18. Jahrhundert* (Leipzig: Peters, 1984), 80–90; *BDok* III, no. 1025, p. 588; Christoph Wolff, *Kanons, Musikalisches Opfer: Kritischer Bericht*, Johann Sebastian Bach, Neue Ausgabe sämtlicher Werke, series 8, vol. 1 (Kassel: Bärenreiter, 1976), 71ff.

45. *Katalog der Sammlung Manfred Gorke*, p. 17.

46. See note 44.

47. Breig, for example, suggests that Bach initially conceived the *Goldberg Variations* as a set of twenty-four pieces. See his article cited in note 38.

48. See Hartwig Eichberg and Thomas Kohlhase, *Einzeln überlieferte Klavierwerke II und Kompositionen für Lauteninstrumente: Kritischer Bericht*, Johann Sebastian Bach, Neue Ausgabe sämtlicher Werke, series 5, vol. 10 (Kassel: Bärenreiter, 1982), 49.

49. See note 20.

50. It is worth noting that apart from the concerto and sonata, the polonaise appears to be one of the most popular types of composition Boineburg composed, copied, or possessed. Further studies from a stylistic point of view are desirable in order to authenticate this anonymous piece in manuscripts from the Landesbibliothek Gotha, including Mus 4 ° 99h/1 (containing polonaises inclusive of his own), Mus 4° 99h/5 (containing BWV 825/7), and Mus 4 ° 21a/21 (containing Fk 12).

51. See Dammann, 94. See also Szymon Paczkowski, "Über die Funktionen der Polonaise und des polnischen Stils am Beispiel der Arie 'Glück und Segen sind bereit' aus der Kantate Erwünschtes Freudenlicht BWV 184 von Johann Sebastian Bach," in *Johann Adolf Hasse in seiner Epoche und in der Gegenwart: Studien zur Stil- und Quellenproblematik*, ed. Szymon Paczkowski and Alina Zórawska-Witkowska (Warsaw: Instytut muzykologii Uniwersytetu Warszawskiego, 2002), 207–24, at 208.

52. I wish to convey my gratitude to Robin for all the help I received from him in the past, and to pay tribute to his huge contribution to Bach studies, which recently culminated in the formation of the Contextual Bach Studies group that he initiated. This group will offer many opportunities to reexamine afresh those already known historical facts and evidence in a completely new light, illuminating what we could not see and showing their real value and significance in the past.

11

A Is for *Apple*: The Search for an American Church Music; or The ABCs of American Church Music: *A* Is for *Apple, B* Is for *Billings,* and *C* Is for *Chapman*

Steve Pilkington

For several centuries running, the apple has served as a symbol for things quintessentially American, an odd fact considering its hometown is somewhere in the mountains of Kazakhstan. Its story, like that of many pioneers, is one of long journeys, domestication, and transformation in the wilderness that once was America. In the nineteenth century Henry David Thoreau said of the apple: "It migrates with man, like the dog and horse and cow: first, perchance, from Greece to Italy, thence to England, thence to America; and our Western emigrant is still marching steadily toward the setting sun with the seeds of the apple in his pocket, or perhaps a few young trees strapped to his load."[1] As waves of pioneers gave way to seas of vernal blossoms, the apple evolved through natural selection and cultivation into "the American fruit" (in the words of Emerson), taking up into itself the very substance of the land while drawing deeply on its ancient store of genes in order to survive and flourish on the New World's farms and homesteads.

While one of the world's oldest fruits, the apple was never specifically identified in the Genesis narrative as the primordial fruit forbidden of Adam and Eve, in spite of its usual assignation by the Christian imagination. The original apple ancestor is thought to be the Asian *Malus sieversii* found in a place far from Eden's garden. Being a wild and mostly inedible fruit, it is unlikely that Adam would have eaten something "sour enough to set a squirrel's teeth on edge and make a jay scream" (to borrow a phrase from Thoreau).[2] It was not until long after the fall that the discovery of grafting by the Chinese in the second millennium B.C. would encourage the evolution of *Malus domestica*. Without this ancient technique of cloning—notching a slip of wood from a desirable tree into the trunk of another—every apple in the world would have continued to be its own distinct variety, since each of the apple's five seeds contains the genetic instructions for a completely new and different type of apple. The botanist Michael Pollan explains that "apples don't 'come true' from seeds—that is, an apple tree grown from a seed will be a wildling bearing little resemblance to its parent. Anyone who wants edible apples plants grafted trees, for the fruit of seedling apples is almost always inedible."[3] While the earliest immigrants to America wisely brought grafted Old World trees to their new home, their seedlings generally fared poorly in the new, less temperate climate. However, by planting the seeds saved from the apples they ate on their ocean crossing, new trees called "pippins" allowed for the miracle of genetic adaptation to occur. As Pollan concludes: "Wherever the apple tree goes, its offspring propose so many different variations on what it means to be an apple—at least five per apple, several thousand per tree— that a couple of these novelties are almost bound to have whatever qualities it takes to prosper in the tree's adopted home."[4]

Such was the case as early as 1781, when Ben Franklin reported the fame of the Newtown Pippin in European markets, a new American apple that had been discovered in a Flushing, New York cider orchard. By the nineteenth century the thousands of orchards that dotted the north and the ever-expanding margins of the west gave birth to a "great apple rush," a consequence of the fruit's happy fecundity. For a while, whenever a homesteader's tree produced a succulent and fair eating apple, it was promptly named, grafted, and merchandised. The story of the Delicious—the world's most popular eating apple—was just such a tale. Bearing mystical overtones, it told of a stubborn seedling found between the rows of Jesse Hiatt's farm in Peru, Iowa, which refused to die even after repeated mowings cut it down. Interpreting its hardiness as a divine sign, the Quaker farmer allowed the tree to grow and fruit, only to discover its apples were a miracle of flavor. Sending four of his apples to a nursery contest in Missouri, Hiatt's fruit won the day, and the formerly named Hawkeye was rechristened the Delicious for its national debut. Even Thoreau would breathlessly exult in those pomocentric days: "Every wild apple shrub excites our expectations thus, somewhat as every wild child. It is, perhaps, a prince in disguise. What a lesson to man! Poets and philosophers and statesmen thus spring up in the country pastures, and outlast the hosts of unoriginal men."[5] No wonder Henry Ward Beecher, one of the greatest preachers of the nineteenth century, came to call the apple "the true democratic fruit," observing that it was happy to grow just about anywhere and "whether neglected, abused or abandoned, [it was] able to take care of itself, and to be fruitful of excellences."[6]

In actuality, the tale of the apple serves as a metaphor for the American experience and how such experience transforms culture. Just as the Old World apple tried out literally millions of new genetic combinations in order to adapt to its new environment, so too have generations of Americans evolved through a similar process of enculturation. As Thoreau acutely observed, "It is remarkable how closely the history of the apple tree is connected with that of man."[7] (As a Transcendentalist, he was probably not even thinking biblically.) Today, the apple continues as a symbol for knowledge, serving as a corporate identifier for one of the most successful and innovative computer companies in the world—Apple's line of Macintosh computers and iPod sound sources are but another manifestation of the fruit's ongoing power over the American imagination. The purpose of this chapter is as simple as it is odd: drawing on a chapter found in Michael Pollan's lively book, *The Botany of Desire*, this chapter attempts to demonstrate that the story of the apple and its transformation into *the* American fruit provides an excellent corollary for examining the search for an American church music. In a time filled with a host of unoriginal musics—mostly "spitters" as the inedible fruits of the wild orchards were called, this chapter also speaks to the need for a sacred repertoire that is "fruitful of excellences."

Any accounting of the American apple will most likely begin with the colorful and free-spirited John Chapman, a nineteenth-century figure later mythologized as "Johnny Appleseed." One of America's few folk heroes, his story is a quaint and curious piece of Americana involving hundreds of miles, millions of apple seeds, and dozen of orchards scattered across the nation's heartland. While European folklore often includes handsome princes and beautiful princesses, America's mythic tales seem to revolve around eccentric and solitary figures found in the wilds of the frontier, like Paul Bunyan, Davy Crockett, and Daniel Boone. Johnny Appleseed was just such a character. Described by an early biographer as having a "thick bark of queerness on him," one of the first engravings of Chapman depicts a short man with long hair and a scraggly beard wearing a burlap sack with holes cut out for the arms and head, cinched at the waist like a dress.[8] Barefoot and holding a sapling like a scepter, his ensemble was crowned by a tin pot serving as a hat. (The American tolerance for eccentrics has a long history that continues to this day.) Indefatigable, Johnny Appleseed perpetually coursed through the unsettled territories of Ohio and later Indiana and Illinois on a mission to fruit the American plains. Traveling sometimes in a dugout canoe, sometimes with a horse in tow, or most often on foot saddled with the seed-bearing leather bags himself, Chapman would typically develop a nursery or two on the banks of a river, leave a designated manager in charge as his young trees matured, and move on with another load of seeds for the next series of plantings. When his supplies were depleted, he would return to the cider mills of western Pennsylvania, where he would sort through back door piles of discarded pomace and prepare for the next foray into the wilderness. While the legends make much of his broadcast seeds, his trees were actually not sown with great abandon but were planted methodically within the confines of a carefully selected nursery site. Having found a good loamy piece of land in an open and unsettled place near a river or creek, Chapman would mark the ground with fences of fallen trees and logs, bushes and vines. So skillfully were his infant nurseries fixed, by the time his seedlings had attained sufficient growth for transplantation, the next wave of settlers would just be beginning to pass through the region. While he charged a small fee for each tree (six cents in some accounts), his altruism also led him to accept old clothing or shoes, simple foods such as corn meal, or even nothing at all. For Chapman, it was more important for a settler to plant a tree than to pay for it. And with an old brogan on one foot and a discarded boot on the other (according to one description), who was a settler to argue with such a character?

While a frontiersman without a rifle or a knife would have been difficult to find, Chapman traveled without any defensive weapon, befriending Indians, bears, wolves, and even black rattlers if the legends are to be believed. Despite his ridiculous attire and some strange ways, Chapman was often greeted like a saint as he moved between white settlements and far-flung Indian villages. Indians treated him with respect and allowed him to move freely through their territories, regarding him as an unusually gifted woodsman and medicine man. Bearing some knowledge of medicinal herbs, he also blanketed the frontier with dog fennel, pennyroyal, catnip, hoarhound, mullein, rattlesnake root, and other healing plants. When asked why he feared neither man nor beast, he replied that he lived in harmony with all people, and that he could not be harmed as long as he lived by the law of love. One account glowingly reported:

> Johnny made friends with many of the Indian tribes and was known to have learned many Indian languages well enough to converse. Memoirs from settlers who knew Johnny well indicate the impression that many Indians held Johnny in a high regard, and that his unusual zeal for serving others led some to believe he was touched by the Great Spirit. For that reason, they allowed him to listen to their council meetings, and he was therefore sometimes able to avert trouble between a tribe and incoming settlers. He is said to have had compassion for the views and needs of both cultures, and was a fine communicator. He possessed a peculiar eloquence and a resonant voice that was persuasively tender, inspirationally sublime, or, when needed, witheringly denunciatory. He had a keen sense of humor and was quick to make a witty retort or a cutting rebuke.[9]

Johnny Appleseed lived everywhere and nowhere, as restless as the American spirit can be. Some nights he could be found under great chunks of elm bark leaned against the trunk of a tree; other times he would put up a temporary tepee while tending a nursery, or he would avail himself of the floor of a settler's cabin. One winter he used the hollowed-out stump of a sycamore. Often he just slept on a pile of leaves next to a log or protective tree. Like a latter day St. Francis, he also maintained a deep respect for wildlife, grieving when he accidentally stepped on a worm or a snake. With such dangers afoot, he found it much safer simply to travel barefoot whenever possible. Known for his own tolerance of pain, he often demonstrated this capacity to young boys by thrusting needles and pins into the leathern soles of his feet. Equally kind to farm animals, he would round up disabled horses, lame and broken-down animals turned lose by settlers who had moved on, and bargain for their food and shelter until the next spring, when they would be led out to some good pasture for the summer or given away to more humane settlers. In Chapman's view, even the smallest of creatures—mosquitoes—were endowed with the Divine Essence, so that to wound or destroy them was to inflict an injury upon some atom of Divinity. As observed by Pollan, "Chapman combined the flinty toughness of a Daniel Boone with the gentleness of a Hindu."[10]

In truth, Chapman's zest for apples was only matched by his passionate faith. A disciple of Emanuel Swedenborg, he himself claimed to have frequent conversations with angels and spirits. Two of the latter, of the feminine gender, had revealed to him that they were to be his wives in a future state if he abstained from a matrimonial alliance on earth. This was in spite of another circulating tale about a ten-year-old child whose family was holding her as a bride-in-waiting for Chapman. Like a biblical prophet, Chapman considered himself a man called "to blow the trumpet in the wilderness." Under his penetrating gaze, he often inquired of the settlers whose cabins he visited if they might like to hear "some news right fresh from heaven," for he always carried Swedenborgian tracts in his waistband and a tattered copy of the New Testament. Drawing inspiration from the first primitive Christians, he believed he was fulfilling his God-appointed commission to preach a gospel of love, his apple trees a living sermon from God.[11] One woman settler cited in an 1871 article in *Harper's New Monthly Magazine* remembered Chapman in this way: "We can hear him now, just as we did that summer day, when we were busy quilting upstairs, and he lay near the door, his voice rising denunciatory and thrilling—strong and loud as the roar of wind and waves, then soft and soothing as the balmy airs that quivered the morning-glory leaves about his gray beard. His was a strange eloquence at times, and he was undoubtedly a man of genius." With a dash of Protestant righteousness she concluded: "If there is a sublimer faith or a more genuine eloquence in richly decorated cathedrals and under brocade vestments, it would be worth a long journey to find it."[12]

Finally, having planted the American wilderness for nearly fifty years, Johnny's own journey ended in an old friend's cabin. According to the *Harper's* article, having entered the cabin, taken some bread and milk, and read the Beatitudes, "he slept, as usual, on the floor, and in the early morning he was found with his features all aglow with a supernal light, and his body so near death that his tongue refused its office." The author then eulogized:

> Thus died one of the memorable men of pioneer times, who never inflicted pain or knew an enemy—a man of strange habits, in whom there dwelt a comprehensive love that reached with one hand downward to the lowest forms of life, and with the other upward to the very throne of God. A laboring, self-denying benefactor of his race, homeless, solitary, and ragged, he trod the thorny earth with bare and bleeding feet intent only upon making the wilderness fruitful. Now "no man knoweth of his sepulchre;" but his deeds will live in the fragrance of the apple blossoms he loved so well, and the story of his life, however crudely narrated, will be a perpetual proof that true heroism, pure benevolence, noble virtues, and deeds that deserve immortality may be found under meanest apparel, and far from gilded halls and towering spires.[13]

With these words, Chapman's hagiographic journey had begun, the once quivering morning glories around his bearded head now a floral aureole for a queer American saint.

Chapman's devotion to the apple had been nearly sacramental—as though the fruit was actually a means to divine grace. He had spoke of it ardently, describing the growing and ripening fruit as a rare and beautiful gift of the Almighty, with "words that became pictures, until his hearers could almost see its manifold forms of beauty present before them" as reported in *Harper's*. Having found the process of grafting a mutilation of God's creation, Chapman purportedly had said of his wild seedlings: "They can improve the apple in that way but that is only a device of man, and it is wicked to cut up trees that way. The correct method is to select good seeds and plant them in good ground and God only can improve the apple."[14] Knowing that the thousands of trees on homesteader's lands were mostly filled with Johnny's wild apples rather than the delicious grafted varieties, this charming tale becomes less about fresh fruit in autumn and more about hard cider in winter. For, in reality, up until Prohibition most apples were not something that people ate but drank. The only reason to plant a tree that produced sharply sour apples ("spitters," in common parlance) was to press the fruit and ferment its juice in a barrel for several weeks. The resultant cider was "hard" or mildly alcoholic, and the drink of choice for thousands of pioneers and settlers. In rural areas cider could take the place of not only beer, wine, coffee, and tea, but also water, as it was arguably more sanitary than some local sources. Orchards established across New England in the earliest days of the colonies had already supplied thousands of barrels of cider to America's settlers, most likely including Chapman's immediate ancestors. As suggested by a speaker to the Massachusetts Horticultural Society in 1885: "The desire of the Puritan, distant from help and struggling for bare existence, to add the Pippin to his slender list of comforts, and the sour 'syder' to cheer his heart and liver, must be considered a fortunate circumstance. Perhaps he inclined to cider . . . because it was nowhere spoken against in the scriptures."[15]

The good news, as far as the apple was concerned, was that the thousands of trees planted on homesteaders' land allowed the fruit to reach down randomly into its ancient genetic storehouse and produce some of the greatest eating apples of all time. Pollan, in concluding his essay on the American apple, explains:

> [I]n the process of changing the land, Chapman also changed the apple—or rather, made it possible for the apple to change itself. If Americans like Chapman had planted only grafted trees—if Americans had eaten rather than drunk their apples—the apple would not have been able to remake itself and thereby adapt to its new home. It was the seeds, and the cider, that gave the apple the opportunity to discover by trial and error the precise combination of traits required to prosper in the New World. From Chapman's vast planting of nameless cider apple seeds came some of the great American cultivars of the nineteenth century.[16]

In turning to American sacred music, one wonders if there has ever been a similar search for "the precise combination of traits required to prosper in the New World," or have American composers been busily grafting Old World stock onto New World musings for the last two hundred years? Certainly the strains of gospel hymns and songs, white and black spirituals, and most folk hymns and religious ballads have an easily identifiable American flavor. Today's large body of contemporary Christian music, based as it is on the music of rock and the commercial sounds of popular culture, is one of the most transparent of all American sounds. But in assessing the various strains of cultivated music, church music comes up distressingly short. One is hard pressed to find even one enduring cultivar in these sacred groves. A list of ten or even five favorite anthems, whether compiled by musicians or congregants, is unlikely to yield a single piece of American music, that is if one is only considering art music outside the recent phenomena of contemporary Christian music (CCM). While the secular strand of cultivated music (repertoire for the concert hall) contains a series of independent and idiosyncratic mavericks such as Anthony Philip Heinrich (the "Beethoven of Kentucky"), Charles Ives, Henry Cowell, Lou Harrison, and John Cage, in the area of church music few composers have divested themselves of their European pedigree with the abandon of the aforenamed writers. Only in the rebellious, "anything goes" decades following the cultural revolution of the sixties does one find such experimentation in the colorful music of William Albright and such lesser lights as Richard Felciano and Daniel Pinkham. In terms of technique and content, America's best church composers have consistently looked back towards the motherland, borrowing heavily from the rich traditions of English cathedral music or even further afield from the musics of France, Austria, Germany, and Scandinavia. In the late nineteenth century, musicians such as Horatio Parker, George Chadwick, John Knowles Paine, and Mrs. H. H. A. Beach produced impressive works of compositional rectitude, which were flawlessly constructed, but their sounds hung in the air like ghosts in search of a meaningful American soul. Even with Leo Sowerby, an American master in the first half of the twentieth century, there was a potential for a music of substance and American style, but ultimately his harmonic language owed more to Claude Debussy's understanding of tertiary harmony than any of the jazz greats of his time. Today it is the greatest irony that some of the most Anglican sounding music comes from the pens of American composers, while the snazziest, more idiomatic sounds seem to flow contagiously from the Englishman, John Rutter. Most often, when considering American church music, one could apply a critical (if snide) remark published after the premiere of *Leonora* (1845), the third opera of the American nationalist, William Henry Fry (1813–1864): "All were delighted with the music, it was so much like an old acquaintance in a new coat."[17]

Interestingly, in the beginning, it was not so. In the person of William Billings (1746–1800), one finds a particularly striking cultivar, a popular singing-school master and a colonial character as colorful as John Chapman. Like Chapman, he, too, came from the same general area of Massachusetts and made a similarly striking appearance, with an inventory of oddities that included a withered arm, one leg shorter than the other, a blinded eye (which brought him the uncharitable sobriquet, the American Cyclops), shortness of stature, and an uncommon negligence of person, perhaps related to a snuff habit. He also seems to have been cheerful, persuasive, indefatigable, full of self-deprecating humor, and, above all, enthusiastic. Worshiping at the same altar of nature, Billings sounded notes similar to those of America's pomocentric folk hero. An autodidact, he famously said: "Nature is the best Dictator, for all the hard dry studied Rules that ever was prescribed, will not enable any Person to form an Air any more than the bare Knowledge of the four and twenty Letters, and strict Grammatical Rules will qualify a Scholar for composing a Piece of Poetry . . . without a Genius. It must be Nature, Nature must lay the Foundation, Nature must inspire the Thought."[18] He also abhorred the grafting of Old World forms onto the tender strands of America's first crop of sacred composition, believing that it was better for a composer to strive for independence rather than inheritance. Like the wild seed of an apple, he said: "For my own Part, as I don't think myself confin'd to any Rules for Composition, laid down by any that went before me, neither should I think (were I to pretend to lay down Rules) that any who came after me were any ways obligated to adhere to them, any further than they should think proper. So in fact, I think it best for every composer to be his own Carver."[19]

And so it was that when Billings published the *The New England Psalm Singer* in 1770, it was a pippin, a musical seedling different from anything that had gone before. It was full of variety, animation, and an exuberant freedom of movement that accorded well with the new spirit of the budding nation. It was also a music that marched to its own drummer, breaking traditional part-writing rules as it went its own, independent way. It represented one of America's first original musical moments—the first tune book containing solely American music wholly by a single composer. His tunes, wide-ranging like the unfolding continent itself, percolated with optimism. Many settings were distinguished by a rugged pioneer energy, bursting with cheer and even humor. These qualities could be found most noticeably in the fuguing tune, which had faired modestly on English soil but flourished in the American Northeast. Produced by many musical amateurs in addition to Billings, the brief and rapid bits of imitation robustly sung were like a vigorous scattering of apple seeds, the tunes themselves decidedly wild like sour seedlings. While popular and highly favored by the colonists, it was Billings who rhapsodized most about the fuguing tune's qualities, which appear repeatedly in his psalm and hymn settings:

> There is more variety in one piece of fuging music than in twenty pieces of plain song. . . . The audience are most luxuriously entertained, and exceedingly delighted; in the mean time, their minds are surprizingly agitated, and extremely fluctuated. . . . Now the solemn bass demands their attention, now the manly tenor, now the lofty counter, now the volatile treble, now here, now there, now here again—O inchanting! O ecstatic! Push on, push on ye sons of harmony.[20]

A quintessential example of Billings's work is the charming and vivacious "Rose of Sharon," a setting of verses from the Song of Solomon, including lines that reference the apple: "As the apple tree among the trees of the wood, so is my beloved among the sons" and "Stay me with flagons, comfort me with apples."

During this same period a text appeared that has been in American tune-books and hymnals off and on for over two hundred years; it too references the apple. "Christ the Appletree," an autumn-crisp paean to Jesus, is a lovely contemplation of redemptive theology, perhaps the inspiration of a poetical farmer standing in the midst of an autumnal orchard;

> The tree of life my soul hath seen,
> Laden with fruit, and always green;
> The trees of nature fruitless be
> Compared with Christ the apple tree.
>
> His beauty doth all things excel;
> By faith I know, but ne'er can tell
> The glory which I now can see
> In Jesus Christ the apple tree.
>
> For happiness I long have sought,
> And pleasure dearly I have bought;
> I missed of all; but now I see
> 'Tis found in Christ the apple tree.
>
> I'm weary with my former toil,
> Here I will sit and rest a while;
> Under the shadow I will be
> Of Jesus Christ the apple tree.
>
> This fruit doth make my soul to thrive,
> It keeps my dying faith alive;
> Which makes my soul in haste to be
> With Jesus Christ the apple tree.

While feeling like it must have sprung from the ground of New Hampshire or Vermont, it actually has been traced back to a London magazine of 1761, although there are no records of it ever having been sung in England during those days.[21] Finding its way across the Atlantic, it became thoroughly naturalized in a number of American settings, beginning with Joshua Smith's 1784 *Divine Hymns, or Spiritual Songs* and continuing with recent treatments by Pinkham and others. (As if in tribute to its roots, its loveliest incarnation is probably Elizabeth Poston's English setting, in which the melody's octave leap is like an arm reaching up to grasp a piece of luscious fruit.) Interestingly, the last verse, possibly altered in the days of temperance, initially read:

> I'll sit and eat this fruit divine,
> It cheers my heart like spirit'al wine;
> And now this fruit is sweet to me,
> That grows on Christ the Appletree.

With these lines, one is brought full circle to Johnny Appleseed and his sacramental zeal for cider and salvation.

In returning to Pollan's essay on Chapman and the evolution of the American apple, one finds a powerful metaphor that seems to be transferable to the American arts, and especially to the music of the church. Speaking of the need for the imported apple to grow ungrafted so that it might find a New World adaptability, he writes:

> In effect, the apple, like the settlers themselves, had to forsake its former domestic life and return to the wild before it could be reborn as an American—as Newtown Pippins and Baldwins, Golden Russets and Jonathans. . . . By reverting to wild ways—to sexual reproduction, that is, and going to seed—the apple was able to reach down into its vast store of genes, accumulated over the course of its travels through Asia and Europe, and discover the precise combination of traits required to survive in the New World. The apple probably also found some of what it needed by hybridizing with the wild American crabs, which are the only native American apple trees. Thanks to the species' inherent prodigality, coupled with the work of individuals like John Chapman, in a remarkably short period of time the New World had its own apples, adapted to the soil and climate and day length of North America, apples that were as distinct from the old European stock as the Americans themselves.[22]

One might immediately ask where in church music history does one find its composers searching to "discover the precise combination of traits required to survive in the New World"? Billings began the process with his six collections of maverick tunebooks that also glowed with a certain patriotic light. While deeply rooted in the Anglo-American singing tradition, his settings came to sound more of America and less of England as he willfully sought his own path. Not surprisingly, his tune CHESTER with its proud text was one of the most popular songs of the Revolutionary War. Regrettably, his many pieces passed out of fashion quickly, his own strain of musical independence—like an apple's experimental ways—was an embarrassment to the next generation of leaders, who sought a more "scientific and correct" form of expression. Lowell Mason and his colleagues, William Bradbury and Thomas Hastings, decried Billings's ineptitudes, finding the fuguing tune a particularly crude and egregious form of music-making. Unlike the apple, which "forsook its former domestic life" in the American wilds, cultivated American church music has deliberately clung to Old World models, repeatedly attempting to graft itself onto European stock.

For at least a century and a half, the Anglican anthem, in its form, style, musical language, and even texts, has been the graft from which "classical" composers of American church music have drawn their materials. One might ask how many times can the well of English cathedral music, especially in its beloved incarnation from the early twentieth century, be drawn upon until the musical content runs dry? A lesson looms from the days of Johnny Appleseed, when hundreds of different varieties of apples with dozens of different flavor qualities were in commerce. Today that prodigality of fruit—apples that bore quirky, self-endorsing names like the Sheepnose, the Oxheart, the Westfield Seek-No-Further, the Hubbardston Nonesuch, the Ladies Favorite of Tennessee, the Clothes-Yard Apple, and Hay's Winter Wine—have all but disappeared. In this century, most grown apples come from the same five or six parents—Red Delicious, Golden Delicious, Jonathan, Macintosh, and Cox's Orange Pippin—the American public and the apple's marketers having voted for a homogenized sweetness and attractiveness rather than variety and interest. Typically, Thoreau, ever the loner's voice, was already complaining about these matters even in the midst of the nineteenth century:

> Apples for grafting appear to have been selected commonly, not so much for their spirited flavor, as for their mildness, their size, and bearing qualities,—not so much for their beauty, as for their fairness and soundness. Indeed, I have no faith in the selected lists of pomological gentlemen. Their "Favorites" and "None-suches" and "Seek-no-farthers," when I have fruited them, commonly turn out very tame and forgettable. They are eaten with comparatively little zest, and have no real *tang* nor *smack* to them.[23]

How many thousands of modern anthems are common, tame, forgettable, and sound with no real *tang* or *smack*? Whole catalogues of American publishers' sacred music could be classified as sweet as well as shallow. Lamenting the miles of modern-day cloned orchards, one horticulturalist warns, "Breeders keep going back to the same well, and it's getting shallower."[24] As originally endowed by Johnny Appleseed, the vast national orchard—"that wildness preserve and riotous breeding ground of apple originality" (in Pollan's words)—has been winnowed down to the small handful of varieties that can "pass through the needle's eye of our narrow conceptions of sweetness and beauty."[25]

If one steps away from the conservative confines of cultivated sacred music—a place of "narrow conceptions of sweetness and beauty"—and looks to America's broad vernacular tradition, one finds a music that, in its roots and unfolding story, nearly parallels the evolution of the American apple. With the birth of jazz, a great cultivar full of *tang* and *smack* appeared, inarguably an American music "as distinct from the old European stock" as the Americans themselves. Like the best American apples, jazz was born when the music of New Orleans reached down into its rich store of styles and rhythms and produced something entirely new, entirely American. New Orleans was the perfect place for such a flowering: wonderfully cosmopolitan, ethnically complex, and notoriously wild, its multicultural din was as much remarked upon as its saturnalia.

Outdoors, one could hear such things as the singing and drumming of dancing slaves on Congo Square; the outdoors brass bands that regularly played for picnics, parades, and funeral processions; and the ubiquitous dance bands that accompanied the events of a polyglot society, which included the French, Creole (a mixture of French, black, and native American bloodlines), white Americans, black Africans, and a bouillabaisse of foreigners from the Caribbean, the Far East, and many parts of Europe. Indoors, in addition to the music found in its three opera houses and the theaters that sported lively shows of minstrelsy (a concoction that could only have been bred in black and white America), extraordinary things were happening in Storyville, the red-light district where 230 whorehouses held a perpetual party fed by a cornucopia of drugs, sex, liquor, and a new seductive piano music. The famous Jelly Roll Morton remembered that he and many of the district's pianists used to hang out after hours at a place called The Frenchman: "We had Spanish [pianists], we had colored, we had white, we had Frenchmens, we had Americans. We had 'em from all parts of the world. New Orleans was the stompin' grounds for all the greatest pianists in the country."[26] As with the wild native crabs, the American thing that helped catalyze all these ingredients into something distinctly American was a three-fold combination of ragtime—"syncopation gone mad," quipped one magazine editor; the music of the black Baptist Church; and the ancient blues. (Although they appeared to have been born around New Orleans, clarinetist Louis "Big Eye" Nelson would say, "Ain't no first blues; the blues always been."[27])

An eyewitness account from the earliest days of jazz is worth reporting. It comes from the autobiography of W. C. Handy (1873–1958), a multitalented musician and publisher who came to be known as "the Father of the Blues." He tells of playing a dance in Cleveland, Mississippi with his band of "musicians who bowed strictly to the authority of printed notes." Late in the evening, Handy's band was asked to take a break so a local colored band of three men could make some music on "a battered guitar, a mandolin and a worn-out bass." He reported:

> They struck up one of those over-and-over strains that seem to have no very clear beginning and certainly no ending at all. . . . Thump-thump-thump went their feet on the floor. Their eyes rolled. Their shoulders swayed. And through it all that little agonizing strain persisted. It was not really annoying or unpleasant. . . . [Soon a] rain of silver dollars began to fall around the outlandish, stomping feet. The dancers went wild. Dollars, quarters, halves—the shower grew heavier and continued so long I strained my neck to get a better look. . . . Then

I saw the beauty of primitive music. They had the stuff the people wanted. It touched the spot. Their music wanted polishing, but it contained the essence. Folks would pay money for it. The old conventional music [printed scores] was well and good and had its place, no denying that, but there was no virtue in being blind when you had good eyes. That night a composer was born, an American composer.[28]

One is reminded of Billings and his own streak of independence, fighting the tyranny of conventional music not because it was printed but because of the rules it represented. This fledgling but popular composer had also found an essence, "the stuff the people wanted."

Along with jazz, baseball and the nation's Constitution bear mentioning, as they comprise a trinity of things that are as American as apple pie. Gerald Early, an essayist, has predicted that Americans will be known for these three things "when they study our civilization two thousand years from now."[29] Ken Burns, America's great documentarian, expands on their character:

[They] reminded us . . . that the genius of America is improvisation; that our unique experiment is a profound intersection of freedom and creativity. . . . The Constitution is the greatest improvisational document ever created. Written on four pieces of parchment at the end of the eighteenth century, it is still able to adjudicate the thorniest problems of the fledgling twenty-first. It set us on our improvisatory course, emphasizing that we are a nation in the process of becoming, always striving to create a more perfect union, always, as the Declaration of Independence mysteriously put it, in *pursuit* of happiness. More than anything, it has helped to ensure our future by making us Americans unusually curious, unsatisfied, experimenting.[30]

Such descriptors return us to Chapman's improvisatory orchards, where great abandon and a rich heritage produced apple art. It is no wonder the apple became "the true democratic fruit" (in Beecher's words) and a metaphor for American possibility thinking. Pollan calls "The American orchard, or at least Johnny Appleseed's orchard, a blooming, fruiting meritocracy, in which every apple seed roots in the same soil and any seedling has an equal chance at greatness, regardless of origin or patrimony."[31] Similarly democratic, a jazz band presents each player an equal opportunity for improvisatory glory, yet in rewarding individual expression it also demands selfless collaboration. Interestingly, neither of these principles are far from the message of the Christian gospel.

In returning to this chapter's true purpose, this brief survey of the American apple's evolution and its primary saint brings forth these additional considerations. First, church music in America must go into the wilds of contemporary Christianity and free itself from its parochialism so that it might be reborn as an American music. One final iteration of the horticultural miracle found in Chapman's immense pomocentric sanctuary draws the musical metaphor:

> By planting so many apples from seed, Americans like Chapman had, willy-nilly, conducted a vast evolutionary experiment, allowing the Old World apple to try out literally millions of new genetic combinations, and by doing so to adapt to the new environment in which the tree now found itself. . . .Whenever a tree growing in the midst of a planting of nameless cider apples somehow distinguished itself—for the hardiness of its constitution, the redness of its skin, the excellence of its flavor—it would promptly be named, grafted, publicized, and multiplied. Through this simultaneous process of natural and cultural selection, the apples took up into themselves the very substance of America—its soil and climate and light, as well as the desires and tastes of its people, and even perhaps a few of the genes of America's native crab apples. In time all these qualities became part and parcel of what an apple in America is.[32]

Many of America's finest composers of sacred music have been intent on taking up the very substance of the Anglican cathedral—beautiful, magnificent, and holy as it is—and placing it in their music while somehow disdaining the desires and tastes of their own people and culture. It is no wonder that contemporary Christian music has swept through America's churches like a ravening fire: it is an American music that fully resonates with the people and the culture of today. While the language of church music should differentiate itself from popular and rock culture, it should, nonetheless, find other ways to express the very substance of America, sounding of its soil, climate, and light as much as Aaron Copland's *Appalachian Spring* embodies an American essence. Looked at from this angle, planting musical seeds instead of well-tried clones can be seen as an extraordinary act of faith in the American land, a vote in favor of the new and unpredictable as against the familiar and European.[33]

Perhaps more than any other American composer, the music of Ives, with its densely packed layers of American marches, hymns, and songs swirling in an aleatoric fog, often sounds of the organic process described above. It is as though the music was trying to reform itself in the very presence of the listener's ears, the composer determined to discover by trial and error the precise combination of traits required for his music to prosper in the New World. At its best, an Ives symphony is one of Chapman's orchards thinking out loud.

Second, the hymn "Jesus Christ the Apple Tree" reminds us:

> His beauty doth all things excel;
> By faith I know, but ne'er can tell

The glory which I now can see
In Jesus Christ the apple tree.

Any music presented in worship should strive for the beauty of Christ and the glory of his being. Like a Delicious apple, it should be excellent, the best of its kind, beautiful and polished, and stimulating and satisfying to the palette. Superior church music should be "fruitful of excellences," using Beecher's wonderful phraseology. At the same time, some portion of the church's music should be immediately accessible and easily understood by all. This would seem to be particularly essential with a religion that preaches a gospel of inclusivity and a society that boasts democratic ideals. As in H. C. Handy's accounting of one of the early moments in jazz—"Then I saw the beauty of primitive music. They had the stuff the people wanted. It touched the spot. Their music wanted polishing, but it contained the essence."—a church musician should be looking for a musical language that speaks to the people, not beyond them.

Much like the paradox of Christ's own humanity and divinity, the music of accessibility is to be balanced by compositions of unsurpassing beauty and timelessness. It is a concept that even the apple orchard understands. Thoreau reported that "[o]ne Peter Whitney wrote from Northborough in 1782, for the Proceedings of the Boston Academy, describing an apple tree in that town 'producing fruit of opposite qualities, part of the same apple being frequently sour and the other sweet;' also some all sour, and others all sweet, and this diversity on all parts of the tree."[34] This tree and its fruits—another Christological metaphor—is the one church musicians must seek. In concluding his own thoughts, Thoreau aptly quotes Francis Quarles's *Emblems, Divine and Moral* (1825):

Nor is it every apple I desire,
Nor that which pleases every palate best;
'Tis not the lasting Deuxan I require,
Nor yet the red-cheeked Greening I request,
Nor that which first beshrewed the name of wife,
Nor that whose beauty caused the golden strife:
No, no! bring me an apple from the tree of life.[35]

Third, these opinions do not imply that sacred music should ever sound like the great vernacular musics of America. The word "sacred" implies all of the following definitions garnered from *Merriam Webster's Collegiate Dictionary* (Tenth Edition): "dedicated or set apart for the service or worship of a deity; devoted exclusively to one service or use; worthy of religious veneration: holy; of or related to religion: not secular or profane; unassailable, inviolable; highly valued and important." What remains true is that the church has never been so poised to create a music of tremendous interest, variety, and excellence. Great apples were produced because the fruit itself was able to draw on thousands of years of genetic information in wild and random combinations. The church possesses this same potential. Never before in its history has such a diverse and broad range of musics been within close proximity of each other: world music of an astonishing range of interest, electronic music, two thousand years of traditional church music, jazz, plainsong, and gospel, these being only the beginnings of a list of possibilities. Joel Cohen, the director of numerous recordings that seek to recover some of the discarded religious music of America, sounds reveille for the American people:

> Americans awake! We have one of the most rich, diverse, and challenging musical civilizations on this planet! We also, unfortunately, have a collective inferiority complex about our popular culture, and a dreary, stifling tendency to make "official" thoughts and "correct" attitudes replace the spontaneous movements of the soul. As a result, the media and the official circuits of distribution often ignore what is best in our musical heritage, and the public has been miseducated to prefer counterfeit culture to the real thing.[36]

If church musicians and their composers were able to ameliorate the many biases that delimit the possibilities for liturgical music, an extraordinary range of superlative compositions might appear, much as the great cultivars of the nineteenth century transformed the taste and the appearance of the American apple.

Fourth, in a similar vein, American church musicians must be reminded that the genius of America is improvisation, that this unique experiment is a profound intersection of freedom and creativity. Worship, whether regulated by the rhythms of ritual or the freedoms of John Calvin, must be fresh, inventive, and vital, and brought to life through a liturgical creativity that embraces stylistic variety. An endlessly repeating cycle of the same tried and true anthems is deadly. Similarly, a monochromatic sound, either in choral tone or in repertoire, is numbing to the ear and the mind. *Tang* and *smack* should not be foreign descriptors rarely applied to the art of worship. To borrow again from the words of Thoreau in the tone of Billings:

> I wish to speak a word for Nature, for absolute freedom and wildness, as contrasted with a freedom and culture merely civil,—to regard man as an inhabitant, or a part and parcel of Nature, rather than a member of society. I wish to make an extreme statement, if so I may make an emphatic one, for there are enough champions of civilization: the minister and the school committee and every one of you will take care of that.[37]

Fifth, Johnny Appleseed was a wild man, a man of nature, and, seemingly, the real thing. While few, if any, musicians will doff their shoes and follow in his footsteps, one may find an unusual model for saintliness in examining his life. A singular man of unwavering faith, his life was a living theology. In an era where truth and beauty have been eclipsed by sentimentality and secularity, his purity of vision and passionate conviction must be applied to the cause of church music. Additionally, all church musicians, like Chapman, are planters of seeds. The public must be educated to prefer the real thing instead of the many counterfeit cultures that are afoot today. If done faithfully, the harvest of spiritual fruit may be as great as the prodigiousness of his myriad orchards.

In concluding his discussion of Johnny Appleseed, Pollan writes: "John Chapman's millions of seeds and thousands of miles changed the apple, and the apple changed America."[38] One hopes that through a similar dance of adaptability involving millions of notes and thousands of songs, church music will change and, in the course of finding its own American soul, its music will help change America.

NOTES

1. Henry David Thoreau, *Wild Apples and Other Natural History Essays*, ed. William Rossi (Athens: University of Georgia Press, 2002), 142.

2. Ibid., 157.

3. Michael Pollan, *The Botany of Desire: A Plant's-Eye View of the World* (New York: Random House, 2001), 9.

4. Ibid., 11.

5. Thoreau, 153–54.

6. Pollan, 48.

7. Thoreau, 140.

8. Quoted in Pollan, 7.

9. "Johnny Appleseed History," www.swedenborg.org/jappleseed/history.

10. Pollan, 33.

11. For a brief discussion of Chapman and Swedenborgian theology, see Pollan, 33–35.

12. W. D. Handy, "Johnny Appleseed, a Pioneer Hero," *Harper's New Monthly Magazine* (November 1871): 830–36.

13. Ibid., 836.

14. Pollan, 15.

15. Ibid., 21.

16. Ibid., 42.

17. Richard Crawford, *America's Musical Life: A History* (New York: W. W. Norton, 2001), 321–22.

18. Quoted in Crawford, 40–41.

19. Quoted in Gilbert Chase, *America's Music*, 3d rev. ed. (Urbana: University of Illinois Press, 1992), 115.

20. Quoted in H. Wiley Hitchcock, *Music in the United States: A Historical Introduction*, 3d ed. (Englewood Cliffs, N.J.: Prentice Hall, 1988), 13.

21. This information is found in Edward S. Ninde, *The Story of the American Hymn* (New York: Abingdon Press, 1921), 120.

22. Pollan, 13.

23. Thoreau, 156.

24. Pollan, 51.

25. Ibid.

26. Quoted in Geoffrey C. Ward and Ken Burns, *Jazz: A History of America's Music* (New York: Alfred A. Knopf, 2000), 27.

27. Ibid., 15.

28. Quoted in part in Ward and Burns, 15.

29. Ibid., vii.

30. Ibid.

31. Pollan, 42.

32. Ibid., 44–45.

33. Ibid., 42.

34. Thoreau, 157.

35. See "Notes" in Thoreau, 158.

36. Joel Cohen, *An American Christmas, 1770–1870*, Erato 4509-92874-2.

37. Thoreau, 59.

38. Pollan, 43.

12

Beauty and Terror: What Have We to Sing; What Has Worship to Pray?[1]

D. E. Saliers

Philosophers and religious thinkers used to speak with confidence about "human nature." Theologians shaped by existentialism insisted on attending to the "human condition." But most theologians have now been taught to think that everything we think, say, or gesture is "situated"—which, of course, is true. Proper caution against "totalizing" is in order. How and what we speak manifests more than we consciously intend; there are hidden voices, presumptions, and powers—secret and not so secret imperialisms—that sound and distort our discourses. Yet music in Christian worship still speaks to the deepest aspects of human life.

Alongside these complexities, Christian theology speaks amidst the devaluing of language itself. We seem to swim in the corruption of human speech—political, moral, media-dominated aesthetic, and religious—in a popular culture of hype and disaffection. And yet, when it comes to certain matters of extremity, the older discourses of "common humanity" reemerge. Liturgical music in particular can be a sustained resistance to the devaluing of language and life. In this chapter I explore how questions generated by the contrasts between beauty and terror in two musical Requiems may illuminate what theology may pray and say. In Benjamin Britten's *War Requiem* and the *Requiem* by Gabriel Fauré I find significant touchstones to questions for theological aesthetics relevant to Robin Leaver's work.

In his *War Requiem*, Benjamin Britten sets Wilfred Owen's World War I poems against texts of the Mass for the Dead. At the point of the Offertory, the music retells the story of Abram and Isaac. "So Abram rose, and clave the wood, and went, And took the fire with him, and a knife." The boy observes the preparations for the sacrifice and asks where the lamb for this offering is.

"Then Abram bound the youth with belts and straps, And builded parapets and trenches there, And stretchèd forth the knife to slay his son." A musical shift interposes the voice of a divine messenger who bids Abram: "Lay not thy hand upon the lad, Neither do anything to him. Behold, A ram . . . Offer the Ram of Pride instead of him." A children's choir joins the baritone and tenor soloists.

The children begin to sing the ancient Offertorium text from the Latin Mass ("Hostias e preces tibi Domine laudis offerimus. . . ." [Sacrifices and prayers we offer, Lord, to you with praise . . . bring them from death to life]. But unlike the biblical ending of the story, there follows a terrifying text, sung by the two soloists: "But the old man would not so, but slew his son,—And half the seed of Europe, one by one." In Britten's musical intensification of the unspeakable, both soloists in broken musical lines, "one by one," repeat the phrase, over the children's prayers. How is it that listeners are drawn to the exquisitely rendered terrible scene—echoing in our memory long after the music ends? It is terror exquisitely made into ordered sound, in a manner that language alone could not. The layering of musical lines, the irony of text and Mass structure, and the instrumentation all fuse into a sonic event greater than the juxtaposition of the words alone, memorable in its aesthetic power. This episode, coming as it does at the point of the offering of gifts, permeates the surrounding musical elements.

Having heard the *War Requiem* performed recently brought back to me why the juxtaposition of the words "terror" and "beauty" is crucial to questions of prayer and theological discourse. Set together, these words point toward the extremities of the world, and our dwelling in it. In this case, Britten's musical art sounds a layered beholding: the texts of terror are musically articulated in the complex beauty and the rituals for the dead and the bereaved. Such a weaving of war poetry into the prayer of the Requiem Mass interrogates our very notion of what a Requiem is. Moreover, I am drawn to hear such a musical work again—knowing that time will deepen such disturbing art, or as novelist William Maxwell might say, "time will darken it." But against Britten let us place the extraordinary setting of the Requiem by Gabriel Fauré. By contrast, this musical setting of the Mass texts seems enveloped in a calm, serene beauty. Here we encounter no dramatic effects as in other large nineteenth-century Requiems, such as those of Berlioz or Verdi. There is only a hint at the Dies Irae ("day of wrath") sequence. Fauré does not offer a musical expression of the final judgment. He did not aim at the terrifying tensions found in Britten; rather, we are embraced by a profoundly elegiac consolation. It is no accident that the word "requiem" is the first and the last word in this work. Even the scoring of the orchestra signals restraint. There are the two solo voices—soprano and baritone, a choir in four parts, surrounded by modest strings with occasional uses of trumpet and horn, alongside harp, solo violin, and a subdued organ part.

Philippe Fauré, writing four years after his father's death, includes a telling phrase in his description of the work: "It comes about that Fauré, unwilling to describe heaven, yet gives us a glimpse of it, because . . . he has eliminated from prayer its passionate element—that is, terror."[2] This observation signals the composer's musical achievement. Arguably the greatest Requiem since Mozart's, one hundred years earlier, Fauré's treatment of death is oriented toward the comfort of the bereaved. Yet it is not sentimental or unreal about death. Despite his not taking the hearers into the apocalyptic ferocity of "Dies irae" and "tuba mirum," we nevertheless understand that death is real, and that loss and perishing are never to be denied.

Unlike Britten, Fauré's unpretentious treatment of the "Hostias et preces" is a chant. And the "Pie Jesu" text is expressed in an achingly beautiful soprano solo over harp and lower strings. Here is musical pathos, but expressed, as it were, within the interiorization of death's reality and the consolation of the liturgical ritual of Christian burial. The concluding "In Paradisum" contains no trace of torment. As one commentator has observed, "Faure's Requiem . . . is perhaps, more than any other, a Requiem without the Last Judgment; the terrors of the after-life are hardly more than touched upon."[3] One could say also that neither does Britten concentrate on the terrors of the afterlife. The terrifying passages sounded there are very much of this world. The slaughter of war is foregrounded precisely by the historical and theological associations contained in the Latin prayer texts of the Requiem. When we hear the musical setting of Owen's poem, "One ever hangs where shelled roads part," the fusion of crucifixion and the picture of the dead suspended soldier is palpable.

It would be easy, of course, to say the Britten holds the terror and Fauré the beauty. But this will not do. For both hold beauty and the terror of death together, but from very different aesthetic and religious approaches. Britten's music also offers a form of consolation, composed as it was after the end of the Second World War and performed in view of the bombed-out ruins of Coventry Cathedral. It is a very public prayer arising out of the devastation of human conflict. Fauré's composition, coming shortly after the death of both his parents, attends to the role of ritual prayer in the process of grief. Taken together, I contend, they have something to teach us about praying and the work of theology in the face of death and "the human condition."

Rainer Maria Rilke's line from the *First Duino Elegy* haunts our project: "For beauty is nothing but the beginning of terror."[4] Perhaps we might add that the terrifying and its aftermath of grief may lead to reappropriation of nearly unbearable beauty. Labyrinthine pathways lead off from here into aesthetic theory, theology, and the limits of language. For now I simply mark the necessity of confronting these very contrasts. The two Requiems are works of musical art that address what theology and prayer require of human beings.

The terror and the beauty lie unacknowledged for most of us, until the conditions of perception come round: characteristically when pain and terror strike by chance, or when we are enraptured by the intrinsic splendor of something other. I shall argue that, *without* the "everydayness" of our ordinary human embodied patterns of knowing, feeling, and acting, intense experiences of terror or beauty by themselves could be deceptive, could "lie" (not tell the whole truth) about how and what the world is.

Three interrelated sets of questions follow: first, how do we come to see relations between the beautiful and the terrifying? Second, how might we speak of the intelligence of human emotions stretched between these extremities (human pathos) by which we gain a "sense of the world"? Deep human emotions such as awe, wonder, grief, compassion, fear, and grateful receptivity are ingredient in a way of being and knowing and intending the world. How do we reason and perceive in and through our emotions, and not simply subject them to critical assessment? Confronting the beautiful and the terrifying are test cases. A third question emerges: can we speak of a poetics of prayed life in which the imaginative powers lead us beyond the tyranny of the "literally given"? Are there ritual practices that open us to beauty and terror, yet hold these in a deepening emotional intelligence (wisdom) that theology seeks?

The deepest things we know are found in the form of defining affections and passions. We could call this a determinate attunement to the world. A person or a society is better known through what is feared, loved, grieved over, and hoped for than through its factually stated ideas and thoughts. I am convinced that there is available to particular communities of moral and religious discourse a "poetics" necessary for forms of human flourishing. A sense of transcendence in and through the finitude of the world will appear, if at all, precisely amidst the contrasts and connections between terror and beauty. Such a *poesis* is, in part, the work of theology grounded in the full stretch of prayer that dares name both.

EVOKING THE CONDITIONS FOR SEEING THE CONTRASTS

Some of us may now be tiring of the rhetoric of terror, especially as it has been translated into the political rhetoric about "terrorism" and our plan to manage it. Yet no one here can quite take in yet the sense of psychic bodily trauma of the towers falling to dust. Even with the endless replication of images of the planes, the towers, and the enormous human reclamation, we still recoil at the thought. That is, our thoughts are not, nor could they be, merely rational. We recoil because we have appraised these events as a deep violation of our humanity.

Everyday mail can shock in its appeal: "Soldiers shot Tamba's father. Then, as his father lay dying, they trained their guns on the tearful boy and forced him to clap and cheer. Later, soldiers killed Tamba's mother. Tamba is one of thousands of children who have incurred unspeakable trauma—in the war-wracked West African nation of Sierra Leone." Dare we say in Jerusalem, the West Bank, and hundreds of other places as well? The term "Holocaust" so dominates our perception of the century just past, and carries with it enormous import for what we must think, how we must now live. To say that the world is not a place of such daily terror is to be deceived.

Public historical events such as my litany and the nightly news recites are not the only terrors, of course. There are profound personal experiences of being strung between beauty and terror. I think of Gerard Manley Hopkins's "Terrible Sonnets," wherein the poet who can sing ecstatically of the beauty of God's grandeur has become his own self-tormentor because of both external and inner psychic perception. The ordinariness of the starting point in "To seem the stranger" seems obvious—ill, away from family, a sense of exile: "To seem the stranger lies my lot, my life."

Here the terror is internalized to self, and the emotions are articulated in physical and bodily images that show the tortured thoughts:

O the mind, mind has mountains; cliffs of fall
Frightful, sheer, no-man-fathomed. Hold them cheap
May who ne'er hung there. Nor does long our small
Durance deal with that steep or deep. Here! Creep,
Wretch, under a comfort serves in a whirlwind: all
Life death does end and each day dies with sleep.[5]

In such poetry we "feel" and hence "think" into the personal terrors that can indeed accompany and compose everyday life. In Hopkins's case, a specific religious sensibility intensifies the human plight—not comforted, yet strung out by that thought of a "carrion comfort, Despair. . . ." The poetry itself becomes a matter of willed resistance, even against experience. What strikes terror in the human heart depends upon what is valued as precious. Hopkins's lines actually hold the terror in the beauty of his linguistic art. The poetic utterance is a kind of ritual in language, marking a difference between simply being overwhelmed and inarticulate, or reduced to silence, and a cry of the soul striving to witness to the extremity.

We live in a world of immensely beautiful and wondrous things. But this same world is also a terrifying world. Side-by-side with senseless loss and despair lie the mystery and beauty of being. There is sheer delight and deep pleasures in the order of nature, the wondrously finite world of human persons, and the lure of significant form in the human arts. The concept of beauty is notoriously contested. Still, human beings go on being drawn to things we call "beautiful." For instance, what is it about a single jonquil in a simple glass vase, a melody by Mozart, the dance of a child, a painting that causes us to see something forever differently, a passage from Mahler, or the voice of your child singing, in imitation of the mother's lullaby—what is it about these things that arrest us? Is it simply subjective approval that prompts the exclamation, "How beautiful?" Or even the stunned silence that follows a first encounter with Van Gogh's "Starry Night?"—what is perceived? We know that not all art requires the evaluative term "beautiful." Our opening passage from Britten's *War Requiem* is not, in any ordinary sense of the term "beautiful." We need a wide range of discriminations here.

In her dense but illuminating book, *Beauty Restored*, Mary Mothersill argues that beauty is a necessary concept in human life. It is more than a disputed term belonging to the philosophy of art. What is perceived and said to be "beautiful" may, of course, be inconsequential in some instances and settings, while possessing spiritual range and power in others. "Some things," Mothersill claims:

> like a pebble or a clear and cloudless sky, have simple souls. They please in virtue of their aesthetic properties, but those properties once noted and appreciated, do not invite prolonged critical analysis. Decorative formal designs . . . may be elegant, intricate, admirable, and yet, once understood, easily forgotten. All persons and some works of art—those to which we pay homage—have souls that are complex, multi-layered, and partly hidden. They are not to be taken in at a glance, and long study leaves room for fresh discoveries.[6]

Perhaps a better way of making the point is with Emmanuel Levinas, who, in speaking of the sheer delight in something outside ourselves, expresses "non-nostalgic nature of desire, the plentitude and joy of the being who experiences it."[7] Wendy Farley's remarkable discussion of beauty in *Eros and the Other* makes this even clearer: "The exteriority of beauty," she observes, "is emphasized by its infinity. The experience of beauty is never exhausted. The expression 'I love you more each day' makes little quantitative sense, but it is a fumbling attempt to evoke the experience of unending freshness that accompanies friendship or romance or motherhood. . . . But beauty is the sort of thing that in and of itself delights the soul."[8] Thus, detachment from self-preoccupation is the source of genuine delight.

Terror and that which terrorizes; beauty that draws us toward its appearance—both challenge our notion of language. Both stubbornly refuse our intellectual theories, especially our causal explanations. But explaining something by way of causal theory is not the only way to understand something. It may in many cases not be a primary form of understanding at all of those features of human experience that bring as a "sense" of world, of society, of self. In this way prayer is not explanation, but tenacious exploration of the contrasts in human experience. And perhaps the ritual prayer of the Requiem Mass (and its Protestant equivalents) is a continuing non-identical repetition of this vulnerable exploration.

The concept of beauty and the beautiful are notoriously difficult to grasp, yet so persistent in human utterances about what affects us and draws our desires in being a human being. The stunned silence before something that attracts powerfully, as well as the silence following the horrible, the profoundly traumatic, may be related in ways we do not ordinarily consider. Something beyond words occurs when we are confronted with forces outside our control. The "unspeakable" can refer to the searingly traumatic, and also to stunning revelatory beauty, and to music that consoles.

Two conditions emerge for seeing terror and beauty. The first is what "befalls" us; the second is "attentiveness." When I think of the second condition, I think of what Simone Weil has taught us out of her own emotional complexities of affliction and beauty. Human attentiveness to what presences and absences are before us she likens to prayer. It is the crucial element in being and becoming human in the world. So the beauty of the world, precisely in the midst of affliction, is "like a mirror . . . [that] sends us back to our desire for goodness." As one of her biographers remarks, "With the exception of Saint Francis, whose life she looks on as 'perfect poetry in action,' she repeatedly castigates Christianity's lack of emphasis on nature's physical splendor. Our very longing for the beauty of the world, in her view, is God-inspired."[9] But if we are to be attentive to the world's beauty—in nature, in art, in persons—then we must be prepared to be subject to physical suffering (*la douleur*) and to distress of spirit (*le mallheur*) "affliction."

Whatever we make of her own self-tormenting thoughts and actions, I cannot help learning from her of the extremities. And these surface precisely in our bodilyness, not in our pure rationality. In fact, these may diminish or even be repressed in our discursive attempt at theory. Thus comingle those conditions that are pressed upon us by events in the world, and by the necessary condition of our coming to attentiveness about ourselves in the world. I have already alluded to how deep emotions may be ingredient in a sense of the world. To understand what we think about ourselves and the otherness of the world, involves our "being affected." Our knowing the world requires emotional capacities.

THE INTELLIGENCE OF THE EMOTIONS
AND A SENSE OF THE WORLD

Without particular dispositions or emotion capacities we would not "see" things about ourselves and the way the world is. Grief and gladness, gratitude and hope, sorrow and pity, jealousy, envy, compassion: these are the stuff of human beings, and indeed forces within societies. How much is presupposed by deep grieving, or by intention and action born of compassion? The having of such capacities certainly involves "feelings" and bodily experience. What makes such emotions function in a sense of the world is precisely their taking the otherness of the world into us. So the grateful heart is both a disposition and a practice. Ludwig Wittgenstein was right in observing that the world of the grateful is different from the world of the ungrateful. Not just subjectively—but in what one is prepared to see, to think, to intend, to resist.

Deep emotions are oriented toward certain elemental facts: we are mortal, our wills are corruptible, we are born and live in ignorance, and, in short, we are embodied and finite. That is the glory and the travail of being human. All great literature and the range of human arts give us our existence in the otherness of the world known most deeply and intimately through our emotions and passions. This is also the place of encounter with the substance of the moral life and with religious concern. The "untutored heart" has its story to tell. The heart schooled in the inhumanity of our age is racked with anguish, and traumatized into silence.

The philosophical traditions shaping our contemporary habits of mind have characteristically drawn category contrasts between reason and passion, thought and feeling, judgment and emotion. Our habits of thought, and especially theories about mind and body, take natural contrasts and make them into what some have called a "great divide." Being rational excludes considerations of emotion. The intellect is to rule the passions. And our rational capacities have been conceived as needing to control our "lower nature." Emotions have typically been regarded as unruly, belonging to our bodily and sensible nature, linking humans to the animal world through the biological urges and drives of our physical bodies.

The idea that our loves and hates, fears and joys are basically disruptive forces in life is a dominant viewpoint—having come to us in popular psychology as well as in religious and moralist traditions. The stability and objectivity of reason is contrasted with the torrent and tempest of the passions. If it was difficult in the seventeenth century to think clearly about the passions, it is even more bewildering in the present. Many competing conceptions of emotion have emerged. Those who speak of the "science" of human behavior, each with its popular counterpart, conceptualize emotions in particular ways.

Still a certain original sense of "passion" is present—referring to those things in life that human beings suffer. In one of its root meanings, the term refers to the state of being that results from something acting vigorously upon us—change, vicissitude, and accident. We seem, then, passive in the face of the passions. Some may be happy—such as certain forms of love, hope, and joy, while others are painful, even destructive, such as fear, grief, pain, and anger. Underlying this way of regarding human emotional life is the assumption that we cannot help being overcome by our emotions, since they are subjective responses to forces both external and internal (Freud's early "force language" heightened sense of causal connections).

The matter of grieving is particularly instructive because grief is an especially complex and ritually embedded case. Anger, jealousy, regret—all these too may be part of a particular instance. But deep grieving over the loss of a parent or a child, or deep grieving over the terror perpetrated on the innocent—these involve a powerful set of thoughts, appraisals, value-laden descriptions of human life, of the circumstances, and contemplation of the consequences of mortality. That's what makes the grieving deep.

All this ought to alert us to the difference between immediacy of feeling and depth of emotion over time. Likewise we need to see that emotions are also narratives of a sort, having an "onset" and durability. Thus, we can discern the difference between "feeling" angry or jealous and being characteristically angry or jealous, or compassionate, or hopeful. One of the most common ways of learning and expressing emotions is in and through how we describe things outside us. That is how poetry and literature work. It is no accident that many religious sacred texts utilize poetry, or at least the powers of heightened speech, to describe persons, events, and the ascribed attributes of the deity. Human emotions can be "schooled," corrected, altered, and matured when we assent to truthful and persuasive re-descriptions of the world.

Emotions, like thoughts and judgments about the world, can be vague or precise, adequate or inadequate, yes, even "true" or "false" to how things are. The more deeply an emotion in this sense is "lived into" the more it involves understanding specific things toward which the emotion is directed, and grasping the social context that prompts, sustains, or alters the emotional regard. So poetry fused to music, and especially ritual texts drawn from sacred scripture, arouses, sustains, and articulates deep emotions by offering evaluative images and descriptions of reality. Because metaphor, image, and symbols are involved, we speak of the power of the imagination in such discourse. To live with and to understand something by a deep metaphor or image of the self in the world requires a range of intelligence that goes beyond bare rationality as such. "Requiem in aeternam" is such an image. Musical and ritual settings can draw out (or diminish) the implicit features of human vulnerability contained in the phrase.

The intelligence of the emotions gives us a sense and orientation to the world and to our questions of how to live in the world. These, I suggest, are suspended between terror and beauty. In the religious domain, we are more accountable for what we are than for what we immediately feel. To say that a person has a deep sense of gratitude, or that a community is magnanimous or hospitable (or full of vengeance and enmity!), is to remark about their character over time. To understand such emotions in their depth, we must see what is true over time. The evidences of our fear, our hope, our enmity, our compassion will be found in our intentions, and the way we perceive the daily world. Part of human maturity is to learn the difference between shallow and deep emotional life. But this, I contend, requires the cultivation of beholding the contrasts.

But lest this maturity become the province only of the intellectually superior, we now turn to address how human practices, especially certain ritual practices, are a key element in negotiating life amidst terror and beauty, affliction and joy. Thus, as Martha Nussbaum contends, "in an ethical and social/political creature, emotions themselves are ethical and social/political, parts of an answer to the questions, 'What is worth caring about?' 'How should I/we live?'"[10] Both of these questions are implicit in the holding together of death and life, terror and beauty, as we find in both the Requiems with which we began.

THE POETICS OF TRANSFORMATIVE RITUALS

Deep human emotions are ingredient in the "poetics" of everyday life. Both the vulnerability to and the assessment of our lived world (personal, social political, cosmic) are at stake in the cultivation of certain human practices. For seeing the world and human life as something other than what is literally given is crucial to having a "sense of life." We are both active and passive toward our lived world. Desire for the beautiful, a passion for truth, for justice, for healing, orients a whole life. But we are vulnerable in these passions. Both contingency and agency are required. So we are lead to ponder the poetics of everyday life, where both the beautiful and the terrifying lie in wait for us.

Permit me a personal story. In a small rural church I once served, one of the respected, but tumultuous, members of the community died a sudden death. After the church funeral was held, we all gathered back at the farmhouse where his kinfolk and friends had come. Food and drink had been lavishly brought to the place. There a large, polyglot crowd assembled. We ate and drank the gifts of the communal food. Stories began about the deceased.

Laughter and tears, quiet solemnity and utter hilarity came and went. Talk about fear of death, talk about what it meant to have him as a friend, what it now means for the family to go on . . . all this in everyday language, drawing upon friendships as well as rivalries, with all the gestures that accompany such a "reconstruction" of a life in a new kind of memory. So it was I came to my realization of what a sacramental meal really means, what "to remember" begins to signify, and how that ritual occasion itself was the embrace of both terror and beauty.

That funeral meal in which joy, sorrow, laughter, song, and the tears of lament comingled is one of the practices requiring both everydayness and the intelligence of emotion. We need such rites that will not shrink from our humanity at full stretch. Here then is the connection with religious ritual that depends both upon a tradition of practice and real humanity brought to the gestures, the language, the interaction, and the shared sense of life. This is why the ritual of Passover Seder or the Christian Eucharist carry this at their heart. These practices—even when *against* experience, against the evidence that there is something to hope in, to hope for, or to bless in gratitude—are central to receiving our humanity.

Miguel de Unamuno speaks in his *Tragic Sense of Life* of the inner connection between the language of human emotion and religious belief in God:

> Those who say that they believe in God and yet neither love nor fear [God], do not in fact believe in Him but in those who have taught them that God exists. . . . Those who believe that they believe in God, but without any passion in their heart, without anguish of mind, without uncertainty, without doubt, without an element of despair even in their consolation, believe only in the God-Idea, not in God Himself.[11]

We should not, I think, regard such human ritual practices of memory and meal as mere "coping mechanisms" or as vestigial projections of infantilism, or as false dependencies on imagined deities. Of course, such human practices can indeed be interpreted this way, and perhaps usefully so when religious practices degenerate into cliché and empty form.

Perhaps the meal of memory that comprehends both terror and beauty is itself one of the few revelatory things we do. The shaping of certain dispositions toward life and our world where grief and hope are found together can be a place of reconfiguring, or liberation back to our full humanity. These are practices in the midst of our bodily everydayness: where memory is more than language, more than mere recalling of past event; where the comingling of the boundaries of our speech about the terrors of annihilation and the deepest gratitude for life converge. Acknowledging that the same capacity that allows the apprehension of exquisite beauty (however embedded in its cultural specificity) is the capacity that opens the abyss of the terrifying is itself a human achievement, but it is also a gift and a grace.

"Humanity at full stretch." This is not merely the province of the intellectual life, nor is it merely conatural with being born. It requires a form of life and communities that practice the emotions so essential to seeing the world in more than its literal surfaces. It can, of course, go either way: toward the world as a prison, as a charnel house, as a "war of all against all"; or, as a created order in which terror and beauty coexist, where human moral maturity and a sense of the transcendent in and through the finite world becomes part of wisdom about existence.

Everydayness is a dangerous thing to which to appeal. For we know so well the inattentiveness, the egocentricity, the dwelling in illusion and delusion that is part of the inheritance of habit. It is the place of presumptive beliefs, of intentions and actions seeking to avoid the disruptions of emotion *and* thought! And yet, we who are tempted to think our way into transcendence, or into the ideas of terror and beauty can be equally deceived. For we too are flesh and blood, our thoughts and convictions are themselves also born by our emotional regard of the world. And reason is always intermingled with what attracts us most. Yes, reason is eros. But the denial of our finite, bodily life is also a distinctive repudiation of forms of thought—about the elemental facts of being human: we are mortal, born in ignorance, with malleable wills and the corruptibility of flesh and soul. It is only in the stretch of seeing the world in its fullness, in critical awareness of our situatedness between the terrifying and the glorious, between the unspeakable and the most desirable, that we come to moral and religious maturity. We do then have some access, though through a glass darkly, to truth and to what constitutes the good for human existence in a world not of our devising. This is in part the work of theology: to continually awaken and sustain the kinds of intelligence required to attend to beauty and terror, to explore and hold forth both the discourses and the necessary silences before God. Authentic liturgical prayer attends to the formation of those capacities to explore, and to continually re-embed us in the rituals that deepen, sustain, and nourish those capacities, those dispositions that awaken and reveal a world beyond cause and effect, beyond the literally given.

What is it to be drawn back to our humanity at full stretch before God and in this world of enemies and neighbors, of hurtful and incomprehensible suffering, of the ecstatic sense of being alive? Here we come finally to see how a passion for truth, for justice, for the good of the other and for all requires all our reason and more. Some aesthetic forms of a prayed theology open this up for us. I have suggested how two contrasting Requiems are touchstones to key features of theological aesthetics.

Beauty can deceive. Terror can drive us to self-torture. But where human lives in time and space are actively receptive to mystery and suffering, we come to respect the knowing and the unknowing, the glory and the fragility of humanity in the whole created order of things. Doxology without lament can be a snare and a delusion. Yet practices that form us in a sense of the world that takes into itself suffering and joy are more fitting to our humanity than is a sense of the world that ignores the suffering, or that takes easy pleasure in the pleasant or the beautiful. There is more than the cold assessment of brute facts. Our humanity is the place of convergence of beauty and terror. When faith speaks truthfully about joy in the midst of tribulation, we pause. When practices make this palpable over time, awe and wonder and the capacity to grieve are restored. To this continuing paradoxical tension we must turn again and again, in art, in prayer, in theological reasoning, and in life.

REFLECTION ON THESE "NOTATIONS"

My colleague, Steffen Loesel, remarked that this essay takes the form of a series of "notations." Each notation suggests a particular way of starting with the musically embodied pattern and themes found in the contrasting Requiems, prescinding into three separable but interrelated domains:

1. conditions of perception,
2. the affective/cognitive reception of what is mediated by musical settings of the Requiem, and
3. connections with the transformative "poetics" of ritual practices that may tensively hold the contrasts of beauty and terror in the face of death.

Returning to Britten's and Fauré's contrasting settings of the Requiem, and our continuing experience of these works over time, perhaps it is now possible to offer specifically theological insights. We first recognize that both settings are dependent upon the *ordo*—the "tensive" structural pattern—of the Western Christian Mass rite for the dead.[12] The Latin texts are "tensive" in themselves, moving as they do from the opening Kyrie through successive ritual modalities (Sanctus, Dies Irae, Agnus Dei, et. al.) concluding with the return to the primary word "requiem." This is especially true of Fauré's selection of texts. Each section of the Mass rite can be "heard" and understood only in juxtaposition with the others. The Christian theology of death requires the cry of "mercy!"—"Kyrie" or "Agnus Dei"—and the affirmation of the paradox of death and resurrection. The Medieval sequence of the Dies Irae sounds the terrors of judgment against the claim of Christ's victory. In this we noted the difference between Britten and Fauré.

Second, the musical setting itself is part of a performed presentational interpretation of the meaning of death. In both cases we find compelling aesthetic features, musical form, and performance worthy of the term "beautiful." Yet the "beautiful" itself is comprised, especially in Britten's range, of dissonance and demanding layers of instrumentation and vocalization, not to mention key and pitch relations of considerable tension. In Fauré the elegiac serenity of the moving tonal forms, the spare instrumentation, the exquisite use of solo voice (and solo violin as well) present us with a non-dissonant beauty. Even here a full musicological analysis would reveal daring elements in view of Fauré's break with antecedent French musical traditions. The main point here is that specific musical settings are particular realizations (performances) of the ritual prayer texts. The music is not an ornamentation of the theological truths; the music is intrinsic to the "content" of those claims. In this sense the music is essential to our reception of holding together death and life, of discerning terror born of not knowing, and the consolations of faith "coming to resolution." This is a knowing, but more than a merely cognitive or "doctrinal" knowledge. The power of these musical settings generates the possibility of an affective knowing, a participation in the "sounded" truth.

A third point of return is to ponder the differences between a dramatic collision of the violence and terrors of war and the liturgical texts, on the one hand (Britten), and attending to the serenity of acceptance born of a transparency of the liturgical texts, on the other (Fauré). Here we regain a specifically theological frame of reference. Can we pray these ancient ritual texts without the Christian (and, for some, the "Christocentric") claims they make? We can certainly appreciate the aesthetic power of these works in performance. But I propose that it is precisely the musical re-presentation of human existence (life and death, the beauty and the terrors of human existence) *coram deo* that illuminate the aesthetic power. There is something more here than simple "aesthetic enjoyment." While it is yet another step to reinsert Fauré's setting into a celebration of an actual funeral rite (and this is quite possible, whereas it is not possible with Britten), I contend that an adequate grasp of the mystery of our humanity at full stretch before God requires precisely the contrasts these two great works of art present us.

No doubt we must keep listening to these works, and keep returning to the ritual contexts of the Christian rites that they contain, in order to grasp the inexhaustibility of the theological claims. Returning again and again, especially in their "live" performance, we deepen our sense and sensibility of the central mystery of Christian faith. The "terrors" of which Rilke and Owen speak in their poetry are more than the fact of death or mortality. But we need both the fierce and demanding beauty of Britten's juxtaposed ironies, and the profound consolation of requiem in God expressed by Fauré to understand the range of prayer, and the stretch of truthful theological claims about the human search for, and journey toward, the God who has embraced death and life—the God who gives requiem *in aeternam*.

NOTES

1. This essay was developed from an earlier version published as "Beauty and Terror," *Spiritus* 2/2 (2002): 181–91.

2. Philippe Fauré-Frémiet, *Gabriel Fauré* (Paris: Rieder, 1929), 50, cited in Norman Suckling, *Fauré* (Westport, Conn.: Greenwood Press, 1946), 177.

3. Suckling, 176.

4. Rainer Maria Rilke, *Duino Elegies*, trans. Stephen Mitchell (New York: Random House, 1980), 9.

5. Gerard Manley Hopkins, *Poems of Gerard Manley Hopkins*, ed. W. H. Garner, 3d ed. (New York: Oxford University Press, 1948), 107.

6. Mary Mothersill, *Beauty Restored* (Oxford: Clarendon Press, 1984), 422–23.

7. Emmanuel Levinas, *Collected Philosophical Papers*, trans. Alphonso Lingis (Dordrecht, The Netherlands: Martinus Nijhoff, 1987), 57.

8. Wendy Farley, *Eros for the Other: Retaining Truth in a Pluralistic World* (University Park: Pennsylvania State University Press, 1996), 81–84.

9. Francine du Plessix Gray, *Simone Weil* (New York: Viking, 2001), 221.

10. Martha C. Nussbaum, *Upheavals of Thought: The Intelligence of Emotions* (Cambridge: Cambridge University Press, 2001), 149.

11. Miguel de Unamuno, *The Tragic Sense of Life*, trans. J. E. Crawford Flitch (New York: Dover Publications, 1954), 193.

12. For the particular sense in which I am using the terms "ordo" and "juxtaposition," see Gordon W. Lathrop, *Holy Things: A Liturgical Theology* (Minneapolis: Fortress Press, 1993), 13–86.

13

Robin A. Leaver: A Bibliography of His Writings

Sherry L. Vellucci

Robin Leaver has a lifelong commitment to his three loves: teaching, mentoring, and scholarship. Examples of his dedication to teaching and mentoring are well represented by many of the authors who have contributed to this Festschrift. His teaching at Westminster Choir College, The Juilliard School, and Drew University occupy a large portion of his time. It is all the more remarkable, therefore, that he is able to maintain the scholarly productivity that is represented in this bibliography.

Robin's earliest published writing was a letter to the editor of *The Musical Times*, penned just before his ordination into the Church of England ministry (September 1964). As a parish pastor he was called upon to write journalistic material for parish magazines and the like, writings that are not recorded here. In 1971 he was awarded a Winston Churchill Fellowship, in order to travel to the United States to undertake research into Johann Sebastian Bach's theological library, especially Bach's own copy of the Calov *Deutsche Bibel*, which is in the library of Concordia Seminary, St. Louis. Ultimately this research led to two books on these subjects, published in 1983 and 1985. The time spent in the United States proved to be a great stimulus to his research and writing, as can be seen from the bibliography that follows. He began reviewing books for various publications as well as writing somewhat popular articles in a journalistic vein, but little by little scholarly concerns began to predominate, and the flow of scholarly articles and books continues to this day.

Despite a publication record that many of us can only envy, Robin remains modest with regard to his accomplishments. In the preface to a bibliography he issued to mark his sixtieth birthday Robin wrote:

> People have often commented on my productivity, as if it is something unusual. Compared with theologians and musicologists of earlier centuries, my writings are much less numerous. If this is a record of anything, it shows what can be achieved when you quietly keep at it. Perhaps I have written too much, and too superficially. If so, then I hope that others will be encouraged to get into the realm of scholarship, prove me wrong, amend my findings, or go far beyond them.
>
> What I have written witnesses to the questions that I have pursued, questions that I could not find answered to my satisfaction, so I felt myself compelled to find my own answers. But I have not finished yet; there are many more questions to be answered, and I intend to address them in the years ahead.
>
> "Bibliography of the Published Writings of Robin A Leaver," Princeton, 1999

We are indeed fortunate that Robin continues to pursue his quest for answers and sincerely hope that he has many more years ahead of him to address these questions.

PREVIOUS BIBLIOGRAPHIES

Leaver, Robin A. [Recent Activities]; [Biography and Bibliography of Bach Studies]. In *Theologische Bachforschung heute: Dokumentation und Bibliographie der Internationalen Arbeitsgemeinschaft für theologische Bachforschung 1976–1996*, edited by Renate Steiger, 152–53; 385–88. Berlin: Galda + Wilch, 1998.

"Bibliography of the Published Writings of Robin A. Leaver." Princeton, N.J.: privately published, 1999.

1964

Letter to the Editor [on hymnody]. *Musical Times* 105 (1964): 437.

1970

Review

English Church Music 1650–1750: In Royal Chapel, Cathedral and Parish Church, by Christopher Dearnley. *Churchman: A Quarterly Journal of Anglican Theology* 85 (1971): 300–1.

1971

Chapters/Articles

"Against the Stream: Heinrich Schütz." *News Extra* (Appleford, Eng.), March 1971.
"From Jew to Christian: Mendelssohn." *News Extra* (Appleford, Eng.), April 1971.
"The Man of Simple Faith: Johann Sebastian Bach." *News Extra* (Appleford, Eng.), October 1971.
"Further Thoughts on B-A-C-H." *Bach: The Quarterly Journal of the Riemenschneider Bach Institute* 2, no. 4 (October 1971): 36–37.
"Falling Foul of the Nazis: Hugo Distler 1908–1942." *News Extra* (Appleford, Eng.), Dec 1971.

Review

Hilfsbuch zum Luther-studium, 3rd ed., edited by Kurt Aland, Witten: Luther-Verlag, 1970. *Concordia Theological Monthly* 42 (1971): 568.

1972

Chapters/Articles

"Genius and Enigma: Beethoven 1770–1827." *News Extra* (Appleford, Eng.), January 1972.
"Getting Out of a Rut: Charles Ives 1874–1954." *News Extra* (Appleford, Eng.), March 1972.
"Leipzig's Rejection of J. S. Bach." *Bach: The Quarterly Journal of the Riemenschneider Bach Institute* 3, no. 3 (July 1972): 27–39; 3 no. 4 (October 1972): 3–7.

Miscellaneous

Letter to the Editor [on a 17th century organ tutor]. *Musical Times*, 113 (1972): 559.

1973

Book

A Short History of St. Mary's Chapel Castle Street, Reading. Reading, Eng.: St. Mary's Castle Street, 1973.

Chapters/Articles

[1972] "Genius and Enigma: Beethoven 1770–1827." *News Plus* (Appleford, Eng.), January 1973.

[1972] "Getting Out of a Rut: Charles Ives 1874–1954." *News Plus* (Appleford, Eng.), March 1973.

[1971] "The Man of Simple Faith: Johann Sebastian Bach." *News Plus* (Appleford, Eng.), April 1973.

"Heinrich Schütz as a Biblical Interpreter." *Bach: The Quarterly Journal of the Riemenschneider Bach Institute* 4, no. 3 (July 1973): 3–8.

"List of Settings of Biblical Texts in the Works of Heinrich Schütz." *Bach: The Quarterly Journal of the Riemenschneider Bach Institute* 4, no. 3 (July 1973): 8–12.

"The Funeral Sermon for Heinrich Schütz." Pt. 1. *Bach: The Quarterly Journal of the Riemenschneider Bach Institute* 4, no. 4 (October 1973): 3–7.

"Reading's Proprietary Chapel." *Oxford Diocesan Magazine* 6, no. 12 (December 1973): 13–14.

Miscellaneous

Letter to the Editor [on Lutheran use of plainchant] *Musical Times*, 114 (1973): 795–96.

1974

Chapters/Articles

"The Funeral Sermon for Heinrich Schütz." Pts. 2–4. *Bach: The Quarterly Journal of the Riemenschneider Bach Institute* 5, no. 1 (January 1974): 9–22; 5, no. 2 (April 1974): 22–35; 5, no. 3 (July 1974): 13–20.

"Bunk, Lies, Falsehood, or, A Great Dust Heap?" [An evaluation of the importance of the study of church history]. *Forum: The Quarterly Newsletter of Church Society, London*, June and September 1974.

1975

Books

Luther on Justification. St. Louis: Concordia Publishing House, 1975. Includes preface by Professor E. Gordon Rupp.

A Thematic Guide to the Anglican Hymn Book. London: Church Book Room Press, 1975.

Chapters/Articles

"The Libretto of Bach's Cantata no. 79: A Conjecture." *Bach: The Quarterly Journal of the Riemenschneider Bach Institute* 6, no. 1 (January 1975): 3–11.

"Tenth Anniversary of a Hymn Book [on the *Anglican Hymn Book*, 1965]." *Home Words* (London), May 1975, 11.

"A Decade of Hymns: Reflections on the Tenth Anniversary of the Anglican Hymn Book." *Churchman: A Quarterly Journal of Anglican Theology* 89 (1975): 108–19.

"More than an Honorable Failure [On the Tenth Anniversary of the *Anglican Hymn Book*]." *Church of England Newspaper*, no. 4243, June 6, 1975.

"A New Hymn Book Every 25 Years." *Church of England Newspaper*, no. 4252, August 6, 1975.

"The Hymn Book Today." *Hymn Society of Great Britain and Ireland Bulletin* 8, no. 8 (November 1975): 133–40.

"Bach's Understanding and Use of the Epistles and Gospels of the Church Year." *Bach: The Quarterly Journal of the Riemenschneider Bach Institute* 6, no. 4 (October 1975): 4–13.

"Bach's *Clavierübung III*: Some Historical and Theological Considerations." *The Organ Yearbook* (1975): 17–32.

"Bach und die Lutherschriften seiner Bibliothek." *Bach-Jahrbuch* 61 (1975): 124–32.

1976

Book

The Liturgy and Music: A Study of the Use of the Hymn in Two Liturgical Traditions. Grove Liturgical Study 6. Bramcote, Nottingham: Grove Books, 1976.

Chapters/Articles

[1975] "A Decade of Hymns: Reflections on the Tenth Anniversary of the Anglican Hymn Book." *IAH* [Internationale Arbeitsgemeinschaft für Hymnologie] *Bulletin* 3 (1976): 79–90.

"Number Associations and the Structure of Bach's *Credo*, BWV 232." *Bach: The Quarterly Journal of the Riemenschneider Bach Institute* 7, no. 3 (July 1976): 17–24.

"Series III Communion." *Anglican*, November 1976, 8. [See also the editorial apology on page 3 of the December 1976 issue].

"The Calov Bible from Bach's Library." *Bach: The Quarterly Journal of the Riemenschneider Bach Institute* 7, no. 4 (October 1976): 16–22.

Reviews

Handbook of Parish Music, by Lionel Dakers, London: Mowbray, 1976. *Churchman: A Quarterly Journal of Anglican Theology* 91 (1976): 284–85.

Christian Worship, edited by B. Howard Mudditt, Exeter: Paternoster Press, 1976. *Churchman: A Quarterly Journal of Anglican Theology* 90 (1976): 332–33.

Hymns for Choirs Arranged for Mixed Voices and Organ, edited by David Willcocks, London: Oxford University Press, 1976. *Churchman: A Quarterly Journal of Anglican Theology* 90 (1976): 336.

Das Deutsche Kirchenlied (DKL): *Kritische Gesamtausgabe der Melodien* I/1: *Verzeichnis der Drucke von den Anfangen bis 1800*, edited by Konrad Ameln, Markus Jenny, and Walther Lipphardt, Kassel: Bärenreiter Verlag, 1975. *Hymn Society of Great Britain and Ireland Bulletin* 8, no. 11 (October 1976): 195–96.

1977

Chapters/Articles

"Celebrating the Reformation." *Churchman: A Quarterly Journal of Anglican Theology* 91, no. 1 (1977): 62–67.

"Bach and the Kirchengesangbuch." *The Bach Society Bulletin* 1, no. 1 [only issue] (February 1977): 1–11.

"A New Bach Source." *The Bach Society Bulletin* 1, no.1 (February 1977): 27–28.

"Isaac Watts's Hermeneutical Principles and the Decline of English Metrical Psalmody." *IAH Bulletin* 4 (April 1977): 54–59.

"Literaturbericht für United Kingdom." *Jahrbuch für Liturgik und Hymnologie* 21 (1977): 234–39.

Reviews

Die Kantaten von Johann Sebastian Bach, by Alfred Dürr, 2nd ed. 2 vols., Kassel: Bärenreiter/ DTV, 1975. *Bach Society Bulletin* 1, no. 1 (February 1977): 30.

Number in Scripture, by E. W. Bullinger, London: Bagster, 1976. *Bach Society Bulletin* 1, no. 1 (February 1977): 30.

Jahrbuch für Liturgik und Hymnologie, vols. 19 and 20, Kassel: Johannes Stauda, 1975 and 1976. *Churchman: A Quarterly Journal of Anglican Theology* 91 (1977): 285–86.

Calvijns Beginsel voor de Zang in de Eredienst Verklaard uit de Heilige Schrift en uit de Geschiedenis der Kerk, by H. Hasper, vol. 2, Groningen: Vuurbaak. 1976. *Churchman: A Quarterly Journal of Anglican Theology* 91 (1977): 286–88.

Program Notes

Program notes on Bach's Cantatas BWV 84, 73, 32 and 158. For a performance by the Taverner Choir and the Taverner Players, conducted by Andrew Parrott. Queen Elizabeth Hall, London, Saturday October 1, 1977.

1978

Books

The Work of John Marbeck. Courtenay Library of Reformation Classics 9. Appleford: Sutton Courtenay Press, 1978.
Catherine Winkworth: The Influence of Her Translations on English Hymnody. St. Louis: Concordia Publishing House, 1978.

Chapters/Articles

"Anglikanse lezingenreeks." In *Samen Leven Evangelish-Luthers Gadboek 1978–1979*, 408–13. Amstelveen: Netherlands, 1978.
"John Marbeck." *News Extra* (Appleford, Eng.), April 1978.
[1977] "Isaac Watts's Hermeneutical Principles and the Decline of English Metrical Psalmody." *Churchman: A Quarterly Journal of Anglican Theology* 92, no. 1 (1978): 56–60.
"The Hymn and the Old Testament." *Hymn Society of Great Britain and Ireland Bulletin* 9, no. 1 (January 1978): 14–16.
"Catherine Winkworth: Queen of Translators 1827–1878." *News Extra* (Appleford, Eng.), July 1978.
"The Valuation of Bach's Library." *Bach: The Quarterly Journal of the Riemenschneider Bach Institute* 9, no. 2 (April 1978): 28–32.
"News of Publications." *Music in Worship: A Quarterly Journal for Christians* 4 (June 1978): 6–7.
Duffield, Gervase. "Latimer House Man Rediscovers 'Resilient' John Marbeck." Interview with Robin A. Leaver. *Church of England Newspaper*, no. 4404, July 21, 1978, 10.
"Bach and Luther." *Bach: The Quarterly Journal of the Riemenschneider Bach Institute* 9, no. 3 (July 1978): 9–12, 25–32. Expanded English version of "Bach und die Lutherschriften seiner Bibliothek." *Bach-Jahrbuch* 61 (1975): 124–32.
"An Ecumenical Hymn Book for the United Kingdom." *Churchman: A Quarterly Journal of Anglican Theology* 92, no. 4 (1978): 340–43.
"Catherine Winkworth's Place in English Hymnody." *The Hymn: The Journal of the Hymn Society of America* 29, no. 4 (October 1978): 214–16.
"Literaturbericht zur Hymnologie für United Kingdom." *Jahrbuch für Liturgik und Hymnologie* 22 (1978): 270–72.

Reviews

Hymnals and Chorale Books of the Klinck Memorial Library, edited by Carl Schalk, River Forrest, Ill. Concordia Teachers College, 1975; *Hymn Books at Wittenberg*, by Louis Voigt, Springfield, Ohio: Chantry Press, 1975. *Churchman: A Quarterly Journal of Anglican Theology* 92 (1978): 95–96.

A Short Survey of English Church Music, by Erik Routley, London: Mowbray, 1977.
Churchman: A Quarterly Journal of Anglican Theology 92 (1978): 190–91.
Six Easy Three-Part Anthems, by A. Greening, Croydon: RSCM, 1977; *Singing on Saturday: A Selection of Music and Readings*, by Erik Routley, Croydon: RSCM, 1977; *Sixteen Hymns of Today for Use as Simple Anthems*, edited by John Wilson, Croydon: RSCM, 1978. *News of Liturgy*, no. 42, June 1978, 6.

1979

Book

The Doctrine of Justification in the Church of England. Latimer Studies 3. Oxford: Latimer House, 1979.

Chapters/Articles

"The German Hymn in English: The Challenge of Catherine Winkworth (1827–1878)." *Hymn Society of Great Britain and Ireland Bulletin* 9, no. 4 (January 1979): 61–65.
"Two Hundred Years of Praise [on Olney Hymns]." *News Extra* (Appleford, Eng.), June 1979; *News Plus* (Appleford, Eng.), June 1979.
[1971] "Against the Stream: Heinrich Schütz." *Music in Worship* no. 8 (June 1979): 10–11.
[1971] "The Man of Simple Faith: Johann Sebastian Bach." *Music in Worship* no. 10 (December 1979): 6–7.
"An English Ecumenical Hymn Book." *IAH Bulletin* 7 (1979): 60–63.
"Olney Hymns 1779, 1: The Book and Its Origins." *Churchman: A Quarterly Journal of Anglican Theology* 93, no. 4 (1979): 327–42.
"Literaturbericht zur Hymnologie für United Kingdom." *Jahrbuch für Liturgik und Hymnologie* 23 (1979): 246–48.

Reviews

Een Compendium van Achtergrond informatie bij 491 Gezangen uit het Liedboek voor de Kerken, Amsterdam: Gerardus Van der Leeuw-Stichting, 1977. *Churchman: A Quarterly Journal of Anglican Theology* 93 (1979): 94–95.
English Church Music 1978, edited by Lionel Dakers, Croydon: RSCM, 1978. *Churchman: A Quarterly Journal of Anglican Theology* 93 (1979): 95–96.
With One Voice: A Hymn Book for All the Churches, London: Collins Liturgical Publications, 1979. *News of Liturgy,* no. 50, February 1979, 6–7.
Short reviews of various periodicals, books and music. *Music in Worship* no. 7 (March 1979): 6–8.
Johann Sebastian Bach: Life, Times, Influence, edited by Barbara Schwendowius and W. Dömling, Kassel: Bärenreiter, 1977. *Churchman: A Quarterly Journal of Anglican Theology* 93 (1979): 190–92.

One by One, by Cyril Taylor, Croydon: RSCM, 1979. *Churchman: A Quarterly Journal of Anglican Theology* 93 (1979): 192.

Short reviews of various books. *Music in Worship* no. 8 (June 1979): 9.

John Taverner: His Life and Work, by Colin Hand, London: Eulenburg, 1978; *A Handbook of Church Music*, edited by Carl Halter and Carl Schalk, St. Louis: Concordia, 1978; *Keywords in Church Music*, edited by Carl Schalk, St. Louis: Concordia, 1978. *Music in Worship* no. 9 (September 1979): 7.

A Handbook of Church Music, edited by Carl Halter and Carl Schalk, St. Louis: Concordia, 1978; *Keywords in Church Music*, edited by Carl Schalk, St. Louis: Concordia, 1978. *Churchman: A Quarterly Journal of Anglican Theology* 93 (1979): 286–88.

Partners in Praise, edited by Bernard Braley, London: Galliard, 1979. *News of Liturgy* no. 58, October, 1979, 5–6.

Jonathan Gray and Church Music in York 1770-1840, by Nicholas Temperley, York: Borthwick Institute, 1977. *Churchman: A Quarterly Journal of Anglican Theology* 93 (1979): 378–79.

Handbook to the Church Hymnary Third Edition, edited by John M. Barkley, London: Oxford University Press, 1979. *Churchman: A Quarterly Journal of Anglican Theology* 93 (1979): 379–80.

Johann Sebastian Bach, by Fred Hamel. 4th ed., Göttingen: Vandehoeck und Ruprecht, 1968. *Churchman: A Quarterly Journal of Anglican Theology* 93 (1979): 380–81.

Program Notes

Program notes on Bach's *Johannespassion* (BWV 245). For performances by the Taverner Choir and the Taverner Players, conducted by Andrew Parrott. *Early Music Centre Festival 1979: The Dignity of Man*. Seven Concerts at St. John's, Smith Square, London, 38.

1980

Books

A Hymn Book Survey 1962–80. Grove Worship Series 71. Bramcote, Nottingham: Grove Books, 1980.

Hymns with the New Lectionary. Bramcote, Nottingham: Grove Books 1980.

Chapters/Articles

"Music in Church Today." In *Anglican Worship Today: Collins Illustrated Guide to the Alternative Service Book 1980*. Edited by Colin Buchanan, Trevor Lloyd, and Harold Miller, 49–52. London: Collins Liturgical Publications, 1980.

with Ann Bond. "Martin Luther and Lutheranism." In *New Grove Dictionary of Music and Musicians*, edited by Stanley Sadie, 11: 365–71. London: Macmillan 1980.

"Ulrich Zwingli." In *New Grove Dictionary of Music and Musicians*, edited hy Stan-ley Sadie, 20: 725–26. London: Macmillan, 1980.

"Accepted for Christ's Sake [on the Doctrine of Justification]." *Church of England Newspaper*, no. 4480, January 18, 1980, 7.

"Supplement to *Hymn Book Survey 1962–1980*: 1980 and the Future." *News of Liturgy*, no. 61, January 1980, 2–8.

"Olney Hymns 1979, 2: The Hymns and their Use." *Churchman: A Quarterly Journal of Anglican Theology* 94, no. 1 (1980): 58–66.

"Sin: In Need of Radical Treatment [on Nos. 9–19 of the Thirty-Nine Articles]." *Church of England Newspaper*, no. 4510, September 12, 1980, 6.

"Welsh and English Hymnody." *IAH Bulletin* 8 (July 1980): 61–62.

"Oxford 1981." *IAH Bulletin* 8 (July 1980): 62–63.

"The Augsburg Confession and the Confessional Principle." *Churchman: A Quarterly Journal of Anglican Theology* 94, no. 4 (1980): 345–52.

"Literatur zur vorbereitung der Tagung." *IAH Mitteilungen* 4 (December 1980): 6.

"Literaturbericht zur Hymnologie für United Kingdom." *Jahrbuch für Liturgik und Hymnologie* 24 (1980): 215–19.

Reviews

Short reviews of various books. *Music in Worship* no. 12 (June 1980): 8–9.

Praying and Singing, by J. D. Crichton, London: Collins Liturgical Publications, 1980. *News of Liturgy* no. 66, June 1980, 6.

A Responsorial Psalm Book for Sundays and Feastdays, edited by Geoffrey Boulton Smith, London: Collins Liturgical Publications, 1980. *News of Liturgy* no. 67, July 1980, 5.

Music of the English Parish Church, by Nicholas Temperley, 2 vols., Cambridge, Eng.: Cambridge University Press, 1980. *Churchman: A Quarterly Journal of Anglican Theology* 94 (1980): 284–87.

Johann Sebastian Bach Concerto for Two Harpsichords and String Orchestra (BWV 1060) and Sonata for Flute and Harpsichord. Facsimile, edited by Hans-Joachim Schulze, Kassel: Bärenreiter, 1980. *Music in Worship* no. 13 (September 1980): 9.

USPG Psalm Project: Church—A Chosen People, London: USPG, 1980. *News of Liturgy* no. 69, September 1980, 7.

New Liturgy, New Laws, by R. Kevin Seasoltz, Collegeville, Minn.: The Liturgical Press, 1980. *Churchman: A Quarterly Journal of Anglican Theology* 94 (1980): 382–83.

1981

Books

Bibliotheca Hymnologica. London: Charles Higham (SPCK), 1981.

English Hymns and Hymn Books: Catalogue of an Exhibition held in the Bodleian Library Oxford. Oxford: Bodleian Library, 1981.

Chapters/Articles

[1972] "Genius and Enigma: Beethoven 1770–1827." *Music in Worship*, no. 17 (September 1981): 16–17.

"Literatur zur vorbereitung der Tagung." *IAH Bulletin* 9 (May 1981): 142.

"Hymns, Organs and Choirs." *Music and Worship*, no. 15 (March 1981): 15–16.

"Music and the Reformation." *Churchman: A Quarterly Journal of Anglican Theology* 95, no. 2 (1981): 182–89.

"Hymn Books in Use in English Churches." *IAH Bulletin* 9 (May 1981): 41–45.

"The Date of Coverdale's *Goostly psalmes*." *IAH Bulletin* 9 (May 1981): 58–63.

"The Hymns of Paul Gerhardt in English Use." *IAH Bulletin* 9 (May 1981): 80–84.

"Bunsen and the Translation of German Hymns into English." *IAH Bulletin* 9 (May 1981): 85–89.

"Oxford and Hymnody: A Tourist's Guide." *The Hymn: The Journal of the Hymn Society of America* 32, no. 2 (April 1981): 70–81.

"Oxford und die Hymnologie: Ein Wegweiser für Hymnologen." *IAH Mitteilungen* 5 (August 1981): 23–32. German version of "Oxford and Hymnody: A Tourist's Guide." *The Hymn: The Journal of the Hymn Society of America* 32, no. 2 (April 1981): 70–81.

"Die Datierung von Coverdale's *Goostly psalmes*." *Musik und Kirche* 51 (1981): 165–71. German version of "The Date of Coverdale's *Goostly psalmes*" *IAH Bulletin* 9 (May 1981): 58–63.

"Literaturbericht zur Hymnologie für United Kingdom." *Jahrbuch für Liturgik und Hymnologie* 25 (1981): 197–201.

Reviews

Gemeindelieder, herausgegeben im Auftrag des Bundes Evangelisch-Freikircher Gemeinden und des Bundes Freier evangelischer Gemeinde, Wuppertal und Kassel: Onckem Verlag and Witten: Bundes-Verlag, 1978. *The Hymn: The Journal of the Hymn Society of America* 32, no. 1 (January 1981): 53–55.

Papal Legislation on Sacred Music 95A.D. to 1977A.D., by Robert F. Hayburn, Collegeville, Minn.: The Liturgical Press. 1979. *Churchman: A Quarterly Journal of Anglican Theology* 95 (1981): 88–89.

A Guide to Byzantine Hymnography: A Classified Bibliography of Texts and Studies, 2 vols., by Joseph Szövérffy, Brookline, Mass.: Classical Folia Editions and Leiden: E. J. Brill, 1979. *Churchman: A Quarterly Journal of Anglican Theology* 95 (1981): 89.

A Panorama of Christian Hymnody, by Erik Routley, Collegeville, Minn.: The Liturgical Press, 1980; *An English-Speaking Hymnal Guide*, by Erik Routley, Collegeville, Minn.: The Liturgical Press, 1980. *Churchman: A Quarterly Journal of Anglican Theology* 95 (1981): 90–91.

Sing With Understanding: An Introduction to Christian Hymnology, by Harry Eskew and Hugh T. McElrath, Nashville: Broadman Press, 1980. *Churchman: A Quarterly Journal of Anglican Theology* 95 (1981): 91–92.

Church Music and the Christian Faith, by Erik Routley, London: Collins Liturgical Publications, 1980. *Churchman: A Quarterly Journal of Anglican Theology* 95 (1981): 92 93.

Music and the Alternative Service Book, by Lionel Dakers, Croydon: Addington Press, 1980. *Music in Worship* no. 15 (March 1981): 17.

Gedenkheft Christhard Mahrenholz. Musik und Kirche 50, no. 4 (July–August 1980). *The Hymn Society of Great Britain and Ireland Bulletin* 9 (April 1981): 219–21.

The Psalms: Their Use and Performance Today, by Lionel Dakers, Croydon: RSCM, 1980. *Music in Worship* no. 16 (June 1981): 16.

The Organ Works of J. S. Bach. vol. 2., by Peter Williams, Cambridge, Eng.: Cambridge University Press, 1980. *Music in Worship* no. 16 (June 1981): 17–18.

Bramwell Brontë's Flute Book. Facsimile, edited by Richard Rastall, Boethius Press, 1980; *Anne Brontë's Song Book*. Facsimile, edited by Richard Rastall, Boethius Press, 1980. *Hymn Society of Great Britain and Ireland Bulletin* 9, (September 1981): 238–40.

Bilddokumente zur Lebensgeschichte Johann Sebastian Bachs, by Werner Neumann, Kassel: Bärenreiter, 1979. *Music in Worship* no. 17 (September 1981): 15.

Amazing Grace: John Newton's Story, by John Pollock, London: Hodder and Stoughton, 1981. *Churchman: A Quarterly Journal of Anglican Theology* 95 (1981): 362.

Program Notes

Program notes on Bach's *Matthäus-passion* (BWV 244) For performances by the Taverner Choir and the Taverner Players, conducted by Andrew Parrott. The Early Music Centre Festival 1981, London, October 17–31, 36–37.

1982

Books

Marbeck's Book of Common Prayer Noted (1550). Courtenay Facsimiles 3. Appleford: Sutton Courtenay Press, 1982.

Music as Preaching: Bach, Passions and Music in Worship. Latimer Studies 13. Oxford: Latimer House, 1982.

Churchman Index 1965–1980. Oxford: Latimer House, 1982.

Chapters/Articles

"Preface." In *Hymns in Today's Language* by Christopher Idle, 3. Bramcote, Nottingham: Grove Books, 1982.

"The Origins of the Tune SAVANNAH." *Hymn Society of Great Britain and Ireland Bulletin* 10, no. 1 (January 1982): 26–30.

"O Gladsome Light." *News of Hymnody*, no. 1, January 1982, 1–2. (RAL was the founding editor of *News of Hymnody* and continued as editor until 1985.)

"Hymns and Readings for Good Friday." *News of Hymnody*, no. 1, January 1982, 5–6.

"Bach's Use of Reformation Hymnody." *The Hymn: The Journal of the Hymn Society of America* 33, no. 3 (July 1982): 178.

[1971] "From Jew to Christian: Mendelssohn." *Music in Worship* no. 21 (September 1982): 10–11.

"Amerikanische Hymnodie: Bericht über die Jubiläumsfeier der HSA in Atlanta." *IAH Mitteilungen* 7 (October 1982): 13–14.

"Folksong and Hymn." *IAH Mitteilungen* 7 (October 1982): 8–9.

"Atlanta 1982 [Report on the 60th Anniversary Convocation of the Hymn Society of America]. *News of Hymnody*, no. 4, October 1982, 4–5.

"Scandinavian Hymnody." Pt. 1. *News of Hymnody*, no. 4, October 1982, 7–9.

"A Newly-discovered Fragment of Coverdale's *Goostly psalmes.*" *Jahrbuch für Liturgik und Hymnologie* 26 (1982): 136–50.

"Literaturbericht zur Hymnologie für United Kingdom." *Jahrbuch für Liturgik und Hymnologie* 26 (1982): 247–50.

Reviews

The ASB Psalter and Canticles Set to Anglican Chant, edited by Lionel Dakers and Cyril Taylor, London: Collins Liturgical Publications, 1981. *Expository Times* 93, no. 5 (February 1982): 158–59.

Short reviews of various books. *News of Hymnody*, no. 1, January 1982, 4.

Der Gelehrte Diplomat: Zum Wirken Christian Carl Josias Bunsens, by Erich Geldbach, Leiden: E. J. Brill, 1980. *Churchman: A Quarterly Journal of Anglican Theology* 96 (1982): 91.

Short reviews of various books. *News of Hymnody*, no. 2, April 1982, 3–4.

The Shaker Spiritual, by Daniel W. Patterson, Princeton, N.J.: Princeton University Press, 1979. *Hymn Society of Great Britain and Ireland Bulletin* 10 (May 1981): 51–53.

American Hymns Old and New, edited by A. Christ-Janer and C. W. Hughes, New York: Columbia University Press, 1980; *American Hymns Old and New: Notes on the Hymns and Biographies of the Authors and Composers*, edited by A. Christ-Janer and C. W. Hughes, New York: Columbia University Press, 1980. *Hymn Society of Great Britain and Ireland Bulletin* 10 (May 1981): 53–54.

Das Deutsche Kirchenlied I/2: Registerband, edited by Markus Jenny, Kassel: Bärenreiter, 1980. *Hymn Society of Great Britain and Ireland Bulletin* 10 (May 1981): 54–55.

Short reviews of various books. *News of Hymnody* no. 3, July 1982, 5–7.

Hymns for Today's Church, Jubilate Group, London: Hodder and Stoughton, 1982. *News of Hymnody* no. 4, October 1982, 3.

Short reviews of various publications. *News of Hymnody* no. 4, October 1982, 6.

Hymns for Today's Church, Jubilate Group, London: Hodder and Stoughton, 1982. *Church of England Newspaper*, no. 4621, November 12, 1982, 8–9.

1983

Book

Bachs theologische Bibliothek: Eine kritische Bibliographie. Beiträge zur theologischen Bachforschung 1. Stuttgart: Hänssler-Verlag, 1983.

Chapters/Articles

"Holy Chant and Psalm." In *Anglo-Catholic Worship: An Evangelical Appreciation after 150 years*, edited by Colin Buchanan, 45–48. Grove Liturgical Study 33. Bramcote, Nottingham: Grove Books, 1983.

"Luther the Musician." In *The Man Luther,* 30-31. St. Louis: Concordia Publishing House, 1983.

"Johann Sebastian Bach: Vier Duette aus dem Dritten Teil der Klavierübung, BWV 802–805." In *Musik—gedeutet und gewertet: Texte zur musikalischen Rezeptionsgeschichte*, edited by Herman J. Busch and Werner Klüppelholz, 31–33. Kassel: Bärenreiter Verlag, 1983.

"Scandinavian Hymnody." Pt. 2. *News of Hymnody*, no. 5, January 1983, 7–8.

"Elements of American Hymnody." *Hymn Society of Great Britain and Ireland Bulletin* 10, no. 4 (January 1983): 90–93.

[1972] "Getting Out of a Rut: Charles Ives 1874–1954." *Music in Worship* no. 23 (March 1983): 6–7.

"Predigt am zweien Sonntag nach Epiphanias, dem 16. Januar 1983, in Vespergottesdienst der Church of St. Anne and St. Agnes in London, in dem, neben anderen Werken Bachs, die Kantate BWV 3 musiziert wurde." *Musik und Kirche* 53 (1983): 185–87. "Walter Blankenburg zum 80. Geburtstag."

"The Routley Service at Westminster Abbey." *The Hymn: The Journal of the Hymn Society of America* 34, no. 2 (April 1983): 110–11.

"Verba Testamenti versus Canon: The Radical Nature of Luther's Liturgical Reform." *Churchman: A Quarterly Journal of Anglican Theology* 97, no. 2 (1983): 123–31.

"Hymn Writers of Today: John Wilson." *American Organist* 17, no. 6 (June 1983): 38–39.

[1971] "Falling Foul of the Nazis: Hugo Distler 1908–1942." *Music in Worship* no. 25 (September 1983): 10–11.

"Olney Hymns: A Documentary Footnote." *Churchman: A Quarterly Journal of Anglican Theology* 97, no. 3 (1983): 244–45.

"The *Jahrbuch für Liturgik und Hymnologie* reaches 25 + 1." *The Hymn: The Journal of the Hymn Society of America* 34, no. 4 (October 1983): 250.

"Theology and Music." *Music in Worship* no. 22 (December 1983): 14–15.

"Literaturbericht zur Hymnologie für United Kingdom." *Jahrbuch für Liturgik und Hymnologie* 27 (1983): 283–88.

Reviews

Short reviews of various publications. *News of Hymnody,* no. 5, January 1983, 6–7.

The Church in the Theology of the Reformers, by Paul Avis, London: Marshall, Morgan and Scott, 1982. *Expository Times* 94, no. 5 (February 1983): 150.

Short reviews of various publications. *News of Hymnody,* no. 6, April 1983, 6–7.

A Study of German Hymns in Current English Hymnals by John S. Andrews, Berne: Peter Lang, 1982. *Churchman: A Quarterly Journal of Anglican Theology* 97 (1983): 89–90.

Beethoven and the Voice of God, by Wilfred Mellers, London: Faber and Faber, 1983. *Expository Times* 94, no. 10 (July 1983): 316.

Christian Hymns Observed, by Erik Routley, London: Mowbray, 1983. *Church of England Newspaper*, no. 4656, July 22, 1983, 12.

Praise and Lament in the Psalms, by Claus Westermann, translated by K. R. Crim and R. N. Soulen, Edinburgh: T. & T. Clark, 1981. *Churchman: A Quarterly Journal of Anglican Theology* 97 (1983): 157.

The Way, the Truth, and the Life: An Introduction to Lutheran Christianity, by D. W. H. Arnold and C. G. Fry, Grand Rapids, Mich.: Baker Book House, 1983. *Expository Times* 94, no. 12 (July 1983): 316.

Luther: Witness to Jesus Christ, by Marc Lienhard, translated by E. H. Robertson, Minneapolis: Augsburg Publishing House, 1982. *Expository Times* 94, no. 12 (July 1983): 377.

Experience and Faith: The Significance of Luther for Undertanding Today's Experiencial Religion, by William Hordern, Minneapolis: Augsburg Publishing House, 1982. *Expository Times* 95, no. 2 (November 1983): 62–63.

Bachiana et alia Musicologica. Festschrift Alfred Dürr zum 65. Geburtstag am 3. März 1983, edited by W. Rehm, Kassel: Bärenreiter, 1983. *Music in Worship* no. 26 (December, 1983): 10.

1984

Books

J. S. Bach as Preacher: His Passions and Music in Worship. St. Louis: Concordia Publishing House, 1984. Revision of *Music as Preaching: Bach, Passions and Music in Worship.* Latimer Studies 13. Oxford: Latimer House, 1982.

Stiller, Günther. *Johann Sebastian Bach and Liturgical Life in Leipzig.* Edited by Robin A. Leaver. Translated by H. J. A. Bouman, D. F. Poellot & H. C. Oswald. St. Louis: Concordia Publishing House, 1984.

The Liturgy of the Frankfurt Exiles 1555. Grove Liturgical Study 38. Bramcote, Nottingham: Grove Books, 1984.

with David Mann and David Parkes. *Ways of Singing the Psalms.* London: Collins Liturgical Publications, 1984.

Music in the Service of the Church: The Funeral Sermon for Heinrich Schütz (1585–1672). St. Louis: Concordia Publishing House, 1984.

Chapters/Articles

"Liturgy and Language: A Postscript." In *Language and Liturgy*, by G. L. Bray, S. A. Wilcockson & R. A. Leaver, 29–34. Latimer Studies 16. Oxford: Latimer House, 1984.

with J. Stange. "Register aller von Heinrich Schütz vertonten Bibelstellen." In *Cantate. Eine Handreichung für Pfarrer und Kirchenmusiker zum Schütz- und Bach-Gedenkjahr*, edited by W. Blankenburg and R. Steiger, 18–25. Kassel: Merseberger Verlag, 1984.

"German Hymnody." *News of Hymnody*, no. 9, January 1984, 6–7; no. 10, April 1984, 5–6.

"Psalm Singing and Organ Regulations in a London Church ca. 1700." *The Hymn: The Journal of the Hymn Society of America* 35, no. 1 (January 1984): 29–35.

"Opinion: Playing Scrabble with Hymns." *The Hymn: The Journal of the Hymn Society of America* 35, no. 2 (April 1984): 114–15.

[1983] "The *Jahrbuch für Liturgik und Hymnologie* reaches 25 + 1." *The Hymn Society of Great Britain and Ireland Bulletin* 10, no. 8 (May 1984): 192–93.

"The Earliest Anglican Communion Hymn." *News of Hymnody*, no. 11, July 1984, 1–3.

"The Routley Collection of Books and Hymnals." *News of Hymnody*, no. 12, October 1984, 2–3.

McKinley, E. Graham. "Making All the 'Right' Moves in the Arts: Music." Interview with Robin A. Leaver on authenticating musical manuscripts, especially those of J. S. Bach. *The Princeton Packet*, September 21, 1984, 6, *Time Off* section.

"Coverdale and the Anglo-Genevan Liturgy of 1556." *Mededelingen van het Instituut voor Liturgiewetenschap Rijksuniversiteit Groningen* 18 (1984): 30–34.

"Literaturbericht zur Hymnologie United Kingdom." *Jahrbuch für Liturgik und Hymnologie* 28 (1984): 229–34.

Reviews

A Study of German Hymns in Current English Hymnals, by John S. Andrews, Berne: Peter Lang, 1982. *Hymn Society of Great Britain and Ireland Bulletin* 10 (January 1984): 172.

Werkbuch zum Gotteslob. 9 vols., edited by Josef Seuffert, et al., Freiburg: Herder, 1974–1984. *Hymn Society of Great Britain and Ireland Bulletin* 10 (January 1984): 172–74.

Hymns and Psalms: A Methodist and Ecumenical Hymn Book, London: Methodist Publishing House, 1983. *News of Hymnody* no. 9, January 1984, 2–3.

Encounter with God, by Duncan Forrester, J. I. H. MacDonald, and Gian Tellini, Edinburgh: T. & T. Clark, 1983. *Church of England Newspaper*, no. 4687, March 2, 1984, 12.

Church Music in a Changing World, by Lionel Dakers, London: Mowbray, 1984. *Church of England Newspaper*, no. 4688, March 9, 1984, 10.

John Stainer and the Musical Life of Victorian Britain, by Peter Charton, Exeter: David & Charles, 1984. *Church of England Newspaper*, no. 4692, April 6, 1984, 12.

Organists of the City of London 1666–1850: A Record of One Thousand Organists with an Annotated Index, by Donovan Dawe, Privately published, 1983. *Music in Worship* no. 28 (June 1984): 13.

Liturgische Spiel-Geistlicher Gesang: Das wissenschaftliche Werk von Dr. phil., Dr. theol. h.c. Walther Lippardt, by Friederike Kiedl. *The Hymn: The Journal of the Hymn Society of America* 35, no. 3 (July 1984): 187.

Short reviews of various publications. *News of Hymnody* no. 11, July 1984, 5–7.

Short reviews of new bibliographical resources. *News of Hymnody* no. 12, October 1984, 5–8.

Program Notes

"Bach and Luther." Program notes for the English Bach Festival 1984. Queen Elizabeth Hall, London, May 10, 1984, 14.

Program notes on Bach's *Magnificat* (BWV 243), and Cantatas BWV 140 and 63. For a performance by The Bach Choir of Bethlehem. Tercentenary Program I, Packer Memorial Church, Lehigh University, December 16, 1984, 3–4.

1985

Books

Duty and Delight: Routley Remembered. A Memorial Tribute to Erik Routley (1917–1982). Edited by Robin A. Leaver and James H. Litton. Carol Stream, Ill.: Hope Publishing; Norwich: Canterbury Press, 1985.

J. S. Bach and Scripture: Glosses from the Calov Bible Commentary. St. Louis: Concordia Publishing House, 1985.

Chapters/Articles

"Bachs Motetten und das Reformationsfest." In *Bach als Ausleger der Bibel. Theologische und musikwissenschaftliche Studien zum Werk Johann Sebastian Bach*. Hrsg. im Auftrag des Kirchlichen Kommitees Johann Sebastian Bach 1985 von M. Petzold, 33–47. Berlin: Evangelisches Verlagsanstalt; Göttingen: Vandenhoeck and Ruprecht, 1985.

"Bachs theologische Bibliothek." In *Ex Libris Bachianis II. Das Weltbild Johann Sebastian Bachs im Spiegel seiner theologische Bibliothek. Ausstellung zum Heidelberger Bachfest 1985*, 13–21. Heidelberg, 1985.

"The Theological Character of Music in Worship." *Duty and Delight: Routley Re membered. A memorial tribute to Erik Routley (1917–1982).* Edited by Robin A. Leaver and James A. Litton, 47–64. Carol Stream, Ill.: Hope Publishing Company; Norwich: Canterbury Press, 1985. Issued separately in 1989.

"Powerful Biblical Hymnody." *News of Hymnody*, no. 13, January 1985, 2–4.

"Lowell Mason's Observations on English Hymn Singing, &c., 1837." *News of Hymnody*, no. 13, January 1985, 4–5.

"J. S. Bach's Faith and Christian Commitment." *The Expository Times* 96, no. 6 (March 1985); 168–73.

"Bach and Hymnody: The Evidence of the Orgelbüchlein." *Early Music* 13, no. 2 (1985): 227–36.

"TV Hymnody: Songs of Praise 1985." *News of Hymnody*, no. 14, April 1985, 1–5.

"The Liturgical Place and Homiletic Purpose of Bach's Cantatas." *Worship* 59, no. 3 (1985): 194–202.

"Coverdale's *Goostly psalmes* and the English Prayer Book of 1549." *IAH Bulletin* 13 (May 1985): 23–25.

"John Marbeck in 1985." In *The World of Church Music 1985: A Collection of Essays*, edited by L. Dakers, 54–59. Croydon: Royal School of Church Music, 1985.

"Bach, Hymns and Hymnbooks." *The Hymn: The Journal of the Hymn Society of America* 36, no. 4 (October 1985): 7–13.

"Heinrich Schütz as Biblical Interpreter." *Bach: The Quarterly Journal of the Riemenschneider Bach Institute* 16, no. 4 (October 1985): 4–7.

"List of the Settings of Bible Texts in the Works of Heinrich Schütz." *Bach: The Quarterly Journal of the Riemenschneider Bach Institute* 16, no. 4 (October 1985): 24–31.

"Schütz and the Psalms." *Bach: The Quarterly Journal of the Riemenschneider Bach Institute* 16, no. 4 (October 1985): 34–48.

"Englische und Deutsche Hymnodie. Ihre gegenseitigen Befruchtungen." *Die Zeichen der Zeit: Evangelische Monatsschrift für Mitarbeiter der Kirche* [Berlin DDR] 39 (September 1985): 223–27.

"Literaturbericht zur Hymnologie für United Kingdom." *Jahrbuch für Liturgik und Hymnologie*, 29 (1985): 256–59.

Reviews

Das Deutsche Kirchenlied (DKL): *Kritische Gesamtausgabe der Melodien I/1: Verzeichnis der Drucke von den Anfangen bis 1800*, edited by Konrad Ameln, Markus Jenny, and Walther Lipphardt, Kassel: Bärenreiter Verlag, 1975; *Das Deutsche Kirchenlied I/2: Registerband*, edited by Markus Jenny, Kassel: Bärenreiter, 1980. *The Hymn: The Journal of the Hymn Society of America* 36, no. 1 (January 1985): 33–34.

Table and Tradition: Towards an Ecumenical Understanding of the Eucharist, by Alisdair Heron, Edinburgh: Handsel Press, 1983. *Expository Times* 96 (February 1985): 151–52.

Short reviews of various publications. *News of Hymnody* no. 13, January 1985, 5–7.
The Master Musicians: Bach, by Malcolm Boyd. London: Dent. 1983. *Soundings* no.
   12 (Winter, 1984-1985): 71–75.
Short reviews of various publications. *News of Hymnody* no. 14, April 1985, 5–7.

Program Notes

Program notes on Bach's *Johannespassion.* For a performance by The Bach Choir of
   Bethlehem. Tercentenary Program II, Packer Memorial Church, Lehigh University,
   March 17, 1985, 3–4.
Program notes on Bach's Cantatas BWV 110 and 65, and *Magnificat.* For a perfor-
   mance by The Bach Choir of Bethlehem. Christmas Concert, The First Presbyter-
   ian Church of Bethlehem, December 15, 1985, 4–5.

1986

Chapters/Articles

with Alfred Bichsel. "Music of the Lutheran Church." In *The New Grove Dictionary
   of American Music*, edited by H. Wiley Hitchcock and Stanley Sadie, 3: 128–29.
   London and New York: Macmillan, 1986.

Program Notes

Program notes on Bach's *B-Minor Mass* (BWV 232); *Komm, Jesu, komm* (BWV 229);
   and Cantatas BWV 172, 87, 21, 102, 51 and 69. For performances by The Bach
   Choir of Bethlehem. Seventy-Ninth Festival, Packer Memorial Church, Lehigh
   University, May 16–17 and May 23–24, 1986, 7–11.
Program notes on Bach's *Christmas Oratorio*, BWV 248/I-III. For a performance by
   The Bach Choir of Bethlehem. Christmas Concert, The First Presbyterian Church
   of Bethlehem, December 14, 1986, 4–5.
Program notes on movements from Bach's Cantatas BWV 29 and 191, and *Christ-
   mas Oratorio* (BWV 248/I). For a performance by The Westminster Choir and
   Westminster Chamber Orchestra, conducted by Joseph Flummerfelt. *Christmas
   at Westminster,* Bristol Chapel, Westminster Choir College, Princeton, N.J., December 14, 1986.

1987

Dissertation

"'Goostly Psalmes and Spirituall Songes': English and Dutch Metrical Psalms from
   Coverdale to Utenhove 1535–1566." DTheol. Diss., Rijksuniversiteit Groningen,
   The Netherlands, 1987 [*cum laude*].

Chapters/Articles

"Der Text von Bach's Kantate Nr. 79: Eine Mutmassung." In *Theologische Bach-Studien I*. Beiträge zur theologischen Bachforschung 4, herausgegeben von W. Blankenburg and R. Steiger, 109–16. Stuttgart: Hänssler, 1987.

"Three Hymnals: Different Denominational Emphasis but One Song?" *Worship* 61, no. 1 (January 1987): 45–60.

"Dykes' NICEA: An Original Tune or the Re-working of Another?" *The Hymn: The Journal of the Hymn Society of America* 38, no. 2 (1987): 21–24.

"Proclamatio Evangelii et Hymnodia: Some Thoughts in Preparation for Lund 1987." *IAH Bulletin* 15 (1987): 35–48. Full text in both English and German.

"Bach, Kirchenlieder und Gesangbücher." Pt. 1. *Musik und Kirche* 57 (1987): 169–74.

"Preface." *IAH Bulletin: Sondernummer, Dankesgabe an Markus Jenny.* (November 1987): [3–7]. Text in both English and German.

"Coverdale's *Goostly Psalmes* and Early English Metrical Psalm Tunes." *IAH Bulletin: Sondernummer, Dankesgabe an Markus Jenny* (November 1987): 54–59.

"Theological Dimensions of Mission Hymnody: The Counterpoint of Cult and Culture." *Africa Theological Journal* 16 (1987): 242–54. See also the summaries: 1) J. Vanden Bussche, "'Proclamatio evangelii et hymnodia': Het 14de Congres van de I.A.H. te Lund, 3–7 Augustus 1987," *Tijdschrift voor Liturgie* 71 (1987): 385–88, especially 385–86; 2) Bertil E. Anderson, "American Hymn Society Visits Scandinavia," *The Hymn: The Journal of the Hymn Society of America* 39, no. 1 (January 1988): 33–38, especially 35–36.

"Literaturbericht zur Hymnologie für United Kingdom." *Jahrbuch für Liturgik und Hymnologie* 30 (1987): 244–48.

Program Notes

Program notes on Bach's Cantatas BWV 31, 82, 95, 130, 180, 184, 190a, 226, and *B-Minor Mass* (BWV 232). For performances by The Bach Choir of Bethlehem. Eightieth Festival, Packer Memorial Church, Lehigh University, May 15–16 and May 22–23, 1987, 8–14.

Program notes on Bach's Cantatas BWV 50, 80, 4 and the *Magnificat* (BWV 243). For a performance by the Westminster Summer Choir and Orchestra, conducted by Robert Shaw. *An Evening of Choral Works by Johann Sebastian Bach*, Richardson Auditorium, Alexander Hall, Princeton University, Princeton, N.J., July 31, 1987.

Program notes on Bach's Cantatas BWV 61, 36, and the *Magnificat* (BWV 243). For a performance by The Bach Choir of Bethlehem. Christmas Concert, First Presbyterian Church of Bethlehem, December 13, 1987, 4–6.

Miscellaneous

Hymnal Supplement II, edited by Carlton R. Young, et al. Carol Stream: Agape, 1987. Robin A. Leaver, contributing editor.

1988

Chapters/Articles

"Bach's Reworking of BWV 67/6 as the First Movement of the *Gloria in excelsis Deo* in the *Missa in A*, BWV 234." *Internationale Arbeitsgemeinschaft für theologische Bachforschung*. Bulletin 2. *Internationale Bachakademie Stuttgart: Parodie und Vorlage. Zum Bachschen Paradieverfahren und seiner Bedeutung für die Hermeneutik, 17–20 März 1988. Referate. Protocolle. Materialien*, Heidelberg, 1988, 50–71.

"Bach, Kirchenlieder und Gesangbücher." Pt. 2. *Musik und Kirche* 58 (1988): 8–12.

[1987] "Theological Dimensions of Mission Hymnody: The Counterpoint of Cult and Culture." *Worship* 62 (1988): 316–31, text slightly modified; and *IAH Bulletin* 16 (1988): 15–52, complete text in both English and German.

"The New Swedish Hymnal." *The Hymn: The Journal of the Hymn Society of America* 39, no. 2 (April 1988): 9–13.

"Vincent Novello and *The Psalmist*." *The Hymn: The Journal of the Hymn Society of America* 39, no. 3 (July 1988): 15–20.

"From the President." *IAH Bulletin* 16 (1988): 2–9. Complete text in both English and German.

"President's Words of Welcome, Lund 3 August 1987." *IAH Bulletin* 16 (1988): 12–14.

"Letters to the Editor." Edited by Robin A Leaver. *IAH Bulletin* 16 (1988): esp. 209, 239–40. Collection of letters of appreciation to celebrate Casper Honders' years as Editor of the *IAH Bulletin* 1974–1987.

"English and German Hymnody: Imports and Exports." *The Hymn Society of Great Britain and Ireland Bulletin* 12, no. 4 (October 1988): 62–69.

Review

Hymns and Tunes Indexed by First Lines, Tune Names, and Metres: Compiled from Current English Hymn Books, by David W. Perry, Croydon: The Hymn Society of Great Britain and Ireland and RSCM, 1980. *The Hymn: The Journal of the Hymn Society of America* 39, no. 4 (October 1988): 60–62.

Program Notes

Program notes for a recording of Bach cantatas BWV 63 and 65, and the *Sanctus* from the *B-Minor Mass* (BWV 232). Performed by The Bach Choir of Bethlehem. *Christmas in Leipzig*, Dorian Recording 90113, 1988.

Program notes on *Johannespassion* (BWV 245) and *B-Minor Mass* (BWV 232). For performances by The Bach Choir of Bethlehem. Eighty-first Festival, Packer Memorial Church Lehigh University, May 13–14 and May 20–21, 1988, 9–14.

Program notes on Bach's *Christmas Oratorio*, BWV 248/IV-VI. For performances by The Bach Choir of Bethlehem. Christmas Concert, First Presbyterian Church of Bethlehem, December 11, 1988, 4–7.

1989

Book

The Theological Character of Music in Worship. St. Louis: Concordia Publishing House, 1989.

Chapters/Articles

"The Lutheran Reformation." In *The Renaissance from the 1470s to the end of the 16th century*, edited by I. Fenlon, 263–85. Vol. 2 of *Man and Music: A Social History*, edited by S. Sadie. London: Macmillan 1989. Translated into Japanese as part of the series *Man and Music: Seiyo no Ongaku to Shakai* [Man and Music: Music and Society in the West]. 12 vols. Tokyo: Ongaku no Tomo Sha, 1996–1998. Vol. 2, *Renaissance: Hana Hiraku Kyutei Ongaku* [Renaissance: The Flowering of Court Music]. Edited by Kazunori Imatani, 1997. Chapter 10, "Luther no Shukyo Kaikaku" [The Lutheran Reformation], translated by Kaori Yoneda, 309–32.

"Choral Music in Worship." *Reformed Liturgy and Music* 23 (1989): 66–68. Korean translation in *Ministry and Theology* (December 1989): 120–23.

"The Revival of the St. John Passion: History and Performance Practice." *American Choral Review* 21, no. 1 (1989): 14–29; and *Bach: The Quarterly Journal of the Riemenschneider Bach Institute* 20, no. 3 (Fall 1989): 34–49. Originally given as pre-concert lecture, "The First American Performance of Bach's *St. John Passion*, Bethlehem, Pennsylvania, 1888," at the Eighty-First Festival of The Bach Choir of Bethelehem, centenary performances of the *St. John Passion* (BWV 245), May 13 and 20, 1998.

"Two Pupils of Rheinberger and their use of the Organ in Performances of Bach's St. John Passion." *The Tracker: Journal of the Organ Historical Society* 33, no. 2 (1989): 18–23.

"A Unique Broadsheet in the Scheide Library." *Papers of the Bibliographical Society of America* 83 (1989): 337–52.

"Literaturbericht zur United Kingdom." *Jahrbuch für Liturgik und Hymnologie* 31 (1989): 229–34.

Program Notes

Program notes for a recording of Bach's Cantatas BWV 56 and 140, and the Motet *Ich lasse dich nicht* (BWV Anh. 159). Performed by The Bach Choir of Bethlehem. *Wachet Auf!*, Dorian Recording 90127, 1989.

Program notes on Bach's Cantatas BWV 4, 11, 43, 169, 249, Motets *Ich lasse dich nicht* (BWV Anh. 159) and *Fürchte, dich nicht* (BWV 228), and *B-Minor Mass*

(BWV 232). For performances by The Bach Choir of Bethlehem. Eighty-second Festival, Packer Memorial Church, Lehigh University, May 19–20 and May 26–27, 1989, 8–15.

Program notes on Bach's Cantatas BWV 63 and 65, and the *Sanctus* from the *B-Minor Mass* (BWV 232). For a performance by The Bach Choir of Bethlehem. Christmas Concert, First Presbyterian Church of Bethlehem, December 10, 1989, 4–5.

1990

Book

Church Music: The Future: Creative Leadership for the Year 2000 and Beyond: Symposium Papers. Edited by Robin A. Leaver. Princeton, N.J.: Westminster Choir College, 1990.

Chapters/Articles

"Lutheran Vespers as a Context for Music." In *Church, Stage, and Studio: Music and Its Contexts in Seventeenth-Century Germany*, edited by Paul Walker, 143–61. Ann Arbor, Mich.: UMI Research Press, 1990.

"A Celebration of Sacred Sound." In Leaver, *Church Music: The Future*, 1990, 5–9.

"Church Music: The Future is Here." In Leaver, *Church Music: The Future*, 1990, 12–13.

"Music for Worship." In Leaver, *Church Music: The Future*, 1990, 17.

"Musicians for Worship." In Leaver, *Church Music: The Future*, 1990, 37–39.

"The Sound of Change." In Leaver, *Church Music: The Future*, 1990, 65–67.

"A Penitential Hymn from the English Exile Congregation in Emden 1555." *The Hymn: The Journal of the Hymn Society of America* 41, no. 1 (January 1990): 15–18.

"The Hymnbook as a Book of Practical Theology." *Reformed Liturgy and Music* 24 (1990): 55–57.

"Hymnals, Hymnal Companions, and Collection Development." *MLA Notes* 47 (December 1990): 331–54.

"'Then the Whole Congregation Sings': The Sung Word in Reformation Worship." *The Drew Gateway* 60, no. 1 (Fall 1990): 55–73. 1990 Tipple Lecture, Drew University, Madison, N.J.

"Parody and Theological Consistency: Notes on Bach's *A-Major Mass*." *Bach: The Journal of the Riemenschneider Bach Institute* 21, no. 3 (Winter 1990): 30–43.

Review

Johann Sebastian Bach. Ehre sei Gott gesungen: Bilder und Texte zu Bachs Leben als Christ und seinem Wirken für die Kirche, by Martin Petzold and Joachim Petri, Göttingen: Vandenhoeck and Ruprecht, 1988. *Theologische Literaturzeitung* 115 (1990): 134.

Program Notes

Program notes on Bach's *St John Passion* (BWV 245). For a performance by The Bach Choir of Bethlehem. Packer Memorial Church, Lehigh University, March 18, 1990, 5–6.

Program notes on the *Christmas Oratorio* (BWV 248) and *B-Minor Mass* (BWV 232). For performances by The Bach Choir of Bethlehem. Eighty-third Festival, Packer Memorial Church, Lehigh University, May 11–12 and May 18–19, 1990, 8–15.

Program notes on Bach's Cantatas BWV 110, 140, and 191. The Bach Choir of Bethlehem. Christmas Concert, First Presbyterian Church of Bethlehem, December 9, 1990, 4–5.

1991

Book

"Goostly Psalmes and Spirituall Songes": English and Dutch Metrical Psalms from Coverdale to Utenhove 1535–1566. Oxford Studies in British Church Music. Oxford: The Clarendon Press, 1991. Revision of doctoral dissertation, 1987. See also: Junko Kikuchi, "Introduction to Robin A. Leaver's *Goostly Psalmes and Spirituall Songes.*" *Musica Ecclesia Reformatae Semper Reformandae* 1 (1999), 28–41. In Japanese.

Chapters/Articles

"Plainchant Adaptation in England." In *The Hymnal 1982 Companion*, edited by R. F. Glover, 1: 177–93. New York: The Church Hymnal Corporation, 1991.

"English Metrical Psalmody." In *The Hymnal 1982 Companion*, edited by R. F. Glover, 1: 321–48. New York: The Church Hymnal Corporation, 1991.

"British Hymnody from the Sixteenth through Eighteenth Centuries." In *The Hymnal 1982 Companion*, edited by R. F. Glover, 1: 365–92. New York: The Church Hymnal Corporation, 1991.

"British Hymnody in the Nineteenth Century." In *The Hymnal 1982 Companion*, edited by R. F. Glover, 1: 417–46. New York: The Church Hymnal Corporation, 1991.

"British Hymnody, 1900–1950." In *The Hymnal 1982 Companion*, edited by R. F. Glover, 1: 474–504. New York: The Church Hymnal Corporation, 1991.

"British Hymnody Since 1950." In *The Hymnal 1982 Companion*, edited by R. F. Glover, 1: 555–99. New York: The Church Hymnal Corporation, 1991.

"Theological Dimensions of Mission Hymnody: The Counterpoint of Cult and Culture." In *The Hymnology Annual: An International Forum on the Hymn and Worship*, edited by V. Wicker, 1: 37–50. Berrien Springs, Mich.: Vande Vere Publishing, 1991. Revision of essay originally published in 1987.

"Bach and Pietism: Similarities Today." *Concordia Theological Quarterly* 55 (1991): 5–22. Originally given as paper at the First Annual Symposium on the Lutheran

Liturgy and Hymnody, January 1990, Concordia Theological Seminary, Fort Wayne, Ind.

"Twenty Years of Psalmody." *News of Hymnody*, no. 38, April 1991, 5–6.

"The Hymn Explosion [in the 18th century]." *Christian History* 10, no. 3 (August 1991): 14–17.

Program Notes

Program notes on Bach's *St. Matthew Passion* (BWV 244). For a performance by The Bach Choir of Bethlehem. Packer Memorial Church, Lehigh University, March 10, 1991, 5–6.

Program notes on the *B-Minor Mass* (BWV 232). For a performance by The Bach Choir of Bethlehem. Eighty-fourth Festival, Packer Memorial Church, Lehigh University, May 10–11 and May 17–18, 1991, 8–17.

Program notes on Bach's Cantatas BWV 147, 61, and *Magnificat* (BWV 248). For a performance by The Bach Choir of Bethlehem. Christmas Concert, First Presbyterian Church of Bethlehem, December 15, 1991, 4–6.

1992

Chapters/Articles

"Charles Wesley and Anglicanism." In *Charles Wesley: Poet and Theologian*, edited by S. T. Kimbrough, 157–75, 241–43. Nashville: Kingswood Books, 1992.

"The Date of Coverdale's *Goostly Psalmes*." In *The Hymnology Annual: An International Forum on the Hymn and Worship*, edited by V. Wicker, 2: 209–16. Berrien Springs, MI: Vande Vere Publishing, 1992. Revised form of earlier published version (1981).

"A Newly-discovered Fragment of Coverdale's *Goostly psalmes*." In *The Hymnology Annual: An International Forum on the Hymn and Worship*, edited by V. Wicker, 2: 218–26. Berrien Springs, Mich.: Vande Vere Publishing, 1992. An abbreviated form of earlier published version (1982).

"Christian Liturgical Music in the Wake of the Protestant Reformation." *Sacred Sound and Social Change: Liturgical Music in Jewish and Christian Experience*, edited by Lawrence A. Hofmann and Janet R. Walton, 124–44. Two Liturgical Traditions 1. Notre Dame, Ind.: University of Notre Dame Press, 1992. Originally given as paper, "The Protestant Reformation," at the conference in honor of Eric Werner's 80th birthday, November 1986, Hebrew Union College, New York.

"New Light on the Pre-history of The Bach Choir of Bethlehem." *Bach: The Journal of the Riemenschneider Bach Institute* 22, no. 2 (Fall–Winter 1991): 24–34 [issued May 1992]. Originally given as paper at the joint-meeting of the American Bach Society and the American Heinrich Schütz Society, April 1992.

"BBC Hymn Sing." *The Hymn: The Journal of the Hymn Society of America* 43, no. 5 (July 1992): 3. Also appeared, under the title "Westminster Records Hymns for

BBC Broadcast," in *Westminster Choir College, The School of Music of Rider College, Alumni Newsletter*, Summer 1992, 4 5.

"Literaturbericht zur United Kingdom." *Jahrbuch für Liturgik und Hymnologie* 33: (1992): 266–71.

"List of the Settings of Bible Texts in the Works of Heinrich Schütz (1985)." In Pasquale Troia, "Panorama Bibliografico Internazionale su Musica e Bibbia," *La Musica e la Bibbia: Atti del Convegno Internazionale di Studi promosso da Biblia e dall' Accademia Musicale Chigiana, Siena 24–26 agosto 1990*, edited by Pasquale Troia, 451. Rome: Garamond, 1992. Summarized in Italian.

"Schütz and the Psalms (1985)." In Pasquale Troia, "Panorama Bibliografico Internazionale su Musica e Bibbia," *La Musica e la Bibbia: Atti del Convegno Internazionale di Studi promosso da Biblia e dall' Accademia Musicale Chigiana, Siena 24–26 agosto 1990*, edited by Pasquale Troia, 451. Rome: Garamond, 1992. Summarized in Italian.

Program Notes

Program notes on Bach's *St. John Passion* (BWV 245). For a performance by The Bach Choir of Bethlehem. Packer Memorial Church, Lehigh University, March 22, 1992, 5–6.

Program notes on the centenary performance of the *St. Matthew Passion* (BWV 244) in Bethlehem, (1892–1992). For performances by The Bach Choir of Bethlehem. Eighty-fifth Festival, Packer Memorial Church, Lehigh University, May 8–9 and May 15–16, 1992, 9–13.

Program notes for a reconstructed Lutheran Christmas Mass at Wolfenbüttel ca. 1620, music by Michael Praetorius. Notes on historical and liturgical background by R. A. Leaver; notes on performance practice by Paul McCreesh. For performances by the Gabrieli Consort and Gabrieli Players, directed by Paul McCreesh. First performance August 29, 1992 at the Festival de la Chaise Dieu in the 12th century Abbatiale. Notes in French, 79–84. Second performance on September 1, 1992 in Great St. Mary Church, Cambridge, [5–10]. Performance recorded by the BBC and broadcast on Christmas Day 1992.

Program notes on Bach's *Christmas Oratorio* (BWV 248/I-III). For a performance by The Bach Choir of Bethlehem, Christmas Concert, First Presbyterian Church of Bethlehem, December 13, 1992, 6–8.

1993

Book

Ars et Musica in Liturgia: Celebratory Volume Presented to Casper Honders on the Occasion of his Seventieth Birthday on 6 June 1993. Edited by Robin A. Leaver and Frans Brouwer. Utrecht: Nederlands Instituut voor Kirchenmuziek 1993. American edition published in 1994.

Chapters/Articles

"A Christmas Service in Dutch and English held in the Scottish Church in Rotterdam in 1801." In *Ars et Musica in Liturgia: Celebratory Volume Presented to Casper Honders on the Occasion of his Seventieth Birthday on 6 June 1993*, edited by Robin A. Leaver and Frans Brouwer, 91–116. Utrecht: Nederlands Instituut voor Kirchenmuziek, 1993.

"Congregational Hymn and Soloistic Aria in the Music of Johann Sebastian Bach." In *The Hymnology Annual: An International Forum on the Hymn and Worship*, edited by V. Wicker, 3: 109–19. Berrien Springs, Mich.: Vande Vere Publishing, 1993.

"Bach and the German *Agnus Dei*." In *A Bach Tribute: Essays in Honor of William H. Scheide*, edited by Paul Brainard and Ray Robinson, 163–71. Kassel: Bärenreiter, 1993.

"Music and Christianity." In *The Blackwell Encyclopedia of Modern Christian Thought*, edited by Alister McGrath, 388–94. Oxford: Blackwell, 1993.

"Renewal in Hymnody." *Lutheran Quarterly* 6, no. 4 (1992): 359–83. Paper originally given at the General Pastoral Conference of the Northern Illinois District of the Lutheran Church–Missouri Synod, May 5, 1992. Summaries appear in *Presbyterian Outlook*, March 8, 1993, 5; *The Lutheran*, May 1993, 53.

"The Chorale: Transcending Time and Culture." *Concordia Theological Quarterly* 56, nos. 2–3 (1993): 123–44.

"English Adaptations of German Tunes in the Nineteenth Century." *IAH Bulletin* 21 (1993): 42–52.

"Hymnody and the Reality of God." *The Hymn: The Journal of the Hymn Society of America* 44, no. 3 (July 1993): 16–21.

Reviews

Theological Music: Introduction to Theomusicology, by Jon Michael Spencer, Westport, Conn.: Greenwood, 1991; *The Emergence of Black and the Emergence of Rap*, edited by Jon Michael Spencer, Durham, N.C.: Duke University Press, 1991; *Black Hymnody: A Hymnological History of the African-American Church*, by Jon Michael Spencer, Knoxville: University of Tennessee Press, 1992. *The Sonneck Society Newsletter* 19, no.1 (Spring 1993): 35–37.

German Sacred Polyphonic Vocal Music Between Schütz and Bach: Sources and Critical Editions, by Diane Parr Walker and Paul Walker. Detroit Studies in Music Bibliography 67. Warren, Mich.: Harmonie Park Press. 1992. *Fontes Artis Musicae* 40 (1993): 345–47.

Program Notes

Program notes on Bach's *St. Matthew Passion* (BWV 244). For a performance by The Bach Choir of Bethlehem. Packer Memorial Church, Lehigh University, March 21, 1993, 6–7.

Program notes on the *B-Minor Mass* (BWV 232), Motets *Ich lasse dich nicht* (BWV Anh. 159), *Jesu, meine Freude* (BWV 227) and *Lobet den Herrn* (BWV 230), and Cantatas BWV 101, 149, 69, 97 and 34. For performances by The Bach Choir of Bethlehem. Eighty-sixth Festival, Packer Memorial Church, Lehigh University, May 14–15 and May 21–22, 1993, 8–13.

Program notes on Bach's Cantatas BWV 63, 190, and Motet *Singet dem Herrn* (BWV 225). For a performance by The Bach Choir of Bethlehem. Christmas Concert, First Presbyterian Church of Bethlehem, December 12, 1993, 14–15.

1994

Books

Come to the Feast: The Original and Translated Hymns of Martin H. Franzmann. St. Louis: Morning Star, 1994.

Ars et Musica in Liturgia: Essays Presented to Casper Honders on the Occasion of his Seventieth Birthday. Edited by Robin A. Leaver and Frans Brouwer. Studies in Liturgical Musicology. Metuchen, N.J.: Scarecrow Press, 1994. American edition of 1993 Dutch Festschrift with slightly different content.

Chapters/Articles

"The Hymnbook as a Book of Practical Theology." In *Exploring Presbyterian Worship: Contributions from Reformed Liturgy and Worship*, edited by Joseph D. Small, 33–38. Louisville, Ky.: Christian Faith and Life Congregational Ministries Division, The Presbyterian Church (U.S.A.), 1994.

Numerous entries. In *The Hymnal 1982 Companion*, edited by R. F. Glover, vol. 3. New York: The Church Hymnal Corporation, 1994. Commentaries on the texts (*) and tunes (+) of the following hymns in the hymnal: 3*, 7+, 9+, 11*, 14+, 23+, 36+, 43*, 46+, 47+, 53*, 53+, 54*, 54+, 58+, 66+, 67*, 71*, 76*, 76+, 77+, 80*, 80+, 87+, 91*, 107+, 124 *, 126 +, 127*, 139*, 151*, 151+, 164+ 181*, 184*, 185* 207*, 207+, 219*, 229*, 230+, 250+, 252+, 258+, 274+, 284*, 301+, 302+, 308+, 313+, 321*, 333*, 334*, 338+, 339*, 343+, 348+, 351*, 355+, 362+, 365*, 365+, 373*, 381*, 388*, 390*, 390+, 396*, 400*, 400+, 402+, 404*, 413+, 414*, 421*, 429+, 436*, 440*, 445*, 445+, 465+, 467+, 471*, 472+, 483*, 486+, 495*, 496*, 510*, 510+, 512*, 515*, 522*, 525*, 526+, 530*, 540+, 543*, 544+, 545*, 558+, 559+, 570*, 572*, 572+, 579+, 601+, 605+, 620*, 626+, 628*, 629*, 634*, 635*, 636*, 639+, 644*, 645+, 646+, 656+, 658*, 663+, 666*, 667*, 668*, 671*, 675*, 677*, 683*, 683+, 687*, 687+, 688+, 695*, 707+, 709*, 709+.

"Look beyond the Expected: Music for Advent and Christmas." *Westminster Notes*, Winter 1994, 1, 6.

"The Funeral Sermon for Heinrich Schütz." *Bach: The Journal of the Riemenschneider Bach Institute* 25, no. 2 (Fall–Winter 1994): 115–29. Revised version of article that originally appeared in *Bach: The Journal of the Riemenschneider Bach Institute* in 1973–74.

"John Bale, Author and Revisor of Sixteenth-Century Metrical Psalms." *Jahrbuch für Liturgik und Hymnologie* 34 (1992–93): 98–106.

Reviews

Neither Voice nor Heart Alone: German Lutheran Theology of Music in the Age of the Baroque, by Joyce L. Irwin, New York: Peter Lang, 1993. *Sixteenth Century Journal* 25 (1994): 471–72.

Musica getutscht: A Treatise on Musical Instruments (1511) by Sebastian Virdung, translated and edited by Beth Bullard, Cambridge, Eng.: Cambridge University Press, 1993. *Sixteenth Century Journal* 25 (1994): 682–83.

Program Notes

Program notes on Bach's Cantatas BWV 49 and 11, and Motet *Jesu, meine Freude* (BWV 227). For a performance by The Bach Choir of Bethlehem. Spring Concert, The First Presbyterian Church of Bethlehem, March 20, 1994, 11–13.

Program notes on Bach's *B-Minor Mass* (BWV 232), the Motet *Singet dem Herrn* (BWV 225), and Cantatas BWV 12, 82, and 129. For performances by The Bach Choir of Bethlehem. Eighty-seventh Festival, May 12–14 and May 19–21, 1994, 8–13.

with Paul McCreesh. Program notes for recording by the Gabrieli Consort and Players, the Boys' Choir and Congregational Choir Roskilde Cathedral, Denmark, directed by Paul McCreesh. *Mass for Christmas Morning: Michael Praetorius, Samuel Scheidt, Johann Herman Schein*. Hamburg: Deutsche Grammophon Archiv. DG 439 250-2, 1994. The text of the U. S. edition is in English only; the German edition has texts in English, German, French and Italian. RAL was the project consultant and was responsible for the liturgical details and the monodic chant.

Program notes on Bach's *Christmas Oratorio* (BWV 248/I–III). For a performance by The Bach Choir of Bethlehem. Christmas Concert, First Presbyterian Church of Bethlehem, December 11, 1994, 6–9.

1995

Book

Elisabeth Creutziger, the Magdeburg Enchiridion, 1536, and Reformation Theology. The Kessler Reformation Lecture, Pitts Theology Library, October 18, 1994. Atlanta: Pitts Theology Library, Emory University, 1995.

Chapters/Articles

"*Agnus Dei* Compositions of J. S. Bach. Some Liturgical and Theological Perspectives." In *Das Blut Jesu und die Lehre von der Versöhnung im Werk Johann Sebastian Bachs*, edited by Albert A. Clement, 233–49. Amsterdam: The Royal Netherlands Academy of Arts and Sciences, 1995.

"Theological Consistency, Liturgical Integrity, and Musical Hermeneutic in Luther's Liturgical Reforms." *Lutheran Quarterly* 9 (1995): 117–38. Abridged in *Luther Digest* 6 (1998): 53–54.

"In Memoriam Adriaan Casper Honders 1923–1994." Written by Robin A. Leaver and co-signed by Frans Brouwer, Jan Luth, and Bernard Smilde. *IAH Bulletin* 23 (1995): 1–2.

"Are Hymns Theological by Design or Default?" *New Mercersburg Review* 18 (Autumn 1995): 12–33.

"Hymnody in Reformation Churches: An Overview of the Primary Historical Contours." *Liturgical Ministry* 4 (Fall 1995): 152–64.

Program Notes

Program notes on Bach's *St John Passion* (BWV 245). For a performance by The Bach Choir of Bethlehem. Spring Concert, First Presbyterian Church of Bethlehem, March 26, 1995, 6–7.

Program notes on Bach's *B-Minor Mass* (BWV 232), *Easter Oratorio* (BWV 249), and Cantatas BWV 137, 130, 169, 79 and 34. For performances by The Bach Choir of Bethlehem, Eighty-eighth Festival, May 11–13 and May 18–20, 1995, 8–13.

Program notes on Bach's *Christmas Oratorio* (BWV 248/IV-VI). For performances by The Bach Choir of Bethlehem. Christmas Concerts, First Presbyterian Church of Bethlehem, December 9 and 10, 1995, 5–8.

1996

Book

Introduction to Musicology: Bibliographical and Research Handbook. Princeton, N.J.: Westminster Choir College, 1996.

Chapters/Articles

7 entries and 48 biographies. *The Hymnal 1982 Companion*, edited by R. F. Glover, vol. 2. New York: The Church Hymnal Corporation, ©1994, 1996. Raymond Glover's "Editor's Note" (p. vii–viii): "To Robin Leaver, a cherished friend, mentor and member of the original Editorial Committee, I express my most sincere gratitude for his valuable contribution to *The Companion*: his vision of its structure

and contents, his constant interest and support in the total project, and his passionate insistence that the book be one of academic and literary excellence."

"Hymnals." In *The Oxford Encyclopedia of the Reformation*, edited by Hans J. Hillerbrand, 4 vols., 2: 286–89. New York: Oxford University Press, 1996.

"Michael Praetorius." In *The Oxford Encyclopedia of the Reformation*, edited by Hans J. Hillerbrand. 4 vols., 3: 321–22. New York: Oxford University Press, 1996.

"Lampe's Tunes." In *Hymns on the Great Festivals and Other Occasions by Charles Wesley and Samuel Wesley, Jr., Music by John Frederick Lampe,* introduced by Carlton R. Young, Frank Baker, Robin A. Leaver, and S. T. Kimbrough, Jr., 31–44. Facsimile of the first edition, 1746. Madison, N.J.: The Charles Wesley Society, 1996.

"Lection, Sermon, and Congregational Song: A Preaching Lectionary of the Dutch Reformed Church (1782) and its Implications." In *Pulpit, Table and Song: Essays in Celebration of Howard G. Hageman,* edited by Heather Murray Elkins and Edward C. Zaragoza, 77–99. Lanham, Md.: Scarecrow, 1996.

"By Gracious Powers [Bonhoeffer]." *The Hymn: The Journal of the Hymn Society of America* 47, no. 2 (April 1996): 3.

Review

Orlando di Lasso's Imitation Magnificats for Counter-Reformation Munich, by David Crook, Princeton, N.J.: Princeton University Press, 1994. *Sixteenth Century Journal* 27 (1996): 1181–82.

Program Notes

Program notes on Bach's Cantatas BWV 4 and 31 and the motet *Der Geist hilft unser Schwachheit auf* (BWV 226). For a performance by The Bach Choir of Bethlehem. Spring Concert, Sunday, March 24, 1996, First Presbyterian Church of Bethlehem, 5–6.

Program notes on Bach's *B-Minor Mass* (BWV 232), and Cantatas BWV 140, 80, 149, 199, 21 and the motet *Der Geist hilft unser Schwachheit auf* (BWV 226). For performances by The Bach Choir of Bethlehem. Eighty-ninth Festival, May 10–11 and May 17–18, 1996, 8–13.

Program notes on Bach's *Sanctus* (BWV 232) and Cantatas BWV 151 and 63. For performances by The Bach Choir of Bethlehem. Christmas Concerts, First Presbyterian Church of Bethlehem, December 7–8, 1996, 4–5.

1997

Book

Introduction to Musicology: Bibliographical and Research Handbook. 2nd ed. Princeton, N.J.: Westminster Choir College, 1997.

Chapters/Articles

"Music and Lutheranism." In *The Cambridge Bach Companion*, edited by John Butt, 35–45, 253–56. Cambridge, Eng.: Cambridge University Press, 1997.

"The Mature Vocal Works and their Theological and Liturgical Context." In *The Cambridge Bach Companion*, edited by John Butt, 86–122, 267–75. Cambridge, Eng.: Cambridge University Press, 1997.

[1990] "The Sound of Change." *The Chorister's Voice* [Newcastle, NSW, Australia], 10, nos. 1–2, June 1997.

"The Failure that Succeeded: The *New Version* of Tate and Brady." *The Hymn: The Journal of the Hymn Society of America* 48, no. 4 (October 1997): 22–31. Keynote address at The Hymn Society in the United States and Canada Annual Conference, Oberlin College, 14–18 July 1996.

"Luther's Catechism Hymns. 1. 'Lord Keep Us Steadfast in Your Word.'" *Lutheran Quarterly* 11 (1997): 397–410. Abridged in *Luther Digest* 8 (2000): 68–69.

"Luther's Catechism Hymns. 2. Ten Commandments." *Lutheran Quarterly* 11 (1997): 411–21. Abridged in *Luther Digest* 8 (2000): 70–71.

Program Notes

Program notes on Bach's *St. Matthew Passion* (BWV 244). For a performance by The Bach Choir of Bethlehem. Spring Concert, First Presbyterian Church of Bethlehem, March 26, 1997, 4–5.

Program notes on Bach's *B-Minor Mass* (BWV 232), Cantatas BWV 4, 42, 43, 51, 129, 195 and the motet *Komm, Jesu, komm* (BWV 229). For performances by The Bach Choir of Bethlehem. Nintieth Festival, May 9–10 and May 16–17, 1997, 7–11.

Program notes on Bach's *Sanctus in D Major* (BWV 238) and Cantatas BWV 65, 91 and 147. For performances by The Bach Choir of Bethlehem. Christmas Concerts, First Presbyterian Church of Bethlehem, December 6 and 7, 1997, 6–8.

Miscellaneous

Unisono: Ökumenischer mehrsprachige Lieder der Christenheit. Graz: Schnider, 1997. A multi-lingual book of ecumenical hymns in 16 different languages. RAL was on the editorial board and edited some English texts.

1998

Book

Liturgy and Music: Lifetime Learning. Edited by Robin A. Leaver and Joyce Ann Zimmerman C.PP.S. Collegeville, Minn.: The Liturgical Press, 1998. Received a

Catholic Press Association Book Award in 1999. Italian translation in preparation by the Vatican Press, Rome.

Chapters/Articles

"What Is Liturgical Music?" In Leaver and Zimmerman, *Liturgy and Music: Lifetime Learning*, 211–19.

"Liturgical Music as Congregational Song 1: Hymnody in Reformation Churches." In Leaver and Zimmerman, *Liturgy and Music: Lifetime Learning*, 281–307.

"Liturgical Music as Homily and Hermeneutic." In Leaver and Zimmerman, *Liturgy and Music: Lifetime Learning*, 340–59.

"Liturgical Music as Anamnesis." In Leaver and Zimmerman, *Liturgy and Music: Lifetime Learning* 395–410. Revision of keynote address given at the Third AGO Seminary Musicians Conference at General Theological Seminary, New York, July 6, 1996; lecture given at the Centennial Convention of the American Guild of Organists in New York, July 6, 1996, under the title: "Christian Memory and Church Music in Contemporary American Context."

[1988] "Bach, Kirchenlieder und Gesangbücher." In *Theologische Bachforschung heute: Dokumentation und Bibliographie der Internationalen Arbeitsgemeinschaft für theologische Bachforschung 1976–1996*, edited by Renate Steiger, 277–93. Berlin: Galda + Wilch, 1998.

"Liturgical Chant Forms in Bach's Compositions for Lutheran Worship: A Preliminary Survey." In *Die Quellen Johann Sebastian Bachs: Bachs Musik im Gottesdienst*, edited by Renate Steiger, 417–28. Heidelberg: Manutius, 1998.

"Johann Walter's Reputation and the Publication of His Music in England and America." In *Johann-Walter-Studien: Tagungs-bericht Torgau 1996*, edited by Friedhelm Brusniak, 145–69. Tutzing: Schneider, 1998.

"Alternatimspraxis"; "Anthem"; "Arie"; "Brooke, William Thomas." In *Religion in Geschichte und Gegenwart*. 4th ed., edited by H. D. Betz, et al. *Band 1: A–B*. Tübingen: Mohr, 1998.

"Luther's Catechism Hymns. 3. Creed." *Lutheran Quarterly* 12 (1998): 79–88. Abridged in *Luther Digest* 9 (2001): 164–65.

"Luther's Catechism Hymns. 4. Lord's Prayer." *Lutheran Quarterly* 12 (1998): 89–98. Abridged in *Luther Digest* 9 (2001): 165–67.

"Luther's Catechism Hymns. 5. Baptism." *Lutheran Quarterly* 12 (1998): 160–69. Abridged in *Luther Digest* 9 (2001): 167–68.

"Luther's Catechism Hymns. 6. Confession." *Lutheran Quarterly* 12 (1998): 170–80. Abridged in *Luther Digest* 9 (2001): 169–70.

"Luther's Catechism Hymns. 7. Lord's Supper." *Lutheran Quarterly* 12 (1998): 303–12. Abridged in *Luther Digest* 9 (2001): 170–72.

"Luther's Catechism Hymns. 8. Confessional Substance." *Lutheran Quarterly* 12 (1998): 313–23. Abridged in *Luther Digest* 9 (2001): 172–74.

"Obituary: William Paul Hays." *The American Organist* (August 1998): 33; *The Tracker* 41 (1997): 3 [published July 1998].

Review

Die Melodien bis 1570, Teil 1: *Melodien aus Autorendrucken und Liederblättern,* vorgelegt von Joachim Stalmann (*Das deutsche Kirchenlied, Abteilung III: Die Melodien aus gedruckten Quellen bis 1680,* Band 1: *Die Melodien bis 1570,* Teil 1), 2 vols., Kassel: Bärenreiter, 1993. *MLA Notes* 54, no. 4 (June 1998): 907–11.

Program Notes

Program notes on Bach's Motets, *Singet dem Herrn* (BWV 225), *Jesu, meine Freude* (BWV 227), *Fürchte, dich nicht* (BWV 228), 230, *Brandenburg Concerto, no. 3* (BWV 1048), and Sinfonias from Cantatas BWV 29, 156 and 209. For a performance by The Bach Choir of Bethlehem. Spring Concert. First Presbyterian Church of Bethlehem, March 29, 1998, 3–4.

Program notes on the *Christmas Oratorio* (BWV 248). For performances of The Bach Choir of Bethlehem. Ninety-first Festival [The Bach Choir Centennial 1898–1998], May 8–9 and May 15–16, 1998, 7–10.

Program notes for the recording *J. S. Bach: Mass in B Minor, BWV 232.* Performed by The Bach Choir of Bethlehem, with The Bach Festival Orchestra, Greg Funfgeld, conductor. Dorian Recordings, DOR 90253 I, II, 1998.

Program notes for the recording *The Leipzig Chorales of J. S. Bach.* Performed by Joan Lippincott, organist. Gothic Recordings, G 49099, 1998.

Program notes for the recording *Bach Epiphany Mass.* Performed by the Gabrieli Consort and Players, Paul McCreesh, conductor. Deutsche Grammophon Archiv. DG 457 631-2, 1998. RAL was the liturgical consultant and edited the liturgical chant. Featured in an article by Bernard D. Sherman, "Re-creating Bach in His Own Element," *New York Times,* Arts and Leisure section, Sunday January 2, 2000, 39 and 42.

Program notes on the Bach's *Sanctus* from the *B-Minor Mass* (BWV 232) and Cantatas BWV 140, 1, and 63. For performances by The Bach Choir of Bethlehem. Christmas Concerts, First Presbyterian Church of Bethlehem, December 5–6, 1998, [7–8].

1999

Chapters/Articles

"Passiontide Music." In *Passover and Easter: The Symbolic Structuring of a Sacred Season,* edited by Paul F. Bradshaw and Lawrence A. Hoffman, 146–80. Two Liturgical Traditions 6. Notre Dame, Ind.: University of Notre Dame Press, 1999.

"Cantata." In *Oxford Composer Companions: J. S. Bach,* edited by Malcolm Boyd, 82–87. Oxford: Oxford University Press, 1999.

"Chorale." In *Oxford Composer Companions: J. S. Bach,* edited by Malcolm Boyd, 92–94. Oxford: Oxford University Press, 1999.

"Missa." In *Oxford Composer Companions: J. S. Bach*, edited by Malcolm Boyd, 297–99. Oxford: Oxford University Press, 1999.

"Reception and Revival. 13. United States of America." In *Oxford Composer Companions: J. S. Bach*, edited by Malcolm Boyd, 405–7. Oxford: Oxford University Press, 1999.

"St. Matthew Passion." In *Oxford Composer Companions: J. S. Bach*, edited by Malcolm Boyd, 430–34. Oxford: Oxford University Press, 1999.

Entries on 13 cantatas: BWV 10, 16, 22, 23, 61, 62, 63, 79, 80a, 80, 101, 137, 156, and 159. In *Oxford Composer Companions: J. S. Bach*, edited by Malcolm Boyd. Oxford: Oxford University Press, 1999.

"Abraham Calov," "Calvinism," "Church Calender," "Consistory," "Hauptgottesdienst," "Jahrgang," "Lutheranism," "Orthodoxy," "Passion," "Pietism," "Internationale Arbeitsgemeinschaft für theologische Bachforschung," and "Vespers." In *Oxford Composer Companions: J. S. Bach*, edited by Malcolm Boyd. Oxford: Oxford University Press, 1999.

"Christophers, Samuel Woolcock"; "Creamer, David"; "Duffield; Samuel"; "Englische Kirchenmusik." In *Religion in Geschichte und Gegenwart*. 4th ed., edited by H. D. Betz, et al. *Band 2: C–E*. Tübingen: Mohr, 1999.

"The *Deutsche Messe* and the Music of Worship: Martin Luther and Johann Sebastian Bach." In *Von Luther zu Bach. Bericht über die Tagung 22.–25. September 1996 in Eisenach*, edited by Renate Steiger, 115–27. Sinzig: Studio, 1999.

Review

The English Hymn: A Critical and Historical Survey, by Richard Watson, Oxford: Clarendon, 1997. *West Gallery: the Newsletter of the West Gallery Music Association*. 13, Spring 1999.

The Hymn Tune Index: A Census of English-Language Hymn Tunes in Printed Sources from 1535 to 1820, by Nicholas Temperley, 4 vols., Oxford: Clarendon, 1998. *MLA Notes* 56, no. 2 (December 1999): 385–87.

Melodien aus mehrstimmigen Sammelwerken, Agenden und Gesang-büchern I, edited by Joachim Stallmann et al. (*Das deutsche Kirchenlied, Abteilung III: Die Melodien aus gedruckten Quellen bis 1680*, Band 1: *Die Melodien bis 1570*, Teil 2). Kassel: Bärenreiter, 1996–97. *MLA Notes* 56, no. 2 (December 1999): 388–91.

Program Notes

Program notes on Bach's *St John Passion* (BWV 245). For a performance by The Bach Choir of Bethlehem. Spring Concert, First Presbyterian Church of Bethlehem, March 14, 1999, 6.

Program notes on Bach's *St John Passion* (BWV 245). For a performance by the Washington Bach Consort, Chorus and Orchestra. National City Christian Church, Washington, DC, March 21, 1999, 25–30.

Program notes on Bach's *St. Matthew Passion* (BWV 244) and the *B-Minor Mass* (BWV 232). For performances by The Bach Choir of Bethlehem. Ninety-second Bach Festival [The Bach Choir Centennial 1898–1998], May 7–8 and May 14–15, 1999, 10–12.

Program notes for the recording of Schütz's *Christmas Story*. Performed by the Gabrieli Consort and Players conducted by Paul McCreesh, in the context of Vespers, ca. 1664. Deutsche Grammophon Archiv. DG 463 046-2, 1999. RAL was project consultant.

Program notes for a recording of Bach's *Christmas Oratorio* (BWV 248). Performed by The Bach Choir of Bethlehem, directed by Greg Funfgeld. Dorian Records. DOR-93183, 1999.

With Paul McCreesh. Program notes on Michael Praetorius's *Mass for Christmas Morning c. 1620*. For performances by the Gabrieli Consort and Players, directed by Paul McCreesh. Performed at Harvard Memorial Church (Boston Early Music Festival), December 12, 1999; Church of the Holy Spirit, Kenyon College, Gambier, Ohio, December 13, 1999; St. Francis of Assisi Church, UMS, Ann Arbor, Michigan, December 14, 1999; Southern Theater, Columbus, Ohio, December 15, 1999; The Church of St. Ignatius Loyola, New York City, December 16, 1999; and Royce Hall, UCLA, Los Angeles, California, December 17, 1999.

2000

Book

Introduction to Musicology: Bibliographical and Research Handbook. 3rd ed. Princeton, N.J.: Westminster Choir College, 2000.

Chapters/Articles

Numerous entries. *Worship Music: A Concise Dictionary*, edited by Edward Foley. Collegeville, Minn.: Liturgical Press, 2000.

"Frost, Maurice"; "Gottesdienst—Reformation"; "Hymnologie." In *Religion in Geschichte und Gegenwart*. 4th ed. edited by H. D. Betz, et al. *Band 3: F–H*. Tübingen: Mohr, 2000.

"Bach Vespers (Gottesdienstplan und Kommentar)." In *Johann Sebastian Bachs Kantaten zum Thema Tod und Sterben und ihr literarisches Umfeld*, edited by Renate Steiger, 237–41. Wiesbaden: Harrassowitz, 2000.

"Johann Sebastian Bach: Theological Musician and Musical Theologian." *Bach: The Journal of the Riemenschneider Bach Institute*, 31, no. 1 (2000): 17–33.

"Thematic Building Blocks: Liturgical, Pedagogical and Political Concerns in Early Lutheran Church Music." *Cross Accent: Journal of the Association of Lutheran Church Musicians*, 8, no. 2 (Summer 2000): 24–36. Paper originally presented at the First International Conference of Frühe Neuzeit Interdisziplinär, Duke University, April 1995. Described as "a wide-ranging and impressively detailed survey" by Steven Saunders in *17th Century Music* 5, no. 1 (Fall 1995): 5.

Review

Liturgy and Hermeneutics, by Joyce Ann Zimmermann, Collegeville, Minn.: The Liturgical Press, 1999. *Liturgical Ministry* 9 (2000): 109.

Program Notes

Program notes on Bach's *B-Minor Mass* (BWV 232). For a performance by The Bach Choir of Bethlehem with The Bach Festival Orchestra. Carnegie Hall, February 7, 2000. *Stagebill February 2000 Carnegie Hall*, 26–28.

Program notes on the performance of Bach's *B-Minor Mass* (BWV 232). For a performance by The Bach Choir of Bethlehem to mark the 100th anniversary of the first complete American performance on March 27, 1900, Central Moravian Church, Bethlehem, March 27, 2000.

Program notes on Bach's Cantatas BWV 21, 31, 80, 97, Motet *Singet dem Herren* (BWV 225) and *Magnificat* (BWV 243). For performances by The Bach Choir of Bethlehem. Ninety-third Bach Festival, May 12–13 and May 19–20, 2000, 9–13.

Program notes on Bach's *Orchestral Suite* (BWV 1068), Cantata BWV 80, and *Magnificat* (BWV 243). For a performance by the Choir and Orchestra of St. Ignatius Loyola, conducted by Kent Tritle. The Church of St. Ignatius Loyola, Park Avenue, New York, October 17, 2000.

Program notes on Bach's *Christmas Oratorio, Pts. IV-VI* (BWV 248). For a performance by The Bach Choir of Bethlehem. Christmas Concerts, First Presbyterian Church of Bethlehem, December 9–10, 2000, 5–7.

2001

Chapters/Articles

"Luther, Martin." In *The New Grove Dictionary of Music and Musicians*, 2nd ed., edited by Stanley Sadie and John Tyrell, 15: 354–69. London and New York: Macmillan, 2001. Newly-written entry.

"Lutheran Church Music." In *The New Grove*, 15: 369–81. Newly-written entry.

"Marbeck, John." In *The New Grove*, 15: 805–6. Newly-written entry.

"Zwingli, Ulrich." In *The New Grove*, 15: 354–69. Revised entry.

"Chorale." In *The New Grove*, 5: 736–46. Revision.

"Chorale Mass." In *The New Grove*, 5: 746. Revision.

"Chorale Settings." In *The New Grove*, 5: 747–63. Revision.

"Figured Chorale." In *The New Grove*, 8: 792. Revision.

"Melanchthon, Philipp." In *The New Grove*, 16: 303–4. Revision.

"Spener, Philipp Jakob." In *The New Grove*, 24: 171–72. Revision.

"Healing in the Music of Johann Sebastian Bach." In *Christ's Gifts of Healing for the Soul: Toward a Lutheran Identity in the New Millennium*, edited by Daniel Zager, 99–114. Fort Wayne, Ind.: Concordia Theological Seminary Press, 2001. The Good Shepherd Institute for Pastoral Theology and Sacred Music for the Church, vol. 1, Journal for the First Annual Conference, 5–7 November, 2000.

[1990] "'Then the Whole Congregation Sings': The Sung Word in Reformation Worship." *Musica Ecclesiae Semper Reformanda* 4, 2001, 11–34 (Japanese), 35–56 (English).

"Music as Proclamation and Acclamation." *Liturgical Ministry* 10 (2001): 73–82.

"The Current Situation of American Church Choirs: Problems of a Changing Culture." *Semoonnan Church Music Institute Journal* (2001). Korean text of a lecture given at the Semoonan Church Music Institute, Seoul, Korea, May 22, 2001.

"The *Deutsche Messe* and the Music of Worship: Martin Luther and Johann Sebastian Bach." *Lutheran Quarterly* 15 (2001): 317–35. Revision of 1999 chapter in *Von Luther zu Bach. Bericht über die Tagung 22.–25. September 1996 in Eisenach*, edited by Renate Steiger, 115–27, Sinzig: Studio, 1999.

Review

The Essential Bach Choir, by Andrew Parrott. Rochester, Eng.: Boydell, 2000. *Cross Accent: Journal of the Association of Lutheran Church Musicians* 9, no. 3 (Fall 2001): 29–32.

Program Notes

Program notes on Bach's Motets, *Der Geist hilft* (BWV 226), *Komm, Jesu, komm* (BWV 229), *Ich lasse dich nicht* (BWV Anh. 159) and motets by Mendelssohn (*Richte mich, Gott*, Op. 78, Nr. 2) and Brahms (*Schaffe in mir Gott*, Op. 29, Nr. 2). For a performance by The Bach Choir of Bethlehem. Spring Concert, First Presbyterian Church of Bethlehem, March 25, 2001, 3–4.

Program notes on Bach's Cantatas BWV 11, 34, 51, 74, 105, 170, and the Motet *Der Geist hilft* (BWV 226). For performances by The Bach Choir of Bethlehem. Ninety-fourth Bach Festival, May 11–12 and May 18–19, 2001, 11–15.

Program notes on Bach's *St. Matthew Passion* (BWV 244). For a performance by the Princeton High School Choirs and Fuma Sacra, conducted by Andrew Megill, Richardson Auditorium, Alexander Hall, Princeton University, Princeton, N.J., June 17, 2001.

Program notes for *Christmas in Leipzig*, reconstruction of Christmas morning, Leipzig, ca. 1740. For a performance by the Washington Bach Consort, conducted by J. Reilly Lewis. December 2, 2001, [9]–[13]. RAL was liturgical consultant.

Program notes on Bach's *Magnificat* (BWV 243), and Cantatas BWV 36, 61, and 191. For performances by The Bach Choir of Bethlehem. Christmas Concerts, First Presbyterian Church of Bethlehem, December 8–9, 2001, 5–6.

Miscellaneous

"Letter to the Editor." *Cross Accent: Journal of the Association of Lutheran Church Musicians,* 9, no. 1 (Spring 2001): 27–28. Response to correct inaccuracies in the review of the *Oxford Composer Companions, J. S. Bach*, by Mark Bighley.

2002

Chapters/Articles

"The Biblical Canticles in Luther's Hymnals." In *Lord Jesus Christ, Will You Not Stay: Essays in Honor of Ronald Feuerhahn on the occasion of his Sixty-fifth Birthday*, edited by J. Bart Day, et al., 23–64. St. Louis: Concordia Publishing House, 2002.

"Johann Sebastian Bach and the Lutheran Theological Understanding of Music." *Lutheran Quarterly* 16 (2002): 21–48.

"Walter E. Buszin and Lutheran Church Music in America." *Lutheran Quarterly* 16 (2002): 153–94. Article received award from Concordia Historical Institute, St. Louis (November 2003), being "recognized as a significant contribution to Lutheran archives and history in America."

"Liturgical Musicology Today: Trends in America and Europe." *Journal of Liturgical Musicology* 1 (2002): 5–32. In English and Japanese. Keynote address given at first conference of the Japan Society of Liturgical Musicology, Tokyo, May 26, 2001.

Review

The Chansons of Orlando di Lasso and Their Protestant Listeners: Music, Piety, and Print in Sixteenth-Century France, by Richard Freedman, Rochester, N.Y.: University of Rochester Press, 2000. *Early Music* 30 (2002): 128–29.

Program Notes

Program notes for Bach's *St. Matthew Passion* (BWV 244). For a performance by The Bach Choir of Bethlehem. Spring Concert, March 17, 2002, 5–6.

Program notes for performances and recording of Bach's *St. Matthew Passion* (BWV 232). Performed one-to-a-part by the Gabrieli Consort, directed by Paul McCreesh. Soloists include Mark Padmore, Peter Harvey, Deborah York, Julia Gooding, Magdalena Kozená, Susan Bickley, James Gilchrist and Stephan Loges. March 19 and 20 St. John's, Smith Square, London; March 22 Centro Cultural de Bélem, Lisbon; March 29 Herkulesaal, Munich; March 31 Snape Maltings Concert Hall, Aldeburgh. Deutsche Grammaphon recording in Roskilde Cathedral, Denmark, April, 2002.

"De Koralen in de Matthäus Passion." Program notes for performances of the *Matthäus Passion 2002* by De Nederlandse Bachvereniging, conducted by Gustav Leonhardt and Johannes Leertouwer. Performed in Haarlem, Naarden, Aardenburg, Utrecht, and Tilberg, 20–30 April 2002, pp. 13–21. Notes translated into Dutch by Pieter Dirksen.

Program notes on Bach's *B-Minor Mass* (BWV 232). For performances by The Bach Choir of Bethlehem. Ninety-fifth Bach Festival, Packer Memorial Chapel, Lehigh University, May 10–11 and May 17–18, 2002, 8–12.

Program notes on Bach's Cantatas BWV 40, 110, 147, and the *Sanctus* from the *B-Minor Mass* (BWV 232). For performances by The Bach Choir of Bethlehem. Christmas Concerts, First Presbyterian Church of Allentown and First Presbyterian Church of Bethlehem, December 7–8, 2002, 4–5. The 50th set of concert notes written for the Choir since 1984.

Program notes for the recording of Bach's *Ascension Oratorio* (BWV 11) and *Two Festive Cantatas* (BWV 51 and 34). Performed by The Bach Choir of Bethlehem, directed by Greg Funfgeld. Dorian Records, DOR-90306, 2002.

2003

Chapters/Articles

Revisions (some substantially re-written) of the following articles: "Anglican Chant;" "Anglican Church Music;" "Anthem;" "Choral Music;" "Chorale;" "Church Music;" "Hymn;" "Liturgical Books II;" "Lutheran Church Music;" "Psalmody;" "Psalter;" and "Service." In *The Harvard Dictionary of Music*, 4th ed., edited by Don Michael Randel. Cambridge, Mass.: Belknap Press of Harvard University Press, 2003.

"Using Historic Music in Contemporary Worship." *Choral Journal*, 43, no. 2 (February 2003): 51–61. Paper originally given at the ACDA conference, San Antonio, TX, March 2001.

"Brahms's Opus 45 and German Protestant Funeral Music." *Journal of Musicology* 19 (2002): 616–40. [Published March 2003]. Revised version of paper originally given as the 2nd Annual Blackard Lecture, Brevard College, North Carolina, February 5, 2000.

Review

Das deutsche Kirchenlied: Kritische Gesamtausgabe der Melodien. Abteilung III: *Die Melodien aus gedruckten Quellen bis 1680*, herausgegeben von der Gesellschaft zur wissenschaftlichen Edition des deutschen Kirchenlieds. Band 1: *Die Melodien bis 1570*, Teil 3: *Melodien aus Gesangbüchern II*, herausgegen von Joachim Stalmann, Hans-Otto Korth, Daniela Wissemann-Garbe, Silke Berdux, Karl-Günther Hartman and Rainer H. Jung, 2 vols. [Notenband and Textband]. Kassel: Bärenreiter, 1998. *MLA Notes* 59, no. 3 (March 2003): 664–67.

Program Notes

Program notes for Bach's Cantata BWV 21 and Motet *Singet dem Herrn* (BWV 225), and Mozart's *Great Mass in C Minor* (K. 427). For a performance by The Bach Choir of Bethlehem. Spring Concert, The First Presbyterian Church of Bethlehem, March 23, 2003, 4–5.

Program notes on Bach's Cantatas BWV 29, 34, 56, 71, 120, 199, and the Motet *Fürchte, dich nicht* (BWV 228). For a performance by The Bach Choir of Bethlehem. Ninety-sixth Bach Festival, Packer Memorial Chapel, Lehigh University, May 9–10 and May 16–17, 2003, 8–10.

Program notes on Bach's *B-Minor Mass* (BWV 232), Cantatas BWV 34 and 191, and four Mendelssohn motets. For performances of The Bach Choir of Bethlehem UK Tour 2003, July 17–31, 2003, 6, 10. Performed in Usher Hall, Edinburgh; King's College Chapel, Cambridge, Sheldonian Theatre, Oxford; BBC Promenade Concert, Albert Hall, London. Tour Program book, 6, 10.

Program notes on the *B-Minor Mass* (BWV 232). For a performance by The Bach Choir of Bethlehem. Performed in the cathedral as part of the St. Albans 22nd International Organ Festival, 10–19 July 2003. Souvenir Programme, 93.

Program notes on *B-Minor Mass* (BWV 232) For a performance by The Bach Choir of Bethlehem. King's College as part of the Cambridge Summer Music Festival July 17–August 16, 2003. Programme booklet, 18.

Program notes on Cantata BWV 199. For a performance by The Bach Choir of Bethlehem. Claydon House, England, July 20, 2003.

Program notes on Lutheran Vespers, with music by J. S. Bach and Mendelssohn. For a performance by The Bach Choir of Bethlehem. Southwark Cathedral, London, Sunday July 27, 2003. RAL also planned the liturgy.

Program notes on Bach's Cantatas BWV 63 and 140 and C. P. E. Bach's *Magnificat*. For a performance by The Bach Choir of Bethlehem. Christmas Concerts, The First Presbyterian Church of Allentown and The First Presbyterian Church of Bethlehem, December 6–7, 2003, 4–5.

2004

Chapters/Articles

"Anglican Chant." In *The Encyclopedia of Protestantism*, edited by Hans Hillerbrand, 1: 65–66. New York: Routledge, 2004.

"Hymns and Hymnals." In Hillerbrand *The Encyclopedia of Protestantism*, 2: 909–20.

"Music, American." In Hillerbrand *The Encyclopedia of Protestantism*, 3: 1327–30.

"Music, Northern European." In Hillerbrand *The Encyclopedia of Protestantism*, 3: 1338–42.

"Musical Instruments and Reformation Worship." *Journal of Liturgical Musicology* 3 (2003): 5–48 [published 2004]. In English and Japanese. Keynote address given at the third conference of the Japan Society of Liturgical Musicology, at Meiji Gakuin University, Tokyo, May 31, 2003.

"Ms. Bach *P 271*, a Unified Collection of Chorale-based Pieces for Organ?" *Bach Notes: The Newsletter of the American Bach Society*, 1, Spring 2004, 1–4.

"Sequences and Responsories: Continuity of Forms in Luther's Liturgical Provisions." In *Worship in Medieval and Modern Europe: Change and Continuity in Religious Practice*, edited by Karin Maag and John Witvliet, 300–28. Notre Dame, Ind.: University of Notre Dame Press, 2004.

"Eschatology, Theology and Music: Death and Beyond in Bach's Vocal Music." In *Irish Musical Studies 8: Bach Studies from Dublin*, edited by Anne Leahy and Yo Tomita, 129–47. Dublin: Four Courts Press, 2004. Paper presented at the Ninth Biennial Conference on Baroque Music, Trinity College Dublin July 12–16, 2000.

"Luther as Musician." *Lutheran Quarterly* 18 (2004): 125–83.

"Carol." In *Key Words in Church Music: Definition Essays on Concepts, Practices and Movements of Thought in Church Music, Revised and Enlarged*, edited by Carl Schalk, 79–81. St. Louis: Concordia, 2004.

"English Hymnody." In Schalk *Key Words in Church Music*, 327–36.

"Metrical Psalmody." In Schalk *Key Words in Church Music*, 423–30.

"Hymnody in English and Dutch Exile Congregations ca. 1552–1561." *Jahrbuch für Liturgik und Hymnologie* 43 (2005): 217–45. Originally given as paper, "Bekenntnis und Beichte im Kirchenlied der Englischen und Niederlandischen Flüchtlinge," at the Johannes á Lasco Bibliothek, Emden, in 1997.

"Genevan Psalm Tunes in the Lutheran Chorale Tradition." In *Der Genfer Psalter und seine Rezeption in Deutschland, der Schweiz und den Niederlanden 16–18 Jahrhundert*, edited by Eckhard Grunewald, Henning P. Jürgens and Jan R. Luth, 145–66. Frühe Neuzeit, Band 97. Tübingen: Niemeyer, 2004. Revision of paper given at the Johannes á Lasco Bibliothek, Emden, in 2001.

Program Notes

Program notes for Bach's *St. John Passion* (BWV 245). For a performance by The Bach Choir of Bethlehem. Spring Concert, The First Presbyterian Church of Bethlehem, March 28, 2004, 6.

Program notes on Bach's Cantatas BWV 4, 106, 182, 31, 119, 102, 103, and 151. For performances by The Bach Choir of Bethlehem, Ninety-seventh Bach Festival. Packer Memorial Chapel, Lehigh University, May 7–8 and May 14–15, 2004, 8–11.

Program notes for Bach's *Christmas Oratorio, Pts. I–III* (BWV 248). For performances by The Bach Choir of Bethlehem. Christmas Concerts, The First Presbyterian Church, Allentown, The First Presbyterian Church of Bethlehem, The Forum, Harrisburg, December 5–6, 2004, 5–6.

2005

Chapters/Articles

"Dutch Singing in 18th Century New York." In *Amsterdam—New York: Transatlantic Relations and Urban Identities Since 1653*, edited by George Karinck and Hans

Krabbendam. Amsterdam: VU Uitgeverij, 2005, 99–115. Revision of paper given at the conference "Parallel Cities: Amsterdam and New York, 1653–2003," in Amsterdam, 31 January, 2003.

STUDIES IN LITURGICAL MUSICOLOGY

Robin A. Leaver, Editor
Scarecrow Press, Metuchen, N.J.; Lanham, Md.
Each volume contains an introductory "Editor's Preface" by Robin A. Leaver.
Ars et Musica in Liturgia: Essays Presented to Casper Honders on the Occasion of his Seventieth Birthday. Edited by Robin A. Leaver and Frans Brouwer. 1994.
"The Way to Heavens Doore": An Introduction to Liturgical Process and Musical Style, by Steven Plank. 1994.
A Theology of Music for Worship Derived from the Book of Revelation, by Thomas Allen Seel. 1995.
Hymnology: A Collection of Source Documents, by David W. Music. 1996.
Biblical Quotation and Allusion in the Cantata Libretti of Johann Sebastian Bach, by Ulrich Meyer. 1997.
Hymntune Index and Related Hymn Materials, compiled and edited by D. Dewitt Wasson. 1998. 3 vols. Also issued as a CD-rom, 2001.
Instruments in Church: A Collection of Source Documents, edited by David W. Music. 1998.
Medieval Music as Medieval Exegesis, by William T. Flynn. 1999.
On the Role of the Organist in Worship (1787), by Daniel Gottlob Türk, translated and edited by Margot Ann Greenlimb Woolard. 2000.
Hymnal Collections of North America, by Tina M. Schneider. 2003.

DREW STUDIES IN LITURGY

Robin A. Leaver and Kenneth E. Rowe, Editors
Scarecrow Press, Metuchen, N.J.; Lanham, Md.
Pulpit, Table and Song: Essays in Celebration of Howard G. Hageman, edited by Heather Murray Elkins and Edward C. Zaragoza. 1996.
St. James in the Streets: The Religious Processions of Loíza, Puerto Rico, by Edward C. Zaragoza. 1995.
The Impact of the Liturgical Movement on American Lutheranism, by Timothy C. J. Quill. 1997. Preface by RAL.
The Language of the Psalms in Worship: American Revisions of Watts' Psalter, by Rochelle Ann Stackhouse. 1997. Preface by RAL.
The Matter and Manner of Praise: the Controversial Evolution of Hymnody in the Church of England, 1760–1820, by Thomas K McCart. 1998. Preface by RAL.
"Bless the Lord, O my Soul": The New-York Liturgy of the Dutch Reformed Church, 1767, by Daniel James Meeter. 1998. Preface by RAL.

The Eucharistic Service of the Catholic Apostolic Church and its Influence on Reformed Liturgical Renewals of the Nineteenth Century, by Gregg Alan Mast. 1999.
Moving toward Emancipatory Language: A Study of Recent Hymns, by Robin Knowles Wallace. 1999.
Two Faces of Elizabethan Anglican Theology: Sacraments and Salvation in the Thought of William Perkins and Richard Hooker, by Bryan D. Spinks. 1999. Preface by RAL.
The Language of Baptism: A Study of the Authorized Baptismal Liturgies of the United Church of Canada, 1925–1995, by William S. Kervin. 2003.
The Reform of Baptism and Confirmation in American Lutheranism, by Jeffrey A. Truscott. 2003.
"With One Heart and One Voice": A Core Repertory of Hymn Tunes Published for Use in the Methodist Episcopal Church, 1808–1878, by Fred Kimball Graham. 2004.

CONTEXTUAL BACH STUDIES

Robin A. Leaver, Editor
Scarecrow Press, Lanham, Md.
The Crucifixion in Music: An Analytical Study of the Crucifixus between 1680 and 1800, by Jasmin Melissa Cameron. 2006.

DOCTORAL DISSERTATIONS FOR WHICH ROBIN A. LEAVER ACTED AS ADVISOR

Dirk W. Rodgers. "John à Lasco in England." Ph.D. diss., Drew University, 1991.
Fred Kimball Graham. "'With One Heart and One Voice': A Core Repertory of Hymn Tunes Published for Use in the Methodist Episcopal Church in the United States, 1808-1878." Ph.D. diss., Drew University, 1991.
David Allan Weadon. "Clarence Dickenson (1873–1969) and the School of Sacred Music at Union Theological Seminary in the City of New York (1928–1973)." Ph.D. diss., Drew University, 1993.
Rochelle Ann Stackhouse. "American Revisions of Watts' Psalter: Liturgical Change in the Early Republic." Ph.D. diss., Drew University, 1994.
Deborah Rahn Clemens. "Foundations of German Reformed Worship in Sixteenth Century Palatinate." Ph.D. diss., Drew University, 1995.
Timothy J. Sidebothom. "Music in the Marriage Rites of Mainline Protestantism (1978–1993): A Theological, Liturgical, and Cultural Analysis." Ph.D. diss., Drew University, 1997.
Alice M. Swartz. "Gerard Sloyan and His Contribution to the American Liturgical Movement." Ph.D. diss., Drew University, 1997.
Philip Edward Yevics. "Lazarus Saturday in the Byzantine Tradition: An Example of Structural Analysis of the Byzantine Triodion." Ph.D. diss., Drew University, 1997.

Paul Richard Powell. "Louis F. Benson, the 1895 Presbyterian Hymnal and Twentieth-Century American Hymnody." Ph.D. diss., Drew University, 1998.

Bruce Reginald Harding. "Change and Continuity: The Development of Tune Repertoire for Congregational Singing in the United Church of Canada 1925–1975." Ph.D. diss., University of Toronto, Canada, 1998.

Seongdae Kim. "Inculturation in Korean Protestant Hymnody." Ph.D. diss., Drew University, 1999.

Larry A. Schmalbach. "When the Roll is Called Up Yonder: Eschatology in the Twentieth Century American Hymnal." D.Litt. diss., Drew University, 2000.

Joseph Francis Watson. "To Love and Praise the Fathers: Patristic Methodology in the Theology of Martin Chemnitz." Ph.D. diss., Drew University, 2001, with distinction.

Kathleen Harmon. "Liturgical Singing as Ritual Enactment of the Paschal Mystery." Ph.D. diss., Drew University, 2001.

Timothy C. J. Quill. "An Examination of the Contributions of Theodosius Andreas Harnack to the Renewal of Lutheran Liturgy in the Nineteenth Century." Ph.D. diss., Drew University, 2002.

Anne Marie Leahy. "Text-Music Relationships in the 'Leipzig' Chorales of Johann Sebastian Bach." Ph.D. diss., University of Utrecht, the Netherlands, 2002.

Jill Suzanne Burnett. "Aspects of the Liturgical Year in Cappadocia 325 to 430 C.E." Ph.D. diss., Drew University, 2003.

Evan Scooler. "J. S. Bach's Changing Conception of the 'Great Eighteen' Chorales." Ph.D. diss., Brandeis University, 2003.

David Michael Buley. "Eloquence as the Essence of Common Prayer: Liturgical Languages of the English Reformation—Humanism, Eloquence and Liturgy in Sixteenth-Century England." Ph.D. diss., Drew University, 2004.

Paolo Michele Bordignon. "Johann Sebastian Bach's Halt im Gedächtnis Jesum Christ BWV 67: A Study of the Sources and their Implications." DMA diss., The Juilliard School, New York, 2004.

Jan Graham. "But for Henry, A Lutheran England? Thomas Cranmer and the Supreme Royal 1529–1540." D. Litt. diss., Drew University, 2004.

Kimberly Bracken Long. "Ravished with the Love of Christ: the Eucharistic Theology of the American Holy Fairs." Ph.D. diss., Drew University, 2005.

Shelley P. Sanders Zuckerman. "Spiritual Formation through Singing the Psalms: A Study of John Brown of Haddington's *The Psalms of David in Metre with Notes (1775)*." Ph.D. diss., Drew University, 2005.

Index

About the Contributors

Gregory Butler is senior professor of music at the School of Music, University of British Columbia in Vancouver, British Columbia. He is author of *Bach's Clavier-Übung III: The Making of a Print* (1990) and numerous articles on the first editions of Bach's works. He has also written extensively on Bach's concertos and is presently researching the composer's Leipzig organ works. He was elected president of the American Bach Society in 2004.

Albert Clement is professor of musicology at Utrecht University and at its international Honors College in Middelburg, the Netherlands: the Roosevelt Academy. He has devoted a number of publications to Bach, among them several books, including *The Blood of Christ and the Doctrine of Reconciliation in the Works of Johann Sebastian Bach*, Proceedings of the International Colloquium in Amsterdam 1993 (1995) and *Der dritte Teil der Clavierübung von Johann Sebastian Bach: Musik - Text - Theologie* (1999).

Stephen A. Crist is chair of the Music Department at Emory University. He served as contributing editor of *Bach in America*, Bach Perspectives, 5 (2003) and contributing coeditor of *Historical Musicology: Sources, Methods, Interpretations* (2004).

William T. Flynn is lecturer at the University of Leeds, Institute for Medieval Studies. He is the author of *Medieval Music as Medieval Exegesis*, Studies in Liturgical Musicology, 9 (1999), which investigates the cross-fertilization of the elementary study of grammar, rhetoric, music, and liturgy, and its effects on the production and interpretation of biblical commentary in the eleventh-century church. He participates in the study group Sapientia-Eloquentia based at the University of Stockholm, which is investigating developments in liturgical poetry from the eleventh to the twelfth centuries.

Don O. Franklin, professor of music at the University of Pittsburgh and past president of the American Bach Society, has published widely on the music of J. S. Bach. Recent essays appear in *Passion, Affekt und Leidenschaft in der frühen Neuzeit,* Wolfenbütteler Arbeiten zur Barockforschung, 43 (2005); *Bach Studies from Dublin,* Irish Musical Studies, 8 (2004); and *Bachs Musik für Tasteninstrumente,* Dortmunder Bach-Forschungen, 6 (2003). As Director of the Bach and Baroque Ensemble, he recently presented the modern premiere of C. P. E. Bach's 1789 Matthew Passion.

Anne Leahy lectures in academic studies at the DIT Conservatory of Music and Drama (Dublin). She holds the Ph.D. from Utrecht University and is also a professional organist, having been director of music at St. Michael's Church, Dún Laoghaire, Dublin, from 1983 to 2006. She is a Fulbright scholar and was the first visiting Gerhard Herz Professor of Bach Studies at the University of Louisville in 2003.

Michael Marissen is Daniel Underhill Professor of Music at Swarthmore College. His publications include *The Social and Religious Designs of J. S. Bach's Brandenburg Concertos* (1995) and *Lutheranism, Anti-Judaism, and Bach's St. John Passion* (1998). Current projects include a study on Handel's *Messiah* and Christian Triumphalism and a book of annotated translations of the librettos from Bach's oratorios.

Daniel R. Melamed is associate professor at the Jacobs School of Music, Indiana University. He is the author of *J. S. Bach and the German Motet,* coauthor (with Michael Marissen) of *An Introduction to Bach Studies,* editor of *Bach Studies 2,* and serves as associate editor of the *Journal of Musicology.* His book for general readers, *Hearing Bach's Passions,* was published by Oxford University Press in 2005.

Steve Pilkington is associate professor of sacred music; chair of conducting, organ, and sacred music faculties; and director of chapel at Westminster Choir College of Rider University. He holds degrees from St. Olaf College and the University of Illinois and is active as an organist and choral conductor.

D. E. Saliers is Wm. R. Cannon Distinguished Professor of Theology and Worship at Emory University, where he is also organist/choirmaster at Cannon Chapel and director of the M.S.M. program. Educated at Yale Divinity School and Cambridge University, he received the Ph.D. degree from Yale University, where he taught before joining the faculty at Emory in 1974. Among his publications are *Worship as Theology* (1994), *Worship Come to Its Senses* (1996), *The Soul in Paraphrase: Prayer and the Religious Affections* (1980), and, most recently, *A Song to Sing, A Life to Live: Reflections on Music as Spiritual Practice* (2005), coauthored with his daughter Emily Saliers.

Kerala J. Snyder is professor emerita of musicology at the Eastman School of Music, University of Rochester. Her publications include the books *Dieterich Buxtehude: Organist in Lübeck* (1987) and (as editor) *The Organ as a Mirror of Its Time: North European Reflections, 1610–2000* (2002). She was founding editor-in-chief and is now consulting editor of the online *Journal of Seventeenth-Century Music*.

Yo Tomita is reader in the School of Music at Queen's University, Belfast. He recently edited Joseph Groocock's *Fugal Composition: A Guide to the Study of Bach's "48"* (2003), and, with Anne Leahy, *Bach Studies from Dublin*, Irish Musical Studies, 8 (2004).

Sherry L. Vellucci (a.k.a., Sherry Vellucci-Leaver) holds a DLS in library and infomation science from Columbia University, where she also taught. She was director of the Division of Library and Information Science at St. John's University until 2004, when she joined the faculty of Rutgers University, School of Communication, Information, and Library Science. Her research and publications are in the area of information organization, with a specific focus on music metadata. Prior to her teaching career, she was director of Talbott Library of Westminster Choir College, Princeton, New Jersey.

Daniel Zager is head of the Sibley Music Library, associate professor of musicology, and affiliate faculty member in the organ department at the Eastman School of Music. He holds the Ph.D. in musicology from the University of Minnesota and has contributed chapters to *Orlando di Lasso Studies* (1999) and *Orlandus Lassus and His Time* (1995).